SOVOK

(The Memoirs of a Liar?)

Kevin McKinney

SOVOK (The Memoirs of a Liar?)
Copyright © 2023 Kevin McKinney. All Rights Reserved.

No part of this publication may be reproduced, stored in a retrieval system or transmitted, in any form or by any means—electronic, mechanical, photocopy, recording, or otherwise—without prior written permission from the publisher, except for the inclusion of brief quotations in a review.

For information about this title or to order other books and/or electronic media, contact the publisher:

Contact Info: Kevin McKinney
Sovokthebook@gmail.com

ISBN:
979-8-9880409-0-3 (paperback)
979-8-9880409-1-0 (ebook)

Printed in the United States of America

Contents

Introduction vii
SOVOK 1
En Route to USSR 2
Leningrad University 6
More Equal Than Others 15
Soviet Shopping 17
Wife to Be 20
Leningrad Student Life 22
Set a Wedding Date 27
Hired By a Criminal 30
Pretend to Be a Student 34
Blood Sample or Be Deported . . . 37
Americana 38
USSR Beyond Leningrad 39
Revolution Day In Leningrad . . . 44
Useful Idiot Master Class 48
Scofflaws At a Wedding 50
Welcoming 1988 54
USSR, Do Svidaniya 55
Final Year At GWU 56
Restaurant Near White House . . . 59
Physicist From Yale 62
Hotel Concierge 64
Bologna Frisbeeing 68

Perestroika Mania 70
A Nascent Cult of Bologna 73
Greet Marina at Dulles 76
Our Bar In Georgetown 78
Kentucky Derby or Exam 83
Russia Becomes a Fad 85
Business with Toolshed 89
First Foray Into Moscow 94
Bologna Bust 99
Bologna to Budapest 101
Soviet Art Exhibit In D.C. 103
Soviet Jazz at Paisley Park 105
Siberian Oil 109
Marc Rich + CO AG 124
The Fugitive 127
Soviet Space Team 129
Russian Far East 131
Pissed on In Public 133
Portrait of Lenin 134
Farther East 137
Star City to W. Ukraine 141
Toolshed v. Tobacco Mafia 145
Betting Pool on Holy Hajj 146
Attempted Communist Coup 152

Mugged By Moscow Police 154	COPPA 223
Transition: Soviet to Russia. 156	Governor Crosses the Pacific 226
Russian Navy's Pacific Fleet 159	Charity / Moiseev Dance 229
Embargo-Busting Gasoline 162	False Narrative In USA 231
Miss Bust / Miss Legs 165	Kazakhstan with Lip 233
Tequila! 167	Solntsevo Mafia 234
Ukrainian Wheat Thieves 168	U.N. Oil for Food — Mogilevich 236
Oil Equipment Thieves 173	False Medical Alarm 238
Beretta 9mm for Gasoline 174	Razzle Dazzle Documents 240
Border with North Korea 180	Pablo's Chechen Fax 244
From Infidelity to Khanka 182	Honor Fight In Minneapolis 245
Rabbit Gets Caught 184	Aluminum Wars 247
Police Escort 186	Paul Tatum's Assassination 254
McHugh Construction 188	Visit to Kraz 256
Train From Odessa 192	Who Has a Spare Key 259
Rigged Casino 194	U.S. Embassy In Moscow 261
Dogfights 195	Real Wedding 268
Hunting Ussuriysk Tigers 196	Whorewacker Does Russia 270
Marc Rich Ousted 198	Exit Sultan 273
"Best Bar In America" 200	Exit Pablo 274
Road Trip Across America 204	Crimea 275
Gerald Metals 207	Bolshoi Ballet 276
Hiring a Roof 209	A Message from Kraz 277
Gerald Moscow Expands 212	Hitlerina 280
Jackalope In St. Petersburg 213	Stops Bullets / Shoot Back 284
Kazakh Zinc 214	Mike Crotch (Stage Name) 286
Privatization, Sort Of 217	Bullets Shot at BiFF 293
Real Wife 220	September 11, 2001 299

- Cursed Prescription Pills 302
- Job Lead from London 304
- Celtic Resources PLC 308
- Small World of Lawyers 312
- Putin Chokes Liberty 313
- Bad Contract / Worse Language 315
- To Produce Gold 317
- Powerful Landlord Perks 319
- Bourbon Street Bar Moscow 321
- Celtic Hits Bumps 323
- Edibles from Night Flight 325
- Banker and Prime Minister 327
- Celtic Hobbles Along 329
- Eureka Mining 331
- Simon Wiesenthal—Jerusalem 333
- Blackjack Blacked Out 336
- A Wild Man In Provence 338
- Kraftwerk In Moscow 340
- The Trinity Sues 342
- Uncle Marijuana Pioneer 343
- Bolshoi Chapter Ends 345
- An Unlikely Diplomat 347
- Arrest Tourists 348
- Zero Gravity Flight 351
- Still Swinging at Celtic 354
- Water Thief In Provence 357
- Body Parts In Our Luggage 359
- Sale and De-Listing of Celtic 360
- Loose Ends 361
- Three Bottles of Wine 363
- First Jew In Outer Space 366
- Random Meeting New Orleans 367
- Texan Teaches Russians 368
- Stock Forger Resurfaces 370
- Chance Meeting In Cannes 371
- MMA Heavyweight 372
- U.S.—Russia Foundation 373
- I Know a Guy 375
- Backstory 376

Introduction

"Sovok" is a derogatory term used by Russian speaking citizens of the USSR to describe the surreal reality that socialism created there. It can also be used to describe a person who never deviates from the official party line in thought or speech. It literally translates into English as dustpan, or (poop) scoop. It is derived from "Sov," as in Sov-iet. It is not a compliment.

Originally the title concept of this book was "Bar stories," because it's essentially a compilation of them. Topics range from as serious as it gets, like mass murder, multi-billion dollar international business deals, criminal syndicates, to the inane, like frisbee-ing bologna at passersby from a balcony nine floors up. There are several instances when the comedic and serious intersect. I will admit that the thought of these tales tied together in a television mini-series influenced me to expand the range of the ones I chose to tell.

The introduction of certain characters might seem unneeded, but I intend to provide evidence that denizens of our planet are without doubt interconnected and have been since before Facebook. Occasionally, I might make a reference to someone simply because I want to acknowledge them and the positive impact they had. Some times it may seem like namedropping, when it is not. I do not expect every section to be interesting to every reader, but I know there will be rapt readers of every section. If a topic arises that's of no interest, flip forward a little. The tone and topic will change and usually quickly.

Once in a while I will mention cultural aspects, which I hope will be educational to non-Russians, but which hopefull will also elicit a nod of approval from Russia savvy readers, who share the same esteem I have for certain aspects of living there, or in some cases maybe a revulsion to it.

My mother taught me by example to seek and embrace the best in every society. She showed me life-improving contributions that people all over the world have made. No ethnicity or culture has a monopoly on the wonderful. My father held a person's word in the highest regard. He drank and gambled, but always did sober what he said he would do drunk. He looked at the business world as a roulette table. As long as you've got a chip in play, you've got a chance.

Several people familiar with some of these stories warned me to change names, locations, and topics. After more than a year of debate, I chose to be guided by the quote on the pedestal of the statue in front of the U.S. National Archives on Constitution Avenue in Washington, D.C., "The price of liberty is eternal vigilance," which in my opinion requires an unobstructed view. This will apply especially to government officials.

I've witnessed very little, but these stories might help connect some dots. Nonetheless, I hereby declare all that follows fiction and will paraphrase Dostoevsky's opening in "Notes From Underground." A reader's question should always be: "Is this rhetoric or reality?" Do research and verify. Then verify and research those who provided the research you verified. Anyone who denies the version of events in this book might be presented with facts. Also, wink wink, a cache of supporting documents, videos, and photographs might be out there somewhere, either on a password protected cloud or stored with loyal friends anywhere in the world. You can choose to not believe, or maybe challenge what's written and find out.

SOVOK
(The Memoirs of a Liar?)

I am a liar. A dishonest person am I. I embellish the truth. I think I suffer from chronic mendacity, but I don't know squat about that disease. I never study and never studied, even though I respect research and scholars.

Almost everything that follows is made up. It is the fiction of a fantabulous fabulist. Think of me as the bullshitter at the end of the bar. If some of the characters' names match actual people, it is only by coincidence. Call me Baron Munchausen.

En Route to USSR

Washington, D.C. 1987
In a closed office of The Russian Department at George Washington University (GWU), a few blocks from the White House, a faculty member and I listened on speakerphone to a male voice with a heavy accent. News that I had been accepted to attend a Soviet university had obviously been leaked.

"When you arrive in the Soviet Union," the voice said, "there's something I'd like you to do, which is to marry a friend so that she can move to America. Will you do that?" I said yes without hesitation. The faculty member, who arranged the phone call, grabbed my wrist and interrupted by shaking her head with a look of fear and disbelief. She muted the mic.

"Do not agree without first very carefully thinking about this," she warned. "I've been to the USSR. This is serious business and could land you in jail there and here."

I unmuted the mic. "Yes, I will do it," I repeated.

Now it was the Russian voice who gave me a warning. "I hope you realize that if you say yes now and decide later to back out, your decision will likely lead to her death, or at best destroy her life."

"If I said I will do it, I will do it." I considered myself engaged to be married to someone I knew nothing about other than her unfortunate citizenship. Both advised me to tell no one.

The voice on the phone was soon revealed to be Arkady Polischuk's, a Jewish Soviet dissident, who was then a correspondent for Radio Free Europe/Radio Liberty. Three years of study with diehard anti-Soviet professors had helped form my opinion that the Soviet regime was every bit as vile as the government of Nazi Germany. I was happy for the chance to help a person, any person, leave there. That is why I instantly agreed to the marriage.

Polishchuk prepared me for what to expect in the USSR. My American brain was incapable of processing what he told me. His descriptions of everyday life and the army of petty enforcers that make it miserable bolstered my resolve to make sure the escape by marriage was a success. Arkady was raised to be a faithful Jew. The Soviet government tried to break his family's faith by imprisoning family members and threatening him in various ways. In order to punish the innocent, they made everything a crime. Arkady evolved into a resolute defender of human rights. To punish him for Judaism, the Soviet government banished him to live in a small village for the blind. Arkady wasn't blind. They ordered him to use his journalism skills to write about the Soviet government's glorious treatment of its blind citizens. Polishchuk honestly described living conditions there in terms that elicited images of abandoned crackhouse squalor.

It was a no-brainer that if I could rescue even one person from the USSR, it had to be done. Polishchuk suggested a list of lies to tell people when I arrived in the Soviet Union, aka disinformation. He advised me to keep a journal and write down to whom I told which lie about my wife-to-be. Then when the inevitable confrontation by authorities happened, the informant(s) would be revealed. One person would hear that I was paid, another that the CIA gave me an apartment, or that I was genuinely in love, etc.

What I didn't know was that the USSR in textbooks and media reports was already dead. As Russian novelist and dissident Aleksandr Solzhenitsyn observed in 1979, "For us in Russia, communism is a dead dog, while, for many people in the West, it is still a living lion." Intelligence agents from the United States may gather correct information, but the "Community" generates custom-made reports to fit whatever narrative their politician-handlers request. Right up until the Soviet Union collapsed in 1991, American intelligence officers promoted the myth that the USSR was a major threat. Whether they believed that to be true or not, who knows? That was the bogus narrative they fed to Congress and major media outlets. Intelligence continued to fabricate and spread the lie of robust communism right up until the day the USSR splintered into fifteen countries, most of which embraced capitalism. There was mass mutiny in the Soviet military, yet Washington struggled to convey what was obvious to even uneducated observers. A cogent voice at the time was author Judy Shelton, whose prescient book, "The Coming Soviet Crash," was published in 1989. It was mostly ignored.

Arkady Polishchuk, I always assumed, was affiliated with the Central Intelligence Agency (CIA), but I never knew for sure and never found out. Polishchuk and other dissidents briefed President Ronald Reagan about the likes and dislikes of Soviet leaders, including their hatred of derision. Faux respect for people with power permeates the culture in Russia. Every official letter opens with a salutation to "The Respected" or even "Highly respected" so and so. The sign off is "With respect." Soviet bureaucrats wielded tremendous power as accuser, judge and jury. The higher the position, the easier it was for an official to wreck someone's life. Ordinary citizens walked on eggshells, I imagine much the way slaves behaved. Reagan's former Soviets advised him to put the "Dis" in dissident, as in disrespect. They fed jokes to the U.S. president that an American couldn't know. During one exchange with Mikhail Gorbachev[1]

---

1 The last Soviet leader.

Reagan asked him if socialism had been invented by scientists or politicians.

Gorbachev replied, "Politicians."

The scripted retort from Reagan was, "Of course it was politicians. Scientists would have had the decency to at least try it on rats first to see that it didn't work."

In the 1980s Soviet universities in a select few cities, including Moscow, Leningrad and Krasnodar, admitted approximately forty American students to study for up to a year. To be accepted into these programs a student had to profess to be a peacenik moron, or at least pretend to be, as was the case with me. We wrote essays in Russian about how much we loved socialism and feigned a desire to get along with Communist slave masters. In actuality, the operators of the educational programs in Leningrad and elsewhere didn't give a shit about what we were going to do there, or even if we were going to study at all. It would be a bonus if the USSR program for foreigners cranked out some useful idiots, aka admirers of socialism. What the operators really wanted was hard currency to do things like circumvent Cold War (COCOM²) sanctions and illegally purchase IBM computers from corrupt European resellers.

Foreign student programs provided cash for someone, but it certainly wasn't the professors. They earned next to nothing. Their low salaries made it easier for students with money to bribe them and secure good grades. The saying about employment in Soviet Russia was, "We pretend to work, and they pretend to pay us." There was also a common Soviet curse, "May you live on your salary alone." Everyone was on the take.

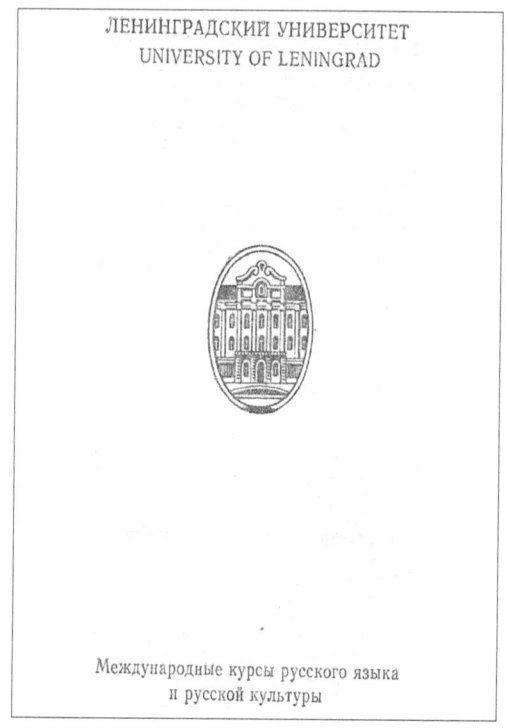

The study program I entered lasted five months, from August, 1987 until January, 1988 at Leningrad State University. Before the semester started, all the American students made their way separately to meet at a hotel in Espoo, Finland, near Helsinki. En route, I

---

2 The Coordinating Committee for Multilateral Export Controls (CoCom) was established by the Western Bloc after the end of World War II. During the Cold War, CoCom put an embargo on Comecon (communist) countries. CoCom ceased to function on March 31, 1994. The then-current control list of embargoed goods was retained by the member nations until the successor, the Wassenaar Arrangement, was established in 1996.

visited a high school friend in England, who was serving as a Russian linguist in the US Air Force. He was married with a young son. He arranged for me to stay with another Russian specialist, Toolshed, who will appear later. After England, I visited my college roommate of two years, J. Dog, who was at home in his native Paris. I learned only in France that he was from a very wealthy family and had a noble title. In the dormitory at GWU he had always been humble.

My last stop before Helsinki was to visit friends in Hamburg. J. Dog's elderly aunt had been a lifelong diplomat. Upon learning I was headed to Hamburg, she suggested I take a lesson on Soviet reality from her friend, a lifelong German diplomat, Dr. Franz Breer. We met and I mentioned the fictitious marriage. He warned me to be wary of entrapment by seductresses. I took his advice to heart and have never abandoned it.

Leningrad University

Over 400 meters long, the Twelve Colleges building of Saint Petersburg University is the largest surviving building from the era. It was commissioned by Peter I in 1718.

The Leningrad State University program was run by New York based Council on International Educational Exchange (CIEE) which employed two American directors, Brad and Edna. Collectively they had spent many years in the USSR. They briefed the students in Helsinki, the day before departure. They claimed their job was to keep us out of trouble and impart their unique knowledge. One of the stated goals of the program was immersion in Russian culture. The directors warned at orientation how strict everything will be once we cross the border from Finland, stating that any illegal activity in the USSR could result in imprisonment and there was very little anyone could do to help us if a student went off script. Admonition number one was "Never exchange your currency for rubles anywhere other than at an official exchange booth!" It was illegal for a Soviet citizen to be in possession of more than $25 in foreign currency. If a person took thirty dollars from an American they could be arrested as soon as they put it in their pocket. The official government-dictated exchange rate comically fluctuated, between 60 – 64 kopecks per dollar. I say comically because there was no currency market at that time on which the Soviet ruble traded. The government just made up a rate. Instead of sharing real life experience, Brad and Edna parroted official warnings, as if they were advising embassy staff in a lecture hall at Georgetown University. In less than twenty-four hours, the opening act of a decades-long adventure awaited me.

On our final night in the West, several of us went out on the town in Helsinki. Chatting with Finns, who all spoke excellent English, they asked what we were doing there. When we told them that the next day we were headed to Leningrad for months, the reaction was uniform and not dissimilar to how someone might react to hearing a confession of incurable cancer, a mixture of pity, disbelief, and dread. The phrase that stuck from my conversations with many Finns was, "A Russian is a Russian even if you fry it in butter."

On the day of departure to Leningrad, we waited for our train on an outside open-air platform. My appearance made me stand out more than any other student. The reason was that the night before I gave myself a wide scrape across the middle of my forehead that was impossible not to notice. Perhaps not entirely sober, I gave a girl a piggyback ride and fell forward while running. My arms were wrapped around her legs and my hands were holding her ankles so I couldn't break the fall. My chest hit the ground first. My shirt ripped open as it slid across the sidewalk. Then the weight from my passenger pressed my forehead into the cement. Still moving forward, a swath of skin was stripped off before we came to a stop. The upside to that story was that my vocabulary in Russian improved because of it. The wound took weeks to heal. Inquisitive Russians continually asked about the scar. To answer, I had to learn expressions like "I lost my balance," and "faceplanted into a sidewalk."

From the Helsinki train station platform, the sight of the approaching Soviet train was ominous and exhilarating. The dark green color of the train was a type of drab not seen in the West outside of prisons. Ubiquitous hammers and sickles seemed to portend doom and elicited visuals of cattle cars plowing through deep tundra snow, hauling hapless people to a brief life of misery in a Siberian Gulag. The train stopped and out stepped stone-faced ticket takers. This was our first interaction with genuine Soviet citizens. That they all remained unsmiling seemed to bolster the admonitions of Brad and Edna to do everything by the book. Combined with the genuine pity that the Finns had expressed the night before, many in the group were already starting to regret not pursuing a semester in France or Italy. As my dad said, there's no such thing as bad experience.

Waiting in Helsinki for the
train to Leningrad

We boarded the Soviet train, destination: Leningrad's Finlyandsky station. Decorations were absent. Everything was industrial and utilitarian. It looked more like the lower decks of a submarine than a passenger train. The staff showed absolutely no signs of joy and via body language conveyed a uniform expression of "I hate my job. I hate my life. But I must do this if I don't want to die."

Historical note[1]:

Our point of entry was Vyborg, which offered our first glimpse inside the USSR. Vyborg was a city of about 80,000 people on The Baltic Sea. It was originally Swedish, annexed by Peter I in 1710. It became Viipuri, Finland from 1919-1940, only to fall again under Soviet Russian control. It had been the site of some serious WWII battles between the Nazis and Soviets. It appeared that not much had been done to rebuild it since 1945. The first thing that struck me, besides a paucity of smiles, was how poorly lit everything was. We were sitting in the stopped train, with the doors to our berths closed. What sounded like an army of border agents could be heard walking past. The commotion they made indicated either overkill or incompetence. We'd soon find out.

There were four passengers in each double-decker berth. When the door slid open, its metal frame crashed into a metal stop, causing the unusual sound of sliding wood with clanking metal. "Dokumenti," was the obligatory first word. They methodically analyzed every page of our passports and visas, stone-faced, but as if somehow they were truly interested. They looked up now and then emotionless to compare passport photos with faces.

Baggage? As everywhere, there was no choice but to let them examine anything they wanted. They could conceivably declare anything contraband. A person in D.C. suggested I bring copies of Mikhail Bulgakov's novel, "The Master & Margarita." They also warned that they might get confiscated. The book was written in the 1930s but was banned in the Soviet Union until 1966 due to its satirical depiction of Stalinist Russia. The agents found them and didn't care. Mostly they were searching for "Tamizdat" which were the smuggled manuscripts of dissidents, living outside the country (Tam means "there," as in abroad and "izdat" means press.) My main concern was they'd take my Walkman and cassettes. They ignored those too. After what seemed like fifteen minutes, they put a stamp on the visa and entry was official. The visa was a separate document because Soviets had a policy to never put a stamp in a foreign passport. They worried that abroad someone could replicate it. They collected visas upon departure.

After the train started moving again, the mood was more relaxed. No one had been thrown off. A few people were carrying Russian language Bibles, which were supposed to be strictly forbidden. The conversation turned more anticipatory about what to

---

1 The reason one can board a Soviet or Russian train straight from Helsinki is that Finland is the only European country whose railway gauge is the same as Russia's which is 1,520 mm (five feet). Nearly all of Europe's trains roll on 1,435 mm. If they cross into Russia, the undercarriages have to be switched out at the border or they can't move. The back story to this anomaly was that while in London in the 1840s, Tsar Nicholas I asked what a train station was. The English replied, "Vauxhall," the name of a railway station. Still today the Russian word for train station is "Vokzal." Nicholas I started building Russia's first railway between Moscow and St. Petersburg, using the five-foot gauge that he thought was in England, but they'd already abandoned it. Therefore Russia still runs on slightly wider tracks, allowing train compartments to be a little more spacious.

expect for living conditions and what kind of food would be available. Some worried about how hard classes would be. I concentrated on how quickly I could find my bride-to-be, Marina, who should be waiting at the station as soon as I step off. Arkady Polishchuk assured me that Marina knew exactly where to stand and even from which car I would exit. While others were discussing the Soviet university experience, I was thinking about how to reply when someone asks how I met a woman who lived in Gatchina, a place I could not legally visit.

Our train pulled into Leningrad's Finlyandaski train station. With a single suitcase, I exited the train and immediately noticed a woman, who looked to be in her early forties nodding with a fixed stare. I walked to meet my fiancée. She confirmed she was Marina. No one seemed to pay attention to us. After some brief chitchat, she gave me a note that read, "The statue in front of Kazansky Cathedral[2]. Wednesdays. 1 p.m." She explained that this location would be our default meeting place in case plans went awry, which they will and always do. "What if I have class?" I asked. "I don't even know my schedule yet." She looked incredulous at the naiveté of the question and told me to skip class. She said that Kazansky was where all the "Fartsovshiki[3]" meet every Wednesday. The word was unfamiliar, but I didn't admit it. She said anyone watching will think I'm trading. I didn't understand, but promised Marina to be there on Wednesday no matter what. She left.

With Marina gone, my attention turned to taking in the sights around the train station. The expectation of a society with extremely strict laws and order promptly changed to "What kind of shitstorm is this?" Instead of armed police on every corner, enforcing order by threatening to shoot jaywalkers, there were throngs of people everywhere. It was indiscernible where the street started and the sidewalk ended. A smattering of maybe a dozen cars were parked haphazardly. There were no delineated parking spots. Intermittent buses and cars didn't slow down at all for pedestrians. Instead, they seemed to accelerate into crowds. The noise from a revving engine sent people scurrying. Grimy men stood around overflowing garbage bins, passing bottles of vodka, which I soon learned did not have screw tops, but instead pop-tops, because who wouldn't finish a bottle of vodka in one go? After chugging from the bottle, a drinker would sniff another's hair or place their nose on their sleeve and inhale deeply. Russians do this to mask the

---

2 **Kazan Cathedral** or **Kazanskiy Kafedralniy Sobor** (Russian: Казанский кафедральный собор), also known as the Cathedral of Our Lady of Kazan. It was one of the most venerated structures of the Russian Orthodox Church on the main thoroughfare of Saint Petersburg, Nevsky Prospekt. Construction started in 1801 and continued for ten years with the intent of making it similar to Saint Peter's Basilica in Rome. After the Russian Revolution of 1917, the Cathedral was declared "The State Museum of Atheism."
3 Fartsovshiki were street hustlers, black marketeers. If something was illegal, they could get it. The Soviet government waged a "War on alcohol" in 1987. Vodka and cognac were extremely scarce on store shelves. Fartsovshiki had everything. They hounded tourists and would try to buy foreign clothes off your back, offering to replace it with low quality Soviet items. They also worked as currency traders. Their rates were at least five times more beneficial for the seller than the official rate offered by the government.

fumes of alcohol by smelling something after taking a shot. Traditionally it is black bread or pickles, but those aren't available on the street. Taking in the exotic scene, I noticed Edna and Brad motioning everyone to a grimy Intourist[4] bus that seemed oddly tall.

As we rode to the brand new dormitory, I asked Brad when we would see the lights of downtown.

"We are in the center of the city right now," he said. "This is it."

It was about as lit up as an oven nightlight set to dim. A city of five million residents had what looked like 50 street lamps and all were of the lowest wattage.

The new dormitory was a complex of three twenty-story towers on Shipbuilder's Street. There was a common lobby on the second floor. One tower was strictly for Soviet students, another housed foreign socialists, Africans and students from Warsaw Pact Countries. Our tower was a mix of Soviets, Westerners, and Hungarians. Hungarians technically should have been in the Warsaw Pact side, but they were considered so Western, as in antisocialist, that the KGB wanted them watched like all other nationalities they considered adversarial. The program directors had repeatedly stressed how lucky we were to live in the "New" dormitory. The other dormitory, Number Six, was walking distance from campus. Returning graduate students impressed upon us first-timers that riding a bus was a small price to pay for not living in Number Six.

Dormitory on Shipbuilder's Street in Leningrad, USSR

When we got off the bus at the new dorm, we first-timers were all looking around confused. Almost all the windows in the door frames were broken, or missing altogether. Shards of broken glass were strewn inside and on the sidewalk. Looking up, perhaps half the windows on an emergency staircase

---

4 Intourist was the official Soviet travel agency. Their mission generally was to make sure that the activities of foreign visitors would be controlled and monitored, so that tourists would see only what the State wanted to show. Phones in Intourist Hotels were tapped and rooms were bugged.

were missing and many others were broken. Inside an entrance, pieces of busted up furniture and abandoned construction materials were visible. One of the experienced grad students commented, "This will be the black entrance," explaining, "The main doors will be locked from sometime around 11 p.m. to 7 a.m. There's always a way in and out. I predict this will be it."

After hours back door
entrance to the "new" dormitory

The group walked around the corner from the broken glass to the main entrance. As is typical all across Russia, the entrance consisted of sets of double doors, four in each row yet only one door is unlocked. There are no arrows or signs to indicate which door to open. You have to pull on them randomly until one opens. Once in between the sets of doors, you have to guess again. It is never the right choice to choose the inside door that was directly across from the outside unlocked door. That would be too easy. Later it was explained that doors opposite each other are never both unlocked to mitigate strong winds.

The first impression of the dorm made us wonder if there was a Soviet equivalent of OSHA. Inside the lobby was a Dezhurnaya who was seated at her desk. She pretended to review the documentation that Edna or Brad presented. She quickly waved us through and we went upstairs one floor to get our room assignments from an administrator with our keys. The staircase did not instill confidence that it could withstand the weight of twenty people. None of the walls and ceilings were congruent. Where there were bricks, the cement was sloppy and haphazard. Exposed I-bars on the stairs weren't parallel. Other first-time students instantly began searching for terms to describe the style of architecture. One suggested, "Pre-dilapidated," another coined the term "Instant shambles." If this building was brand new and the returning students considered it superior to Number Six, what lay ahead was ominous.

Room assignments were slowly announced and keys were handed out. They parked me in a room with two Russians on the ninth floor. Elevators were already broken, or maybe had never worked. As I trudged up the staircase with my suitcase, I was grateful to not be on the 20th floor. So many construction flaws were visible that it seemed doubtful the building could remain upright for five months. Inside room 907 my roommates, Slava and

Sergei, were reading when I entered. They pretended to not have been informed that an American would be the third in their room. All the roommates of foreigners were hand-picked and expected to report on our activities.

They were trained to detect possible espionage as well. Slava was a local Leningrader and Vladimir Lenin wannabe. He had the same cheesy mustache and shabby beard. He wore Lenin's famous puffy hat with the short brim and was short enough to suffer from Napoleon syndrome. Sergei was from Pskov, which is an historic Russian city near the border with Estonia. In its history of over 1,000 years, Pskov had been the capital of its own Republic. It was considered a Russian bridge to Europe. Sergei seemed to be less enthusiastic about communism. Little Slava constantly parroted the party line. It was curious to meet someone whose speech and mannerism had clearly been programmed. John Candy's character, Tom Tuttle, in the 1985 movie "Volunteers" wasn't a ridiculous caricature after all.

After speaking to Sergei and Slava, I looked around the suite. We shared a common kitchen, toilet, and shower with two other people, who were administrators from a Russian language program in Pecs, Hungary. They stayed in a smaller room to the right upon entering. Despite everything allegedly being new, the shower floor was rust stained and looked as if it had been there ten years. A piece of broken mirror was taped to the wall. That was the only mirror. There was a kitchenette, equipped with a plastic sink and a single coil electric stove. On an open shelf, there was a bag of loose tea, salt and sugar, one glass cup, one metal cup and a pan for boiling water. There was no food and no refrigerator. Nothing smelled pleasant, especially the hot water when there was any. It wasn't outright putrid, but an odor of decay permeated everything. The plastic pipe under the sink was exposed. Sergei warned me to avoid the roach poison that was next to it. Everyone warned to never drink unboiled Leningrad tap water. It contained Giardia.[5] Worse than the disease were the pills to treat it. The pills cause a violent reaction to alcohol consumption. Giardia and the cure needed to be avoided.

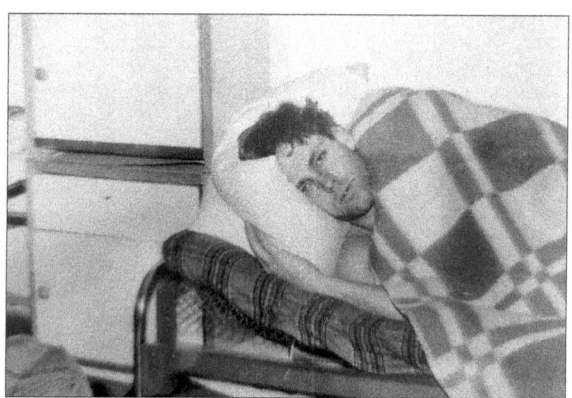

The finest thin wire mesh cot, aka dormitory bed. It would probably be considered inhumane in American prisons.

When I sat down on my new "bed," my butt sagged to just above the floor. It was like a loose trampoline and hard to get out of. It

---

5   Giardia is a microscopic protozoan parasite that can cause violent diarrhea for weeks.

wasn't a bed, but a cot with an elastic metal mesh, hidden by a sheet and thin blanket. There was no light switch for the toilet stall. To turn the light on or off, one had to screw in or unscrew the bulb by hand. Lightbulbs were considered a sign of wealth, as was toilet paper. If those items were left unattended anywhere in public, they'd be stolen instantly. When someone was among the three or four percent lucky enough to own a car to park, they had to take the windshield wipers off, because they'd also be stolen instantly.

While putting my things away, there was a knock on our door. Slava and Sergei looked at each other suspiciously and didn't move. I opened up and recognized a student from our group that I'd seen in Helsinki. He stood there with a panicked look on his face, asking in English "You're with the American group, right?!" I nodded yes. He motioned for me that I should go out in the hallway with him. Down the corridor to the right, about 5 meters away, there was a wide area that housed a garbage chute in the middle of a landing next to an emergency exit staircase. At the opposite end to the left were the elevators and main staircase. We stood by the garbage chute, out of earshot. Diego introduced himself. He grew up in Colombia and was studying at Harvard. We noticed the trash chute was already completely clogged. It had been built at a slant instead of perpendicular. The end of a metal pole was sticking out of a hole that had been punched in the cement pipe. It was lodged in and guaranteed that trash from higher floors would also get stuck even if the clog from nine and lower was cleared.

Diego confessed the reason for the panic on his face in a stream of consciousness that he unleashed without punctuation or breaks in a slight Spanish accent in English:

"Have you seen the toilets I took a shit in the one in my room and the turds are just sitting there like it's some kind of examination table it really stinks I don't know if I'm supposed to push it in with my hand or what is this disgusting device I don't want to insult my Russian roommate by asking him to clean up my shit and they were right about no toilet paper I'm glad I brought my own what am I gonna do this is horrifying."

The need to test out the plumbing hadn't happened to me yet. I suggested we go back to my room and ask a roommate to show us how the toilet worked. The toilet in my room functioned properly, but that was luck. Instead of a bowl filled with scent-diminishing water, Soviet toilet users dropped their wares onto a dry porcelain table. To remove excrement from the table, one lifted a stopper on top of the water tank behind, which action resulted in a deluge that pushed the odiferous matter into a hole at the front. This action often caused splashing, which contributed to the already substantial stench. We quickly learned that almost every toilet in the dormitory required some kind of hack to operate. Some had no water at all. Diego was lucky that water flowed to his. He ended up lifting the stopper by hand and the toilet worked. The well-equipped kept a bucket handy.

Not all in the dormitory was gloom, doom, and failure though. To everyone's surprise, the elevators started working intermittently and occasionally for several days in a row before breaking down again. The elevator doors seemed paper-thin, almost like Japanese walls. Every part of the elevator seemed like it was constantly strained. Stepping in, the floor dropped slightly. The high-pitched electric motor that shut the doors quickly sounded like it was running at triple the speed it was supposed to. The doors clanged shut with a collision that sounded like it would be painful to have your hand in. Once the cabin started moving, the sound of cables being stressed was non-stop. It swayed slightly from side to side almost as if it was in free fall, like there were no tracks holding it in place. Eventually most of us chose to walk, even when the elevators were working.

After studying the dormitory, a few of us wandered out together to investigate the neighborhood. The area was all new construction. If there were remnant buildings from before the 1917 Revolution, none were visible. Everywhere were massive apartment blocks between twelve and twenty stories high, many of which stretched an entire city block with at least ten different entrances. Shipbuilders Street had four-lanes of traffic in each direction, divided by a median with a short fence. The size of the road seemed commensurate with the dense population, but in reality only about four percent of Soviet citizens had private cars. Almost all traffic was gasoline buses and electric trolleybuses that were always stuffed with passengers.

One thing that was admirable about the culture of Soviet public transportation was that the elderly and mothers with young children never had to ask for a seat. Volunteers immediately stood up and abandoned their seats. They didn't offer. They just did it. As a healthy young man, there was almost no chance to get a seat on public transportation, except maybe on the last trip at the end of the day. Buses and subways were generally so crowded that it took advanced planning to get near the exit to be able to jump off. To push through the crowd, you had to ask everyone blocking your way, "Are you getting off at the next?" which implied that you were and they'd let you pass. If you didn't ask, the other passengers would assume you're rude and block you.

More Equal Than Others

About a five-minutes walk from the dormitory was the Pribaltiiskaya Hotel, which is on the coast of The Baltic Sea. It was built by Swedes so it had unusual features for the USSR like functioning elevators and light fixtures with bulbs in them. It was part of Intourist, i.e. one had to have permission or a foreign passport to enter. Adjacent to the hotel was a Beriozka shop[1] where a guard was stationed inside the entrance, seated at a desk. To enter, the rule was to show a foreign passport, visa, and currency declaration. That was the rule. In reality, the drawers of the guard's desk were full of bribes that he took to overlook paperwork deficiencies. But getting past the guard wasn't what prevented most Soviets from risking a shopping excursion to a Beriozka. Law enforcement watched the entrance from inside their black Volga[2] that was always parked nearby.

Even without seeing passports, it was obvious who was a foreigner and who was local. Foreigners smile. As Russians became more comfortable about cultural differences, they'd often ask "What in the fuck are you foreigners always smiling about?" The men in the Volgas were usually hoping to make big money by nabbing a high value black marketeer, but they almost never took the risk of buying something on their own. The Volga guys usually just took their cut from the guard at the end of the day.

Pribaltiiskaya Hotel on the shores of the Gulf of Finland, Baltic Sea

---

1 Beriozka shops sold Western goods for foreign currency or credit cards only. Regular citizens were not allowed to shop there or even enter.

2 The Volga was the preferred car of most bureaucrats. Locals could identify which organization the car belonged to by license plate. Henry Ford said of the Volga, "It's entirely a tractor and not entirely a car."

Intourist's purpose was to prevent foreigners from interacting with average Soviets and to present a false face. If a Soviet citizen could get to an Intourist guest unhindered, they could do something like ask for toilet paper and reveal the genuine state of society. Near Intourist sightseeing bus stops, young children gathered to beg foreigners for another deficit item, chewing gum. We called them Gumchiks. They knew the word for gum in ten different languages. That Gumchiks weren't banished was a sign that the government was softening. Adults probably wanted to ask for deficit items too, but they stayed clear out of fear of being labeled a collaborator, which could lead to unemployment, or worse. Intourist barred regular citizens from their oases, because locals would be shocked to see things like relatively clean well-lit public restrooms with toilet paper. They didn't exist anywhere else. Beriozkas with well stocked store shelves, and cashiers who put purchases in sturdy plastic bags, was an unthinkable luxury.

Another type of store that was off-limits to regular Russians only accepted "checks" as payment. Checks were given to Soviet citizens who worked and earned foreign currency abroad. In lieu of cash, the Soviet government issued checks to the earner. For example, when Czechoslovakian tennis player Martina Navratilova made it to the semi-finals of the U.S. Open Tennis Tournament in 1975, her government was essentially Soviet. If her prize was $100,000 USD the socialist state took it all and gave her between 5% and 10% in checks, because it was illegal to possess more than $25 in foreign cash. Communist party elites used the state's budget, i.e. Navratilova's winnings or our tuition, to travel abroad and purchase whatever they wanted. They also dictated what was sold in Beriozkas and Check stores. Regular citizens were told how superior all Soviet products were to those found in the West. The elite structured institutions like Intourist to ensure that the majority of people never had the chance to discover how big that lie was.

Soviet Beriozka stores were for non-citizens only

Soviet Shopping

A typical line that immediately formed in front of a store after something scarce went on sale. People would queue without knowing what they were buying.

On the rare occasion that something popular and edible went on sale, the supermarket "system" was overwhelmed by demand. Hours-long lines would form instantly. Many people who got in line didn't know what was being sold. They innately knew that people wouldn't get in line for something that wasn't valuable. Instead of asking, "What's for sale?" The question was, "What are they giving out, or letting us have?"

Without knowing the ins and outs of making a purchase, it was almost impossible to buy anything in a Soviet store. Let's say a deli counter in a store placed 2,000 unspoiled hotdogs in a display case, with a limit of six per customer, but the hotdogs were sold by weight, no line would form and no numbers were given. Instead, a hoard of people would crowd the counter. Three or four workers behind it would choose at random who got to order. If you were lucky enough to get served, they'd weigh the order, calculate on an abacus how much it cost, and place your order out of reach on a shelf behind them. The price would be on a piece of paper next to your order. But the clerk would not give you a written price, instead they'd announce how much you had to pay. You had to remember that exact number and get a receipt for it from a cashier on the other side of the store. You couldn't pick up your order unless you brought a printed receipt that matched the price they had told you. There was always a substantial line for the cashier, too. It might seem easy to remember something simple like five rubles 72 kopecks, but with other people jostling you around and who were also mumbling numbers to themselves while hard of hearing cashiers loudly asked other customers to repeat their memorized prices, staying focused was challenging. There was also the real threat of the cash register running out of paper, which halted all sales.

Just because you managed to get a receipt, didn't mean you'd be leaving the store any time soon with your order. There was still the task of pushing your way through the crowd and trying to get the attention of a clerk to hand it over. It was easier to press forward with a receipt in hand, because the crowd knew you weren't slowing them down. Once up front, it was still not easy to get the attention of a clerk to retrieve your purchase. They were still taking orders and working the abacus. Two hours was not an unusual supermarket visit for just two or three items. Whenever something useful went on sale, a small band of opportunists would gather near the store's exit and offer to pay three or four times more for what you just purchased. It was an implied convenience fee.

The fastest shopper was a Russian babushka, grandmother. Their ability to plow through crowds was unparalleled. Whether in a crowded market or on an overstuffed bus, a babushka got to where she wanted with more determination than anybody. Only a fool would dare to not step aside in the path of a babushka. Their forcefulness elicited reverence, especially from American students, whose sense of personal space boundaries prevented them from acting like a human battering ram. Babushkas were honey badgers.

To repeat the curse, "May you live on one salary," it was a sad reality that pensioner babushkas did. In 1980s Leningrad there were more widows from WWII than any other city. Nearly the entire adult male population of Leningrad died fighting German Nazis during the siege and blockade that lasted almost 900 days. A fixed income pensioner babushka had seen and experienced everything from cannibalism to torture. Many remembered eating rats and drinking puddle water to survive. If something good went on sale at a state store, bet everything in your wallet that babushka will get to the front of line immediately. We American students had a deep and genuine admiration for babushkas and formed a consensus that she was the world's most uniquely skilled woman to play American Football.

The only ruble products in abundance without lines, and for cheap, were propaganda posters and lapel pins. Every socialist sound bite could be purchased for next to nothing. Busts and statues of famous leaders filled the shelves. There was zero demand, except mostly from ignorant foreigners, who admired the skill of the artists, while having no idea about the message. Some of my favorites were posters from bygone communist party sessions in the grand hall of the Kremlin, where they met to pretend that their assembly could command an economy to perform exactly as the document they drafted. A poster admonishing to "Implement the plan of the 27th session of the CPSU[1]!" might be surrounded by identical ones from the 25th and 22nd sessions, which too had failed. They reminded me of Charlie Brown's[2] eternal gullibility that he'd be able to kick the ball.

---

1 Communist Party of Soviet Union
2 Charlie Brown was a character in an American comic strip series, Peanuts. Charlie's antagonist, Lucy, often offered to hold in place an American football, so that Charlie could kick it. Each time he attempted to do so, Lucy would lift the ball, causing Charlie to fall on his back.

Propaganda stores sold pins, buttons, and posters like these. On the rare occasions there were customers in them, it was almost always curious foreigners.

If the store was a hairdo, it would have been a pathetic combover. On display were aisles and aisles of baranki[3] and rows of the worst pasta. Things that one didn't need much of, like baking soda and salt, were in abundance. Soviet shelves rarely contained anything one would want to eat. Pepsi-cola was mostly always available, but the caps were made with the same precision as the dormitory. The bottles usually leaked and the contents tended to be flat and stale. Pepsico built factories in the USSR for barter, receiving Stolichnaya vodka in return. Pepsi marketed Stoli as a premium brand, but in fact Russians didn't consider it near top quality. There was a Soviet version of orange Fanta that was pretty good. Therefore it was very difficult to find in ruble stores.

Central planning worked perfectly, on paper. In reality, Soviet economic indicators were useless. Coal production, for example, showed that the Soviet Union was producing billions of dollars worth of coal. What their statistics didn't show was that a large percentage of that coal was being used for coke to both make steel and to provide energy for steel mills, which steel was used to make more earth-moving machines that in turn were used to boost the production of coal. How many miles did the gerbil run on the wheel? Bureaucrats consider remaining busy success. Producers expect to create and sell goods.

A couple blocks across Shipbuilder's Street from the dormitory was a Soviet grocery store.

In 1972 Pepsi Co gave Soviets their soda in a barter deal for Stolichnaya vodka. The Soviets got the worst of that deal.

---

[3] Baranki are dried, crunchy bagel rings. They can be dipped in tea, or eaten as a cheap source of calories.

Wife to Be

When it was time for the first Wednesday rendez-vous at 1 p.m. with Marina, I hadn't yet ventured to the city center and didn't know the landmark Kazansky Cathedral. An American grad student in our program who had previously done a semester offered to show me the ropes and escorted me on a bus to Nevsky Prospekt[1]. As soon as we got off the bus a fartsovshik immediately recognized us as foreigners and approached, saying something in English. The grad student snapped, "Piss off!" I commented that she seemed extremely rude and asked if she knew him. She explained that if you treat one nicely, others will never leave you alone.

"There are always more and they're always watching," she warned. I'd never seen so many people cram daytime sidewalks, except after a sporting event. It looked like stadium crowds walking up and down Nevsky. One thing was certain. No one was at work. Automobile traffic was very light, but there were almost no jaywalkers. This was due to the fact that pedestrians had no rights on the street. The fact that someone owned a car implied they had connections. Some poor schlub on foot who got injured or killed by a car owner had little chance of getting a court date or criminal hearing for the driver. The threat was very real and people scattered when cars approached. Drivers of all types of vehicles seemed to derive a perverse pleasure by accelerating into people and watching them flee. The grad student warned me about this and advised me to look for blue and white street signs that showed a person walking down a set of stairs, which indicated there was an underground crosswalk, i.e. no need to be on the street and risk getting run over.

Near the meeting place with Marina, I thanked the grad student for her help. She disappeared into the crowd. While I waited, at least a dozen fartsovshiks made some kind of offer to engage in illegal business. I hadn't yet grasped that it wasn't impolite to tell them to fuck off, so they just kept coming. The most common offer was to buy jeans in exchange for shkatulki[2], which were expensive in dollar stores and a favorite of Western tourists. Shkatulka, which they pronounced in English like locker box (lacquer box), meant nothing to me. I couldn't understand why so many people were trying to sell or trade them. One man wearing new jeans and a jeans jacket stood out. He was

---

1 Nevsky Prospekt is the main thoroughfare of Leningrad / St. Petersburg. The equivalent of Paris' Champs-Elyesees or New York's Fifth Avenue.
2 Hand-painted lacquer boxes. The most intricate boxes at the time could sell for $500 or more.

also sporting clean new Adidas running shoes. After a little chit chat he made an entirely different kind of offer. He proposed to pay me to buy things for him in the Beriozka. He said he would provide the cash, if I was willing to make the purchase. It was an intriguing and enticing offer. Students were given a stipend of 16 rubles every two weeks. That amount of money could buy 320 bus or metro fares, or two taxi rides. The program organizers had either cynically, or wisely, told us at enrollment that no extra cash was necessary because everything would be provided for, including spending money. Because of the "You won't need money" fib, I had brought only about $350 with me. The Beriozka was eating that up so fast, I'd be broke in a few weeks. The young man with the jeans spoke in an accent I'd never heard. I asked and he said he was from Estonia. Our conversation ended when Marina arrived. She politely told the Estonian to piss off.

Marina said, "I hope you don't mind a bit of a walk. Follow me and stay quiet." Once we got on a less crowded side street, she looked back to see if anyone was following us. She didn't say much as we zigzagged South through the city for at least an hour, arriving in a remote and mostly people-free area. The sights along the route revealed formerly gorgeous but fading facades, which couldn't mask their crumbling interiors. The sad reality was the entire city desperately needed restoration, even on new construction.

We arrived at the building where one of Marina's trusted friends had left us an empty apartment. Before entering, she warned me to say nothing and to absolutely not smile if we encountered someone. There was no one in the staircase and we entered a fourth floor apartment. Marina got right down to the business of marriage. She didn't ask why I had agreed to it. She acted as if she knew someone had paid me on her behalf. Her manner was more as if she was advising an employee than a complete stranger doing a favor. She instructed me to go to ZAGS[3] as soon as possible to set a wedding date. I had only been there a week and we were already setting the date? I had my doubts. It seemed that Polishchuk's plan was absurd. I suggested that maybe we wait a few weeks, for the sake of optics. Marina brushed off my concerns and repeated, "Go to ZAGS next week on Tuesday." She gave me the time and place, as well as another emergency address for Thursdays, in case she ever failed to show up at Kazansky on Wednesdays at 1. Before leaving her friend's apartment, I noticed a large clear glass jar of some kind of hazy wavy liquid that I'd never seen before. Marina poured herself a glass, drank it and asked if I'd like one too. She called it "Mushroom tea," explaining that it contains bacteria which regenerate themselves when water is continually added. I declined, suspecting it might be Giardia infested. We agreed to meet at ZAGS the next week and I left alone, promising not to smile at anyone.

---

[3] ZAGS The State Registry of Acts of Civilian Status, also known as The Palace of Marriages (and divcorce)

Leningrad Student Life

My Leningrad State University Student ID

Outside the dormitory I ran into Diego, who asked me to go on a Beriozka run to help carry cases of Lowenbrau back to the dorm. I gladly agreed. After only a week, Diego had become a regular and knew all the guards. His Russian roommates were afraid to enter the store or even to wait outside. When we entered, the guard didn't ask to see passports. Diego confessed that he'd started giving the guard a pack of Rothman's cigarettes every time he left. This trip was no different. On the way back to the dormitory, he suggested we walk behind the buildings, away from Shipbuilders Street where there were no sidewalks. We passed an abandoned high-rise construction site between the Beriozka and dormitory. It faced the shore of the Baltic Sea. We had a beer or two there, waiting to see if the men in the black Volga would investigate. They didn't. I noticed that Diego had used a credit card to buy about $200 of booze. I asked him if his parents would be livid when they got the bill. He replied that they would never see it. His card statements were sent to an accountant in Miami. I admired the fact that someone with deep pockets, who could be anywhere in the world, was standing around an abandoned Soviet construction site, drinking canned beer.

We took the haul back to the dorm and returned to the construction site with two other students. After a little digging around, we found a stash of semi-rotted lumber that was dry enough to light. We built some makeshift benches. It was illegal for us to be there, to steal wood, to have a fire, and to drink in public. The police never bothered us. After several beers and swigs of vodka, I revealed my intention to marry Marina. The disinformation plan to track informants was instantly derailed. Instead of unique specific stories to individuals, I had told three people the truth.

Near the bonfire close to an
abandoned construction project

Students in the dormitory were expected to perform duties for the benefit of all. A reality of communism is forced labor. Its implementation could be benign, like in the form of a Subbotnik[1]. Soviets cynically referred to forced labor as "I'm working for that guy." The student party leader ordered me to clear all the garbage off the floor. Rats had been spotted climbing out of what had become for them a ladder of garbage, instead of a trash cute. When I mentioned this to the dorm leader, she insisted that any mention of rats was baseless subversive anti-Soviet propaganda, promulgated by deceitful foreign elements. With the rat argument removed, I tried to shirk my duties by pointing out that it was rather excessive to walk trash down 9 floors of stairs. Jokingly, I asked if I could just throw it onto the street from the emergency staircase. The dorm kommandant nodded yes, but with the caveat that I could only do so only after the main entrance was locked for the night. It was so much fun throwing garbage onto the street, I invited others to join in.

Clogged garbage chute in the dormitory, up through which climbed rats and roaches

I mentioned to a West German friend, Nick, what the kommandant had said about rats. He built a trap and caught one, which

---

[1] From the Russian word for Saturday, Subbota. Subbotniks were days that Soviet citizens were expected to involuntarily perform some activity for the benefit of society. Derisively, people referred to it as "Working for that guy." Cynically, a Subbotnik could mean that citizens were forced to weed the garden of a party leader's home, whereas no citizen was allowed to own either a garden or a separate home.

he victoriously waved in her face as proof that rats were climbing up the garbage chute. She scolded him for engaging in propaganda and declared, "It is despicable that you dared to bring a rat from West Germany in an attempt to damage our reputation."

On the second floor of the dorm was a common cafeteria. Every type of student could eat together. People with connections rarely ate there, because most of the tasty and edible ingredients were already sold out the side door. What was served to students for free was mostly unwanted leftovers. The hand dishwasher in the cafeteria washed only one side of a plate and then stacked them. Flimsy aluminum silverware always felt to the touch as if it had been dipped in lard. The cafeteria wasn't so much about food, but a chance to hear the experiences of other students. Uncharacteristically, I went to the cafeteria by myself one evening and saw no Americans or Hungarians, who also lived on the 9th floor. With nowhere to sit, I walked around for several minutes with a tray until finally noticing a couple open seats at a table of Africans. I asked them in Russian if I could join them.

"As long as you don't mind sitting with a monkey," was one's reply.

Taken aback, I asked, "What the hell are you talking about?"

"Are you a Russian racist?" another asked.

"No. I'm not even Russian. I'm American."

With that, the conversation changed from hostile to cordial. They switched to English, which was forbidden. I was happy to make contact with people from another tower. One guy introduced himself as the son of a diplomat from Ghana, another was from Zimbabwe and a third from Angola. After eating, I took their room numbers and gave them mine. Out of habit, I stuck the end of the pen in my mouth. One of them asked, "What does that remind you of?" I thought to myself, "Oh shit, I hope he doesn't think I'm interested in gay sex." I told him I didn't understand. He got a little more explicit and asked if I like Rastafarian culture and if I wanted to "visit" Jamaica. I asked what he was thinking. He replied that he could show me better than he could tell me. He suggested we all go upstairs to their room. Off we went.

The kitchen of the dormitory's cafeteria

Officially, I was supposed to have a permission slip to enter other towers, but this was Soviet Russia. The dezhurnaya didn't even look up as we passed. A widely cited quote about Russian law enforcement that originated in the 1800's, but has remained true ever since, is "The severity of Russian laws is softened by lax and random enforcement." The quote is generally attributed to Russian author Mikhail Saltykov-Schedrin[2]. However, some suggest the quote could be attributed to an author as early as the era of Peter I in the early 1700s.

In the room, the Africans pulled out a ceramic jar filled with hash. Brad and Edna's numerous admonitions to never do anything illegal evaporated. Arkady Polischuk and Dr. Breer warned that trickery and entrapment were the backbone of the KGB. I quickly crumbled when the Africans filled a bowl and lit it, offering me a smoke. They could have been collaborators, but no one knew about Marina, except for the three students I got drunk with. There was no reason for entrapment. We smoked up. As they were explaining that Soviet soldiers returning from the war in Afghanistan were bringing back hash and heroin, I heard less and less of the conversation. My thoughts were drifting to every horror story I'd heard about Soviet stings and set-ups. Paranoia kicked in and visions of being in a prison cell stuffed with men that had tattooed knuckles took over.

It seemed the Ghanaian could sense I was scared. He showed me his diplomatic passport and told me not to worry. He was untouchable and willing to take all the blame. He said he hated heroin and refused to deal it. Hash was another story. He had at least a half kilo in the jar. Another guy tried to lighten my mood by playing a song with the stereo's treble all the way up, making it sound like something was sizzling. He said that in Zimbabwe they called that sound setting "Frying fish."

When I made up some excuse to leave, they offered me a free chunk of hash. They seemed like great people, but I was suspicious and paranoid. I expected to open the door and see police waiting to arrest me. I asked if I could come back the next day and pick up a taste. They cordially invited me to return any time. As I walked out of their room, I was saying to myself, *You enormous moron. You are going to jail. There will be a cop waiting downstairs. This was a set-up. The guard on the 2nd floor is going to stop you and won't let you return to your tower. They're going to want to know who you were visiting and pressure you to tell how and where you got stoned."* I walked back completely unhindered and encountered no one. Safely on the ninth floor, I went directly to Diego's and exuberantly told him about the incredible connection.

The next night Diego, another American and I were in the Africans' room. During our visit, multiple nationalities stopped by. The Africans declared their smoking device a "peace pipe." We talked and laughed for hours. I remembered a scene from the South African movie "The Gods Must Be Crazy," when a rhinoceros attacks a campfire and stamps it out. I asked about it. The Zimbabwean told me

---

2   Author and satirist who wrote under the pen name Nikolai Shchedrin. He died in 1889. His quote is still accurate today. Saltykov-Schedrin is considered to be like a Russian Mark Twain.

that the scene was accurate, claiming many cultures in Southern Africa believe that rhinos used to have fur, but one day it got burned off. When a rhino sees a fire, it will stamp it out or dump a mouth full of water on it. An American laughed at that. The Zimbabwean admonished him in a heavy accent, "Don't laugh. That's nature!"

The Zimbabwean told us about another uniquely African animal that hides under ashes with its asshole exposed. Like an angler fish that has a built-in lure, this Zimbabwean creature, he claimed, has what looks like a seedling in its powerful anus. If a chicken or other bird tries to pluck what looks like a sprout, the animal will snap its bunghole shut tight and suffocate the bird. He added that it also has a skunk-like defense mechanism. If someone gets too close, he warned, it can unleash a horrific fart blast that would send anyone running. We all laughed and got the same serious reply, "Don't laugh! That's Nature!"

Multi-nationalities enjoying the African "Peace Pipe" in Leningrad

Later in the evening a Polish girl popped in. When she learned that Diego was from Cali, Colombia, she went to retrieve some Colombian students who lived on a lower floor. The Polish girl returned with three Colombian communists, who started a conversation in Spanish with Diego. The Africans passed around the peace pipe very hospitably. We stayed until late. When we returned to our tower, Diego told me about his conversation with his countrymen in Spanish. He said, "Back home, these people want to kill my family. There is no way I could have had a civil conversation with them there." He declared it a fascinating encounter and I believe they eventually became friends.

Set a Wedding Date

Because I'd committed to operation Marina, I reluctantly had to abandon any hopes of spending more time in the East Bloc and African dorm tower. The risk was too big to continue. As soon as our wedding was registered, I knew that the KGB would be paying a little more attention. Being denied fun times with interesting people caused me to hold a little grudge against Marina, even though I was the one who agreed to the marriage.

The reality of Soviet life was reflected by the most common slang words to describe it: "Bardak" (mess), "Durdom" (madhouse), and the mainstay "Sovok[1]" (dustpan). While asking for simple things that weren't available, like toilet paper and shampoo, the indoctrinated parroted the same script, "in principle, everything can be purchased in the Soviet Union." Ubiquitous use of the term "in principle" fascinated me. How could there be such a disconnect with reality in so many people? Former Soviet dissident Natan Sharansky called this "Doublethink." In public people parrot the party line, but in private they say and think the opposite. Instead of replying honestly, which would have been "You will find nothing good on the shelf of a Sovok store," they ran with the doublethink answer, "In principle." Alexander Solzhenitsyn[2] observed the phenomenon a little differently, "The solemn pledge to abstain from telling the truth was called socialist realism."

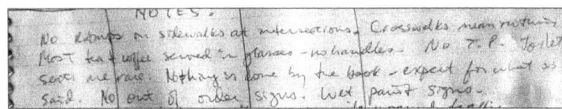

Quote from my journal: "Nothing is done by the book, except for what is said"

People on the street were genuinely kind and courteous. It is worth noting because after visiting numerous other Russian cities, I concluded that it was a particular quirk of Leningrad. The memory of the siege during WWII seems to have left behind a culture of camaraderie and caring. But also because of the siege, Soviet officials intentionally removed street signs and printed bogus maps. They did this to ensure that it would be difficult for invaders to navigate. Printing an

---

1 Sovok is a play on the word Soviet. It translates to English as 'Scoop' or 'Dustpan,' but is generally used to describe any otherwise indescribable situation or policy, uniquely Soviet. A usage would be to answer why a sign reading "No seating available" would hang on the entrance of a completely empty restaurant. Sovok, a Soviet thing.
2 Solzhenitsyn was one of the most famous Soviet dissident authors. He wrote openly and honestly about Soviet life. Despite being a soldier in the Red Army and having reached Eastern Germany in February 1945, Soviet military intelligence officers arrested him for having criticized Stalin in private letters to friends and family. He was sentenced to eight years. .

accurate map of a Soviet city was considered an act of treason and sabotage. Therefore street signs were mostly absent. This could also be attributed simply to Bardak, but most believed it was due to intentional military geographic disinformation. Even major landmarks were omitted from whatever primitive maps there were. There was no way to easily find an address without the help of locals. If you asked someone for directions, it was not uncommon for them to escort you until it was certain you would not get lost again. A kind woman did just that, and walked me to ZAGS (Wedding Palace).

Marina was waiting outside. It was an official looking building with extra tall doors. I felt more trepidation than I'd expected. What if there were interrogators? They could separate us and easily find inconsistencies about how we met and why we were planning a wedding so quickly. I suggested that we memorize a brief story that we could stick to. Marina was unbothered and said, "Let's go find the office that deals with foreigners." A guard was sitting inside, who didn't check our IDs and pointed to a half open door down a wide hallway. A stern looking woman inside was writing things at her desk on some kind of form with lined paper. She was using a ruler. Marina knocked and sheepishly greeted her, exuding obligatory respect and asking permission to approach. "Documents," the woman demanded without saying hello. I set down my passport and visa, and Marina hers. After a short once over, the woman asked why we had chosen that branch of ZAGS and not another. A universal trait of bureaucrats is finding a reason to not work. Government officials in the USSR wanted to garner a reputation of being difficult to deal with. If word got around that they were helpful and cooperative, they'd be swamped. They had to ensure that their demeanor was terse and unpleasant.

Marina explained that because I was registered[3] in this woman's ZAGS district, and because it was impossible for me to enter Gatchina, that location was our only option. She examined my visa and filled out a pre-printed form. She handed it to Marina and snapped "Goodbye" with finality. Marina grabbed me by the arm and led me out. Outside, Marina showed me the paper. The date was set for two days after the expiration of my visa. This seemed catastrophic and I said as much to Marina, who corrected me, saying that the meeting had gone better than expected. Just getting any wedding date was a success. Confused, I told Marina that it was impossible to change my visa. She calmly explained that ZAGS only wanted a bribe. "Make it worth her while and she will bend," Marina said with confidence. She suggested that with an official date, we should start being seen together, especially at student parties.

---

3 Foreign visitors to USSR (as in today's Russia) are required by law to notify the government where they will live and for how long. Hotels do this at check-in. Soviet citizens were issued domestic passports which contained a stamp called "Propiska," registration of residence. Authorities were empowered to change a citizen's residence as desired. Graduates of trade schools and universities would be sent to whichever locations the Politburo deemed specialists were needed. Propiskas in Moscow and Leningrad were coveted.

Eyes would be on us and it would be helpful to have many people corroborate.

It seemed an easy thing to do, but it wasn't. Almost no one had a telephone and it took an hour or more to get from the dorm to another safe apartment she arranged near Elektrosila. If someone was not at home, it wasted hours. I mentioned to Marina another possible snag was that she didn't look like a student and might not get past the dormitory's dezhurnaya. She rolled her eyes.

We met the next day at Kazansky. Marina suggested we go for lunch where government officials would likely be. She took me a couple blocks away to the European Hotel (now the Grand Hotel Europe). On the restaurant door, signs proclaimed "Sold out" and "No seats available." I asked what other places we could go to. She looked at me with incredulity and asked why anyone would believe what was written on a sign. She asked for a three-ruble banknote or a pack of cigarettes. Yes, there really was a three-ruble note. I gave her a three and she slipped it into the maitre d's hand. He held the door open and pointed us towards any table in what was an almost entirely empty restaurant. Why would they intentionally turn customers away? I asked. Restaurants didn't rely on customers to thrive or fail. Rent and utilities were subsidized. Food ingredients at state prices were almost free. Menu prices were set by the state. They'd earn much more by selling their food at market prices to friends and family. In every industry, the saying was "They pretend to pay us. We pretend to work."

Marina taught me the basics. To get into a restaurant, if they didn't know you, it was necessary to demonstrate a willingness to overpay by bribing to enter. Restaurants tried to repel business. It was more profitable to stay empty. To hail a taxi, show two fingers. That indicated you'd pay double the fare of the government installed meter. Without at least two fingers, no one would stop. Three fingers (triple the meter) was for later at night. If three fingers didn't work, hold out a pack of Marlboro Reds or Dunhills, brands sold only in Beriozkas. With an outheld pack of cigarettes, it wasn't too uncommon for a rogue city bus driver, who'd abandoned his route, to stop his empty bus as a taxi. Bus fare was five kopecks. Foreign cigarettes cost the equivalent of a hundred and fifty riders or more, which the driver didn't collect anyway. It was basic economics. If a parked taxi refused to take passengers at any price, that meant they were selling something out of the trunk, which was most likely vodka. The sign to buy alcohol, or a desire to get drunk, was to flick the side of your neck with your index finger, or slap it with a couple fingers. On one of the more memorable empty bus rides, the driver blasted the song "Tenderness" by General Public while smoking a joint behind the wheel with one of my fellow American students, Liza.

After lunch, Marina and I walked to the Nevsky Prospekt metro station, across Nevsky from Kazansky Cathedral. She went down the escalator to the metro and I walked across the street to again observe the ongoings of the black marketeers.

Hired By a Criminal

The Estonian was there. He stood out. In a sea of drab, he looked blinged. We made eye contact. He approached, repeating his offer to pay me for Beriozka runs. He said he'd give me a bottle of gin or rum right there as an advance. I couldn't see how he could possibly have a stash of booze, so I asked where he kept it. He pointed to his brand new car, a Lada Devyatka (aka VAZ-2109 Sputnik), a small four-door hatchback. It was the color of burnt peanuts. He was in his early 20's. It took most people ten years of connections and money to get a new car. Noticing that his car even had windshield wipers, I accepted his offer. He introduced himself as Raivo.

He opened the car and removed a blanket to reveal cases of gin and rum, as promised. He also had boxes of shoes. Raivo offered to discuss business over a cup of coffee. I hadn't seen coffee since leaving Helsinki. On the way to the Hotel Sovetskaya, Raivo stopped to pick up his girlfriend Nina. When we got to the hotel, the guards and staff there acknowledged Raivo with welcoming nods and waved him through to a completely empty restaurant. A waitress appeared as soon as we sat down. The coffee was freeze-dried, but served by a courteous staff in a clean restaurant. It was a luxury. Raivo told me one of his businesses was reselling things from Beriozkas. He wasn't worried about guards, but the KGB agents that monitored the stores could turn nasty on him at any moment, wipe out his operation, bankrupt him, or worse. An American with a currency declaration was pretty much untouchable. My assistance would greatly mitigate his risk.

Raivo promised to reward me. I apologized that I probably couldn't help because before entering Russia, I changed all my dollars into Finnish Marks, intending to blow it all during our last night in Helsinki. Finns and Estonians are not known for being dramatic, or for showing emotion in general. But when Raivo heard me say I had a Finn Mark declaration, his eyes lit up and he declared it, "Excellent!" pulling from his pocket a wad of Finn Marks. At that moment, I began working as a part-time Beriozka shopper for Raivo the Estonian fartsovshik. It was a perfect set up. For me it wasn't illegal. It may have been illegal for Raivo, but not immoral.

Conveniently, the first Beriozka he chose was the one next to the dormitory. The job had benefits, too: Free booze and private transportation. I showed him the dorm and gave him my room number. He said he would send Nina to look for me in the future. She was Russian and looked like a student. Raivo didn't want extra attention by being seen in a dorm full of Americans.

Two or three times a week I'd ride around with Raivo, making random purchases on his behalf. One day in the Hotel Moscow's Beriozka at one end of Nevsky Prospekt, an underground movie translator named Pavel approached me and asked if I would buy all of the store's blank video cassettes for him. He promised to pay me a huge amount. Even though my currency declaration was for a fraction of the purchase price, I agreed. Pavel gave me the money and told me where he'd be waiting outside. Copy machines and cassettes, both video and audio, were highly regulated and scarce. They could be used to spread and promote ideas of rebellion, as well as forbidden foreign movies, which were sort of the same thing. State censors allowed almost no American films, but famously blundered by officially allowing "One Flew Over The Cuckoo's Nest." The censors assumed that the audience would understand Milos Forman's masterpiece as a condemnation of American society. Soviet audiences thought the movie was an allegory about Sovok.

Usually, there might be five or six VHS cassettes on sale at one time. Pavel's purchase that day was dozens. I bought them all and struggled to carry the boxes up the street to where we were out of view of the guys in the black Volga. I was floored when Pavel handed me the equivalent of an average person's yearly salary, 1,400 rubles. The University program gave us 16 rubles every two weeks. I made sure to let Pavel know how to contact me if he needed anything in the future. When I told Pavel that he'd been extremely generous, he shrugged it off and declared rubles worthless. He offered the best exchange rate I'd heard, 5:1. Near the dormitory 3 ½ : 1 was the average.

Pavel sold smuggled foreign movies that he and a small crew translated and overdubbed. A month or so after buying the cassettes for him, Pavel reached out, asking if I could decipher what he claimed was complicated dialogue from an American TV show. He said their best English language experts couldn't understand what was being said. It was a TV show called "Moonlighting" with Bruce Willis. In Pavel's crammed studio, where there were approximately 20 VCRs running at once, one of the English experts turned on the scene that had them stumped. I started shaking with laughter. It was Pig Latin![1] I explained how it works and walked out of Pavel's studio grinning.

In the group of Americans there was an aspiring male opera singer, Jock. He was an excellent conversationalist, great drinking partner, and talented Russian speaker. He heard through the grapevine about my intended bogus marriage and confided that he was gay and wanted to meet a Russian sailor. I was sincerely scared for him. Homosexuality was illegal and punishable by prison. All that could

---

1 Pig Latin was a popular American language game in the 1950's. Usually, the first consonant of a word is cut off and added to the end of the word, plus the letters "Ay." In Pig Latin the language would be pronounced Igpay Atinlay.

be done was to wish him safety and happiness, but I remained worried about him.

Another American student claimed he had visited an underground club where he snorted heroin with punk rockers. My interest in heroin has always been zero, but I loved the fact that a club like that could exist and operate, despite bans on music, drugs, and assembly. Unsanctioned clubs were officially forbidden, but the KGB allowed some to operate under the false belief that if they allowed anti-Soviet songs to be performed, they'd be better equipped to combat the message. An unlikely promoter of the Leningrad underground music scene at the time was American Joanna Stingray,[2] proof that one person can make a difference.

Raivo continued to show me interesting places, like one of Russia's first pizza cooperatives[3] on the far South side of the city, not far from the airport. Eventually, I got comfortable enough to ask Raivo if he had any sway at ZAGS to change my wedding date. He didn't, but was certain that he could find an in via the Kazansky crowd. Raivo reported the woman's first and patronymic[4] names, Larisa Sergeevna, and that she loved imported tea. He also knew the best shop in town for tea was the Ship Chandler (Albatross) at the port, which was a variation on a Beriozka. Its purpose was to sell food items only to the crews of international commercial ships. Raivo, of course, had a connection there too.

Raivo (r), Estonian black market hustler, aka my employer.

After buying the tea, I asked Raivo if his source about Larisa Sergeevna would soften her up to improve the chances of success. It seemed it might offend her to just arrive with a bribe. Raivo said, "No. I will drive you to ZAGS now." En route, Raivo coached me on how to speak, what not to say, and how to act. I thought that Marina should be there too. Perhaps I was jeopardizing the operation by going solo. Raivo scoffed, explaining that the opposite was true. It was better if I went alone. Bureaucrats are afraid of stings. Raivo

---

2 Stingray was an American woman, who befriended all the major underground rock artists in Leningrad. She was known to bring equipment from the U.S., delivering much needed deficit items like guitar strings, cassettes, and recording equipment. In 1986 she released in the U.S. the first recording of Russian rock music, a double album called "Red Wave" featuring a side each of four Leningrad bands.

3 In the final years of the USSR, the government began to allow a very small number of Cooperatives, state sanctioned for-profit businesses.

4 It is impolite in Russian to refer to someone you don't know by their first name only. Official nameplates in offices generally show only last names and initials. A person's patronymic name is taken from their father. Sergeevna meant that the ZAGS official's father was named Sergei. The son of Sergei would be Sergeevich.

predicted that Larisa would be more willing to accept a bribe in the presence of a lone foreigner. Raivo considered it preposterous for someone to suspect that Soviet law enforcement would send an American to entrap a bureaucrat. I felt compelled to at least warn Marina, but Raivo remained adamant that we were proceeding correctly. He declared my concerns horsefeathers and dropped me off at ZAGS, certain that if I stayed on script the job would get done.

In the lobby, I could see that again Larisa Sergeeva was in her office alone. I tapped shyly on her door. She seemed a little stunned when I called her by her proper name. She looked up and said, "I'm listening." I stated that she must have erroneously entered the wrong date the last time we saw her because the date she set was past the expiration of my visa. I asked if she could please possibly re-check the registry to see if she might have overlooked an earlier date, perhaps one in December. As I continued, I pulled the box of assorted teas from the bag, placing it on her desk and saying, "since you are doing us such a great favor, I thought perhaps you might accept a little gratitude in advance." She examined the tea, and then studied the register. Placing the tea on a shelf behind her, she announced that an earlier date had indeed been overlooked. Marina and I were rescheduled to be wed on December 22. I thanked her, took the new pre-printed form with the date and time and walked out of her office on air, and with swag. I was ecstatic. Not because we could get married, but because I had just swayed my first bureaucrat. It was liberating to get a poker-faced bully to bend.

When I next saw Marina and informed her, what I'd done at ZAGS, I thought she'd be angry. Instead, she basically said, "I told you so. The woman wanted a bribe." After letting just two people know about the wedding date, chatter started circulating. What came back to me was that the American program directors, as well as my roommates, were already asking everyone questions about Marina and me. There were questions about my class attendance as well, which was close to non-existent. Students were being instructed to report everything they heard about Marina and me either to the U.S. Consulate or University administrators. This prompted me to start attending classes, which also provided the opportunity for me to meet students I hadn't met before and tell them lies about Marina, which I hoped they'd relay.

Pretend to Be a Student

Having become accustomed to riding with Raivo and taking taxis, it felt strange riding a packed bus to the University. A man on the bus absolutely reeked. I whispered to a Russian friend that the passenger really stank. She shrugged it off and explained, "He probably lives in an apartment with no running water." Listening to lectures was challenging. It was about halfway through the semester and I attended a class for the first time called Stranovedenie, or National Studies. The students changed the course name slightly to "Strashnovedenie," which means something like horror studies. The class was basically an endless presentation of Soviet propaganda, with the professor extolling the superior socialist way of life. Subject appropriate, the professor was known to be among the most corrupt on campus. I attended the class once and took a photo mid-lesson that most considered emblematic. The minds of the students were anywhere but in that class.

It was easy to reject everything they attempted to teach in Strashnovedenie. Even the professor knew what came out of his mouth was bullshit. Socialism's fatal flaw is that it ignores human nature. No amount of bloviating can nullify the fact that people won't work hard for a stranger's benefit. Dostoevsky simplified that observation by asking which scenario would motivate an individual to take action faster, a) his own toothache or b) an urgent need to rescue earthquake victims in China? Rescuing earthquake victims would be more beneficial to humanity overall, but not likely.

American students suffering through a lecture about the virtues of socialism

Soviet textbooks touted as a hero a boy named Pavlik Morozov, who reported to authorities that his farmer parents stored grain in their basement. This was a crime because all grain was property of the state, whose mission was to feed the masses. The result of the policy was that five million people starved to death in the early 1930s. Whether Pavlik was a propaganda myth or real, the state portrayed him as a martyr, claiming that his family murdered him for reporting their activities to the GPU, which Soviet agency was likely the model on which Göring based Nazi Germany's Gestapo. In 1987, Pavlik Morozov's story was still taught in textbooks, but his image was mostly absent in propaganda shops.

In the courtyard outside the study halls, students gathered to smoke cigarettes. Near the smoking area it was not uncommon to see dogs with various electrical wiring in their heads and bodies. The world famous dog psychologist Ivan Pavlov had lived in St. Petersburg / Leningrad and work in that discipline continued there.

The stated goal of our educational exchange program was "Immersion in Soviet culture." Attending classes and studying were therefore inconsistent with the mission statement. I showed up at another class I'd never been to about mid-way through the term and was asked whether I was enrolled by the professor, whom I'd never seen. I confirmed that I was and stated my name. She looked it up on the list and stated "I don't think I've seen you before" and started the lecture. The rumors that professors did not give any merit to attendance were true. It seemed like a fantastic system until you realized that medical schools operated the same way and some day you might need a skilled doctor.

I'd arrive at campus, intending to attend classes, but places like the Hermitage[1] and the Russian Museum were just across the Neva River on foot by bridge. The allure was too much. Other students discovered a beer bar near campus on Vasilievsky Island that actually had beer on sale for rubles, but if you didn't arrive there by 10:00 a.m. for the opening, the day's allocation sold out quickly. The students who went there raved about the experience of drunken conversations with local riffraff. The ambience sounded enticing, but I've never been a fan of drinking in the morning. All agreed the toilets were godawful and advised to only pee outside in the courtyard.

After word spread about the engaged American, a Russian student named Olya sent a request to meet me. She claimed to have married an American the year before. When I finally met Olya, she told me her husband's name and that he was a student from Yale. We had a student in our group from Yale, whom I asked if she had ever crossed paths with Olya's husband. She hadn't, and added that the Russian program at Yale was quite small. She was pretty certain that she knew everyone. To me, that added up to Olya being a KGB plant. I never told her anything truthful about Marina. However, we did speak occasionally on the outside chance her story was real. Olya lived in the number six dorm, so we didn't meet too often.

The frequency of Beriozka runs for Raivo ramped up and he seemed to be raking in more cash than ever, as in average yearly salaries every few days. I was amazed at how many times I could use a single currency declaration and no one questioned it. About three months into our cooperation, Raivo showed signs that he was under some kind of pressure. Nina

---

[1] The Hermitage is the largest art museum in the world and in pre-Soviet times was the royal Winter Palace.

wasn't her happy usual self either. Then Raivo showed up at Kazansky by taxi and told me he had sold his car. He asked for my phone number and address in the U.S. He said he would make contact again soon, but was leaving Leningrad for a little bit. After a week or two of his absence, I became worried and hoped to find him through Nina, but I'd only been to her apartment building once on that first day. I had no idea where it was. I never saw Raivo again.

Group of Soviet and American students in the dormitory

Blood Sample or Be Deported

At some point in the semester the AIDS hysteria reached the USSR. They implemented a policy that all foreigners in the country for more than a week needed to take a blood test. Without an HIV negative result, you'd be forced to leave the country. Brad or Edna, or both, proved to be quite useful. The Soviet testing method was to draw blood with the same syringe multiple times. The American administrators insisted that testing be delayed until single use, individually wrapped, sterile syringes were delivered from the USA. When the syringes arrived and blood samples were drawn, American observers stood watch and ensured that each was used only once and destroyed afterwards. Those drawing blood muttered incessantly about how wasteful Americans were and whelped that we were needlessly destroying perfectly good syringes.

After blood samples were submitted, the administrators warned us not to panic if the test results were bad. The Soviet AIDS test had approximately an 8% false positive rate, which made me wonder what the false negative rate was. All the test results came back negative. No one was sent home and life returned to "Normal."

Americana

Wandering around Gostiniy Dvor[1], which was always very crowded, I noticed a woman looking at me. Once we made eye contact she walked deliberately through the crowd. Standing in front of me, she said, "Congratulations. Your team won." Confused, I asked her what she meant. Before walking away, she asked, "Aren't you from Minnesota?" I'd never seen her before. About a week or so later, I learned that the Minnesota Twins baseball team had won the world series against St. Louis.

A friend and I were drinking at the top floor bar of the European Hotel when we recognized an actor from a popular American TV show called "Cheers." Instinctively we yelled, "Norm!" his character's name and how he was always greeted on the show. He was surprised to meet "local" Americans and asked questions about life in Leningrad. After bemoaning to him the state of cuisine, he went to his room and returned with a box of Ritz crackers and an aerosol can of Cheez Whiz[2]. My friend and I took it back to the dormitory, where we hid behind the garbage chute to prevent someone from spotting our treasure and asking us to share. We felt some guilt, but not much. When I was younger and shopped with my mother, if I had even suggested to her that we should get Cheez Whiz for the house, she would have thwacked me on the head and told me to not eat plastic. I never ate it before or again. When I mentioned the incident to my dad, he observed, "The most flavorful sauce is starvation."

---

1 Russia's original shopping mall. It opened around 1770 and has operated continually ever since. It is approximately 850,000 square feet / 78,000 square meters.
2 Cheez Whiz is the brand name of an American processed cheese that was launched in the early 1950's. According to Reference.com Cheez Whiz contains 27 ingredients. Cheese is not listed as one of them.

USSR Beyond Leningrad

As part of the immersion program, we took a brief tour to Moscow and Rostov-na-Donu as well as to three other Soviet Republics. Yerevan, Armenia was the first stop outside of Russia. As we were descending to land at the airport, single homes with cars parked in a driveway and occasional swimming pools were visible. In all of Leningrad, I'd never seen a home with a fenced in yard and a car parked in the driveway. It was intriguing how they could get away with being blatant Soviet scofflaws. The USSR was all about conformity, collectivism, and equal misery. Yerevan was full of individuals and small businesses.

A map of Yerevan wasn't really needed to wander the city. Our hotel was on top of one the highest peaks and was also quite tall itself. It was visible from just about everywhere. The weather was very warm compared to Leningrad, as in the 60s F. Most of us immediately went for a walk around the city, because the hotel told us we were three hours early for check-in, even though we'd arrived slightly late.

Almost immediately, we were amazed to find a café with outdoor seating, good service, and open tables. The food was not just edible, but delicious. No need to bribe even. Real coffee was served in Ibriks (Dzhezve). Lavash bread and lavash pizza tasted better than anything in Leningrad and it was available without standing in line. Western music played over decent sounding speakers.

People weren't afraid to engage in conversation and even criticize Soviet life. At that time the governor of California was Armenian, George Deukmejian (from 1983 – 1991). Yerevan was proud of him and they joked that there were more Armenians in California than in Armenia. When we got back to the hotel to put our suitcases in the room, my roommate and I turned on the television. TV was a rarity in the Leningrad dorm. There was one communal TV. None of the Americans watched it. Each dorm room, however, was equipped with the hallmark delivery system of communist propaganda, a radio with one channel, "The Lighthouse." Tuneable radios were scarce and the USSR jammed at will broadcasts like Radio Free Europe, Radio Liberty, BBC, and Voice of America, even though they publicly claimed to have stopped doing so. Yerevan gave us the first chance to channel flip. We were stunned to see American TV shows with Turkish subtitles.

Ever since the Turkish genocide against Armenians in 1915, Armenians have not held Turks in the highest regard. As my roommate and I were marveling about the fact we were watching a popular contemporary American TV show in English, our hotel door burst open and a 280 pound Armenian walked across the room and turned our TV off. He announced, "That is Turkish shit. Don't watch Turkish shit in Armenia."

"No! That was American shit," we protested. "And we're American."

"Well, why are you wasting time on shit when you can learn about Armenia? Come to our room for some Armenian wine." We took the invitation.

The big man's friend was waiting for him in a spacious room down the hall. They were from a village, and in Yerevan to sell their homemade wine from somewhere half-way across the country. They'd obviously been sampling their wares most of the day. Their Russian was dreadful but understandable. The wine was in wide-mouthed 10 liter glass jars. As they tried to pour it directly into the omnipresent Graneniy Stakan[1] they'd at first spill, then once over target they'd over pour and spill some more. Their room's coffee table and floor were drenched in wine.

"Isn't that wasteful?" we asked, suggesting maybe they could use a pitcher.

"Don't worry," they explained, "We have 200 or so liters here, but we also have at least a thousand more in our van." The wine was awful, but effective. It was cloudy white and had a hint of yellow to it. I called it "Armenian sweat wine" in my notes about Yerevan. I'm sure that in our wine chugging session we settled any conflicts that may have existed between Armenia and America. We thanked them for the hospitality and stumbled back to our room.

Before we could fall asleep, two Russian women in their late twenties walked in. This was surprising because we had learned to lock the door after the Armenian TV censors had barged in. The women started yelling, calling us thieves. They walked into the hall, announcing loudly, "We've been robbed. We've been robbed. Help!" Our wine merchant friends were the first to emerge and they immediately defended our good names, without even knowing what was happening. We had a brief stand-off with the women and wouldn't let them back into our room. Other people emerged and someone went to fetch a manager.

The hotel admitted that they were overbooked. US dollar paying foreigners via Intourist took precedence over ruble paying Soviets. While we were forced to wait to check in, the hotel staff was busy clearing out the rooms of Soviet guests and didn't bother to tell them about it. In Soviet hotels, the rule was to leave keys with the dezhurnaya when you left your room, but they weren't always there, or they might take gratuities to ignore protocol. The two women who accused us of

---

1 A striated drinking glass that holds 250 ML or about 8 ounces. Across the USSR there were soda vending machines, which for a 15 kopeck coin would dispense a glass full of sweetened carbonated water. The glasses were communal. After someone drank their glass full of soda, they'd return the glass to the top of the vending machine for the next customer.

stealing their stuff hadn't left their key. The hotel had given us a duplicate.

After the first night, we went on a field trip to an avante-garde museum. While my friend and I had been chugging sweat wine, several other students had gone to a nightclub where they were offered and consumed some kind of hallucinogenic pills. Several students bought those pills to pop during the rest of our, um, trip. I refused, but one of my better friends tried one with breakfast. In the art exhibit, he stopped in front of an exhibit and with a look of panic told me that the painting was moving. He sat down on a bench and stared forward with a scared look on his face. I examined the image that was causing him fear, a painting of the face of a multi-colored fish with its mouth agape. I walked in front of my friend, put my palms on my cheeks and waved them like gills, while opening and closing my mouth like a fish. He stared with undeniable fright and said "I am going to kill you," but he couldn't move and stayed on that bench with a scared expression for about an hour.

Sitting in another outdoor cafe on a hill, we watched with curiosity as a garbage truck driver below drove around, emptying the contents of garbage cans onto streets and sidewalks. He left the garbage, but took the cans.

After Yerevan we went to Lvov (Lviv), Ukraine. It's a very scenic city with an almost 800-year history, the most recent century of which is not to be envied. Until 1939 it had been part of Poland. In 1939 the Soviets invaded and, in 1941, the Nazis. The city suffered massive damage with over 100,000 Jews murdered. Because Stalin had starved to death millions of Ukrainians just six years earlier, it was understandable why many locals would want to side with Stalin's enemy. It's not clear why, though, Ukrainian Nationalists started killing Jews before the arrival of Nazi Einsatzgruppe C, who was guilty of murdering more of the Jewish population than any other entity. The locals chose to blame Russians for all the bad that had happened there.

Fellow student getting his weight checked on a sidewalk in Lvov, Ukraine.

While on a bus tour of the city, the local guide told us about the sights in English. There was a KGB agent on board, in the form of an Intourist overseer. She interrupted the guide's speech and instructed her threateningly to speak only Russian. The guide nodded and continued, in English, "To your right you will see the city's Opera House . . . ." The agent was glaring at her, but she refused to say one word in Russian. Walking around town, we got the same treatment. If we spoke to someone in Russian, they'd respond with shoulder shrugs and a blank stare. If we told them we were Americans and could communicate only in Russian or English, then they'd speak Russian. I experienced the same treatment in Prague a few years later.

The meltdown at Chernobyl had happened a little over a year prior and it had devastated the food supply. Our hotel in Lvov only sold "Sandwiches," which consisted of a single piece of black bread, topped with a small slab of pork fat into which they had drizzled fish oil for extra nutrition. We bought trays of those sandwiches only to eat the black bread underneath.

The takeaway oddity in Lvov was signs everywhere advertising the movie, Crocodile Dundee. It was unusual to see any movie ad, but especially a foreign one in color. What also stuck out was the title's translation, "Dundee who goes by the sobriquet of Crocodile."

Speaking Russian in Lvov may have elicited the silent treatment, but in Tallinn, Estonia, it caused outright hostility. Estonia is a country of only 1.3 million people. For a country that small which has been conquered countless times, it's amazing they still have a local culture. An underlying fear and distrust of outsiders permeates everything and causes a type of reserve in people that is palpable. Like their Finnish neighbors, Estonians are not known for dramatics. Displays of emotion are rare. They have a reputation of being unflappable. A common Russian joke told to demonstrate the terseness of Estonians is that a Russian passenger boards a train. His space is in an overnight sleeper car for two. An Estonian is already in the compartment when the Russian enters and says, "Good evening." The Estonian says nothing. The next morning when they awake, the Russian says, "Good morning." The Estonian gets up, walks out and slams the door behind him, muttering to himself, "Fucking Russian chatterbox will not shut up."

Old town Tallinn looked well preserved and was/is one of the more beautiful, quaint places in the world. We visited the nearby beach on the Baltic Sea, where strong winds blew snow that felt like high velocity rice pelting our faces, so we decided to return to old town. While we were exploring Tallinn, Marina somehow managed to catch up with us. I was so shocked that I forgot to pretend that she was my fianceé. As I was asking her how she had found us, she mumbled under her breath, "Show that you're ecstatic to see me. Kiss and hug, dumb ass. People are watching. After faking some theatrics, a snowball hit me in the back. A few students on the other side of the street were taunting Marina and me to start a snowball fight. Someone threw a fast one at me. I ducked and it hit a passing police car on the driver's window. The policemen got out of their car and we were expecting to shell out at least a few rubles, but instead the police returned snowball fire. Marina unintentionally hit one of the officers in the chest. She was visibly scared. When the officer took it in stride and fired one back at her, she was laughing uncontrollably. Hitting a Russian policeman with any kind of projectile would almost certainly result in a beating.

Marina flew back to Leningrad. We took a train, making a stop in Nizhniy Novgorod, which is home to another of Russia's major Kremlins (fortress), which is over 500 years old. Soviet engineers were building a bridge directly into the side of the Novgorod Kremlin, an unthinkable act. It would be like witnessing Italians erecting a parking ramp on St. Peter's Square in Vatican City. But this was Russia. The most memorable thing that happened in Novgorod was when we turned on the hotel TV, Weird Al's music video parody of Madonna was on. He was singing "Like a Surgeon."

After a snowball fight with Tallinn policemen. Estonia.

Revolution Day In Leningrad

1987 Revolution Day. "Celebrating" 70 years of preventable misery.

A classmate and I getting in the "Spirit" of Revolution Day.

When we returned to Leningrad, preparations had begun for the "Great October[1]" Socialist Revolution, the most important holiday of the year for doublethinkers and zealots. New Year's was the true favorite, but politics wouldn't allow for that to be said. Whereas Americans celebrate freedom on the fourth of July, Soviets embraced and bolstered totalitarianism for their country's birthday. It was like a nationwide political convention of the identically-minded. The party had held complete and unchallenged power for decades, but it would be suicide to point out the fact that not one of their plans, promises or predictions had ever come true. Vapid slogans were repeated ad nauseum every November 7. It was a master class in the art of brainwashing: Repeat lies. (Perhaps more importantly) Quash dissent.

---

1 Soviet fervor to change every aspect of society did not spare their calendar. The new government ordered the calendar switched on February 1, 1918, which date then became February 14, 1918. The "October" Revolution took place October 25, 1917, but under the new calendar was November 7.

The slogans, emblazoned everywhere, were generally written in bright red (probably to represent the bloody nature of Soviet socialists). They seemed to vie for the highest level of absurdity. A ubiquitous mainstay was "Lenin lived. Lenin is alive. Lenin will continue living." Celebrations of nonexistent economic successes were common. "The five-year plan has been implemented!" Another part of the propaganda formula was to push for consolidating ever more power in a centralized government. "All power to the Soviets!" For a thorough decoupling from reality, a poster was hung on the Winter Palace[2] depicting children, who thanked Lenin for their happy childhood. Not long after he took power, Lenin's comrades shot to death and bayoneted the Tsar, his wife, and their five children. That was just their terror rehearsal.

An American spoof movie about Asian communists, whose name I forget, but whose line I remember, contained a scene with a somber party leader telling a crowd, "We all must do what we must do, for if we do not, what we must do does not get done." It seemed like satire, but there was a popular Soviet poster that stated, "Economy should be economical." An endless stream of slogans blared over citywide loudspeakers all day and on the radio. No matter what was announced, the crowd followed with cheers of "Ura!" (Hooray). Inventing ridiculous Soviet slogans made a fun parlor game, but real ones were generally comic enough.

God Bless America t-shirt.
My Revolution Day attire

Before leaving D.C. for Leningrad, a regular customer at a restaurant where I worked gave me a custom-made t-shirt with an American flag under which was written in Russian "**Бог Хранит Америку**," a loose translation of God Bless America. That was my attire for November 7. I walked down Nevsky Prospect with my coat open. Passersby definitely noticed. Many pretended not to. Some would make brief eye contact and convey tacit approval. A brave few would openly give a thumbs up. Before heading out to witness

---
[2] A residence of the last Russian Tsar, Nicholas II and his wife Alexandra.

the day, my roommates hinted that displaying that shirt might get me arrested or beaten up.

In the days before November 7, roommates Sergei and Slava, ratcheted up their display of devout communism. Slava put another portrait of Lenin over his bed. The news of Wall Street's Black Monday[3] reached Leningrad, with a delay. Soviet news outlets reported the event as if the American economy had completely collapsed. On hearing the news, Sergei started cheering and dancing. I didn't know why and looked at him with curiosity. Gleefully, he said to me, "I told you it would happen. Capitalism has failed." A week later the market had substantially recovered, but the Soviet narrative remained that the final demise of America's economy had begun.

After having jumped for joy at the perceived collapse of the dollar, I was flabbergasted when Sergei had the chutzpah to ask me to buy vodka for him at the Beriozka so that he could celebrate November 7. It wasn't surprising that he wanted to use my access, but that he would suffer the embarrassment of asking his adversary to do something he should be able to do himself. I couldn't let the opportunity pass and presented to him what I considered odiferous facts.

Sergei: "you are an avowed Soviet patriot. Days ago you cheered what you thought was the extinction of capitalism. You exalt the superiority of socialism. Now, in order for you to celebrate the birth of the USSR, you have the extreme effrontery to ask your declared enemy to go into a store in which you are not permitted to buy a product made by your countrymen, but which you cannot obtain, and you want me to pay for it with a currency that is illegal for you to possess. Did I understand you correctly?"

Like a dog fixated on a treat, he heard none of that and asked, "Will you get the vodka?" He was so worried that I'd forget, he left a note as well, along with a much coveted loaf of bread. It read: Kevin! Buy for me, pleas [misspelled], a bottle of champagne and vodka. Lend a hand- help me, please. I need it by November 7. I went home and will be back tomorrow evening. In the table (sic) lies a tasty loaf of bread. Eat it. Sergei."

I got booze for Sergei.

In almost all Russian dwellings there are windows as well as vent windows, which are called fortochkas. As an invention the fortochka is a practical piece of Russian architecture. Weather, of course, is unpredictable and in the USSR central heating was turned on and off on predetermined dates. The outside temperature didn't matter. If October 10 was the starting date for heat and it was still warm outside, it could be 90 degrees F in an apartment. Opening an entire window might invite thieves, or wind could cause them to shatter, so a fortochka was left open to allow a slight breeze. It was too small for anyone to crawl through. Our dorm room had double windows and for-

---

[3] On October 19, 1987 the New York Stock Exchange lost 22.6% of its value. The market started to rebound the next day and by the end of the year was slightly up.

tochkas. To chill the vodka, Sergei placed the vodka I bought for him on the frame between the fortochka windows. Sergei's friends started arriving as I was about to leave to check out the big rally downtown. I looked back and saw Slava reaching for the vodka bottle from the fortochka. The main window somehow blew open. Whoosh! The bottle fell from the 9th floor and could be heard shattering on the sidewalk below. It was a moment of profound Schadenfreude. Their looks of dejection and despair were comical, but I feigned sympathy.

Soviet Russia could be confusing. The Great "October" Revolution's anniversary was celebrated on November 7. The Bolshevik Party, which means majority, took power when they were the minority political party. The majority party that lost was the Mensheviks, which means minority. Both parties were founded in St. Petersburg. They didn't relocate. The city in which the Bolsheviks took power was Petrograd. After taking power, they renamed it Leningrad.

The signal for the Bolsheviks to commence the revolution and oust the Tsar was a single shot from a naval cruiser ship's cannon. The ship was called the Aurora and is a floating museum still today. It is moored on the Bolshaya Nevka River in the city that is St. Petersburg again. The joke about the Aurora was that its cannon was the most powerful weapon in history. A single shot turned the world's largest country into shit for 75 years.

The names of the rivers, which didn't change, are also nonetheless confusing. The largest, widest and deepest river is The Neva, which is the Finnish word for "Bog." The "Bog" has a powerful current and is navigable by seaworthy ships. The two other rivers are variations of the same name. One is Bolshaya Nevka and the other is Malaya Neva. Bolshaya means big and Malaya means small. Russian words that end in the letter "A," can be made diminutive by changing the ending to "ka.[4]" It's difficult from the names to conclude which is larger, the big little Neva, or the little main Neva?

It was interesting to catch one of the last full blown November 7 rallies. With Soviet dissidents like Polishchuk advising the West, and more importantly leaders like Reagan heeding their advice to unleash blunt criticism for the first time, Soviet leader Mikhail Gorbachev was compelled to implement a policy called Glasnost[5]. It is a point of historical debate whether Gorbachev knew Glasnost would lead to the collapse of the USSR or whether he genuinely believed that by openly enumerating government policy failures, central planners could better fix them. None of the elite grasped that central planning itself was their main failure. Glasnost meant death for doublethink and doublespeak.

---

4 One diminutive word, known the world over, stems from the Russian word for water, "Voda." Vodka is small water

5 Openness. This was a revolutionary policy that allowed for citizens to state obvious facts, like that socialism had been a complete failure for 70 years.

Useful Idiot Master Class

Former Soviet citizens, living in capitalist and democratic societies combined their deep knowledge of Soviet life with profound insights into what made their adopted new societies better. Glasnost gave them an opportunity to share their ideas. Knowledgeable scholars were starting to be allowed to voice their opinions to an audience that had mostly never heard formal dissent or any alternatives to socialism. As cogent people emerged to state valid ideas, useful idiot[1] Phil Donahue waltzed onto the political stage with a cagey Soviet sidekick, Vladimir Pozner.

I'm not sure if Donahue was just stupid, cynical or an immoral opportunist, but he co-hosted a gimmick of a television show called the "Telebridge." For the time it was technologically cutting edge. A 1987 Zoom conference. The telebridge showed a live audience in the US and a live audience in the USSR. Reagan's administration had declared the Soviet Union the "Evil Empire." The Soviet leadership wanted to refute that and similar claims. Donahue was the perfect sap to defend the Soviet position, a useful idiot.

At the beginning of the broadcast, the camera showed the Soviet audience. Donahue explained for people in the West that the audience members had been randomly selected by the show's producers on the streets of the Soviet Union. What he didn't mention was that their phone numbers were taken and the Soviet producers called them later to invite them on the show. "They're all here freely" was Donahue's bogus narrative. To Westerners, that sounded reasonable. To anyone who knew even a tiny bit about Soviet life it was laughable. Regular people didn't have telephones. If their numbers were recorded, authorities knew where they worked and lived. No one except the likes of Andrei Sakharov would dare make

---

1 Useful idiots unwittingly succumb to manipulation and propaganda that lead them to take and support causes that they do not comprehend.

a comment that strayed from party doctrine, especially on live international television.

Pozner knew the Soviet audience would chirp out nothing but parrot speech, but he nonetheless pretended that Donahue's observations about the audience were correct. Donahue's ignorance was the backbone of the show. He asked a series of inane softball questions that were likely fed to him by his more intelligent co-host. Donahue's inability to ask a single difficult question made the Soviets look better, as did his shameful inability to refute blatant lies. Someone spoke of religious freedom in the USSR. Donahue could have easily asked them why Kazansky Cathedral had been converted into the state atheism museum or why Soviet filmmaker Sergei Eisenstein's movie "Enthusiasm" showed socialist zealots destroying a church, releasing its bells from their towers and smashing on the ground below, as frenzied hordes removed icons and crosses and broke them into pieces. Had Donahue asked how those facts were consistent with religious freedom, it may have helped build honest discourse.

Shows like Donahue's are show business for simpletons. Propaganda and lies were served to him and Donahue just nodded as a reflection of the vacuum in his head. The telebridge was a setback for the cause of liberty. For the Soviet government, it was a public relations success. The consensus among all who watched in our dormitory, Soviets and Westerners, was that the commercials by the sponsors were the most interesting aspect of the broadcast.

Scofflaws At a Wedding

We hosted a sendoff party in Diego's room for a group of students from Great Britain. The garbage chute landing served as an overflow party room. The Africans showed up with their peace pipe. I recall watching with laughter a tipsy Scottish girl try to put the moves on Diego, whom she didn't know was gay. At some point in the festivities, Jock (the aspiring gay opera singer) arrived with his new boyfriend, a sailor from Murmansk who was in uniform. Jock said he stopped by to say hello and have a few drinks before taking a train with his new boyfriend to Riga, Latvia where they intended to spend the weekend together. Homosexuality was a prisonable offense. The sailor was AWOL. Jock's visa didn't permit travel outside Leningrad. There was some serious potential downside to their escapade, but as the Russian saying goes: The severity of Russian laws is mitigated by lax and random enforcement. All that could be done was wish them safe travels.

Rumors swirled as the wedding day with Marina approached. People were relaying all kinds of stories. I needed to file some paperwork at the US Consulate. At the entrance, an American woman, State Dept. employee, berated me for wearing a Reagan - Bush '84 campaign pin on my coat. She said it was offensive to the Soviets, and besides, the campaign was long over. I thanked her for letting me know it was offensive to socialists. When I met whomever took the paperwork, they mentioned in passing that filing a false petition for a foreign spouse was punishable in the U.S. by up to ten years. I submitted the documents.

Students started telling me that Brad and Edna were advising and maybe even instructing American students to not attend the wedding. They warned that the wedding was not a justification to skip classes and would be grounds for punishment. Pavel the movie pirate warned me that my roommate Sergei was a KGB informant, who found Pavel and desperately asked him for compromising material on me. Brad even took the unusual step of waking me up in my dorm room to berate me for not attending that morning's class. I thought he'd looked for me specifically, but I later learned that there were only two or three Americans on campus that day and he was livid. I wrote about Brad's wakeup call in a journal, noting that I was hungover after drinking a bottle of cognac with Manoli, a half-Greek half-Russian from Boston. I also noted that Brad mentioned the ten-year punishment for a fraudulent wedding.

When the wedding day arrived, I was pleased to see nearly every student from our program waiting for Marina and me at ZAGS. Their presence was an enormous heartfelt gesture. I didn't think it was for me, but understood their presence to be an act of defiance, a salute of many middle fingers held high for the consulate staff and university admin. Before the ceremony, I wandered the reception hall and greeted and thanked as many people as I could. When the thought of exchanging vows entered my mind, I realized I didn't know how to say, "I do" in Russian. Panicked, I asked the students I knew to be the most fluent what I was expected to say. They didn't know either. The ceremony started before I could find out.

Mercifully, the bride recites her vows first. The opening commitment seemed to go on and on for about 3 minutes. I was thinking, "How in the hell am I going to remember and repeat all of that?" When the wedding clerk finished reciting the vow, my full attention was on what Marina was about to say, which was, "Da." That was it?!? Da?? Relief. After a brief ceremony we were legally married. Stamps were put in our passports and a slew of documents was issued, signed and stamped. All that remained for me to do was submit them to the American consulate along with a petition for a foreign spouse. Marina knew whom to bribe on her side.

At least half of the student group attended the wedding reception at The Pribaltiiskaya Hotel, near the dorm. When I had first bribed the restaurant manager there, I introduced myself as a member of the American consulate. I didn't want them to think of me as just a student. There were some confused looks when Marina and I arrived and the restaurant manager greeted us, saying "Good evening Mr. McKinney from the American Consulate." We had booked the whole place, but there were strangers seated at nearby tables. Their fixed stares and menacing looks did not go unnoticed. They were different types of wedding crashers.

A few of the people who attended Marina's and my wedding, even though warned not to.

My close friends knew that I was miserable and unfairly resented Marina for the loss of freedom she represented. I didn't care much for her and regretted having committed myself to the task. Therefore my friends rubbed it in and made the situation worse. A tradition at Russian weddings is to declare "gorko," which means bitter. The implication is that the newlyweds aren't kissing enough. When someone yells "gorko" the bride and groom are expected to kiss. Diego got the ball rolling and giggled as I glared at him angrily for saying it. My eyes told him, "You son of a bitch. I'm going to kill you for this." Moose picked up and "gorko"-ed us too. Then Manoli. Then Schtuck. Over and over they taunted with gorko. I recall wanting to assassinate half of the room. They would not stop. Had the tables been turned and I could force a miserable friend to kiss a woman he found repulsive, I most certainly would. At least the incessant toasts provided a reason to down lots of vodka shots.

Russians claim that a wedding is not valid unless a fight breaks out. The logic is that emotions and passions are unusually intense at weddings, therefore a fight will certainly somehow be provoked. No one fought at our wedding, or at least I don't recall one. I also do not remember leaving the Pribaltiiskaya, but remember portions of the honeymoon. We went to an entirely average two room apartment. I passed out on a couch and Marina went to sleep in a bedroom. We didn't speak.

After dozing off, I heard her stumbling or maybe falling en route to the toilet, where her vomiting was loud enough to make me semi-awake. It was likely a culmination of nerves mixed with copious amounts of vodka from all the "gorko" calls. If the apartment had been bugged, her puking would have been the only sound they heard.

When we awoke it was almost sunset. Leningrad is so far North that it gets dark around 2 p.m. in the Winter. We were both still slightly drunk and likely experienced the "Shampoo effect[1]" with the help of one of the favorite breakfast drinks of Russians, cognac. We were aware that we had taken an irreversible step and that our fates were linked for at least another year, but we didn't like each other a whole lot. Marina went back to Gatchina and I headed to the dorm. She guided me on a zigzag route to the metro station to see if we could detect anyone following us. We noticed no one.

The next day was Christmas Eve, but not for Orthodox Russians. In my family Christmas Eve is the bigger celebration and I wanted to call home. It was a regular Soviet Thursday and it took most of my day to make a ten minute phone call from the Central Telegraph that was located just off of Palace Square. It had a wall of glass-doored phone booths and rows of benches in the waiting area. To place a call, one had to declare ahead of time the duration of the conversation, provide passport information, the country and

---

1 The Shampoo Effect was coined by a friend from Chicago. He claims that when one first washes dirty hair, more shampoo is required to generate lather. After rinsing, however, a small droplet is sufficient. He equated lather with intoxication and alcohol with shampoo.

phone number, and pre-pay. The price per minute to call the USA was six rubles. Our stipend was sixteen rubles every two weeks. Lines were long. The cashiers also served telegram senders. If the operator reached a busy number, your call might be put to the back of the line. The people you were calling might not be home. No refunds were given. If you really wanted to have an international phone conversation, all one could do was wait and hope. To spend five hours or more to make a single phone call was not unusual.

Eventually my call went through. When a connection was made, they'd announce it over a loudspeaker. "Citizen McKinney. Cabin fifteen." After the door to the booth shut, a light came on, or was supposed to. Lifting the handset, a KGB monitor, who pretended not to listen afterwards, instructed, "Speak!" My mom had answered. I spoke briefly with her first, then dad, my brother, aunts and uncles, etc. Near the end of the call mom came back on and threw a curveball of a question at me, which she may have intended as a joke, but I suspect was rooted in a mother's intuition of which she had an abundance. She asked, "You didn't do something stupid like marry Olga from the Volga did you?" Mercifully my time was up and the line went dead. The call cost approximately the equivalent of an average worker's two-week salary.

That stamp made our marriage official

Welcoming 1988

New Year's Eve is by far Russia's biggest holiday. For our 1987 into 1988, my friends from Hamburg, Germany visited us in Leningrad. They knew the truth about Marina and pretended to be jubilant about our marriage. I took it to heart and have never abandoned it. The Germans stayed at the Pribaltiiskaya. Marina's mother joined us. The only time we met was briefly at ZAGS. As a native of Leningrad, who survived the siege, that was the only subject she wanted to discuss, especially with real live Germans, with whom she'd never had the chance to speak. I foolishly agreed to translate.

What the German military did to the city and its civilians was an undeniable atrocity on par with any of the concentration camps. No decent human could possibly defend the actions of the Nazi military. However, when Marina's mother was asked for her opinion on Holodomor in Ukraine, when Stalin killed more faster than Hitler had Jews, or the invasion of Finland, she claimed it didn't happen and was western anti-Soviet propaganda. She knew only the sanitized Soviet version of WWII, which was that while the rest of the world stood idly by Soviet forces fought Nazi Germany until they reached Berlin. Then the Americans and British arrived to claim part of the victory.

Bringing up the pre-war pact between Nazi Germany and the USSR[1] was intolerable heresy for Marina's mother. She became so unhinged and hostile that she had to be physically restrained. Marina calmed her by saying that my German wasn't good enough to know what I had translated (even though it was my own statement). We were all too drunk blah blah. Marina's mother left shortly after midnight and we enjoyed a pleasant rest of the night. Russians didn't find out that the pre-WWII pact existed until the early 1990s, more than fifty years after the fact. Regarding the Soviet – Nazi battles, I would invoke Henry Kissinger's observation on the Iran – Iraq War, "It's a pity they both can't lose."

---

1 The Molotov - Ribbentrop Pact was signed on August 23, 1939. It was an agreement of non-agression between Nazi Germany and The USSR, as well as to partition Poland between the two signatories.

USSR, Do Svidaniya

We left the USSR the way we came in, by train. At the Vyborg checkpoint, agents took all the Soviet military items they found, mostly Red Army hats. After we crossed into Finland, the guy I was traveling with, Paul, changed into a full officer's uniform, with the overcoat and hat. He smiled and said, "They didn't find these."

When we walked into our hotel in Helsinki, we were elated to see a familiar face smiling at us. Seated in the lobby was one of our African buddies, who had a smirk on his face that said, "Yes. I'm all that." He could see we were pleasantly flabbergasted. He laughed and reminded us, "I told you I have a diplomatic passport." We went for drinks with Robert that night. I never saw or heard from him again.

I flew back to Minnesota for a brief belated Christmas with my family. Before I could even start recanting what I'd seen and done, my mother looked me in the eyes and said, "You did marry Olga from The Volga. That was stupid." I hadn't even admitted it yet, but she knew. She thwacked her finger on my head and walked away. I explained my motive to my father, who said he approved. Mom was more concerned with putting weight back on me. She was at the airport and didn't recognize me when I got off the plane. Even with Raivo's restaurant connections, my weight had fallen by about 20%.

Final Year At GWU

I flew to D.C. where I was still enrolled at GWU. I had nowhere to stay and called around from a payphone at National Airport, looking for a couch until I could find a place to live. I found one in an apartment in a neighborhood called Adams Morgan, or as locals called it, "Madam's Organ." I slept on the couch. A ringing phone woke me the next morning. My friend had left and he had no answering machine. It had been ringing for a while, so I answered it. It was Arkady Polischuk, asking if I knew the status of Marina's petition. I hadn't even informed my parents yet where I was staying. I didn't ask how he found me. He instructed me to call the State Department to ask if they would provide any information.

After several calls, I found the office that oversaw Leningrad. The person confirmed that the petition had been delivered from Leningrad to Washington but was under review. He said there were numerous reports of the marriage being suspicious and casually mentioned that proof of fraud was punishable by up to ten years in prison, saying it in a tone that indicated he knew the marriage was fake. I thanked him for the information, hung up and immediately called Arkady in a panic.

"Arkady! They're threatening me with ten years in jail. What do I do?" Without emotion, he said, "Fuck the State Department and fuck their empty threats. They cannot prove love. You'll be fine." To rattle their cage, he promised to send a telex to the Helsinki Commission on Human Rights, which was a Soviet-centric watchdog not used to receiving complaints from American citizens about their own government. Arkady's telex with my signature expressed outrage that the U.S. State Department was preventing me from being together with my beloved. That Arkady knew my friend's telephone number and therefore where I lived had me rattled.

I left the apartment and was constantly looking over my shoulders. When I arrived at the GWU, the Russian studies department head saw me in the hallway and called me into her office. She had my report card from Leningrad, which was issued by Oberlin College—Five A's and one B+ in phonetics, which was fair because I absolutely could not pronounce the Russian word for dust (Пыль). The GWU professor told me that some students had filed a complaint to CIEE[1], the organization that ran the program. Their letter asserted that they had never seen me attend certain classes. There was no need for me to deflect, but I didn't know that yet. I protested that the grades were legitimately granted by Soviet professors, who had their own methodology. I was worried that the credits wouldn't be applied. GWU had suspended me once for a semester to review what they believed was academic fraud. I took 18 (3 extra) credits at GWU, while simultaneously enrolled in correspondence language courses at the University of Minnesota. When U Minnesota transferred legitimately earned credits, GWU considered it fraudulent. After proving that I knew the material, they reinstated me. I lost a semester. Now the tables were turned. I was receiving credits for subjects I had not learned, but GWU ignored the allegations of fraud and defended me with no investigation.

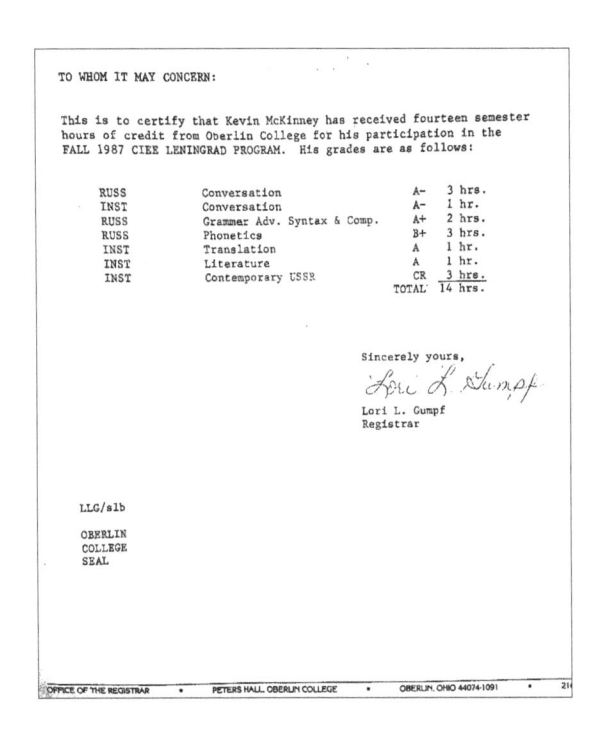

```
TO WHOM IT MAY CONCERN:

This is to certify that Kevin McKinney has received fourteen semester
hours of credit from Oberlin College for his participation in the
FALL 1987 CIEE LENINGRAD PROGRAM.  His grades are as follows:

     RUSS       Conversation                   A-    3 hrs.
     INST       Conversation                   A-    1 hr.
     RUSS       Grammer Adv. Syntax & Comp.    A+    2 hrs.
     RUSS       Phonetics                      B+    3 hrs.
     INST       Translation                    A     1 hr.
     INST       Literature                     A     1 hr.
     INST       Contemporary USSR              CR    3 hrs.
                                        TOTAL        14 hrs.

                                   Sincerely yours,

                                   Lori L. Gumpf
                                   Lori L. Gumpf
                                   Registrar

LLG/slb
OBERLIN
COLLEGE
SEAL
```

The temporary living arrangement turned permanent for the semester. There were numerous Ethiopian restaurants and clubs in Adams Morgan. Fellow students and I sampled them all, but Selam became our favorite. Many Ethiopians there had studied in Moscow at Patrice Lumumba University. It was a novelty for us to speak Russian in Washington with Africans. They taught us phrases in Oromo and Amharic, as well as the eskista dance. A couple friends and I had become regulars. We wanted to support them financially by inviting a larger crowd. We had probably sixteen in our group, so they sat us in a different section. A waitress we'd never seen before came to the table and asked in unpolished English, "Why you come here?" It seemed that we might not be welcome.

---

1   The Council on International Educational Exchange, based in New York City

I told her that we loved the food, service, music and eskista. She walked away without saying anything. After a nervous intermission, she returned with several bottles of champagne and announced that it was a gift, on the house, saying they were happy to have us.

Because I didn't know what my address would be in Washington, I gave people my parents' address in Minnesota. The first piece of forwarded mail was a postcard from Darlinghurst, New South Wales. I didn't know any Australians. The card expressed sincerest thanks. The sender reported that he was healthy and doing well in a suburb of Sydney. Signed-Raivo.

A couple weeks later a letter from the U.S. Consulate in Leningrad arrived. It was a response to an Arkady telex I didn't know about. It was signed by Vice Consul Joyce D. Marshall with a cc:Ambassador Matlock. The letter stated, "What we have done is send all the materials relating to the case to the U.S. Immigration and Naturalization Service in Vienna, Austria. …We did this because we received information which clearly required further investigation."

Arkady unleashed a campaign to portray as a villain anyone who doubted Marina and me. When I discussed with him face to face the State Department's letters to me, he assured me that they were stalling for time as they looked into my bank accounts for evidence of financial gain, which could be used to prove fraud. There weren't any payments, so they would eventually have to cave in and issue a visa to Marina. Arkady always stressed that love cannot be proved or disproved.

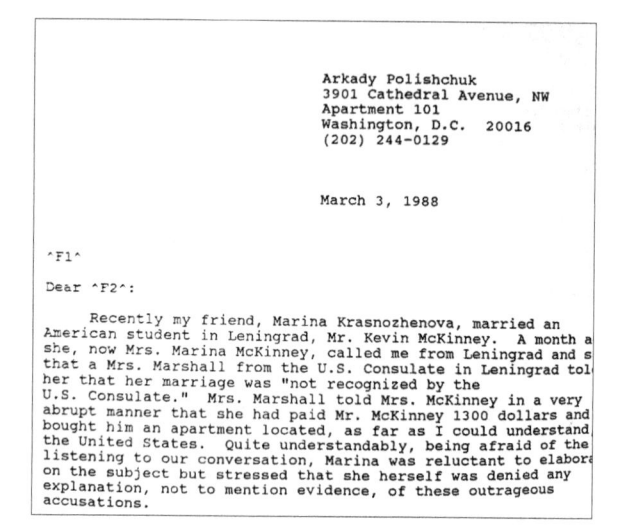

```
                    Arkady Polishchuk
                    3901 Cathedral Avenue, NW
                    Apartment 101
                    Washington, D.C.  20016
                    (202) 244-0129


                    March 3, 1988

^F1^

Dear ^F2^:

    Recently my friend, Marina Krasnozhenova, married an
American student in Leningrad, Mr. Kevin McKinney.  A month a
she, now Mrs. Marina McKinney, called me from Leningrad and s
that a Mrs. Marshall from the U.S. Consulate in Leningrad tol
her that her marriage was "not recognized by the
U.S. Consulate."  Mrs. Marshall told Mrs. McKinney in a very
abrupt manner that she had paid Mr. McKinney 1300 dollars and
bought him an apartment located, as far as I could understand
the United States.  Quite understandably, being afraid of the
listening to our conversation, Marina was reluctant to elabor
on the subject but stressed that she herself was denied any
explanation, not to mention evidence, of these outrageous
accusations.
```

A template for letter blast, intended to prevent charges for a fake marriage

The next piece of forwarded mail had a cancel stamp from New Canaan, Connecticut. Olya and her husband were real. Two things she wrote proved to me that she was genuine and exploring life in America. The first was that a simple thing impressed her very much. Toast. There were no toasters in the USSR. Her other observation was that store clerks were incredibly kind. She mentioned buying perfume. When the sales clerk tossed in free samples, Olya declared it wonderful that a stranger gave her presents.

Restaurant Near White House

I returned to my old job waiting tables during the lunch shift three days a week at The Barrister. The interior was not fancy and the food was slightly better than average. Located two blocks North of the White House, the patrons were not average. They were mostly the who's who of D.C. The U.S. Chamber of Commerce across the street had a dedicated telephone line behind the bar. There was a warning on the handset, "To be answered only by members of USCC." From 2–5 p.m. the place was mostly empty, except for Chamber of Commerce staff who could nearly always be found at the bar until closing time. Chamber members considerately kicked me some translation jobs, which got my name into a network of Russian speakers, which was a burgeoning business.

The Barrister's owner, Vince, was an Italian restaurant veteran who had worked his way up from waiter. He offered very little in the way of formal training, but instead worked side by side every day with his bartenders, wait staff, and kitchen. If he saw something he didn't like, he'd tell you, but not as criticism. He'd say it was a way to improve tips. Two things he demanded were to get menus and water on the table immediately, and requests for condiments were always a top priority, because a hungry person was easy to anger if you made them wait for exactly what they ordered.

Vince was constantly short-staffed and often prodded me to find willing students to wait tables. I had met a woman from Crimea, Elena, who had previously been an aspiring Olympic swimmer. She came to the US as a tourist and simply did not return. Her English could have kindly been described as primitive, but she was desperate to find any job. I lobbied Vince to hire her. At first he declined, because of language. I took a menu for her and compiled a restaurant vocabulary list. After studying for a few weeks, she convinced Vince to give her a chance. He reluctantly agreed, but on condition that I work the section adjacent to her so that I could translate if she ever got in a jam.

```
THE BARRISTER RESTAURANT
   818 Connecticut Avenue, N.W.
      Washington, D.C. 20006

DAVE KERR                        223-4344
```

Bar Manager who gave a Crimean Lesbian her first job in the USA

The bartender and manager, Dave, could be short-tempered. The Barrister was a bustling downtown D.C. establishment that served a demanding clientele, who expected high-paced service. Dave didn't think Elena should work there. After taking her first drink order, she proudly walked to the bar's service station and awaited Dave. When he was ready to dedicate a few seconds to her, she announced, "Toot her up." Dave asked, "What?!?" Elena repeated, "Toot her up." Annoyed, Dave summoned me, pointed at the table and told me to find out what the hell Elena's customers ordered. I explained to them the language situation and asked them to repeat their order, which was "Two Dewars. Up."

The next confusing incident occurred when someone failed to write the daily special on a sign. Elena asked Dave what it was. He replied that it had been eighty-sixed. Elena didn't want to make him mad, so she asked me why Dave told her he "Ate six specials." I explained that eighty-sixed meant that the restaurant was sold out and didn't have any more, which for a Soviet was completely understandable. I didn't know the origins of the number's usage, though.

Serving a table with two women, one American and one, whose accent I recognized as Russian, Elena shot me a quick question that I answered in Russian. The American was visibly annoyed and asked me, "Do you really need to do this? We're just trying to have lunch." I had no idea what she meant, but apologized anyway. She said, "You know!" and dismissively turned her eyes from me. I found Vince and advised him that one of my tables was unhappy and I didn't know why. He asked me to point them out. Vince recognized her and told me, "That's Susan Eisenhower. She does business with Russians, and probably thinks you're spying on her." He was right.

The front of the Barrister had a glass-roofed sidewalk veranda. For the wait staff it was the best rotation because it generated the best tips. A mostly bald man in his sixties was an almost daily customer. He ordered a double Johnny Walker neat in a tumbler, with ice in a snifter and a soup spoon on the side. Dave had his order ready before he ordered it. Nonetheless the man went through the ritual of vocalizing it every time. He wasn't my table, but he stopped me as I walked past. Handing me an envelope, he said "I hear your Russian is pretty good. Please open this envelope at home in private and keep the contents confidential. It was a CIA employment application. I threw it in the trash. I suspected that maybe Arkady had sent him, but when I asked Dave, he said the man had been a regular for years.

A letter arrived with my actual D.C. address. Arkady had been busy again. It was from the acting ambassador of the U.S. Embassy in Moscow. It was several pages long and written largely in legalese. Part of it read that if "...the inquiry determines that the marriage is, in fact, invalid for purposes of immigration, the application for an immigrant visa must, by law, be denied under section 212(a)(19) of the Immigration and Nationality Act." The references to specific laws and the possible punishments associated with them caused me to panic.

An immigration lawyer was a Barrister regular. I asked her if she could spare some office time to consult on a matter concerning a foreign spouse. She said yes and "My rate is $175 per hour." That was a lot of money for me, but I agreed. It was easy for Arkady to say "Fuck 'em" and they can't prove love, but the threat of ten years in jail seemed very real. In her office, I told the lawyer the whole story of Marina and me. Her response was, "I cannot believe you did this." She offered to draft an affidavit for me, instructed me to get it notarized and submit it to Immigration and Naturalization. To add to my relief, she said she would not charge me for her time, because it was such an insane story. She printed out the document and repeated, "You will not be prosecuted if you submit this, but the petition will be withdrawn." I left her office feeling liberated. There was a clear way out.

All kinds of thoughts and emotions were circulating. I decided to walk the two or so miles back to the apartment in Adams Morgan to think about what the affidavit meant. Yes, it provided a way to avoid jail, but it also meant failing to keep my word. What could I tell Arkady, Marina, and most importantly, myself? At the time, there was a Soviet Trade building on Connecticut Avenue, just north of Dupont Circle. I walked past it and the USSR sign repulsed me. My original resolve returned. I remembered tearing up the affidavit on the Taft Bridge and watching the pieces flutter down to the Rock Creek Parkway below. There must have been a second copy. While reviewing my archives, I found the unnotarized affidavit still intact.

Elena and I became close enough to give each other nicknames. She called me Perdun and I called her Bzdunka, "Farter" and "Farteress." Within weeks of her having started waiting tables, Bzdunka became language independent. Vince allowed her to work solo. I took another job and we drifted apart.

Physicist From Yale

After receiving the ambassador's letter, a couple more weeks passed without any news. Final exams were approaching. Out of nowhere, a professor named Vernon W. Hughes from the Physics Department at Yale University called me in Adams Morgan. He said, "I've met your wife. I know her to be a brilliant and wonderful person." He said he would be in Washington and asked if we could meet for tea to discuss the situation with Marina. I jumped at the offer. Professor Hughes said he'd be in D.C. in a little less than two weeks. Two weeks was an eternity for me then.

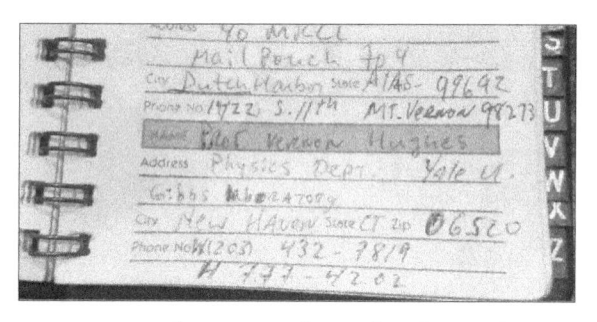

It turned out my wife was familiar with plutonium. A physics professor from Yale University deemed her worthy of assistance.

Arkady revealed nothing about Professor Hughes, but it had to have been him who connected us. We met for tea at the Watergate Hotel. The professor never mentioned Arkady or once let on that he knew the marriage was fake. He praised Marina's intelligence and her good nature. It surprised me when he mentioned her skills in plutonium research. How and where could Marina and Professor Hughes have met? He stated that some documents had been prepared on behalf of Marina and me. He asked if I might be available the next morning to possibly put my signature on them. I would have been ready to sign them on the spot.

The next morning I met Professor Hughes at an office building a short walk from campus. In a conference room a dozen or so documents were laid out on a table, awaiting my signature. I read them all. Each was a variation on the same theme: "How can the U.S. government violate my rights like this? This is an outrage." The Hughes team had selected Congressmen, Senators, White House staff, State Dept. and INS officials. I didn't know whose office I was in and don't remember the name of the company. It had to have been some kind of lobby group.

After the letter blast, I received written replies from four Senators, Claiborne Pell, Dave Durenberger, Rudy Boschwitz, and Barbara Mikulski, all of whom pledged support. The offices of a few congressmen called and acknowledged they had received my information, but didn't commit one way or another to my cause. Within a month, the team of Professor Hughes could claim success. Marina's immigrant visa had been approved. Like tearing up the affidavit, I wondered if I'd misremembered Professor Hughes when I started writing about him.

I found his name in an old address book. Professor Hughes was real and worked at Yale University's Gibbs Laboratory. When I looked him up on the internet, I read that he passed away in 2003. His extensive obituary in the New York Times listed his numerous accomplishments. He had been nominated for a Nobel Prize several times. "...famed nuclear physicist Robert Oppenheimer was once asked to critique the Yale Physics Department. The blunt Oppenheimer gave a less-than-glowing review. He said the only person he had any respect for was Vernon Hughes.[1]"

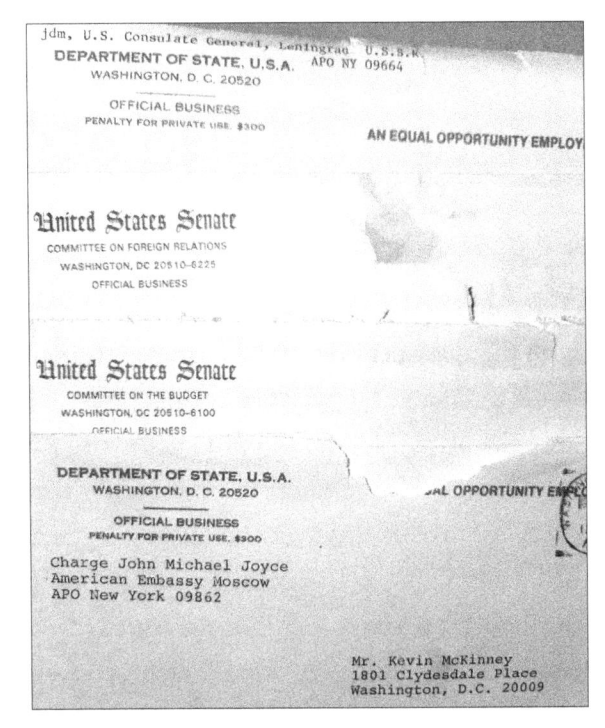

Arkady's Correspondence

---

[1] Source: Yale News. William Sullivan. April 2, 2003

Hotel Concierge

At the end of the academic year, my friend Matt with the apartment in Adams Morgan returned home to Orange County, California. He let me keep the place until the end of June.

Many GWU students were aware that the Washington, D.C. driver's license agency had a gaping hole. If someone cared to climb through it, falsified legitimately issued drivers licenses could be obtained. The process involved two steps. The first was to present an application with a valid out-of-state license. A representative of the D.C. licensing agency verified the information matched the out of state license. If it did, they'd stamp the form and send the applicant to another office down the hall for photos and to make payment. The trick was to write the application in erasable ink. Once stamped, you could change the information to anything you liked between offices. The only catch was you had to use a friendly address where the recipient would let you retrieve it when it came in the mail. I didn't drive in Washington and had no car. But it would have been a wasted opportunity to not avail myself of the "System." The erasable ink method was not a myth.

In the final days in Adams Morgan, a friend of a friend asked for a couch for a student from France who wanted to spend a few days in D.C. He'd just spent a year in Wyoming. I let him stay there. I have no recollection of how we connected, what he looked like, or even his name. I only recall that he was polite and orderly and that our paths barely crossed. The day he departed, I may have not been there or slept through it, he left the keys and title to a 1974 Ford LTD Station Wagon with Wyoming plates. The title could be signed over to anyone, i.e. I could sell the car. I didn't want a car. But after a cursory analysis, a car registered to a foreigner in Wyoming with a legally licensed but untraceable D.C. driver's license, some opportunities could arise. I kept the car and used it to move my things across the Potomac River to where I moved next, Rosslyn, Virginia.

A friend from university had a two-bedroom apartment in a compound called River Place. It had 1,700 units in four ten-story cross-shaped buildings. There was a common area, convenience store, and pool in the center. Across the highway was the Iwo Jima memorial, Arlington National Cemetery and what was then a U.S Army post called Fort Myer. The compound was fenced in and had manned security gates at either end. Our landlord had a policy that he would not rent to students. To get a rental agreement, my roommate Dee printed up business cards from a construction company that didn't exist and bestowed upon himself the title of General Manager. Dee's father was a neurologist and professor at NYU and supported his son financially. Dee had one rule, never mention to his father that Dee was a boxer, who trained at a gym where he was the only white guy. If Dee's dad found out, he would be cut off. I told the landlord that I worked Soviet counterintelligence at the FBI. After saying a few phrases to him in Russian, he agreed to a two-year rental agreement.

My friend Gregot asked me to apply for a job at the Capitol Hyatt hotel. They needed people so bad, they'd pay him for the referral. At the interview, I agreed to whatever position needed to be filled. Almost everything they offered required union membership. I refused. The only non-union position they had was setting out complimentary urns of coffee and trays of pastries by 5:30 a.m. on "VIP" floors for guests with what they called gold passports. It was a terrible job, but it was non-union. I took it. Other than the hours, I didn't mind it at all and even got used to waking up at 4:45 a.m.

The gold passport service was managed by the concierge department. After setting the coffee and pastries out, there wasn't much to do except verify every once in a while that some jackass hadn't left a spigot running or made a mess. To kill time, I'd go to the lobby and chat with the concierge, who most often on duty was a woman from Ireland named Anne McMeekin. I'd bring her coffee and pastries and we talked a lot. Eventually when there was an opening at the concierge desk, Anne kindly lobbied management to hire me. She claimed that my knowledge of other languages would be helpful. In reality, I had no qualifications for the job. But with Anne's backing, the position was mine.

Her knowledge of Washington was encyclopedic. She was the human precursor to Google. She had developed a system of rolodexes: Two for restaurants, one for theaters and concert halls, one for tours and transportation, and one for museums. She kept the desk stocked with maps and guidebooks. She also had an elaborate system for kickbacks for referrals, but was highly ethical in that she would never recommend something for money only.

The Capitol Hyatt is a convention hotel. The concierge desk was at the bottom of an escalator past which a thousand people might walk daily en route to the convention halls. The stream of random questions was often overwhelming for me. Before I could even look up an answer, I had to first determine in which rolodex. Whenever any kind of reservation was made, Anne insisted that all information be entered into her leather-bound log book. I felt uncomfortable having to ignore a customer, who was waiting while I was writing, but Anne was steadfast in the log rule. During the down times, she would review and critique every entry. Her fixation on maintaining a meticulous log book led me to dub her "The logger."

Watching her interact with every kind of person for several months, as well as learning her rolodexes was a master class in concierge hospitality. She demonstrated a very Irish way of remaining polite, while answering stupid questions, ambiguously insulting them at the same time. After having dealt with thousands of guests, I knew all about tourist attractions that I'd never visited and had memorized hundreds of restaurants I'd never tried.

One such restaurant was The Powerscourt in an Irish themed hotel called The Phoenix Park. It was a two-minute walk from The Hyatt. People got tired of eating in the hotel and wanted to walk somewhere, anywhere that was outside. Anne assured me that she recommended Powerscourt not because it was Irish but because it was excellent. I referred so many people to Powerscourt that the manager visited and invited me and a date to have dinner there, for free, that was the first time I learned that complimentary dining was a perk of the position. I invited a Venezuelan girl from GWU. The food was outstanding and the interior elegant. At the end of the meal, Seamus the manager came to our table. The girl looked at me quizzically when he announced, "There'll be no charge for the meal, Kevin. It'll be a pleasure to see you anytime." I told her nothing and enjoyed the aura of mystery that Seamus' comment had created.

A concierge position opened at The Carlton, which was much closer to campus. The hotel was a couple blocks from The White House at 16th and K Streets. It's The St. Regis today. Instead of conventioneers, it was an upscale boutique hotel with highly personalized service. I mentioned it to Anne and she told me to go for it. She was established at The Hyatt and had no interest in leaving. I submitted an application.

Weeks passed and no one called. I asked the friend who worked there if the position was still open. It was. I returned to The Carlton in person and asked the concierge manager for an interview. He told me that my age and experience suggested I could not possibly know the city on a level commensurate with the demands of their sophisticated guests. I said, "Try me." He asked a series of questions about what recommendations I'd make for certain atmospheres, types of cuisine, location, etc. Although I had never been inside almost any of the places I chose, he nodded with approval nearly every time. I could tell you the flavor profile of the rattlesnake salad at 19th and Pennsylvania or the friend alligator at Washington Harbor. I'd never tried either. With all credit to Anne's tutelage, I got the job.

Unlike at the Hyatt, restaurant managers visited us often. A recommendation from The Carlton's concierge was a feather in the cap for most restaurants. It was good business. If we tried a place and liked it, we'd be more likely to recommend it. We could use that relationship to get a reservation at a popular place on a Friday night, when others failed. We looked good to the guest, who said "My secretary tried to book a place, but they're full. I don't suppose you could try." Everybody's reputation as truly full service improved when we succeeded. The doorman, bellman, and I formed a Jeeves[1]-like team. We took pride in fulfilling most any request. It just required a guest brave enough to ask, which most weren't.

Carlton lobby

---

[1] Jeeves was the ultimate resourceful butler character in novels by author P.G. Wodehouse.

Bologna Frisbeeing

With a business card as a Carlton concierge, I got in the habit of going to the most expensive places in Washington for free. My roommate Dee complained that he couldn't afford to go out with me. Most places would chop his bill in half, by association, but they were still too expensive on a student's budget. To save money, he suggested we start eating at home before going out. He recommended buying budget foods like other students, maybe bologna or canned tuna. Dee bought them. We ate the tuna, but by the time we looked at the bologna, its expiration date had long passed. Dee was about to put it in the trash, when he had a eureka moment. He asked out loud to himself whether bologna could be thrown like a frisbee.

Our ninth floor balcony faced the compound's north sentry post, which I'd guess was thirty yards from the building. Beyond the shack was a guest parking lot where the Wyoming LTD stayed most of the time. Inside the compound, in front of the guardhouse a courtesy golf cart was usually parked. Occasionally a guard or doorman would drive it to look for parking infractions, or maybe drive an elderly guest from the parking lot to a remote entrance. Our apartment was at the end of the building, directly across from the gated entrance. We could look through a large window and see the guard(s) below. The door to the balcony opened to the inside and was to the left of the window. A wall blocked the guard's view of the door. From their angle it was not possible to see if the door was open or closed. Mesh was attached to the railing that allowed us to see out, but not for people to see in.

Dee trotted out on the balcony, bologna in hand, and without aiming launched a slice frisbee-style. I didn't watch. Dee reacted overjoyed, laughing so hard he almost blew snot out of his nose. "That was guh-reat!!" he announced, returning to the kitchen for the rest of the pack. I joined him and we took turns challenging each other with different targets. A new hobby was born.

What had begun as a budget reducer turned into an entertainment expense. The next day I went to the supermarket and bought every brand and type of bologna. It was the only item in my basket. At checkout, the woman who rang up the purchase put her head down, slowly shaking her head and pressing her lips as if to convey tacitly that she sympathized with the plight of the bologna eater.

Dee and I couldn't wait until after sundown to test the new frisbees. Initially we wasted a lot of ammunition just trying to aim at any random target. With practice, accuracy improved. We learned that trying to throw with too much force for extra distance would cause the bologna to rip and lose its aerodynamic properties. An elegantly dressed woman was walking from the guest parking lot. She was about twenty feet past the guard house when Dee let loose a slice that kerplopped with vigor six inches in front of her foot. The woman froze, staring with bewilderment at the piece of lunch meat that had just fallen from the sky. Her gesturing was like that of a pantomime. She was clearly failing to come up with any plausible explanation to what had just transpired. She looked up, down and around, shook her head, and walked past the piece of bologna on the asphalt.

We managed to avoid the guards' attention for weeks. Rats and birds probably ate the evidence and we had been careful to always crouch down behind the mesh to remain invisible from below. When we were throwing, it was a rule to always keep the lights off. We got on the radar screen when I landed a beauty that slapped and stuck on the windshield of a car that was awaiting a parking pass in front of the crossarm at the entry. A perfectly round slice of bologna had landed right in front of the driver's field of vision. The guard stuck his head out of the window and looked to the heavens for clues, of which there were none. We hung it up for the night and looked forward to another day.

I can't imagine how those slices of bologna got on the pavement.

Perestroika Mania

Away from the bologna launching pad, official Washington was astir about international summits between Reagan and Gorbachev. The Carlton was geographically symbolic of Reykjavik[1]. It was half-way between where the Soviet Embassy was then and The White House. In the basement of The Carlton there was a barber shop called Mr. Pitts. Milton Pitts was known as the president's barber. Hotel employees knew when someone high up in the government was about to get a haircut, because the Secret Service would sweep the lobby and size up the employees. The Secret Service provided us a non-public number to use in case we needed to report anything.

A Soviet delegation had stopped in for drinks. Luther the doorman, or maybe J.T., found that one of them had left behind his man purse, or oversized wallet. In Russian slang the item is referred to as "Pidorastik," derived from the word for faggot, Pidor. Russians use the term not so much to insult homosexuals, but to deride those who carry them. Luther handed me the purse and said it contained Russian stuff. Therefore it should be my job to find a way to return it. I may be misremembering the name, but I believe it belonged to Lev Vainberg, who was some kind of economic advisor to Mikhail Gorbachev. I reported it to the Secret Service and said that it would be in the concierge's safe. Within a couple hours, Vainberg (?) arrived with several people to claim it. He asked in broken English if I was holding his wallet. I handed it to him. He opened it and examined the contents. Pulling out six or seven hundred dollars and fanning the cash, he announced in Russian to his entourage, "I told you that Americans are idiots. They didn't take anything." I said nothing. Later I told the doormen that the Soviet official had declared them idiots for not stealing. They thought about it briefly and replied, "I don't steal because I have to live with myself."

Many famous people came through the hotel. Off the top of my head I recall meeting or at least seeing Elizabeth Taylor, Michael Jackson, the president of Angola, Olivia Newton John, George H.W. Bush, James Baker, Woody Harrelson, Bob Costas, etc. A singer whose face I knew well from a band I listened to called 10,000 Maniacs had asked me to do something and left her room number. When I saw that she was registered as

---

[1] In 1986 U.S. president Reagan and Soviet leader Gorbachev met in Reykjavik, Iceland to discuss nuclear arms reductions. The location was chosen because it is half-way between Moscow and Washington, D.C.

Helen Kerns(?), I wondered how many other people registered with aliases, and how.

Late one evening Richard Gere called and requested a discreet doctor to make a house call. He was registered under his own name and was in one of the swanky corner suites with Cindy Crawford. He claimed she had hit her head on the sink after stepping out of the shower. The scenario was not likely, but I said nothing and sent the doctor. Later, Richard Gere came to the concierge desk and examined my name tag. He then looked me in the eyes and said something like "Kevin. This will not be mentioned." Until now, it never was.

A political conference just ended and the valet parking attendants were swamped. It was a service catastrophe because none of the attendees had stayed after. All of the hotel's staff were running cars, even the general manager. I helped as well. The first car I retrieved belonged to Walter Williams, an author and professor whom I'd come to know and admire via a newspaper subscription that my grandmother had bought me. I got out of his car. Mr. Williams gave me his claim ticket and a $10 tip. It was hotel policy to not recognize celebrities, but I went unprofessional and told him, "I know who you are, Professor Williams. I am a fan, and my grandmother in Minnesota's a bigger fan." I asked if, instead of a tip, he might sign a note to my grandmother, who introduced me to his writings. Walter smiled, popped the trunk of his car and grabbed a copy of his then new book, "All It Takes Is Guts." He wrote a note to Jane and signed it. Throughout the course of her remaining two or three years, she reminded me every time we spoke how much she cherished that book. At that same conference, I retrieved the car of Patrick Buchanan, who was sort of a cheerleader for all things American. The black Mercedes-Benz he drove didn't seem consistent with his public commentary.

As a student of politics, it was interesting to eavesdrop on the conference. Experts spoke at length about their profound observations on a variety of topics. Their presentations were unlike anything I'd read or heard in major media outlets. Having to rely almost exclusively on revenue from advertising doesn't leave much room for thoughtful, or even worse, unpopular ideas. Moneymakers like The Washington Post and New York Times can't afford to present first-person expert presentations and scientific analyses. As H.L. Mencken noted, "No one ever went broke underestimating the intelligence of the American public." Major media corroborates that observation.

Pop narratives, which are usually untrue, make money. People prefer to consume propaganda, because it's less painful and easier than in-depth learning. The top stories in the late 1980s that were endlessly repackaged to sell papers or attract viewers were variations on: 1) Reagan was a demented warmonger whose anti-Soviet policies will lead to a World War III nuclear holocaust. If you didn't believe that you hated peace; 2) AIDS was going to kill everyone soon. If you didn't believe that you hated gay people; 3) Crack cocaine was unleashed on black communities by the CIA. If you didn't believe that you were a Klan member. Earlier in the decade, the Acid Rain scare had been a major revenue generator. It was predicted to destroy all the world's forests within five years. They overplayed that hysteria by presenting an easily verifiable time frame. I'm not saying that gloom and doom doesn't exist, but merchants of alarmism kill a lot more people than that about which they warn. In the late 1980s the nascent Global Warming[2] industry started to be foisted as acid rain disappeared.

U.N. Predicts Disaster if Global Warming Not Checked

PETER JAMES SPIELMANN   June 30, 1989

UNITED NATIONS (AP) _ A senior U.N. environmental official says entire nations could be wiped off the face of the Earth by rising sea levels if the global warming trend is not reversed by the year 2000.

Coastal flooding and crop failures would create an exodus of "eco- refugees,'' threatening political chaos, said Noel Brown, director of the New York office of the U.N. Environment Program, or UNEP.

He said governments have a 10-year window of opportunity to solve the greenhouse effect before it

Globalwarming 1989

---

2   Read the hysterical predictions of Peter James Spielman of the Associated Press from 1989 and compare them to reality .

A Nascent Cult of Bologna

It had probably been four months since I had seen her when I ran into Elena in the small convenience store at River Place. She was with a Russian man, who was aghast when I opened my arms to hug her and joyfully yelled, "Bzdundka!" (The Farteress). The man was her brother-in-law, a Soviet dissident author named Alexander Suslov. He had written a book called Plakun City that was not welcome in the USSR. He and his family had somehow escaped and he was working for Radio Liberty. It turned out he was a very close neighbor to Dee and me. He and his family lived in a penthouse on the tenth floor, which was one floor higher than ours and directly across the hall. It was an unbelievable coincidence. Suslov had acted as guarantor for Bzdunka, who was not living in a studio apartment in the same building but far away on the 8th floor. I was very happy to see her again and invited her to check out our place and meet Dee.

After brief introductory small talk, Dee poured her a drink and offered her some bologna to throw. Bzdunka accepted both. We turned the lights off and looked out the window for signs of trouble. Dee noticed a boy, who looked to be in his early teens, hiding behind a pine tree. He remained in one place, periodically looking up at the balconies, which were only on the 9th and 10th floors. We checked back several times. The kid was still there. River Place management had definitely assigned someone to try to solve the mystery of flying bologna.

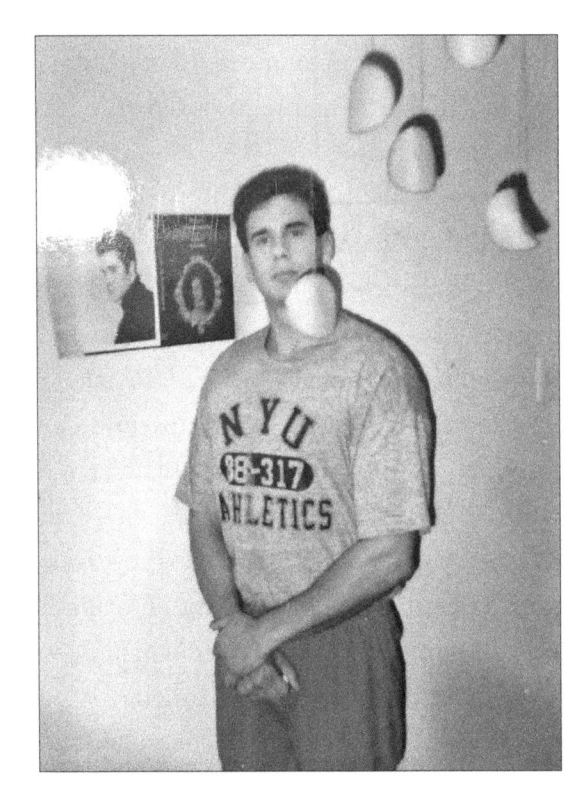

Bologna Mobile

As a New Yorker, Dee was well versed in the culture of befriending the doorman in an apartment building. We generally entered and exited only through the back service door, which was closer to the local metro station, but Dee had wisely gone out of his way to bring gifts and otherwise befriend our building's doorman, who was an Ethiopian that Dee had reverently nicknamed, "Chief." Before throwing any bologna, Dee declared, "We gotta first go see Chief." I didn't know him, but Dee assured me that Chief was gold. Bzdunka went back to her studio. Dee and I went to the lobby to ask Chief if he'd heard or knew anything. I surprised him by asking how things were going in Ethiopian, a phrase his countrymen had taught me in Adams Morgan. Dee explained the nature of our visit. Chief's smile turned serious.

He knew all about the kid by the security hut. River Place held weekly staff briefings. Chief said that the issue of bologna had come up more than once. Resident complaints were rising and management pledged to take action, going so far as to promise upset residents that there would be no further incidents. All staff had been advised to remain alert. Chief cautioned us. "Be very careful. They are serious." Dee thanked him for the information and gave him a six-pack of beer, which he was quite adept at consuming off camera.

Knowing that we were being watched made throwing bologna more fun. I fetched Bzdunka and warned her to be extra careful and to not laugh loudly. We could not reveal our position. With lights off, we took a pack of Oscar Mayer onto the balcony and watched the watchman relocate. He abandoned the pine tree and took position behind the bushes in front of the guest parking lot. We took turns launching slices. Like a variation on the game Whack-a-mole, we bologna flingers were crouched down below the mesh, remaining invisible. As soon as the kid was looking in a different direction and it seemed safe to quickly throw, one of us jumped up and launched their meat missile. A reasonably accurate throw could be executed in less than two seconds.

As bologna began dotting the asphalt around the guard shack and hanging in the trees, the antics and tactics of the detective became increasingly more hilarious. Taking cover in the bushes hadn't worked, so he pretended to leave altogether. We could clearly see that he hadn't left and was standing behind the guard shack. We looked for backup. No one. The biggest threat to revealing ourselves was laughter. We watched as every few minutes the kid popped his head out from both sides of the shack and scoured the top two floors with his eyes, desperate to catch someone in the act.

A car pulled up to the guard shack and was waiting for the gate to open. The bologna spotter was behind a pine tree at our two O'clock. Dee launched a beauty. He was up and down in 2 seconds. It was as accurate as a laser beam, splatting on the car's windshield, inches in front of the driver's field of vision. It had made a perfectly circular landing. There were no folds. Dee had demonstrated cold cut flinging virtuosity. The security guard stuck his head out of the window, looked up at the top floors and then made a gesture to the kid, conveying the question "What good are you?"

The boy shrugged. We were convulsing with laughter behind the mesh. The car's driver removed the bologna with his left hand and waved it at the guard in a manner that he was suggesting it was the guard's fault. The guard's reaction said, "I got nothing."

The driver was in complete befuddlement. Levitating lunch meat was indeed confusing. We didn't press our luck that night. In fact, we refrained from throwing for a few weeks. We assumed correctly that, with no activity, the compound's management would see the detective as a budgetary waste, and the bologna sleuth would come to feel like a chaser of wild geese. Chief kept us updated. As predicted, the compound chose not to maintain the mission, but allocated funds for a maximum of ten hours per week.

Relying on Chief's reconnaissance, and as soon as the kid burned his ten hours, we were emboldened to launch a bologna blitzkrieg. Fifty or so pieces of bologna dotted the asphalt, guard hut, and parking lot. Our barrage had gone off completely undetected. When the guard finally noticed, he looked completely defeated. He didn't even look up and returned to his post. Dee was elated and declared us victorious. He snapped a few photos on a 35mm camera.

Eventually the Arlington, VA police showed up to inventory the scene. We could see them scrutinizing each unit at our end of the building. Concerned that the police might somehow figure out that we were guilty, Dee announced that he was hiding our stockpile of ammunition in the pan tray of the kitchen oven, after which he began referring to it only as, "The Vault." The perception of our adversaries' determination to investigate us was seriously inflated. We truly expected the police to return with a search warrant. We also wondered whether fingerprints could be lifted off bologna. Dee was so impressed with the photo of the bologna array, he ordered 8" x 10" enlargements for us.

Greet Marina at Dulles

Arkady invited me to discuss Marina's upcoming arrival. He wanted to make sure I'd be in Washington and that I had a driver's license. I didn't tell him I had two. He outlined the plan: A car would be parked in the guest lot at River Place. They'd leave the key in an envelope with the doorman (hopefully Chief). Arkady would call to advise the make, model and license plate. I was to drive the car to Dulles Airport and greet Marina. When we met in the airport, we were to perform a reunion scene, worthy of an Oscar nomination. After holding hands across the parking lot to the car, Arkady gave me an address in Silver Spring, Maryland, where I'd drop off Marina. A taxi would be waiting there to drive me home.

In what could have been a snafu, the car they provided was a red Jeep Wrangler with a manual transmission. Luckily, I learned to drive in a 1948 Ford pickup and could handle a clutch. Marina's flight was on time. She made it through. We did the theatrics and got in the car. The first thing she said to me was, "Really? A fucking Jeep?" When I asked what she meant, she explained that she had the impression from Soviet propaganda that everyone in America was Rockefeller and expected to be riding in a Cadillac limo. I drove her to the address in Maryland and never saw her again, nor spoke to her.

Despite the fact that Marina lived in Maryland, and my address was Arlington, Virginia, the divorce papers filed on our behalf purported our joint address as in Washington, D.C. The legal requirement for divorce was a minimum of six months. Our divorce court date was set for six months and one day after Marina's arrival. Arkady was concerned that INS interrogators might question the veracity of our statements. To ensure no trip ups, he created a virtual apartment for us to memorize. I remember being impressed by the cunning behind what Arkady considered likely questions, like "Is your kitchen sink a single or double? Is the faucet a ball or double knob? Is there a medicine cabinet in the bathroom? Does it slide open or have a door or doors? Do you keep drinking glasses in a cupboard and are they standing upright or upside down? Where do you keep toothbrushes and what color is the other's?" I mastered "Our" apartment's layout. They'd hired an attorney for Marina. She'd never have to face questioning.

I arrived at divorce court alone. The courthouse was a few blocks from The Hyatt. I was looking forward to answering any and every question with aplomb. Marina's lawyer and I were the only two people in the room, besides the judge and court reporter. The judge asked if there were any disputed assets or children. We both affirmed there were neither. The judge asked, "Irreconcilable?" We both repeated the same word. The judge said, "Granted." That was it.

I never thought to research Arkady Polischuk[1] until I started writing this. He wrote two books about his experiences as a dissident: "While I Was Burying Comrade Stalin" and "Dancing On Thin Ice." The former was finished just before his death in 2020.

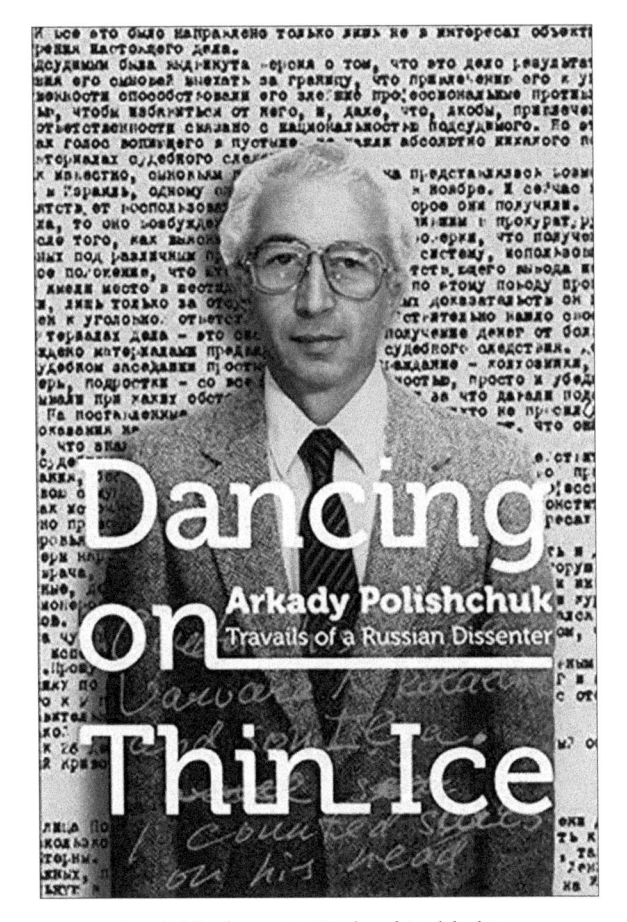

Available from McFarland Publishing

Available from McFarland Publishing

---

1 https://howardlovy.com/arkady/

Our Bar In Georgetown

Our favorite bar in Georgetown c. 1990. Sadly gone

Through his boxing connections, Dee had met a retired Irish boxer named Kelly, who worked as a bartender at a bar called The Guards. It was a sort of a powerbroker meeting place. Most of the patrons were wealthy Georgetown locals or lobbyists on expense accounts. Kelly would ensure deep discounts for Dee and his crew by padding other peoples' tabs. We GWU student regulars, i.e. friends of Dee at The Guards were at least twenty years younger than the average customer. The bar had a political reputation as leaning towards establishment elderly Republicans. Nonetheless, Dee had become so enmeshed with the staff of The Guards, in the days before cell phones, he gave out the bar's phone number as his own.

To celebrate my divorce, Dee summoned the usuals: Juanjo, a business student from the Basque region of Spain. Juanjo left no doubt that he had every intention of returning home after graduation. He began almost every conversation with, "Ju know. In my country. . ." and then would proudly attribute some honorable universal human trait to being unique to Basque people.

There was Don the Saint, who was either a Canadian, or native of Detroit, depending on who asked. He never committed. The Saint had attended school in Hong Kong and Japan. After enough drinks, Don would recite anticommunist political quotes in Cantonese. I didn't understand a word, but always enjoyed listening to them. We once got stuck in an elevator together, drunk. When the rescuer's voice came over the intercom, Don replied in Chinese. I followed his lead and pleaded for help in Russian.

Our only "local" friend, Joel, had graduated high school in suburban Virginia. He'd grown up in French-speaking Switzerland and then moved to Central America, where he became fluent in the local Spanish dialect. We hadn't known that Joel spoke Spanish until some Salvadoran customers, in a toilet of a bar called Las Rocas (another favorite) in Adams Morgan, thought they could safely insult us. Joel heard disparaging comments directed at us and let loose a barrage in their native slang. They bought us a round. Dee called Joel "Motherfuckin' Tee." It stuck. Las Rocas was famous for two things, cockroaches and pad-locked metal grates over the urinals. We wondered if they locked them to prevent customers from stealing urinal cakes. We could come up with no better explanation. For the Saint's bachelor party, we made a stop at Las Rocas by limousine.

I'm with The Saint, JJ, and Joel Teeee!

One of Dee's best friends from NYC visited D.C. often and stayed with us on the couch. Alphonso. Al was a broad-shouldered, mean-looking black man whose voice did not fit. His speech was almost like that of a cartoon character. Al was a serious aficionado of classic literature. I loved hearing his takes on authors like Dostoevsky and Gogol. As sharp as his understanding of the texts was, his pronunciation of authors' names was butcherous.

Dee, Al and I had our own way of mocking racists by buying for one another stereotypical gifts. Dee the Jew started it by bringing Alphonso a watermelon, telling him "I hear your kind likes to eat this sort of thing." Al followed up by bringing me a six-pack of Guinness. Occasionally we'd forget that not everyone was in on the gag and let loose one of our inside joke comments in public, causing anyone who heard to look at us with disgust. For example, if we had been in public and seen the news story about the black snipers in D.C. who randomly shot people, one of us likely would summarize the story with a ridiculous comment like, "Their kind always does that sort of thing."

On the day of my divorce, Dee was waiting at the bar of The Guards. He already looked a little wobbly when I arrived. He claimed he'd already put away at least eleven of Kelly's Rusty Nails[1]. We never ordered nails anywhere else. Kelly used high-end scotch and just a drop of Drambuie. Everyone else made them too sweet.

The divorce celebration ended in three of us fleeing the area. We'd been drinking for hours and behaving like our usual jovial selves, when a stranger angrily told Alphonso, "I don't appreciate you hitting on my girl, Nigger!" Al could handle himself, but Dee the boxer jumped at the opportunity to apply his

---

1 A Rusty Nail is an alcoholic cocktail made from a mixture of scotch whisky and drambuie, a scotch whisky based sweet liqueur that contains honey, herbs and spices. The traditional ratio is two parts scotch, one part drambuie.

skills on a deserving recipient. Al, Dee and the angry moron stepped outside. I followed them a few seconds later, intending to de-escalate the situation. Before I could even get to the exit, the man's head snapped backwards and caused a solid pane of glass to shatter. The guy fell unconscious to the ground. Dee had one-punched him.

Al was mad for having been denied the chance to express himself. Within what seemed like seconds, we heard a siren headed our way. It was likely from the GWU hospital that was six blocks away. We knew that the guys we stuck with the bill would understand our reason for abandoning them. Al's car was parked a couple blocks away. More sirens could be heard. Al suggested we drive by. Dee deemed it too risky. Al smiled and offered a solution. He popped the trunk of his car and retrieved two pairs of Groucho glasses[2]. It was camouflage commensurate with the mission. I sat in the backseat, as Al drove by the scene of the knockout. Through lensless Groucho glasses, Dee and Al watched paramedics load the asshole on a stretcher into an ambulance. No police were present.

We didn't dare go near The Guards for a few weeks. When we finally mustered the courage to return, we brought an expanded entourage, which included two of our extra-large football player friends from Howard University. Dee didn't go. One was among my favorite drinking partners, a native of New Orleans named Roddy. He was a defensive lineman and weighed about 275 pounds. Roddy and I had a mutual goal to introduce our relatives to one another. His grandmother in Louisiana was an unabashed lifelong marijuana smoker and my uncle had bought acreage next to Minnesota's Nemadji State forest, where he grew it. Roddy brought samples to grandma in New Orleans and she relayed her best regards to the residents at the other end of the Mississippi River.

Al had been back in NY for weeks when Dee decided to return. When he entered, Kelly and a female bartender started the slow clap. The applause spread. About half of the bar knew the man that Dee had knocked out as a human turd. They were certain he'd never come back and for that all were grateful.

The owner and general manager, however, tried to pressure Kelly to keep us away. They thought students deterred their bread-and-butter customers, older Republicans. The G.M. told me that D.C. used to have a law that existed into the early 1970s that it was illegal for a man and woman to speak to one another in a bar, if they hadn't entered together. They'd have to agree non-verbally to walk outside, and then enter together in order to speak. I asked one of the older regulars, a Republican lobbyist, about stodgy laws. He rolled his eyes and pointed out that Washington D.C. was 100% under Democrat control since 1961. He bemoaned the fact

---

2 A tribute to comedian Groucho Marx. His namesake glasses have thick black frames, without lenses, tall bushy fake eyebrows, and a large rubber nose that covers an average sized nose.

that those guilty of implementing bad policies habitually try to project them onto those who opposed and changed them. The Civil Rights Voting Act was a prime example. We students were allowed to stay.

Among our favorite conversation partners were two women, Karen and Jean, who drank in The Guards almost as often as we did. Dee and I estimated them to be in their early 50's. Karen would only allude to her past. She led us to believe she was an Italian mafia widow from New Jersey. She drove a mid-1970s green Cadillac, which by itself was admirable and enviable. but it also had a custom horn that played the refrain from the song, Quando Quando Quando which made the vehicle ooze with style. Jean was a lobbyist either in the medical or pharmaceutical sector. They both knew the Guards' owner and when they found out about potential blacklist, they too stood up for students.

We had covered a plethora of topics with Jean and Karen over several months, even occasionally disappointing ourselves by agreeing to meet at a different bar. The Guards always beckoned us back and made us regret trying someplace new. Karen arrived one day with her daughter, who was attractive and close to our age. Dee was almost drooling and focused all of his attention on her. I made up a reason why I had to leave and walked home to Rosslyn, passing along the C & O Canal[3]. I remember and mention the canal because it was a relic from the days of common sense safety. There were no railings to prevent someone from falling into the water that was five or six feet below. There was a lot of pedestrian traffic in the day, but almost no one walked the canal at night. If a drunk fell in, climbing the wall to get out would be an almost physical impossibility. I staggered along the canal's edge many times but never fell in.

I left for classes the next day and saw that the door to Dee's bedroom was open. He had not been there overnight. I returned in the late afternoon and saw no change. A safe bet to connect with friends was to return to The Guards. Sure enough, there sat Dee, The Saint, and See-Say. See-Say was a student at Howard U. His mother was Swedish and his father an ambassadorial level member of the diplomatic corps of Sierra Leone. When he saw me, See-Say grimaced and motioned with his eyes in Dee's direction. I asked Dee where he'd disappeared to and he replied, "I think I've had twenty-one nails." That wasn't an answer.

Reminding him that we'd left him in the company of Jean, Karen and the daughter the night before, I asked what happened. Dee confessed to spending the night amorously and provided details. He said that during intercourse, she had vigorously slapped him open-fist on his back, repeating "Sooo good! Inside me." See-Say or The Saint requested clarification if he was referring to the mother

---

3 Opened in 1815, the Chesepeake and Ohio Canal runs parallel to the Potomac River. There were no railings along the edges, because mules and horses pulled barges on ropes.

or the daughter. Visibly annoyed by the question, Dee said "The daughter, of course."

Dee once hooked up with a female psychiatrist he met at the River Place pool. When he returned to the apartment, he described the sexual encounter thusly: "Dude. She gave me such a blowjob. I couldn't have done it better myself."

Dee, Nick the W. German rat trapper, and Bzdunka

Kentucky Derby or Exam

There was a final oral exam required for a GWU diploma in Russian. It was rumored to be grueling and I was concerned I might fail. It was scheduled for a Friday. A party girl friend, J.J., from Bowling Green, Kentucky had two tickets to the Derby that were about twenty rows up from the finish line. Seats like those at face value were a once in a lifetime opportunity. In order to get there, though, I had to skip and reschedule the oral exam, which was a recorded interview on no predetermined topics. Students were expected to be able to converse about anything.

I reported that I'd fallen ill and left for Kentucky. Paying for the flight ate up most of my cash. It was the beginning of the month. I'd just paid rent. In Louisville the day before the Derby, I felt obligated to reciprocate for the ticket and picked up a tab for J.J. With no betting cash, I decided to call my dad for help, making up a cockamamie story, that I was cramming for the Russian final and hadn't been able to takeshifts waiting tables. Whatever he gave me I bet on Easy Goer to win, who came in a close second. I returned to D.C. hungover and broke, with just enough money for Metro fare. There was a message on the answering machine from one of the Russian language professors, at whose house we often drank vodka shots and ate zakuski[1]. He said he was going to administer the make-up test and advised me to take a couple shots before, to loosen the tongue. His message made me feel like I'd already passed.

A couple blocks from the GWU library where the final exam interview was about to happen was a block-long office building with a street level mall called 2000 Pennsylvania Avenue. Wollensky's was the closest bar to the library. I sat down by myself and ordered a Guinness and a shot of vodka. Next door there was a coffee shop with an Arkanoid video game that Juanjo and Dee were addicted to. As I "prepared" for the exam, Dee noticed me. He called me "Liam," which he took from the movie Spinal Tap, when someone referred to the band's manager, Ian, by the wrong name. In fact, Dee called most everybody Liam.

I told Dee that it was the biggest day of my life. Four years were on the line. I'd prepared by partying all weekend with J.J. at the Kentucky Derby and losing all my money. Dee was considerate and mindful of the situa-

---

1   Small bites to be eaten after drinking shots of vodka. Typically pickles, marinated mushrooms, black bread, and salamis.

tion's gravity. He ordered several more rounds and told me not to worry. He was buying.

When I arrived for the final, I was not tipsy. I was drunk. My breath reeked of alcohol. Recognizing my condition, the department manager, who'd set me up with Arkady Polishchuk, looked at me with disbelief. She said, "Markovich couldn't be here. You're on with Irina Semionovna!" Markovich was the amenable professor who'd given the advice to loosen up a little. Irina Semionovna was the professor who'd told me to drop her class immediately because in her estimation, I would never graduate. She was generally hostile towards my academic regimen.

In the exam room there was a tape recorder and microphones were sitting on the interview desk. Irina Semionovna often wore thin frameless reading glasses. When I stood in the doorway, waiting for her invitation to be seated, she stared, examining my face. Then she dropped her glasses to the bottom of her nose and stared more intensely. Without saying anything about my definite intoxication, she instructed me to sit down, turned on the recorder and began the exam.

After a brief exchange of typical introductory niceties, she got an evil smirk on her face and asked if I was aware of the ecological catastrophe that had taken place at Chernoby and could I please enlighten her about what caused it. Inside, I was crescendo screaming, "You enormous THUNDERCUNT!!" I didn't know nuclear meltdown terminology in English. I spewed some gibberish for several minutes, thinking to myself that I should just walk out and forget about graduating. I don't remember any topic other than the gut punch with which she started.

The evening after the exam my dad called to check on how I thought it went. Judging by the tone of his voice, I could tell he knew I'd bullshitted him about the week before and the need for money. I confessed that the allure of seats at the finish line of the Kentucky Derby was too powerful, so I went. He said, "I know. I noticed you on the screen at the telecast and wondered how you scored those tickets. Well done!"

The recording of the conversation with Irina Semionovna was reviewed by a panel. Test results were posted on the wall outside the office a few days later. En route to look at the bulletin, I passed a classroom where a classmate sat crying alone. She was talented and studied hard. I took her tears as a foreboding. I was prepared to see "FAILED" next to my name. Instead, I had scored highest and the girl was crying because she came in second. She considered it unfair, because I skipped class and rarely studied.

Russia Becomes a Fad

With the piece of paper (diploma), official Washington allowed me to work at more serious venues. The program taught how to not only translate propaganda from Pravda and Izvestiya, but to interpret their deeper meanings. Insights could be gleaned from not only what was written, but also from omissions. Since returning from Leningrad, I had been hired to translate texts on numerous topics. If stumped, I could just ask a native speaker for help. The Fish and Wildlife Service hired me to interpret for a visiting Soviet salmon expert. Forewarned about the topic, it was easy to study and memorize the English and Russian terminology related to fish spawning.

Repeating U.S. - Soviet political mumbo-jumbo like "The plenipotentiary committee's solemn determination to employ their powers-of-attorney as temporarily acting executors of the directors responsible for pursuing the policy of an abatement in tensions," was as easy as an unblocked lay-up for Michael Jordan. I contributed to a book project called "The Human Experience.[1]"

One of the first test drives of the diploma was for a Soviet advisor to George H.W. Bush. A lobbyist had arranged an audience in the Old Executive Building, next to the White House. They needed an American-born citizen as interpreter. He offered to pay $750 to interpret for a delegation from Moscow. Outside of a really hot poker game, I'd never earned that much money so fast. I didn't hesitate to accept, after which he said they'd require my passport, social security number, and home address and let me know if I'd been cleared within twenty-four hours. I was a little nervous. Having to pass a background check in order to work was a first.

The group from Moscow had hired a lobbyist to get an audience with Nicholas Burns. No one warned me about the agenda. I was confident that I could at worst wade through any topic. In the lobby of the OEB I met my clients, who represented a recently formed bank called Menatep. They informed me that the purpose of their trip was to get approval to transfer US dollars internationally with an authorized correspondent bank, hopefully a Wall Street major. I understood.

Before entering the office of Nicholas Burns, I put some Copenhagen chewing to-

---

1 Released in 1989 by the Quaker US/USSR Committee the book was a compilation of short stories by well-known American authors like William Styron, Joyce Carol Oates, John Updike, Alice Walker, Wendell Berry, Garrison Keillor, and more. The only Soviet authors Americans may have possibly heard of were Yevgeny Yevtushnko, Bella Akhmadulina, and Bulat Okudzzhava.

bacco in my mouth. I started the habit when I was about ten years old. There was none in Leningrad, so for a nicotine fix I started smoking cigarettes, and hated them. We were called in immediately and I had no chance to get rid of the chew in my mouth.

Mr. Burns had his own interpreter and there was no need for me to be there. As they discussed U.S. banking regulations and Soviet legislation, tobacco infused saliva was dripping down the back of my throat. I wanted to spit it out, but couldn't. The conversation seemed to go on forever. By the time it was over, I'd pretty much swallowed it all. When we got up to leave, a Secret Service agent said to me, "You're the first Russian interpreter I've ever seen with a chew."

We had a few hours between meetings, so I invited the trio to lunch at The Guards, on me. Whenever I interpreted for visiting Soviets, I always invited them for at least a drink or two, at my expense. I intentionally wanted to drive home the point that a poor student in America had more purchasing power than the Soviet elite. The fact that they had international passports meant they were powerful and successful back home. Even so, most lived on $5 per day of discretionary spending. They laughed when they heard the accounting term, per diem. In Russian it sounds like "Let's fart." To save money, none ever went out to eat. Instead, they'd do things like boil ramen in their hotel room's coffee maker.

After lunch with the banking trio, I reached for the tab. We had several drinks each and I knew it would be out of reach for the average Soviet to pay it. Instead, the leader of the group snatched it out of my hand. I was very surprised and maybe a little insulted. He reached into his coat pocket and pulled out an envelope of hundred dollar bills. He noticed my amazement and with a wink, said "When you're in Moscow, we'll let you pay." Mikhail Khodorkovsky was the first Soviet I encountered with money. The two others with him were Platon Lebedev and Leonid Nevzlin.

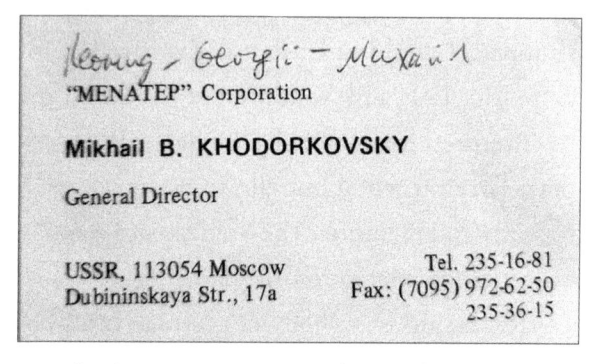

A freelance interpreting job introduced me to someone who'd later become famous

The Menatep bank meetings took us to The Library of Congress. I knew who the director was, James Billington, from his book about Russian culture, "The Icon and the Axe." It covered six centuries of Russian cultural history and is considered indispensable to any scholar of that country. At University it had been the most tedious but fascinating book for me. Khodorkovsky and his crew were discussing convertible equity loans, privatization of state entities via vouchers and open joint-stock companies, shareholder vehicles, leveraged buyouts, IPOs, etc. I'd learned Soviet Russian for the U.N. and picked up street hustler lingo in Leningrad, but these people were speaking Wall Street, which was a Russian that didn't really exist yet.

Humiliated, I had to admit that I was incapable of interpreting the subject. I apologized repeatedly but had to tap out. Mr. Billington offered encouragement and said something like, "Keep with it. You'll come back stronger." Khodorkovsky was clearly disappointed that the meeting was about to fail because his American-born interpreter didn't have a capitalist's vocabulary. He pleadingly pointed at a business plan and repeated a simple word, "Aktsiya," (a share of stock). I'd never heard that either. Private ownership didn't exist in the USSR. Every time I've watched Jen Psaki answer questions on topics about which she clearly knows nothing, which is almost always, I imagine that she is me and I'm rambling on at the Library of Congress.

The lobbyist for Menatep reported afterwards that he understood that the lexicon was new, i.e. no hard feelings. Nonetheless, it was devastating for my confidence. The lobbyist also shared with me the conclusion of Nicholas Burns' office, which was that Menatep lacked the wherewithal to become significant enough to merit the status of correspondent bank. Within a few years of that meeting in the OEB, Menatep became one of Russia's leading financial institutions and Mikhail Khodorkovsky went on to repeatedly vie for, and be declared, the title of Russia's richest person.

The next interpreting job was another subject that didn't exist in Russian, baseball. The first ever Soviet national team had a game scheduled against the George Washington Colonials. Before the game, I asked a professor for a list of baseball terms. He too had no idea, but by relying on intuition, he predicted that the words would be the same as in English. He was right. The Soviet team was horrible. They never scored and GWU could have continued scoring for days, but didn't. After declaring a gentlemanly decision to end the game, one of the Russian players threw a language curveball at me, asking why a pop fly that is easy to catch is called a "Can of corn.?"

The next interpreting gig was symbolic of the era. The president of a D.C. firm that called itself IBD, International Business Development, was hosting a Moscow-based entity called ETM, which stood for Fuck your mother in Russian (Eb Tvoyu Mat'). IBD was a one-man band, T.D. He received partial funding from the lobbyist whom I'd failed with Menatep. T.D.'s budget was limited. The lobbyist suggested he hire me to interpret at a deep discount.

---

2   According to MLB.com a "Can of corn" is a routine fly ball. When 19th-century clerks at groceries and general stores were looking for an easier way to reach canned goods on high shelves, they started using long, hooked sticks to pull them down. After dropping the cans toward them, they would catch them in their aprons -- just like a fly ball.

Neither ETM nor IBD had any assets. I didn't understand how they met. Their summit was reminiscent of a Russian joke about how commerce is conducted. One party promises to buy 100,000 bottles of vodka and the other agrees to deliver it. After signing a contract, one goes to look for vodka and the other to look for money. ETM and IBD spent days investigating potential cooperation. They were ready to ink deals for medical devices, used cars, two-way tourism, and anything else neither one had.

ETM's owner had flown with his own interpreter, Anton, whose command of American slang was excellent. That was unusual. I asked him where he'd learned American. He said he was an underground movie translator (like my friend Pavel in Leningrad). Anton's knowledge was even deeper. IBD didn't need me if ETM had Anton. We exchanged phone numbers and I forgot about him.

A few months after the ETM visit, Anton called me very early one morning from Gander Airport in Newfoundland, Canada. He said his flight was landing in D.C. in a few hours and hoped to meet up. Well, in fact, he admitted that he didn't just want to meet up. He hoped that I'd lend him my couch because he didn't have money for a hotel and didn't know anyone else. I agreed. Dee wouldn't care if someone we didn't know from Moscow stayed with us.

I also saved Anton $40 in cab fare by picking him up in the Frenchman's LTD. The Wyoming tabs were expired and I'd racked up at least $500 in parking tickets. Anton had no idea what he could do to make money, or why he was in Washington. His visit with IBD convinced him that with the border slightly ajar, it was the time to seize an opportunity, even if he didn't know what that opportunity was.

My first-year dorm at GWU was directly across the street from Tower Records, one of the world's biggest retailers of albums, CDs and movies. It seemed Anton would appreciate the wide selection. He bought every recent release he could. He was certain he'd be the first to bring them to market in Moscow, which guaranteed a higher profit. He spent all he had and flew back. He made me promise to contact him if I ever returned to Moscow, and I made him promise to forewarn us next time he wanted a couch.

Dee and several of us Guards regulars were sipping rusty nails when a member of our crew arrived. He confronted Dee about the back-slapping overnighter with Karen's daughter. He pointed his finger at Dee and straight out accused him of lying, saying, "You weren't with the daughter. You did the mother. I know it." Dee looked stunned and responded, "She swore she'd never tell!" The other person said with a smirk, "She didn't. I found out."

Business with Toolshed

The U.S. Air Force Russian linguist, Toolshed, whom I met in England en route to Leningrad, finished his military service and enrolled at the University of Maryland. There was debate about how he earned his name. One version was that he used the vernacular from his native St. Louis area, which described unpleasant people as "Tools." Others maintained he acquired the moniker during a military training exercise where they pretended to be POWs and his job was maintaining the tool shed. To this day, he's still referred to either as Toolshed or Shed, but never only Tool.

He started Maryland as a senior. Previously he'd attended Westminster College in Missouri, famous as the location where Winston Churchill first used the term "Iron Curtain" in a speech. He was expelled from there after a conviction for stealing a horse. The circumstances seemed understandable. There was an all-girl college, William Woods, in the same town as Westminster. Shed planned to stay overnight at William Woods, but found he couldn't. With no taxis in Fulton, Missouri late at night, he borrowed a horse, which was misunderstood as theft.

From Westminster he transferred to Tulane University in America's party city, New Orleans. Shed's academic career did not thrive there. He did, however, achieve a student record for bar debt. He persuaded numerous bars to let him drink on credit by convincing them that his wealthy family would settle up. When the bills came due in 1984, Shed owed over $10,000, a sum which calculates into 2022 dollars to about $28,000. Toolshed's father was a retired U.S. Army Captain and recipient of a Silver Star for gallantry in Germany during WWII. He paid the bills, but on condition his son made one of two options: Military or Monastery. Shed knew his father had little respect for the Air Force and less for Russians, so he joined the Air Force and requested to become a Russian specialist.

We'd spent only a week or so during the evenings in England, but it was difficult to forget his driving or the mischief he dragged me into. When Shed arrived in the Washington metro area in the late 1980s, we reconnected. He found a job at an alphabet soup firm called B.A.S.E. Corp (Bridge for American Soviet Enterprise). Its business model was identical to those of IBD and ETM. B.A.S.E.'s mission was to identify anything in the USSR that Americans would pay for, or vice versa.

Bridge for American Soviet Enterprise, one of a thousand such fledgling firms at the time

Compared to other such businesses, B.A.S.E. was first-class. It had a manager and two salaried employees, Shed, and a recent immigrant, Victor, who had been an architect in Moscow. Victor's resumé included buildings that had actually been constructed based on his designs. What truly elevated B.A.S.E. was that its president held an MBA from an American University that people had heard of. When Toolshed told me about B.A.S.E. Corporation, I will admit to being jealous. It sounded like a badass company for the times. I had a diploma, but Shed had two-sided business cards, one in English, one in Russian. In the USSR, any business card was the sign of a player. But B.A.S.E.'s Two-sided bilingual cards with working phone and fax numbers demanded attention. For the era those cards were hot like a cryptocurrency with a catchy name.

Toolshed and Victor the architect were scheduled to visit Moscow. Victor had used his extensive network to arrange for the B.A.S.E. team to give gifts to powerful bureaucrats all over the city. His influence was such that the deputy Mayor promised to open the front doors of Moscow City Hall for the B.A.S.E. delegation. There were no goals or agenda, but expectations were high that major deals were coming. Shed invited me to visit B.A.S.E. headquarters to see the operation firsthand. He even hinted there might soon be an opening for me.

Two days before they were set to leave for Moscow, I visited. Victor the architect was full of anticipation because their printer called to report the imminent delivery of his new business cards. The courier arrived. With the excited anticipation of a child opening a present on Christmas morning, he opened the box of cards to inspect the aesthetics. The English side looked impressive and impeccable. Then he flipped it over. He froze. He looked horrified and stared in disbelief. He started stammering and stuttering. He couldn't get the word out of his mouth. Toolshed took the card from him and read the cyrillic with curiosity out loud: "Fpiktor."

Victor was devastated. For him the trip was doomed. No man could expect success with a typo on his business card. Shed suggested he use it to his advantage and claim that Fpiktor was his American nickname. It showed that he had street cred in the USA. Victor was inconsolable and contemplated not traveling. The name stuck.

The two returned a couple weeks later with genuine prospects. Fpiktor's contacts at the Union of Architects offered a couple recently finished hotels. Some decision makers had traveled a little and knew Marriott and Radisson. If B.A.S.E. could persuade those chains to enter the USSR, a deal could be made to take some already built hotels on the cheap. They gained access to a warehouse with thousands of paintings. The curator was willing to let them go on consignment. The last prospect was a clothing design center. There were no brochures or photographs, but Fpiktor considered their work top notch. Fashion advice from a man who wore drab polyester and white vinyl shoes was the least encouraging prospect.

Toolshed had surreptitiously been hired by Johnson & Johnson. He agreed to relocate to their European headquarters in the Netherlands after graduation from Maryland. B.A.S.E. considered him treasonous. To save face, I agreed to at least work there part time so Shed looked honorable for finding a replacement.

Toolshed fit in with the crew at Guards. He spent more time there and on our couch than in College Park. Dee spoke often about how impressed he was with Toolshed's ability to pass out in his clothes. He'd take off his jacket, keep his tie on, only slightly loosening it to sleep. When the alarm went off, he'd spring up, tighten his tie, and run to the bathroom for a French shower[1]. On the way out the door, he'd grab his jacket. On a slow day it would take him five minutes to be ready for work.

Even though he was supposed to be across town in College Park, Maryland, he signed a month-to-month rental agreement for a studio in a River Place to save time commuting to drink with us. His apartment was in the same compound, but our units were as far apart as possible. Shed's place wasn't ideal for bologna, but its proximity to Wilson Boulevard / Highway 110 provided an opportunity to reach moving targets. There was also a sentry post below, but Shed's place had no balcony and was on a lower floor.

Leaving for work around 5 a.m., I ran into Bzdunka, who was just returning home. She looked frazzled and was surprised to see me. She'd been to a club near Dupont Circle called the Badlands with her gay neighbors, Jamie and Johnny. Bzdunka had been exposed to cocaine and debauchery. She told me, "There is too much freedom in the USA." I didn't have much time and quipped back, "There's no such thing as too much freedom. Who got hurt? Who wasn't free to leave?"

Shed had been living in River Place for weeks, but his clothes were still in his old bedroom at a house he and other students rented in Maryland. For a graduation gift, his father, who owned a Ford dealership outside of St. Louis, sent him what was a prototype race car, the Merkur XR4Ti[2]. After closing the Guards one night, Shed suggested we drive

---

1 Wash one's face only and put enough water on one's hair to make it look combed.
2 Wikipedia: The **Merkur XR4Ti** is a performance-oriented 3-door hatchback sold in North America from 1985 to 1989. A product of the Ford Motor Company, the car was a version of the European Ford Sierra XR4i adapted to U.S. regulations.[2] The XR4Ti project was championed by Ford vice president Bob Lutz.

to Maryland to pick up his clothes. I'd never been to U Maryland, so I agreed.

Instead of taking the usual fastest routes, New York Avenue / Highway 50 or Rhode Island Avenue / Highway 1, Shed thought it would be smart to avoid police and instead drive through Northeast Washington, home to the highest crime rates in the United States at the time. It was number one for murder and the epicenter of the crack epidemic. The demographics of D.C.'s population was just under 90% black, and I'd guess 90% of the white population lived in Northwest.

There was no GPS and Shed didn't know where he was going. It didn't take long for the police to notice two white guys in a rare European sports car at three in the morning, stopped at a crack dealing intersection. While Shed tried to decide to go right or straight, potential carjackers and crack dealers examined his car, as did two police officers who were parked about a block up the street, staring at us with incredulity. Shed decided to go straight. As soon as his car moved past the police, they did a quick U-turn and pulled up behind us, without even turning on their lights. I told Shed to act sober and he told me to shut up.

When Toolshed rolled down the window, the officer didn't ask for his license but instead if he'd lost his mind.

Toolshed slurred, "I'm sorry, but who do you think you are?"

The officer couldn't believe his ears and explained, "I'm trying to keep the murder rate down. And I can't believe that on top of being stupid, you're drunk. I can take you to jail. Just leave," he pleaded. "I'm trying to help all of us."

Shed wasn't having any of that. He continued his sloppy tirade, "Listen to me carefully. You have no idea who I am. You can't just expect someone like me to roll over. I need your name and badge number. This is not over."

Baffled, the policeman looked to me for help, and asked me to please just get him to drive the hell out of there without stopping anymore. Shaking his head, the officer returned to his car.

Toolshed, however, demanded the last word. He got out of the car and motioned to the policeman that he wanted to say something. The cop stuck his head out of the window and signaled that he was listening. Toolshed pointed his finger at him and said, "You've had it," got back in the car and drove away.

When we got to the house in Maryland, we drank more and passed out. I woke up in Shed's old bed in the early afternoon. I walked out into the living room where some of his roommates or friends were watching a basketball game. I asked where our friend was and they said they didn't know. I joined them watching the game. A short time later, a top player got viciously elbowed in the face and was knocked unconscious. The announcers were wondering if the player would return to the game. The crowd and TV audience anticipated some serious drama when he regained consciousness. As he opened his eyes and sat up, a parabolic microphone clearly caught his first word, which was "Mite," or perhaps

"Maite." What he was really saying was "I'm all right." From under a pile of clothes, Toolshed emerged saying the same thing, "Mite." Upon seeing Shed, his roommate from Germany started shaking his head, saying "I heff never seen somsink so wahnsinnig (insane). You drank much beer and drove ze car."

The XR4Ti was short-lived. Shed managed to pull a maneuver that smashed every corner of the car in a single accident. He wanted to demonstrate to a female passenger the car's ability to outpace traffic from a cloverleaf on-ramp. He turned too sharply and accelerated too much, causing the car to spin out. The rear left hit the guard rail, the car spun around and the front right hit it too. Facing oncoming traffic, he tried to quickly turn around and drove the rear right into the wall and as he was turning back into the flow of traffic a passing car crashed into the front left.

First Foray Into Moscow

Dee and I both forgot about the bologna that had been in the "Vault" for weeks. We learned that warm bologna is flaccid and does not provide the aerodynamic characteristics required for distance and aim. We experimented with bargain and generic brands. The results of our research showed conclusively that Oscar Mayer was the gold standard.

My dad only visited me in D.C. twice. I was happy that Dee and Shed got to meet him. My father's boss, Woody, was the CEO of an insurance company in Omaha, which owned a ten-seat private plane. Woody drank Miller Lite on ice every day from morning until evening, when he switched to red wine. His physique resembled that of a tick that was unable to pull out of an artery. When he wore a suit, it looked like it was stuffed with a baseball umpire's chest protector. When Woody rolled through town, he threw fifty and hundred dollar bills around like Al Czervik, the character played by Rodeny Dangerfield in the movie Caddyshack.

In D.C. for a $5,000 per plate fundraiser, Woody purchased a table for eight. He didn't care about the dinner. He only wanted the recipient to know who the generous donor was. Woody knew I lived in Washington and asked me to round up a few bodies to fill his table.

When my friends and I arrived at the event, Dee was excited to immediately recognize Jackie Mason, a comedian. Dee and I crashed a lot of these types of parties for free drinks. Lobby groups and wealthy donors served free food with open bars every day. If we kept quiet and didn't bother anyone, D.C. establishment types seemed to appreciate that at least someone took advantage of free stuff.

When beef kebabs were served, Woody was buzzed. He struggled to get the end piece off with his fork. It popped up in the air and launched to a few tables over, splatting between the breasts of a heavily bejeweled socialite, who was wearing something that looked like a custom Chanel dress. Woody saw where his kebab cannonball had landed and got up to approach the other table. Instead of apologizing profusely, he instead pulled out his wallet and started flinging hundred dollar bills, offering to pay for a new dress and dry cleaning. Woody returned to his table.

Making small talk, Woody said, "I hear you're going to Moscow soon." When I confirmed that was correct, he continued, "They tell me there are some very talented musicians over there. Find me one." I was surprised that Woody was interested in music. We'd once been at a lake resort in Okoboji, Iowa where a live band was playing. Between songs Woody approached the band and asked how much they earned. They told him and Woody paid them triple the amount to leave, which they did. I remember Okoboji well. While Woody and the adult entourage played golf all day and cards at night, I was an almost teenager who was stuck watching his four year-old son. Live music was the highlight of that trip and he killed it. I also remember wondering why the only thing people talked about was the death of Elvis Presley that happened while we were there. Woody told me to keep my ears open in Moscow and if I heard something special to let him know.

Afterwards, I asked my dad how Woody had become interested in music, he replied, "He found out that money can be made from it. There's a music guy in Omaha named Chip Davis. When Woody saw his plane, he asked what business the owner of it was in. He became interested in music when he found out it can buy planes."

I accompanied B.A.S.E. president, Kurt, and Fpiktor on a ten-day trip to Moscow. The only contact I had there was Anton and I forgot to bring his number. Fpiktor's people put us up in an Apartment near the "Airport" metro station, where there were no planes and there was no airport. After showing Kurt and me the amenities, our hosts left. I suggested we go walk around and explore the neighborhood. Kurt agreed. We then found out that we were locked in. We searched the apartment for a key to the door, but couldn't find one.

When they came to retrieve us the next day, we mentioned that we didn't find it very hospitable for them to have locked us in. Oops. They said that was an oversight. I asked about the "Airport" section of the city and they explained that it was a bus station from which one could ride to Moscow's four main airports.

Fpiktor's business ideas started through connections at the Union of Architects. Each profession in the USSR had union headquarters that were like socialist-style country clubs. Only a tiny fraction of a percent of the population could be members. The original building for the Architects was finished at the end of the 1800s. The interior was beautiful and spacious. During Soviet times they added wings and made other changes with clashing styles and designs. By the late 1980s it looked like a Frankenstein's monster of Architecture, but it had a well stocked ruble bar.

One of the main hustlers there was a Jewish mobster named Marik. He didn't wear an Adidas tracksuit, which is also known as a Balkan Tuxedo, but most of his minions did. Marik's favorite word was "Slysh," which loosely translates as "Listen here." His plan to profit from the city's art collection was based on primitive logic and simple facts. Most people in Moscow didn't have any money. Even if they did, they wanted foreign stuff. Americans had money and liked foreign stuff. Kurt and I were Americans so we should get the job of choosing which paintings Americans would buy.

The basement bar of the Union of Architects Club

Marik's team drove us to a sprawling, cavernous, multi-purpose, factory / warehouse. Machines whirred and people wearing dusty white smocks and cloth hats walked to and fro. We followed the host for several minutes until we passed through a set of open double doors, big enough for a city bus to drive through. There were thousands of paintings. Some were framed, some were in subframes, others rolled up. Numbered tags that showed the artist and title were at the end of each row. It was uncharacteristically well organized for something Soviet.

They sat us in front of a stage with seating for about thirty people. Marik's curator friend offered three genres: Soviet Realism, Still Life, and Portrait. We chose "Whatever you thought best." I'd visited exactly four major museums and knew little about any single artist other than my mother's favorite, Marc Chagall. The workers professionally presented hundreds, if not over a thousand, stunningly beautiful, original paintings. After selecting approximately fifty, the same stage then became a fashion runway. We were supposed to rate clothing. Dee had taught me to never buy trousers that weren't lined. Shed swore by Gitman Brothers shirts. That's all I knew about clothes. Kurt laughed with incredulity when he assumed the role of runway critic. His qualifications were his MBA. While he rated fashion, I took photos of the paintings we'd selected so that I could show them later to galleries in Washington.

Fpiktor arranged a meeting with a Georgian deputy mayor of Moscow, whom I remember as Ordzhonikidze(?) He offered to create joint ventures with two hotels, one was near Kiev Train Station, the other near the rowing canal near Krylatskoe which was built for the 1980 Olympics. When I mentioned that Radisson Hotels and its owner were located in my native city, Minneapolis, they took that as a guarantee of a successful deal and gave B.A.S.E. an "Exclusive" to find an operating partner for the Slavyanskaya Hotel.

Marik took us to dinner at the second-floor banquet hall in the Belgrade Hotel[1] (Today the Golden Ring). One couldn't really yet call the regulars there mafia, but none of them worked, had a title, and instead of cash they paid for everything in favors. A person off the street would never get in. One of the leaders was a Chechen named Musa. At the

---

[1] The Belgrade Hotel was two buildings on opposite sides of the street, which mirrored each other. It was located on Smolensk Square, which is home to the Ministry of Foreign Affairs, one of the iconic "Seven Sisters" building, also known as the Stalinist Wedding Cake style of architecture.

Union of Architects, everyone showed reverence to Marik, but around Musa IR WAS Marik who was reserved.

Kurt and I were seated at a table with a guy named Fabrik, an associate of Marik and close friend of Fpiktor. Fabrik warned me not to approach the head table uninvited and definitely to never kiss or hug Musa. I didn't understand why he thought it necessary to warn me about kissing Musa. He explained. The last time B.A.S.E. representatives were in the Belgrade restaurant, Musa said something flattering about Toolshed, just to blow smoke up his ass, like an Italian in New York might say, "Look at this kid. Everybody loves him." Drunken Shed took Musa's words as an expression of forever friendship so he walked up to him and kissed him on the lips. Everyone in the room gasped, waiting for Musa's signal on how to react. Musa waved off his guards and let it slide. I promised Fabrik I would not kiss Musa.

Fabrik mentioned he was working a computer deal and asked me to convince Kurt to meet his contact. Technology was a non-existent integral part of B.A.S.E.'s business. Kurt agreed. The next day we all met at an apartment inside the "House on the Embankment.[2]" The apartment owner was a concert pianist originally from Kishinev, Moldova. No one told me who he was, but the large apartment and concert grand piano in his living room suggested he was some kind of bigwig.

His name was Leonid Chizhik. He had just visited W. Germany where he astutely noticed a price gap between Munich and Moscow. The price of cutting-edge IBM i486 and B70 computers was triple or more in the USSR. The problem was that there was a ban on exporting the latest technology to Warsaw Pact[3] countries. American legislators pushed for the Capitalist Bloc to implement multilateral export controls, known as Cocom[4] sanctions. The bottom line for us was that if we got caught, the fines would bankrupt everyone in the room, especially since only Kurt had any money at all. I recalled a researcher at Leningrad U boasting to me about his "Illegal" IBM 386, but I didn't understand the significance at the time. I knew it was possible, but had no idea how.

While they continued to discuss computer smuggling, I asked Chizhik if I could play his grand piano. I played an American standard called "Blue Room." As I played, Fabrik whispered in my ear, "Do you have any fucking idea whose piano you're playing? Stop." I did not have any idea other than it belonged to a wannabe computer smuggler. Chizhik said, "I recognize the song. Remind me who wrote it." I told him it was Gershwin. Instantly he said, "That was absolutely not Gershwin." Chizhik

---

2   Дом на набережной. When built, it was the tallest residential building in the USSR. It is located across the Moscow River from the Kremlin and was one of Russia's most prestigious addresses.
3   Albania, Bulgaria, Czechoslovakia, East Germany, Hungary, Poland, Romania, USSR.
4   Seventeen countries agreed to restrict the export of these technologies: Australia, Belgium, Canada, Denmark, France, West Germany, Greece, Italy, Japan, Luxembourg, Netherlands, Norway, Portugal, Spain. Turkey, United Kingdom, United States

sat down and played a snippet of Gershwin's "Someone to Watch Over Me" that gave me goosebumps. His virtuosity was HOLY SHIT!! level. Fabrik casually mentioned that Leonid was the first jazz musician allowed to perform in Tchaikovsky Hall.

House on the Embankment, Moscow. Chez pianist Leonid Chizhik

While Fabrik was telling me about Chizhik's pedigree, he located a reference book and found "Blue Room," which he announced was written by Rodgers and Hart. Leonid added, "I told you it wasn't Gershwin."

Jazz in the USSR was generally forbidden and associated with freedom. I was surprised when he presented me with several of his albums that had been released on Melodiya[5]. Leonid played an original composition. His style reminded me of Chick Corea. His technique was on par with the greatests of all time, like Oscar Peterson and Art Tatum. I took two copies each of his vinyl albums and promised to record demos in the U.S. Woody could expect a call.

Chizhik joined us for drinks and dinner a few days before we left Moscow. I was curious how difficult it had been to earn official recognition as a jazz musician. He said that in the 1970s the KGB had thrown a cavalcade of detractors at him during his concerts. People threw things at him, punched, kicked, slapped, and verbally intimidated him in general. Agents planted in the audience would boo. He said the more they tried to beat down his spirit, the better he played. Leonid Chizhik had the attitude of a punk rocker like Iggy Pop with the chops of Vladimir Horowitz. One of a kind.

Maestro Leonid Chizhik with my mother and niece, Julia

---

5 The Soviet State recording monopoly

Bologna Bust

When I returned to Washington, Dee and I hosted a holiday party. Shed was about to move to the Netherlands. Many others would also soon leave the city. Nick, the German from Hamburg, who trapped the rat in the Leningrad dorm, joined us. He was in a graduate study program at GWU. The Saint was headed to China. Joel was staying put in D.C. He had launched a catering company. Roddy and See-Say from Howard U, and at least a half dozen girls we'd rounded up with the slickest pick-up line, "Do you want to frisbee bologna off our balcony?" which worked almost every time.

We hyped the party as a bologna-palooza. Dee and I prepared pass trays that had only bologna on them. We left the lights on, balcony door open, and no one ducked after launching. Alcohol and crowd numbers made us feel invincible. Most of the partygoers were oblivious to the fact that the launch pad had been under investigation for over a year. The crowd was a melange of mortadella: numerous nationalities, black, white, straight, gay, rich and poor.

After much prodding by me, Ludmila from Moscow finally agreed to try planting a slice of bologna on the roof of the guard house. I accompanied her to the balcony and proudly watched as she flung her first Oscar Mayer frisbee. As soon as it was airborne, a floodlight lit up our faces and a voice over a megaphone announced, "This is the Arlington Police. We've seen the bologna. We're coming up." Ludmila more than panicked. She told me, "I absolutely cannot interact with the police. Get me out of here immediately." I wanted to thank her for giving me a reason to shirk the responsibility of dealing with the police.

We left without saying anything. No one knew that there was about to be a surprise police visit. Right outside the door to the left there was a staircase a few feet from our apartment door. I guided Ludmila to the eighth floor, where we ran down the long corridor to Bzdunka's apartment. I figured a Russian would hide a Russian, but Bzdunka wouldn't open her door, even though she spoke to me from inside. When I angrily railed on her afterwards, she admitted that she had a naked woman with her and hadn't yet told anyone she was lesbian.

Ludmila and I walked down another set of stairs to the service entrance/exit, from where we safely put her in a taxi. After that, no one ever saw her again. Our mutual friend Inga from Odessa had spent lots of time at Ludmila's house, where she lived with her mother. A few days after the bologna scare,

Inga called Ludmila's mother to check in. The mother said, "I don't know you and please do not call here ever again." Inga's conclusion was that Ludmila evaporated into the NSA.

Back on the 9th floor, I peeked around the corner to see if the police were still there. They were gone. I didn't know what to expect when I walked in. I was pretty sure there'd be hostility towards me for having fled. Even though Ludmila's horror was the genuine impetus for doing so, I didn't expect them to believe it. I was surprised to hear that the party seemed to be mostly uninterrupted and going strong.

I entered sheepishly, expecting anger. Instead, they were high-fiving, smiling, and cackling. Toolshed got in my face and in a black D.C. accent blurted defiantly and loudly, "It was bologna!" and started laughing uncontrollably. Dee was anxious to tell me what happened but it took him some time to gain his composure. We had unleashed a full-fledged airstrike. The River Place security guard was outraged and livid. He only wanted to hear, "You're under arrest."

Two policemen and a security guard confronted Dee, while Toolshed stood nearby. Dee said that every time the policeman mentioned the word bologna, he would cut them off, saying things like, "To gain clarity, please tell me explicitly what we're being accused of, or charged with." As soon as he heard the word bologna, he'd interrupt and deflect. "So let me get this straight. You're saying that instead of making sandwiches, we used lunch meat as projectiles?" The police dropped the word and tried to coax a confession by saying things like flying objects, items, projectiles, etc. Dee replied in kind, switching to banter about cold cuts and the like. The guard, who had remained silent, lost it and snapped, "These motherfuckers have been throwing bologna. It was bologna!" The police and Dee made a handshake deal with the police that no more bologna would be thrown for no charges. That was the last time we threw. When they left, the miffed guard muttered angrily all the way down the hall, "It was bologna!"

About the same time, Moose from Leningrad U invited me to meet up with him in Bologna, Italy. No joke. I don't remember what he was doing there, but he loved it there. I agreed to fly over. A day or two before my departure, our landlord called to report he'd received a copy of a cease and desist letter from the management of River Place about us throwing bologna. I promised him we'd quit, and when I mentioned that I wouldn't even be around for a while because I was leaving for Bologna, Italy there was a long pause as he processed what I'd said. In a confused tone, he asked, "Why are you people obsessed with bologna?"

Bologna to Budapest

The name and address of the hotel in Bologna where Moose was waiting for me was in my suitcase that Alitalia lost. They also re-directed me on another airline through Switzerland, where I got stuck for two days. In the days before cell phones, it was very difficult to maintain contact. I called Moose's mother in Boston and he called mine. By the time we found out where the other was, Moose had moved to another city. I wandered around Bologna for a day. It is a beautiful city, but I wanted to be with friends. The closest place where I had an open invitation was Pecs, Hungary, so I decided to go there.

At the train station in Bologna, they told me I had to first get to Vienna, and then book a ticket to Budapest from there. Hungary was still East Bloc, so they couldn't sell me a ticket. Arriving in Vienna early in the morning, it shocked me to see so many people drinking beer with breakfast. It seemed there was a bottle of Stiegl on every table. The train to Budapest departed so soon, I didn't even get to have a breakfast beer.

About two hours outside of Vienna, the train stopped at the Hungarian border. Passport control came through. When they saw I had no visa, they ordered me off the train. I sat alone with my suitcase in a locked room and watched the train depart. I was certain they'd send me back to Vienna. A border agent entered and sternly recited Hungarian law about attempted entry without a visa. When I showed panic, he started to laugh. He pointed outside to a waiting white Volga (Soviet car) and told me he'd give me a visa and taxi ride to Budapest for $50.

Arriving in Budapest, there were thousands, if not tens of thousands, of people in the street. They were carrying flags that had the Soviet emblem cut out of the middle. They were celebrating the demise of socialism. There were no hotel rooms anywhere. I still had a Hyatt employee ID card as a D.C. concierge, which I showed to the front desk of the Budapest Hyatt. They said, "We always recognize fellow employees" and gave me a room at a rate of something like $35/night. My friends in Pecs sent a car to pick me up the next day.

In Pecs, the students we shared the floor with in the Leningrad dorm prodded me to confess that the Americans were government employees and spies. They couldn't believe that any Westerner would voluntarily live in those conditions. I not only admitted that we were spies, but presented them with tools of the trade. Before leaving Washington, Alphonso took me to the bargain store where he found the Groucho glasses he and Dee wore after the knockout incident at the Guards. I intended to wear them when I met Moose. Besides, one never knows when Groucho glasses might be necessary in international travels. They're like a parachute. You hope you'll never need them, but will be glad to have them when you do. We wore them on a city bus in Pecs, telling each other nonsense phrases in Russian, English, and German, and managed to keep straight faces. Afterwards, the Hungarians declared us "Fekete Macska Bandajo," the Black Cat Gang.

Agents of the "Black Cat Gang, undercover, in Pecs, Hungary

About the same time as I was roaming around with Hungarian women in Groucho glasses, Toolshed was on his first mission for Johnson & Johnson, which was to drive an old fire truck loaded with personal care products from the Netherlands to Ukraine, where they'd purchased their first Soviet factory.

Hungarian girls can't resist Groucho glasses

Soviet Art Exhibit In D.C.

When I returned to Washington, B.A.S.E. put me in charge of identifying art galleries to host a sales exhibition of the Soviet art pieces we'd selected. I visited numerous galleries and showed the photographs. An Irish woman had a gallery near Dupont Circle. It was close to Embassy Row and deep-pocketed clientele with discretionary spending for art. She rose quickly to the top of the list of candidates. Marik's reaction, was "Fuck the Irish. We need an Eastern European with a gallery.

I found a Yugoslavian woman with a smaller gallery almost across M street from the Four Seasons Hotel in Georgetown. The address was good. They went with her, whose name was Maria. The address appealed to me as well. It was less than two blocks from the Guards.

Fabrik and his wife, Alka Seltzer, immigrated and moved into a place in suburban Virginia. They needed to keep busy, so they took over the art project. The gallery owner, Maria, knew all about life under communism. She sized up Alka Seltzer and took advantage of her. For one thousand dollars cash and no paperwork, she took Alka's $20,000 sable coat as "collateral." Maria promised to return the coat after collecting money from art sales. Maria and Fabrik set prices. The lowest was around $3,000, the highest nearly $30,000.

There was no market, but the artists were generally well known and the pinnacle of talent. Considering that we'd acquired the entire exhibit for the cost of shipping and favors, it appeared likely that there would be a substantial pie to slice up afterwards. B.A.S.E. provided a small advertising budget. Everything Soviet-related was hot. It was easy to park articles about the opening in local print media.

"In the Garden" by Klara Vlasova c 1960   The artist was awarded a Pushkin Medla on May 17, 2016 by presidential decree No. 233 for the "cultural enrichment of the nation."

The prospect of becoming major art dealers drew Marik and Musa to Washington. The Chechen - Jewish connection arrived to see firsthand how Fpiktor and Fabrik were coping with their new terrain. None of the four knew English or the city. I was their Russian-speaking concierge and tour guide.

Fpiktor had a purple-ish high-mileage two-door Ford hatchback from circa 1981. The LTD with Wyoming plates finally got booted on a busy part of Connecticut Avenue. It was in a no parking zone, possibly a bus stop, when I abandoned it. I estimated the final tally of parking tickets to be nearly $1,000. It had been a real value and money-saver. I owe the French student more than gratitude for leaving it to me. I felt no sadness about losing it. It was more a pleasure to see how its story ended, which was a certainty.

In Moscow Musa and Marik never paid for anything. Their world was based on favors, connections, and barter. Cash wasn't necessary. In D.C. their ties weren't worth much, but at least got them a car and driver, plus an interpreter. We rode around, crammed five in Fpiktor's two-door. Marik was bigger than Musa, but Musa sat in front wearing a Balkan tuxedo. The visitors were annoyed that I showed them famous tourist attractions like Capitol Hill, the Lincoln Memorial, and White House. They wanted to see real life.

At my direction, Fpiktor drove us into a notorious crack neighborhood where prostitutes and dealers openly walked the street. As soon as we stopped curbside and rolled down the windows, salespeople crowded around. Musa and Marik wanted to know everything. From the middle of the back seat, I translated to hookers and crack dealers a flurry of questions like "What cut does your pimp take?" or "Do you pay protection to someone to be able to work?" As their replies were becoming more open and honest, two bodybuilder-sized metro police officers motioned us out and ordered us to put our hands on the car. There were some theatrics involved. They kicked at our feet and patted us down. Fpiktor was nervous. It was his car. They angrily informed us we had no business visiting "Their" neighborhood. They threatened us with vague unpleasantries and ordered us to leave.

We got back in the car and left. Musa was impressed with how polite they were, even though they had no reason to pull us out of the car or search us. Fabrik used the incident to teach me the Russian word for the verb "To frisk." He explained that in Soviet prisons, inmates were patted down and searched every day at 8 a.m. Many or most prisoners were Jewish. Eight in Hebrew is Shmone, so the prison slang verb became "Shmonat," something like getting eighted. D.C. quickly bored them. The real mafia was in Brighton Beach. I stayed behind, while Fpiktor, Musa, Fabrik and Marik headed north to New York.

Soviet Jazz at Paisley Park

Reminding Woody of his offer to finance a musician, I called him to inform that I'd found one. His reply went along the lines of "Ya. ya. Kid. Call my secretary, Nancy. She'll take care of everything." He gave me her direct line and didn't speak to me about it again. Woody didn't even want to listen to his albums.

The most famous studio I knew was Prince's Paisley Park. I had no idea what recording entailed, or cost. Leonid said he preferred evenings and estimated two six-hour sessions would be sufficient to generate a good demo. I booked them from six p.m. to midnight. Woody's secretary sent a check to Paisley Park and booked a ticket for Leonid. The costs of his hotel in Minneapolis would be reimbursed, she said.

The recording project gave me the opportunity to visit my parents. My music loving mother played one of Leonid's albums and declared him world-class. She had an old upright from the 1940s. Leonid played a couple songs on it for her. She was like a super fan whose hand was kissed and they declare, "I'll never wash my hand again." My mom said she'd never play that piano again. Before she passed away in 2016, she made me promise to keep "Leonid's" piano safe. I have it.

To prepare for the recording session, Leonid wanted to rehearse on a concert grand. My aunt Gayle (dad's little sister) at the time was the property manager of the city's top jazz club, The Dakota. The club was only open in the evenings. Gayle was sure that Lowell the owner would let him practice and he did. As Leonid played the Dakota's piano, I did crossword puzzles at the bar. Lowell listened and told me, "You've got somebody."

On the way to Paisley Park, the maestro requested a bottle of vodka, ice cold. We stopped at a liquor store and grabbed a liter of Stoli, a bag of ice, and a styrofoam cooler. Leonid was wearing a gray polyester suit, with black vertical stripes. Its style would have been obsolete before it was released in 1963. He insisted on carrying the cooler himself, pointing out that I wasn't his valet. We arrived at the receptionist of Paisley Park. The woman behind the desk looked like she was wondering if she should call security. After briefly eyeballing us, she probably assumed we were lunatic Prince chasers.

I announced that we were there for the Leonid Chizhik recording session. Surprised, she summoned the engineer. He didn't do a good job of disguising his reaction to Leonid's appearance either. The styrofoam cooler he was holding also didn't bolster the impression of a super talent. The engineer showed us the equipment and layout of the studio as Leonid and I put down a few shots of vodka. After three or four, he declared himself ready to warm up and entered the adjacent room.

It was unusual to watch him play behind glass and not hear it. He was in a separate soundproof room. I asked the engineer. He said the monitor needed to be on. When he turned on the sound, the piano sounded tinny and high-pitched. If the final recording was going to sound like that, I wanted a refund of Woody's money. The engineer assured me that afterwards, he could fix whatever sound we wanted. Leonid warmed up by playing snippets of several different originals. The engineer said to me, "Wow! That's chops."

Not joking, I asked "What are chops?" He laughed and appreciated what he thought was dry humor. I repeated, "I don't know what chops are."

Incredulous, he said, "This is a first. You're supposed to be a producer and you don't know what 'chops' means? It means talent, innate talent."

Before starting his first full song, Leonid returned to the control room for another shot or two. The engineer complimented him on his skills. In Russian, Leonid apologized to me for what he considered was playing like shit. He didn't want to risk missing the demo session by admitting it, but he had seriously injured his left thumb in a bar fight in Munich. He said, "Some goddamn Nazi called me a kyke and dirty Jew so I punched the snot out of him and I really hurt my thumb" He told me not to worry about it, though. He escaped before the Polizei arrived.

Before starting to play for hours non-stop, Leonid took a full glass of vodka. Placing it on the floor next to the piano bench, he looked at the control room and through the monitor enthusiastically repeated the phrase Yuri Gagarin[1] uttered before launching into space, "Поехали!" (Let's go). The first session yielded about a 70 minute cassette of originals and a few covers. The standout for me was his version of "All The Things You Are," but that was probably because I knew it.
https://www.youtube.com/watch?v=cPN7oolnIcU&ab_channel=%ED%97%88%EB%A6%BCTV

My brother joined us for the second session. He remembers the engineer answering the phone in the control booth. He told the caller, "He's playing. Take monitor room B." My brother is convinced that Prince popped in for a listen to Leonid Chizhik.

Paisley Park converted the DAT tapes to cassettes. I sent them overnight to Omaha. Woody didn't listen to them but in turn gave them to someone else, who would form Woody's opinion for him. Nancy called and instructed me to find a business attorney and talent attorney. My brother's friend was a music lawyer, known

---

[1] Soviet cosmonaut who became the first person to travel to space in 1961.

to have an excellent ear. We hired him. He listened to the demos and was enthusiastic about Leonid's future in the U.S. Privately, he confided to my brother that he thought Leonid's left thumb sounded a little weak.

To remain consistent with the corporate style of the era, we formed ECM Corp. using the first letter of each of our last names. Woody agreed. The name was of no concern to him. Leonid and I thought it was a very respectable name.

Rumors trickled back through Woody's network that the demo cassettes reached Blue Note Records, who considered signing their first Soviet artist. Woody instructed the attorney to start due diligence on Leonid's recordings, which revealed that a label in Washington State was selling Chizhik's music under contract with Melodiya. It was a legal nightmare. The Soviet Union was collapsing, along with Melodiya. A legitimate U.S. firm held a valid claim to Leonid's work. Woody didn't want the potential headache and bowed out. If the legal issues could be sorted out, he'd jump back in. That was the end of Leonid's American jazz career. He accepted the position of "Professor Chizhik" at Germany's national music institute in Munich. My last copy of the demo cassette was taken by an Odessan in Minneapolis whose initials are Igor Goldstein. If he didn't lose it, he should return it. The DATs (Digital Audio Tapes) I still have, though, but nothing to play them on.

When I got back to Washington after recording Leonid, Fabrik reported that Brighton Beach had not gone well. Booba, the owner of one of the area's main mafia hangouts, the National restaurant and nightclub, shut the place down for the night as soon as he found out Musa and Marik were in town. It had been like a homecoming ball for Soviet gangsters. Far from home, Musa uncharacteristically drank. There were no alcohol averse Chechens around to give him criticism for violating the tenets of Islam by getting drunk. One of the New York Russians complained that the Italians continually demanded more payments to let him operate his window washing company in Manhattan. Drunken Musa acted like he was at home in Moscow and ordered the window washer to arrange a Razborka[2] with those "Italian punks."

When it was time to meet the Italians the next day, Musa had to be shaken awake. He was still drunk. Fabrik described the scene as surreal. Musa the Chechen mobster was sleeping in a three year old girl's bedroom that was decorated with My Little Pony. The father was a friend from Moscow who had gone straight in the U.S., as in abandoned mafia life. When Fabrik reminded him that he had called for a razborka with the Italian mafia the night before, Musa quickly determined they all needed to urgently return to Washington to find out what was happening with the art gallery. They

---

2 Razborka is a settling of accounts. In American street gang terminology, it would be a rumble.

hightailed it out of Brooklyn in Fpiktor's beat up hatchback.

Georgetown's first Soviet art exhibition was a success, for Maria the Yugoslavian. We estimated she sold over $200,000 worth of paintings. The unsold ones remained on the walls of the gallery that she rented . . . and abandoned. Maria skipped town, leaving the paintings on display in the space on M Street.

To make the situation crazier, the financial backer of B.A.S.E., a man named Karl, filed a lawsuit against Kurt to recover profits that didn't exist. When Karl subpoenaed Fpiktor and me as material witnesses, we laughed, realizing that the USSR didn't have a monopoly on absurdity. When I translated the text of the warrant from Karl's lawyer, Fpiktor laughed harder than I'd ever seen him laugh. He had a great sense of humor but I had never seen him fall apart so much that he couldn't speak.

We contacted Maria's landlord and explained the situation. He let us retrieve the paintings without question. When they arrived from the USSR, Fabrik was the addressee, so he signed for them when we took custody.

Marik et al acted honorably, or perhaps felt remorse for rejecting the Irish gallery. They let me choose for myself about $25,000 worth of paintings in lieu of pay. It was what they estimated would have been my cut if Maria hadn't absconded with the money. I took three, two of which went to family members. One of the pieces was by Klara Vlasova, who has a museum named after her and pieces on display at the Russian Museum in St. Petersburg. On May 17, 2016 she was declared a national artist by presidential decree No. 233.

Siberian Oil

The office of Wisconsin Senator Robert Kasten called me to act as an emergency interpreter. The one they had scheduled got into a car accident. They needed a replacement immediately. I took it. The agenda was a joint venture called White Nights, which had been formed to drill oil in the Tyumen region of Siberia. The Soviet partner was an oil and gas entity called Varyegan Neftegaz, which owned the permits but didn't have the necessary finances, equipment or personnel. The lead partner on the American side was Phibro Energy, a subsidiary of investment bank Salomon Brothers, which in the late 1980s was the most profitable firm on Wall Street. Geological surveys of the region conducted with the aid of U.S. satellites indicated that the drilling equipment required might fall under export sanctions, like Cocom for IBM. Representatives from the Oklahoma office of Parker Drilling were in the Senator's office asking for permission to export the equipment that the venture needed to deploy.

By evening, they determined that the venture could go forward. Whiskey and glasses were brought out. Toasts were made. I remember not wanting to drink on an empty stomach and the Senator insisting that no guest in his office should refuse a drink. After hoisting a glass to the new venture, the group went to dinner. I learned to never be hungry while interpreting. Everyone wanted to talk to the Russians and I was the only interpreter. The best I could do was sneak a small piece of bread here and there.

My dad had been pushing me hard to join the FBI. He was convinced that if I worked there for two years and quit, using "Former FBI agent" as a resumé filler would be a door opener. Living in Washington taught me that the government sucks, but to placate my father I'd gone to a few FBI interviews. One was in such a dangerous part of the city, my taxi driver refused to take me all the way. The building looked abandoned. The portrait of J. Edgar Hoover on the wall of the interview room was eerily reminiscent of Felix Dzerzhinsky's that I'd seen in a KGB office. The questions the FBI asked seemed inane, random, and bizarre. It was as if the job description was to fill the shoes of Cato Fong, Inspector Clouseau's assistant in the Pink Panther movie series.

Mercifully I never had to descend into the political cesspool known as the FBI, which uses law enforcement as a front for its own criminal activities. White Nights offered me a job. They didn't know what my position would be but wanted Americans that spoke Russian. They knew where the job was, though. Raduzhny (Rainbow city), Siberia. Entry-level FBI positions paid $18,000/year at that time. White Nights offered $72,000 plus free business class travel to just about anywhere we wanted to fly during monthly time off. I accepted. Moose called from their headquarters in Houston to congratulate me. He was already working there.

I intended to shock my mother with the announcement I was moving to Siberia. Her reaction was ho-hum. While dropping my stuff off in Minneapolis, I tried a Hail Mary to sell the remaining paintings. There was a premier art broker named Dolly Fiterman, who agreed to give them a serious consideration. She hemmed and hawed for a half hour, but rejected them on the basis they weren't her genre, which was obvious from looking at the contemporary works in her gallery. She declared them exquisitely done and expressed regret. I had to ship them back to Fabrik. B.A.S.E. died shortly thereafter and I never found out if Karl or Kurt prevailed in their court battle over nothing.

A copy of the Wall Street Journal that my dad kept, with a front page article about White Nights

White Nights claimed the title of the first U.S.-Soviet joint venture. Several others followed right on their heels, like the brilliantly named restaurant, TrenMos, whose founding partners lived in Trenton, New Jersey and Moscow, Russia. Pizza Huts started to pop up in late 1990, which actually made sense. The chain was owned by Pepsico, who had bartered Stolichnaya vodka in exchange for building Pepsi bottling plants in the USSR in the 1970s. American Armand Hammer of Occidental Petroleum had also been dabbling in Soviet business for decades. His activities were enigmatic. He built the international trade center complex in Moscow for no apparent benefit to himself. People speculated that he was a communist, CIA agent, or both. McDonald's entered the USSR as a Canadian entity.

At the start of operations White Nights was flying so many employees from Moscow to Nizhnevartovsk and back that the company chartered a dedicated Tupolev 134 plane. Employees flew in to Moscow from all over the U.S. and Canada and stayed at the Cosmos Hotel[1], from where a bus would take us directly to board the flight. There was a melange of skill sets, geologists, accountants, roughnecks, engineers, MBAs, translators, and logistics managers. Most of the veterans referred to non-management as "Oil field trash." Many on the White Nights team had extracted oil all over the world.

Some rig workers and I asked a waitress in the bar of the Cosmos Hotel what drinks they served. She proudly replied, "Everything: Beer, champagne, vodka, cognac, and wine." We asked specifically what kind of wine. She replied, "Both: Red and white." One of the rig workers had worked in Saudi Arabia and told us how the name for the Screwdriver cocktail came to be. Alcohol in Saudi Arabia is completely forbidden. American oil field workers smuggled vodka and mixed it with orange juice. There's no silverware on an oil rig, so they mixed it with a screwdriver.

The first-timers to the Soviet Union who thought the Cosmos was decrepit and drab were in for a schooling in Siberia. An Intourist bus delivered us to Moscow's Sheremetyevo II airport. The main Sheremetyevo (international) airport was built for the 1980 Olympics. It had a hideous interior. The feature everyone noticed was the ceiling. Five-inch deep copper colored rings about a foot in diameter were welded together and suspended from the roof. Its Feng Shui effect was unequaled. The departure hall at Sheremetyevo 2, which was for domestic flights, resembled an architect's rendering of the Starship Enterprise from the TV show Star Trek. The main difference was the airport building had more windows.

Changing a tire on White Nights' chartered plane in Syktyvkar

The crew that operated the White Nights flight was based in Syktyvkar, Komi Republic, where the plane had to stop for refueling and to switch crews. In Syktyvkar, they proudly provided free copies of the Komi newspaper, which was written in the local language. I doubt anyone knew the place existed, let alone that it had its own language, which is

---

1 One of Moscow's main Intourist Hotels. It was built for the 1980 Olympics. Its style was industrial and shaped like a concave semi-circle. It had a reputation with Soviet Muscovites as offering world-class luxury. Joe Dassin performed at the hotel's opening in 1979. Most Russians think of Joe Dassin, by the way, as French. He was a native New Yorker.

a variation of Finnish written in the Cyrillic alphabet. At GWU they taught us there were over one hundred languages in the USSR and over five hundred dialects that ranged from Asian, Arabic, Finnish, Farsi, French, Eskimo, Georgian, Turkish and Armenian, for starters.

It was obvious that the flight crew from Syktyvkar had struggled to create an announcement for us in English. Non-Soviet visitors to Komi during Soviet times would have been rare. After takeoff from Syktyvkar, I approached the crew to volunteer to rewrite their spiel for them. They barely spoke or read English. I suggested drafting an announcement for them, in English, but written in Cyrillic letters. Anyone who reads Cyrillic and tries to read English phonetically will struggle to not sound like a caricature of a Russian with a heavy accent. Ай рекоменд ю рид зис аут лауд энд хир уот ю саунд лайк.

With their new scripted announcement in Cyrillic, I suggested they rehearse a little, and then try it out on the passengers. I returned to the cabin and told everyone what I had done and that they should react positively to reinforce what a great job the announcer did. Figuratively and literally, everyone was on board. "Attention please. On behalf of our crew based in Syktyvkar we welcome on board rednecks and oil field trash. Our blue flight special's destination today is Nizhnevartovsk. To make your flight more enjoyable, please let us know if you're interested in joining the Syktyvkar mile high club. Thank you for listening." The passengers applauded and the crew was encouraged. They used the announcement many more times.

When we landed in Nizhnevartovsk, it was late August. The temperature was around 70F. I remember thinking that Siberia's frigid reputation was undeserved. The first snow fell on September 7. The temperature was tolerable on and off after that for a month or so, but the trend was nosedive.

Raduzhny (Rainbow City) was home to the American administration of the joint venture. It is located at sixty-two degrees North or about two hundred miles South of the Arctic Circle. In 1990 the population was about 30,000. When White Nights arrived and rolled out its equipment, the juxtaposition of socialism and capitalism was on full display.

Raduzhniy, aka "Rainbow City" in Western Siberia

Houston put up prefab offices with satellite dishes on the roof. Rows of brand new Ford F-150s were parked nearby. Many locals made houses out of and lived in segments of oil pipeline. Cows wandered unpaved roads of sand and mud. White Knights took every available hotel room for six months forward. French behemoth Sodexho[2] catered for most of the expat employees. The crew that served White Nights came from Portugal. There was one restaurant in town and one grocery store. What Sodexho served for breakfast on an average Tuesday included more exotic and fresher ingredients than most of the locals had seen in their lives.

Roughnecks and drillers lived in prefab houses on site at the rigs. Management offices were in prefab buildings too. They had water filtration systems. Entry-level personnel and Russians lived in local hotels or apartments, three or four in a room. As much crude oil flowed from the tap as did water. What streamed from the faucet looked like running maple syrup.

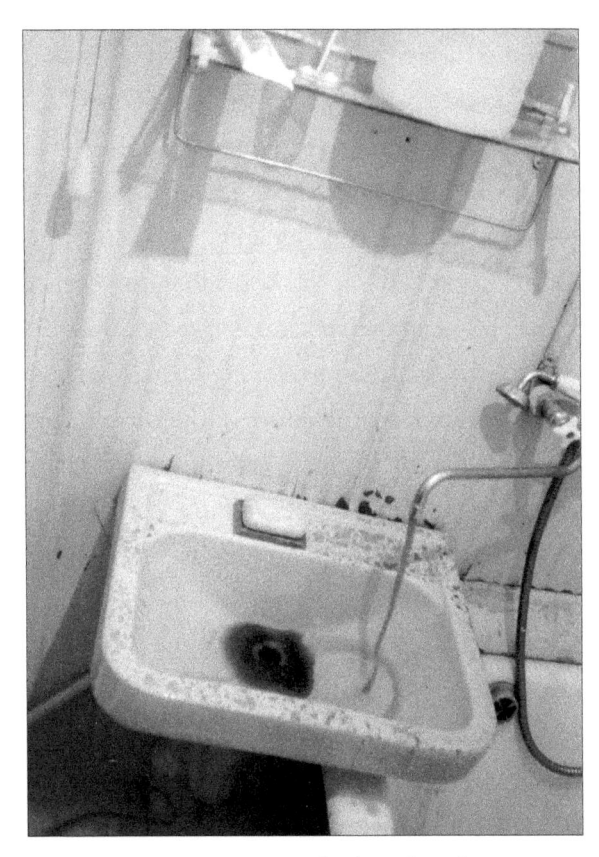

Cleaning schedule sign-off sheets in public toilets were as common as toilet paper.

Tap water in our Raduzhniy hotel. No. Boiling doesn't help, and it might light on fire.

Toilets were emetic, especially in warm weather. They were so universally foul, that we

---

2 An international food service company based in Paris, France that employs over 400,000 people.

developed a rating system called the IVR scale, for Involuntary Vomit Reaction. If the stench caused someone to throw up it was a 10. If you gagged and wretched, it was 7 - 9. Most were from 3 – 6. In an upscale restaurant in a big city like Nizhnevartosk a 2 might be encountered. A clean scentless public toilet was like Bigfoot. If anyone claimed to have seen one, it was fake.

The venture hired me without a job description. After a few days in Raduzhny, they sent me thirty miles or so west to a river port called Novoagansk, where White Nights operated a small warehouse. There were only two American employees there and neither spoke Russian. One was a lifelong oil man from Texas, Glen. I'd say he was close to seventy years old. Having lived and worked all over the world, he was unflappable. He was also expert at keeping track of inventory. The other expat was a meathead from Wyoming or Montana who loaded trucks. The venture used radios to communicate. Glen and his assistant didn't need translators to do their job. The truck drivers knew the locations of all the rigs.

Management sent me to Novoagansk, a town of about ten thousand people on the Agan River. My mission was to gain favor with the river port, which was at the end of the same street as the warehouse. The port was an independent entity, but their customers were few. The woman in charge of operations was Larisa. She had a full grill of steel teeth. I'd guess she was in her early forties. River navigation could freeze up at any time in Autumn and barges were lined up to be discharged. Larisa chose which cargoes got priority.

Her office was the cabin of the port's only crane. She had customized it with carpeting, throw pillows, a coil stove, posters and paperwork. She had two phones and a multi-channel radio. When I met her, I couldn't stop thinking about the first Russian textbook we had at GWU, "Russian for Everybody" (Русский язык для всех). There was a section in it about a female crane operator, Kranovshitsa. I skipped over it. When the language professor ripped on me for not knowing the word, I asked, "Who would ever need to know the word for female crane operator?" It turned out that I did and she worked in a Siberian village.

Most of what was needed to support drilling operations was delivered by rail to Nizhnevartovsk, about 120 miles from Novoagansk. The irony of the region is that although it sits on oil reserves like Saudi Arabia's, gasoline and diesel were scarce. The crude from the ground got pumped by pipeline to refineries thousands of miles away. Only a fraction of it returned to the area. Larisa's port emptied barges of diesel into large tanks from which it would be pumped into ten-ton tanker trucks (approximately 2,500 gallons). The tankers were then dispatched to drilling rigs, whose electric generators operated on diesel.

Permission to enter Larisa's crane office was a sign of enviable access. The town was abuzz about the arrival of Americans. She was happy to share tea in the crane with me. Hosting a foreigner boosted Larisa's prestige and importance when people found out about my visit. She agreed to send a few truckloads of diesel to our rigs right away, but indicated that more than a request would be expected to ramp up deliveries. Official payments for diesel deliveries were made by cashless contractual accounts. It made no difference to her where she dispatched the trucks. The company she worked for got paid, not her. For more diesel she wanted cash, imported goods, and sex. I told Glen about the sex. He knew her physique and steel mouth, but matter-of-factly commented, "If you are a team player, then get up in there."

Sensitive business should never be discussed electronically, so I drove to HQ in Raduzhny, where I requested grease money for Larisa, or at least access to Sodexho's food container to get her a few gifts. The reply was rigid and final, "No! We don't bribe." Some paper pusher recited the Foreign Corrupt Practices Act[3] to me. I thought that they were putting on a show because they thought the room was bugged, so I wrote the request on a piece of paper. The manager crumpled it up and handed me a written copy of the FCPA. I couldn't believe they were in Russia and expected to work bribe free. The FCPA exists because the U.S federal government believes that corrupting foreigners is their job. If private companies are allowed to do it openly, failures in life like John Kerry won't be able to direct kickbacks from foreign aid to friends and family. For the Washington corrupt, eliminating the FCPA would bankrupt a lot of bureaucrats.

The family that ran the hotel in Novoagansk

There was one store in Raduzhny and none in Novoagansk. Every once in a while truckloads of Haake Beck canned beer from Germany showed up. When it did, I bought several cases of beer, vodka, and cognac and returned with it to Novoagansk, where we lived in a tiny six-room two-story hotel not far from the river. It was nestled in an old birch forest and looked like a stereotypical Siberian scene. It was only a ten minute walk to the warehouse down an unpaved sandy road. The

---

3 The Foreign Corrupt Practices Act of 1977, as amended, 15 U.S.C. §§ 78dd-1, et seq. ("FCPA"), was enacted for the purpose of making it unlawful for certain classes of persons and entities to make payments to officials to assist in obtaining or retaining business. Specifically, the anti-bribery provisions of the FCPA prohibit the willful use of any means in furtherance of any offer, payment, promise to pay, or authorization of the payment of money or anything of value to any person, while knowing…

hotel was run by a mother - daughter team. They cooked, cleaned, washed clothes, and enjoyed learning about life in the USA.

In the little hotel there was a room permanently reserved for two men from Abkhazia[4]. They arrived every few weeks with loads of fruits and vegetables. The price in Novoagansk was quadruple what they could get at home. The locals were grateful to have fresh anything. The Abkhazians appreciated that the police didn't shake them down for a percent of their take, which they could have. Selling something higher than prices set by the state was called speculation and was a prisonable offense. Profit meant prison. They said that being able to operate freely compensated for the horrible weather. One's name was Nugzar from Sukhumi, which is on the East coast of the Black Sea.

Reindeer fur traders an hour north by boat from Novoagansk, Siberia

Two workers from the river port took me for a ride on the Agan in about a fourteen foot two-seat boat. One drove while the other sat on the covered bow, holding a shotgun. We headed North at about twenty miles an hour and passed around our first bottle of vodka. The guy on the bow saw an animal on shore and fired the shotgun at it. The recoil from the blast almost tipped the boat over. After about forty minutes, we arrived at an Eskimo village. There were less than twenty homes. They offered us reindeer everything. I hadn't expected to visit an Arctic reindeer market and had almost no cash. After choosing a pair of knee-high boots, I offered them cash rubles. The Russians waved me away and told me to pay them after we left. The locals didn't understand or use money. One of them told me, "I have a nephew in Leningrad, who understands paper. Here we want to be paid with something useful." Expecting I'd have the chance to return, I left behind a reindeer parka that fit me. A few weeks later the river froze. I never was able to return there.

Boating on a remote section of the Agan River, Western Siberia

---

4 A semi-tropical region on the Black Sea in Northern Georgia. It was one of the Southernmost territories of the Soviet Union.

A Russian tourist showed up in the Novoagansk hotel and tried to impress Glen's sidekick by opening a beer bottle with his eye socket. The American roughneck nodded his appreciation, poured the beer into a glass and took a bite out of the beer bottle's neck, grinding the glass with his teeth. The Russian's eyes were all the way wide, as were mine. After washing down the glass dust with the beer he'd just poured, the American opened his mouth and stuck out his tongue to show he was blood-free.

Larisa and I had become business friends (nothing more) but HQ sent me to interpret on the main rig. The rigs operated 24/7. A few hundred yards from them there were stand alone encampments of forty or fifty people. Shifts were twelve hours a day, every day. If someone wanted to go to town during free time, it meant sleep deprivation. The drilling superintendents were Dennis and Cambo. Both had worked all over the world. Dennis had been in Kuwait when Saddam Hussein's army invaded. He said he "Hid" from the Iraqis, who were trying to capture American hostages, by sipping cocktails and sunbathing on a rooftop deck of the tallest hotel. After U.S. troops liberated Kuwait, Dennis flew back to the U.S. The New York Times put a photo of him stepping off the plane on the front page.

Dennis and Cambo had requested a translator to train a crew of oil hands from Ivano-Frankovsk, Ukraine. The Ukrainians had worked on a Soviet rig, but it was a little different than what Parker Drilling used. On an American rig the drill operator stands behind glass with his support team. When a segment of pipe gets all the way down, the crew locks it in place with a collar to prevent the possibility of it falling down the hole. About the last two feet of each pipe segment is several inches wider so it can be clamped.

There are no muddy roads in the winter.

On rig platform 256, the American crew was quick to haze me as the new arrival. They asked if I was familiar with the "Bulldog Nelson" wrestling hold. They said it was similar to a full nelson. They claimed it was necessary to learn in case first-aid was needed. There could be an explosion, they explained, and the bulldog nelson was the best way to evacuate someone. To demonstrate, a 300-pound Oklahoman in brown overalls with a tin of Copenhagen in his bib told me to turn around and put my hands in the air. As soon as I did he locked me in a full nelson and pretended to hump my ass. The test was to see how hard the new guy fought and wriggled to get away.

The Ukrainians all spoke Russian. They tried and failed to trip me up with slang so they switched to teaching me x-rated military cadences from their days in the Soviet Army. There was a lot of idle time when drilling. I taught the American rig hands how to read Cyrillic and swear in Russian, and taught the Russians and Ukrainians similar things in English.

The Soviets considered the technology on American rigs antique because they used spinning chains to rotate the pipes. Soviet rigs were automated. Cambo explained why the chain method was preferable to automatic, but the Ukrainians refused to accept it. We visited a Russian rig. Neither Dennis nor Cambo were impressed.

After just a few days, my job on the rig was over. Before heading back to Novoagansk, Dennis gave me a White Nights superintendent's uniform, dark blue overalls with an American flag patch on the right shoulder and a Soviet on the left. The White Nights logo took up most of the back and showed a chess knight. It was a gift with strings. He wanted me to make his rig a diesel priority. He and Cambo had contracts that included incentives to, as they said, "Get deeper cheaper." Running out of diesel would be catastrophic to their upside. I told Dennis that I could get his reserve tanks full, but I didn't want to pay out of pocket. Also there was the shackling no bribes policy. He offered $100 per truckload, cash, as in off the books. A handshake united us. The promise of cash didn't motivate me, but demonstrating that I could run circles around the no-bribers did. For personal pride I also wanted to show Dennis that I wasn't a bullshitter. It was all a game.

The sudden appearance of a fleet of new Ford F-150s had caused a stir all across the region. Everywhere I stopped, a driver would approach and say, "I'm not trying to rob you. I just want to see the car." The automatic windows, decent sound system, and heated seats elicited the most admiration. I'd seen how Larisa dispatched fuel trucks and came up with a plan to make Dennis happy, and fast. When a tanker truck picked up a load, Larisa wrote the number of liters in a log for the accountant to invoice. She only gave the driver a rig number for delivery. No one at the receiving end took any paperwork or measured how much was offloaded. The transactions were cashless. The drivers told me they could just empty their tanker on the side of the road, if they wanted to, and no one would know.

About ten miles from the port, on the main road to all the rigs, I started parking my Ford on the side of the road, hoping a tanker truck would drive by. While waiting it was not uncommon to see a herd of hundreds of reindeer cross the road. When a loaded tanker truck neared, I'd get out and wave the driver to stop. They always did and were only too happy to think they'd get the chance to look under the hood and offer advice on how to fix a foreign car. Russian drivers have to be among the most resourceful on Earth. With a pocket knife, pack of gum, and piece of duct tape, they can fix most anything.

When a tanker driver stopped to investigate the feigned breakdown, I'd make up a story about why I thought my car was broken, but wasn't. Then the conversation would turn to: by the way, how'd you like a case of beer or bottle of vodka to be redirected to Dennis' rig where you could drop that load faster? I don't recall one driver that refused. Within a few days, Dennis was set for the winter. The first time I left on break, he honored his pledge. I used the money to buy more gifts. The guy who took me on the boat had just become a first-time father. I used some of Dennis' money to buy baby clothes from Neiman-Marcus for them. His wife couldn't believe such things existed. For me it was like using a Rolls-Royce to pick up a hitchhiker.

On one of the rotations out of Russia, several of us, including Cambo and Dennis, got stranded in Moscow's Sheremetyevo airport overnight. We couldn't exit because our visas had expired. We could only pick up new ones in the U.S. Bored, I decided to have "passengers" with fake names paged. There were no flights at three in the morning, but nonetheless I repeatedly went to the information desk and asked their help locating one of the idiot foreigners in our group who'd wandered off and got lost. After dropping a name on the airport staff, I'd hurry back to Cambo and Dennis, whom I'd tell, "Wait for it. . . "After a minute or so the airport wide bells would chime, indicating an announcement was about to be made. In English with a Russian accent, a woman's voice requested passenger Hugh Janus to return to the departure area, left side. Shortly thereafter, Mike Hunt, Ben Dover and Phil MacCracken also all went astray.

Nizhnevartovsk, one of the most oil-rich regions on Earth. On the banks of the Ob River, Western Siberia

The next assignment was dispatching trucks from a rail cargo station in the much bigger city of Nizhnevartovsk, about 90 miles South of Raduzhniy. There was a Beriozka-like store in town that accepted rubles. The prices were too high for most locals. With a railway station and a port on the massive Ob river (7th longest in the world) the city was better supplied than anywhere else in the region.

The railyard office was all-female, except for the general manager, Gennady Mikhailovich. He was rarely there. It seemed he spent every day going back and forth to Raduzhniy. He drove it so often that he knew every curve and pothole. I never figured out what needed to be transported in his small Lada that couldn't fit in one of his fleet of trucks. I suspected a mistress and that he had many other conversations that weren't suitable for the telephone. The only time Gennady Mikhailovich was certain to show up in the office was Friday afternoon, when drinks were being poured.

For whomever worked the rail head, White Nights kept a furnished apartment in downtown Nizhnevartovsk. I preferred it to the hotel. It had hot water that wasn't brown most of the time. I thought it was one of the best posts. I didn't tell anyone, but there was a festering boil in my armpit that had been getting bigger for days and it suddenly expanded to the size of a tangerine. It was very painful. White Nights employed a medic in Raduzhny, but I didn't want to drive for two hours and I also didn't want to see a local doctor. I figured that if I soaked it in hot water, it would explode by itself. I sat in a tub full of hot water, swigging vodka and hoping the thing would burst. Instead, it got much bigger and started throbbing even more. I chugged more vodka to numb the pain, but couldn't tolerate it. To relieve the pressure I jabbed it with a sewing needle. The pulsating mass exploded into the tub water. The relief was instantaneous. Strands of white, red, green, brown and black of who knows what were suspended in the water. It looked like a science project. I dried the hole and plastered Neosporin on it.

In Raduzhny, I mentioned the armpit and thought it would be one of the more bizarre health stories. Word got around fast that one of the rig operators arrived at the medic's office cupping his package with a bloody crotch. He was afraid to show the wound, which he got during heterosexual sex. The woman was on top and pulled off. When she dropped back down, her coccyx bone hit him perfectly on the tip, causing the base of his penis to rupture and spray blood all over the room. Another driller later reported hearing the man scream, "She broke my dick." Cambo said he feigned compassion and asked, "Can I look at it?"

An average one-way car trip from Nizhnevartovsk to Raduzhniy took me about two and half hours. The road to Novoagansk was flat, pothole free and straight. The road from Nizhnevartovsk was full of surprises: black ice, potholes, hills, and curves. On New Year's Eve I had forgotten to fill up my truck. There was a big party in Raduzhny, but not wanting to risk running out of fuel in –40 weather, and with no one on the roads, I decided to stay put. By 6 p.m. Gennady and I had been drinking for hours. All of a sudden he insisted that he'll drive me to the New Year's party. I did not want to be a passenger in rural Siberia in a Lada with a drunk driver.

There was no way to convince him to let me stay. I expected us to become spring flowers[5] (**подснежник**). His Lada, which is a light and flimsy car, had a 70hp engine. The USSR tried selling Ladas in Western Europe. When crash tests were performed it scored 0 out of 16. On the road to Raduzhny he never slowed down. The roads were covered with compacted snow and ice. On sharp turns, his car drifted into the oncoming lane of traffic. The speed remained steady. I reminded him that he was drunk. He told me not to worry

---

5 Literally translated, it is a thing under the snow. Generally, the term refers to the Snowdrop flower. Cynically, in Siberian vernacular, it refers to someone who froze to death while walking home drunk and whose body was only discovered after the thaw.

because he knew every cop. He got us there safely and fast. After two drinks, he left for Nizhnevartovsk.

About the only thing I remember from their New Year's party was that the yee-haw style of music grated on my ears. I approached the one black man at the party, hoping to commiserate about the painful sounds. Suggesting that he couldn't possibly like that shit, he shook his head no and with a slight Texan accent said, "Come on, man. There ain't nothing wrong with a little two-step."

On the next rotation in, our plane from Syktykar landed around 5 a.m. in Nizhnevartovsk. It was the end of January and the temperature was around fifty below Celsius. Everyone had slept during the flight. We got off the plane, expecting to board a warm bus. There were no cars and no people. Usually when it's that cold, there is no wind. A slight breeze made the temperature unbearable. The group started to walk quickly towards the airport building. The airline crew was yelling instructions for us to stay in place, falsely claiming that a bus was about to arrive. We could see there was no bus. Everyone was desperate to get out of the cold. All the airport doors were locked. The cold really bit. Shivering turned into convulsions. One of the Texans noticed a bus gate with no barbed wire and climbed over it. He saw our bus waiting nearby on the other side and summoned everyone to follow. We abandoned our luggage and jumped the gate. It looked like a prison break. We later found out that the airport staff had passed out drunk.

During that stint, I worked at the main transportation base just outside Raduzhniy. We lived in a Soviet hotel that had the worst living conditions in the company. It was 100% occupied by White Nights. There were no thermostats. To ensure it never got too cold it was often unbearably hot, like ninety degrees Fahrenheit. Our diesel Fords could never be turned off or they couldn't be restarted. The small fleet of running engines provided a constant industrial din for sleep ambience. Sunlight was almost non-existent. Daylight hours lasted about three hours from 11 a.m. until 2 p.m.

Knowing that I was about to jump in a warm car that had been running all night, I didn't put on a hat or zip up my jacket. As I walked to the car, I started shivering from the more than minus fifty degree temperature. Across the street there was a small single family home. In front of it there was a skinny man crouched down wearing only a speedo. He was patting himself with snow. My eyes locked on what he was doing. He noticed my amazement and started slowly sticking more snow on his body. I couldn't handle the cold, dressed. At the transportation base, I told the locals what I had seen, as if it was unusual. They were surprised that I didn't know that snow baths warm you up.

A Texan named Stiopa had been working at the transportation base since the beginning. He was a fellow graduate of the Russian program at GWU. He constantly injected humor into the mundane. At the only restaurant in Raduzhny one evening, we happened to meet a drunken listener from the KGB office that worked in the office that monitored our radio transmissions. They had a staff of dedicated English speakers verifying that when we talked about dispatching drill bits and sections of pipe, that was what we were really doing. I didn't think anything of it and wasn't surprised.

The next day Stiopa's voice came over the radio, requesting confirmation that I was receiving. As soon as I told him to go ahead, he started speaking in the voice of Marvin the Martian from the Bugs Bunny cartoon and recited some of his best known lines like, "Listen to me human. I intend to eliminate you with my ilonium Q-34 space modulator. Over."

My response was, "Come again, Stiopa. I didn't copy."

He replied, "Where is the kaboom? There was supposed to be an earth shattering kaboom."

We suspected that the KGB "Experts" spent a long time trying to decipher his message.

Several containers of office furniture and copy machines arrived in Nizhnevartovsk for White Nights. Gennady demanded that I come see him asap. It wasn't a telephone conversation. He was waiting for me with his buddy, who was the head of local customs. The two had calculated that the official duty on the content of the containers was $1,800,000. They wanted to offer White Nights a deal. In exchange for a copy machine with a declared value of a little over $100,000, Gennady's friend would erase their bill altogether. I knew it was more than a longshot, but I wanted to keep Gennady on my good side. I promised to try.

The director of White Nights in Siberia was Glenn Miller. He was uniformly deemed affable. Everyone considered him a good egg. I requested a private conversation and joked that it wasn't about a broken dick. To prepare for the meeting, I wrote the details of Gennady's proposal. That way I wouldn't need to vocalize the offer and the likely bugs in Mr. Miller's office couldn't pick up the conversation. He had a reputation as a straight shooter. His reaction to the customs tax reduction didn't disappoint. He read it carefully and started shaking his head yes. I thought there might be a chance. Then he tapped the paper with his index finger and shook his head no. He declared, "This here," he paused while still tapping his finger, "is a fucked-up deal. Ain't taking it. It's a fucked-up deal. Yes indeed. This is a fucked-up deal." That was that. Final decision. No appeal.

An American auditor from Arthur Anderson stayed in my room at the hotel for a week or so. He was from Indianapolis and didn't speak Russian. He could not believe how chaotic Siberian life was. I told him about the offer to avoid import taxes. He admitted that part of his job was trying to detect irregularities and report them. Houston was mad at him because he rejected as a business expense one of the director's payments for his sports car.

Gennady was speechless when I told him his offer was rejected. He thought I'd failed to properly convey it. He reminded me that his friend was the highest ranking official so there was no possibility of criminal recourse. He asked, "What's wrong with Americans?"

White Nights went bankrupt two or three years after it was launched. The parent company, Phibro, made an announcement that the bankruptcy was due to the fact that the Russian government imposed higher tariffs than had been agreed to. Numerous economists, lawyers, and accountants have demonstrated that full compliance with the Russian tax code can lead to an obligation to pay up to 140% of a company's income. The severity of Russian laws cannot be mitigated if you obey them.

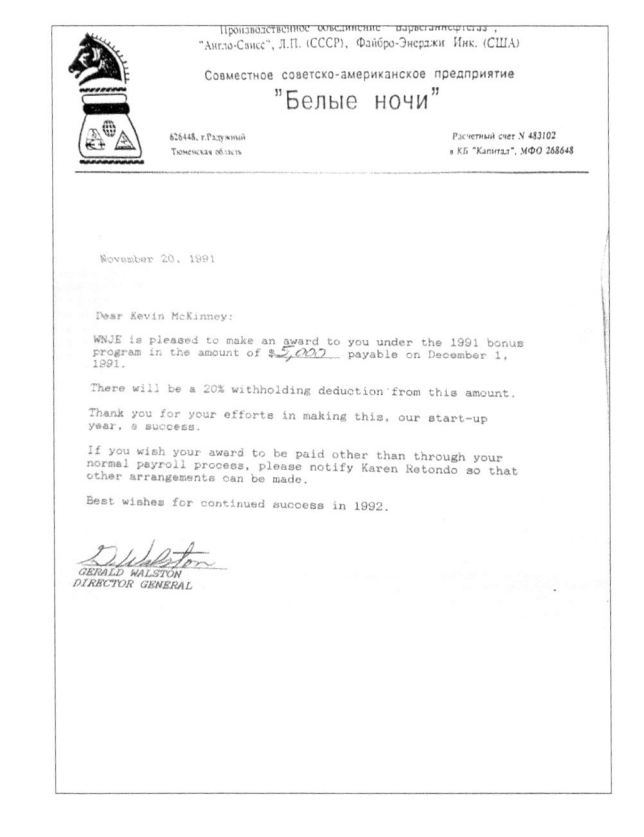

Marc Rich + CO AG

Katia K

Stunned by the White Nights experience, I sat in my Minneapolis townhouse, wondering what to do next. London-based headhunter, Scott Eversman, called to ask if I would be interested in an interview with Marc Rich + Co in Zug, Switzerland. The man's accent was unmistakably American. I suspected it was Toolshed, drunk, and that he'd changed his voice to prank me. "Fuck off, Toolshed. You're not funny," I said.

The man on the line asked, "Do you know Jim? (Shed's real name)" It turned out that the two had served in the U.S. Air Force together and that Shed had recommended me to his firm. The connection with Shed was cause for doubt. I told him, "If you're serious, send me a ticket. I'll go wherever." The next morning a courier brought me a business class ticket to Zurich. I had never heard of Marc Rich and neither had any of the friends I asked.

A driver met me at the Zurich airport and delivered me to the headquarters of Marc Rich + Co. Daniel, the son of one of the founding partners, took me to lunch for a casual interview. He asked questions about specific things I'd done at White Nights that I thought only I knew, like "Did you really use your own money to make things work?" or "How'd you get in with the crane operator? You got a lot of diesel." I was baffled. I asked him how he knew these things. He said they operated a joint venture there as well called

TMR, whose partners were France's major oil company, Total, Marc Rich + Co, and a Soviet entity. Daniel's job offer was succinct, "We know what you do and want you to do it for us." When I mentioned that it had been frustrating to watch White Knights needlessly shackle themselves, he replied, "I can assure you that we are not that kind of company." On a handshake, he hired me. With no contract, I accepted. When I told him I already had a visa, he said, "See you in Moscow."

I had no idea who'd hired me. There were multiple billionaires in the firm, but I didn't know that. The motivator for me was being able to play the Soviet game. Making things work gave me more pleasure than money. It didn't matter what the job was. I looked forward to fixing problems for Marc Rich. There is no equivalent of the Foreign Corrupt Practices Act in Switzerland.

In the Moscow office of Marc Rich + Co no one knew who I was or that I'd been hired. I'd found my way there on my own. It seemed like I'd been duped and had flown to Russia for no reason. Daniel finally got free. I basically asked him "What the fuck?!" He reacted positively to my angry tone, saying that he liked to test the resolve of new hires by messing with them in various ways. He ordered his assistant to find me a desk and book a room at the Penta hotel, which was $350/night.

The offices were on several floors of the International Trade Center, Russia's premier business address that was funded by American Armand Hammer. The company kept phone lines open with offices worldwide. Long distance calls then cost something like $5/minute. If someone wanted to talk to Rotterdam, for example, an operator would tell the other end to pick up and connect the call. It seemed like an unnecessary expense to me, but making phone calls was very challenging. It could take up to an hour to secure a dial tone. To dial long distance you had to first press 8 and wait for a second dial tone. About 90% of the time you'd hear a busy signal after pressing 8. Even when a successful 8 got you a second dial tone, 90% of the calls didn't go through. Leaving the phones connected was a necessity. Not being able to speak to a decision maker for hours could result in lost profits of enormous amounts of money.

On my desk I put a tin of Copenhagen (a brand of chewing tobacco). Almost instantly the tallest man in the office was standing over it. As he greedily reached for it, he realized that he didn't even know who I was and hadn't asked if he could have some. He said, "Obviously you're American. May I have some?" As he stuffed a large pinch into his upper lip, I watched a Russian co-worker gawk at him, because from her angle it must have looked like he was vigorously picking his nose. He introduced himself and said he was from Denver, Colorado. He and I had the only full-time American passports in the Moscow office. The place was the antithesis of politically correct. With the combination of Colorado and being Jewish, he became known as Mountain Hebe. The Mountain was also applicable to his build. He was two meters tall, or six foot seven. My name was either Prairie Mick or Makhuini, which is something like McDick in Russian.

Daniel called me to the office to say. "I need you to go to Switzerland real quick. Tell Lada (his assistant) to book you a ticket asap." I asked if I should check out of the Penta hotel, to save money. The question stunned him. He didn't think that small. He told me to do whatever I thought best and said, "Go to Zug."

A driver took me to the airport in Moscow and I returned to Zug. While I waited for over an hour to meet the person that seemed to not expect me, I wondered if Marc Rich was a wise career decision. Daniel's partner took me into his office and asked how I liked working for them in Moscow. I hadn't started. He handed me a manila envelope with over one hundred thousand dollars cash in it and said, "Throw that in the Moscow safe, OK? See you later." A little stunned, I got up to leave. Just as I was about to walk out, he added, "Make sure you don't declare that going through customs."

On the flight to Moscow, I wondered what would happen if I just walked away. They'd given me more than a year's salary in cash. I figured a company that can risk a hundred or so thousand with a new employee can also afford to pay to have it retrieved, and also

thieves are despicable. I walked through the green channel at Sheremetyevo airport and delivered every note. After putting the cash in the safe, Daniel told Ira, an office manager, to find me an apartment and get me a company American Express card. I still didn't know what my job was.

The first person to give me a task was ZNB. He was a Yugoslavian graduate of Cambridge University in England. During our first meeting, ZNB described metals smelters, railways, ports, and ships to me in condescending terms. His oversimplified presentation, which I appreciated, reminded me of Nigel Tufnel from the movie, Spinal Tap, asking for large bread. I asked ZNB if he'd ever watched it. Not only was he familiar with the movie, he was fluent in all its nuances. He could cite from memory just about any quote. The lingo of Spinal Tap dominated our communications for years.

```
MARC RICH+CO AG

            KEVIN McKINNEY
                 Manager
            Transport Department

                          Tel.:    253 21 00(52)/ 945 4508
                                   253 25 88(94)/ 940 2633
International Trade Centre   Fax:  253 2095/ 96 /97
Office Building, Office № 1604   Telex: 413988 RICH SU
Krasnopresnenskaya nab., 12            413793 RICH SU
123610 Moscow                Teletype: 611230 MARCRI
```

The Fugitive

When I learned details of the background story about why Marc Rich fled the United States to Switzerland and took his company with him, I regretted not knowing it before I was hired. It would have made me more eager to work for him. Marc Rich's biography is titled, "The King of Oil." His "legal" problems began when Jimmy Carter was pretending he had the skills to be president. A popular phrase in Russia is that the only thing worse than an idiot is an idiot with initiative. Jimmy Carter sadly remained busy throughout his folly of a presidency. As Albert Einstein observed, "Great spirits have always encountered violent opposition from mediocre minds." Mediocre is probably too kind for Jimmy.

When Carter took office in 1976, the price of crude oil was $13/barrel. By the end of Carter's four-year term, it was $37/barrel. The House and Senate would not support Carter's calls for socialist tinkering in the oil market. Cogent humans knew with certainty that his policies would decimate the economy. To circumvent Congress, Jimmy Carter took the initiative to issue an executive order that restricted the trade of crude oil and products. As Milton Friedman pointed out, "One of the biggest mistakes is to judge a policy by its intention rather than its result." On cue, Carter's executive order led to predictable and preventable energy shortages, tripling the price of crude and everything else.

For political theater, Carter installed 32 solar panels on the roof of the White House in 1979. To the ignorant, his base, it looked great. In reality the electricity generated by his budget busting gimmick was sufficient only to heat the water used in the White House's dishwasher.

While Carter was implementing bad ideas daily, Rudy Giuliani was masquerading as a principled conservative. He worked for the U.S. Attorney's Office, which filed a complaint[1] against Marc Rich + Co. The majority basis of Giuliani's complaint referenced no laws, but violations of Jimmy Carter's executive orders. When Reagan was inaugurated, the first thing to happen was the release of American hostages that were held by Iran and whom Carter had failed to free. The first executive order that president Reagan signed was No. 12287 "Decontrol of crude oil and refined petroleum products." It nullified Carter's disastrous overreach. Supporters of

---

1 http://www.thesmokinggun.com/file/pardon-me-marc-rich-indictment

liberty and conservatives celebrated the fact that Reagan wasn't just a talker. It took a few years, but the price of crude fell back to $14/barrel under Reagan.

Rudy Giuliani had political ambitions. He worked in the notoriously tyrannical U.S. Attorney's Office in the Southern District of New York, which pursued criminal charges against Marc Rich for violating Jimmy Carter's executive orders that were arguably criminal and unconstitutional themselves. People will say anything, but what they do is always the truth. If Rudy was a Republican, he would have dropped the case against Marc Rich + Co. on Reagan's first day in office. Instead, he used Carter's socialist piece of paper to monetarily shake down one of America's most successful trading companies, Marc Rich + Co. for a very long time. The Carter - Giuliani alliance asked the court to impose a fine on Marc Rich of fifty thousand dollars per day until he provided potentially incriminating evidence against himself, evidence which Giuliani's team failed to find with search warrants and likely did not exist. The U.S. Attorney's Office probably relied on a disgruntled former employee as their credible informant.

Decent Americans had no beef with Marc Rich + Co. The company did fun things like create the Jamaican bobsled team. Jamaica's #1 export was bauxite, aka aluminum ore. Marc Rich + Co AG signed a ten-year deal to buy all of it. As a show of Swiss - Jamaican cooperation the aluminum department came up with the idea to fund and train a Jamaican bobsled team. The bauxite deal innocuously expanded the world's supply of beer can material and automobiles. Reality would be bad optics for people like Giuliani. Articles in the sensationalist mainstream media hinted that Marc Rich + Co was engaged in all kinds of nefarious activities. The truth doesn't sell papers. In 1993 a movie was released about the Jamaican bobsledders called "Cool Runnings." I never watched it, but I wonder if it revealed the Marc Rich connection. My friend Anton made the first translation of the movie, calling it "Крутые Виражи."

After over a year of $50,000 per day fines, the King of Oil left New York and relocated to a freer jurisdiction, Zug, Switzerland. Rudy the RINO (Republican In Name Only) and the U.S Attorney's office had chased out of town what was arguably the world's largest commodity trading company and with it at least a thousand high-paying jobs. No politician could admit that they were the architect of a fiasco like that and expect to survive. Ergo Rudy spent almost the next two decades deflecting from his lack of scruples, and continued to allege Marc Rich + Co was involved in all kinds of things that weren't true. For the U.S. Attorneys Office, I'd use a line from Frank Capra's movie, "Meet John Doe," which is (you're) "Like dogs. If you can't eat something, you bury it."

Soviet Space Team

In Moscow at the Penta Hotel, I remembered my pledge to call Anton after I started watching a classic comedy movie from 1966 called "The Caucasian Captive" on TV. The movie was captivating and one of the funniest things I'd ever seen. I called Anton from ETM to tell him I was in town and asked him if he'd seen the movie. He diplomatically compared my question about the movie to asking an Englishman if he'd ever heard any songs by The Beatles. He said, "You can watch that any time. I've got a much more cultural outing planned for you. Be ready in an hour."

Officially, the USSR and its laws still existed, even though the looming collapse seemed a foregone conclusion. Anton's driver drove us beyond the outer ring road around Moscow and we kept going for another thirty minutes. We turned onto a tree-canopied road that indicated the area was important militarily. During WWII and since, Soviets planted trees that grew tall enough and whose branches grew wide enough to hide from aerial view whatever convoys or traffic might be on the road underneath. Anton refused to tell me where we were going. We pulled up to tall dark green gates, emblazoned with the ubiquitous red star with a hammer and sickle. As he got out of the car to enter the adjacent guard house, telling me "Stay here. Don't say anything to anybody." He returned with permission to open the gate, but warned me again, "Don't say anything."

Star City, Russia. Apartment building where most cosmonauts lived

Once we were past the gate, he welcomed me to Star City. The name meant nothing to me. It is home to the Russian space program. Anton introduced me to the Popovich family. Marina Popovich was the first Soviet woman to break the sound barrier. She set 102 aviation world records. Her husband Pavel had been a contender to make the historic first flight into space, which Yuri Gagarin took. Pavel Popovich took the fourth. Their daughter Oksana was Anton's friend. A guy named Smolo showed up. He was one of the computer programmers for the Mir space station.

We downed shots of vodka. Unbeknownst to me, Marina replaced the regular vodka in my glass with Ukrainian moonshine (Samogon). It was eighty-five percent alcohol. She waited with a camera for my reaction to downing the shot. Right after I drank it, my eyes got as wide as silver dollars. My stomach burned. I had a grimace on my face when she snapped the picture. She was proud of having caused a smuggled American to wobble with moonshine. She stuck the photo on her kitchen wall as a sort of trophy. Oksana, Anton, and Smolo returned me to the Penta.

Son J.P. in the control module of the MIR Space Station

Cosmonaut Pavel R. Popovich. One of the world's all-time great toastmasters.

The centrifuge in Star City's cosmonaut training center. For years Smola repeatedly and unsuccessfully tried to get me to climb in.

Marina Popovich

Russian Far East

My first assignment for Marc Rich was to secure a port agreement in Nakhodka, Russia's Far East. The port is seven time zones forward from Moscow on the coast of the Sea of Japan. The first leg of the trip is a nine-hour flight to Vladivostok, followed by a two to three hour drive through very hilly, heavily potholed, and often washed out roads. Nakhodka is farther East than any part of China. Its name is a misnomer. It means "find" in Russian, as one might declare after locating treasure, "What a find!" The city is no find, but the natural beauty of the area is.

Until 1992, the entire region was closed to anyone who didn't have special permission. It had been closed since 1952. The only time an American officially visited was in 1974 when president Ford arrived for a summit with Soviet premier, Leonid Brezhnev, aka the "Unibrow," or "One-browed wonder." None of my co-workers could tell me what to expect there, because no one had ever been there.

The first thing I noticed after landing at the Vladivostok airport were papier-mâché fighter jets parked between mounds of dirt. They were designed to fool reconnaissance photography. I imagined that the U.S. intel community would declare the paper planes either real or fake, depending on who ordered the report. En route to Nakhodka, we drove through Shkotovo-17, which made me curious. Every city in the USSR with a number after it signified some kind of secret defense activity. This was no different. It was a home base for the Russian Pacific fleet, which included nuclear submarines.

The time difference was brutal. The work day there started at 2:30 a.m. Moscow time. I found the port administration building and sought the deputy director. Directors never conduct business. I managed to get an audience with the deputy fairly quickly, but he sent me to the commercial director. I sat in his reception area for about four hours. He walked past me as he left for the day and said "Come back tomorrow."

The next day I sat in the reception area again for over two hours. He popped his head out and said, "I have a window of a few minutes. Make it fast." I told him we were just starting our operations in the Far East and that we needed a port agreement to load bulk metals for delivery to Japan and S. Korea. He told me the rate was eighteen dollars per ton. I protested. The deputy director had told me the rate was $7 or $8. The commercial director would not budge. I went back to the deputy director, who said his hands were tied and that I had to deal with the commercial director. Annoyed, I jumped on a plane back to Moscow.

When I arrived at the office, ZNB asked what rate I had secured. I told him, "None," adding "The commercial director was a dickhead, so I left." ZNB nodded as if he understood, replying, "That's too bad. You're going to return there today to get that port agreement. The cargo's already on its way." Fuck!

The seven hour time difference, nine hour flight, and three hour car ride are more physically draining when you do them two days in a row. Like a schmuck, I sat waiting in the commercial director's reception room at Nakhodka Port. A big burly bearded beer-belly type walked by the receptionist and entered his office without knocking. He was inside for less than five minutes. When he emerged, he handed me his business card, asking, "What are you doing waiting around for this dickhead? We run the port. Come see me in an hour."

The office was a ten minute drive from the port administration. They had name plates on the door for several companies. The main one was Magdia, taken from Magnitogorsk Steel Works and Dialogue, which they chose because it's the same in English and Russian. Another entity was called Prok. That name came from the boss, nicknamed Noisy. He knew two things in English, P.R. (public relations) and OK. That's why he named his company Prok. Magnitogorsk is a huge factory that by Russian standards is relatively close to Moscow, like a two hour flight. It produces over ten million tons of steel per year. With that kind of throughput, it seemed that was their source of influence at the port. All of them had business cards from at least three different companies.

Magdia invited me to lunch in what wasn't a restaurant, but more like a clubhouse. In the middle of the room there was a large round table for sixteen people. Two or three 4-tops were off to the side. Noisy, the main man, ordered a bottle of vodka for the two of us. It was a foil top bottle, as in not resealable. Most vodka brands in Soviet times didn't have screw tops, because who wouldn't finish a bottle of vodka in one sitting? It wasn't until Pepsi did the Stolichnaya deal that they considered producing screwtops. Even then, domestic Stoli was made with one-time foil caps.

Noisy asked me where I was staying. I told him, "The Nakhodka," which was an Intourist hotel. He told me to get out of that dump and stay in his boutique hotel that had air conditioning, a stocked bar, and a 24 hour cook. I suspected his group might be interested in more than port fees, but I didn't know what. After a bottle of vodka, we returned to their office. They had the port's letterhead and a template contract. They put in our company details, printed it and then Noisy took me to the commercial director's office to have him sign and stamp the rate of six or seven dollars per ton. The commercial director was wide-eyed and looked scared when I walked in with Noisy. I sent a telex to Moscow "Mission accomplished" and spent another sixteen hours in transit.

Pissed on In Public

During the early days of Marc Rich + Co Moscow there were three decent foreign or joint-venture restaurants. The Spanish Bar in the Hotel Moscow[1] was the best. It was just off of Red Square and had views of the Kremlin. A department head from Swiss HQ was visiting. I'll call him "the Californian." He invited about a dozen people from the office for drinks as a get to know everyone kind of session. We took the private room on the second floor and were seated around a large round table. They served San Miguel beer for an exorbitant price. The bill was going to be substantial. The Californian and I were the only two capable of paying it. I wasn't sure if it would be expensable. I asked him if we were going to split it. He suggested we make a bet, which was whoever goes to the bathroom first, pays. To make it a level start, he said we should both empty our bladders and then drink an equal amount of beer. I agreed.

We were similarly sized. Intense pressure had me squirming in my seat. I was certain the bet was lost. Another two or three minutes was all I could hope for when I felt a splatter under the table. I looked across the table at him, gesturing the question, "Are you really pissing under the table in front of a dozen people?" Unfazed, he repeated the bet, "I said the first one who **goes**." I picked up the check.

Someone from the Swiss office shrugged that off that story as amateur for him. The famously strict Swiss police had stopped the Californian for drunk driving. While performing the sobriety test, asking him to walk a straight line, he walked directly to the officer's open car door, whipped it out and pissed on the seat. I retold both stories to a mutual friend and general manager of a famous upscale Moscow brothel called Night Flight. His reaction was, "That's nothing. He's pissed right here on my bar many times, when the restaurant was full of people."

---

[1] The Hotel Moscow was famously depicted on the label of Stolichnaya Vodka. It has since been demolished and replaced with a Four Seasons. The Stolichnaya label showed only one half of the building's facade. The legend goes that when the architect presented to sketch to Stalin, he agreed to it all, but put an 'X' over an archway on one of the top floors. The architect was so afraid to anger Stalin that he built an archway on one side and a colonnade on the other.

Portrait of Lenin

A driver from Marc Rich showed up at my apartment the day I was scheduled to leave for Juanjo's (GWU) and Anita's wedding in Chinchon, Spain, a small town a little South of Madrid. The driver had a one-way ticket to Riga, Latvia. There were instructions and an envelope for an official in the port of Ventspils, which is on the Baltic Sea. I'd been to Latvia a few times. Riga impressed me because it was the first former Soviet city to have a full-service car rental agency. A representative would greet you with the keys and escort you to a new European car. You could walk across Russia from Kamchatka to Kaliningrad and not find a rental car agency.

The bag I checked in Moscow was almost overweight. It was full of bottles for the port and a wedding gift. When I lifted it off the claim belt in Riga, I almost threw it over my shoulder. The consolation was that I hadn't put the envelope in the suitcase.

Right before leaving the port director's office, I noticed a portrait of Vladimir Lenin still hanging on the wall behind him. It caused me to momentarily commit time travel, feeling like I was in the Leningrad ZAGS. I told the director that Latvia was independent already. He could feel free to throw Lenin in the trash. It was as if he'd forgotten it was there. He took it off the wall, handed it to me, saying "Get rid of this cocksucker." I didn't know what to do with it. I asked if maybe I could retrieve it on my next visit. "No!" was the reply. "Throw him in the Sea. Wipe your ass with this face. Just get him out of here." It was an "original" framed oil on canvas. I set it on the back seat and drove to Riga. It couldn't be sold. Anyone with money or a brain hated Lenin. It might have some future historical value, so I decided to give it as a wedding gift.

It was faster to fly through Moscow. There was a Lufthansa flight to Madrid that day through Frankfurt. It would be a close call, but I bought the ticket anyway. In the 1990s there were two Moscow Sheremetyevo airports. One was for domestic flights. Two was international. Riga had only recently split from the USSR, so the flight from there still landed at Sheremetyevo One, which was a minimum of a ten minute drive to Two. Airport Two handled more passengers than it was designed for. It was built for the 1980 Olympics when there were few private cars. After socialism died, there was an explosion of private cars. Traffic was a new phenomenon. Outside the airport it was chaotic.

A company driver took my empty suitcase. The security checkpoint at SVO Two was as orderly as a deli counter in a Soviet supermarket when something good went on sale, and for a few years it was like that all the time. The only thing I had for baggage was the Lenin painting, but I offered a luggage handler twenty bucks to get me to the front of the line. He put Lenin on his metal cart and told me to follow him so close behind it would be like he was walking on my feet. He plowed through the crowd like a babushka. He caused some bruised calves and ankles. He put my single item on the X-ray scanner belt, took the twenty and disappeared into the crowd. I picked up Lenin and headed to the check in counter.

Juanjo's Lenin

The baggage handler had tossed aside some players from a Croatian soccer team, whose flight to Zagreb was right after the Frankfurt flight. Eastern Europeans know when someone tried to make them smell the glove. They knew I'd jumped the line, which potentially could have made them late and they were not happy about it. The Lenin portrait probably pissed them off even more. Marc Rich Moscow employed several Yugoslavians. I recognized many of the curse words the Croatians used to describe the way I passed them by. I got my boarding pass and got in the long line for passport control.

The passport lines were orderly, actual lines instead of crowding. The Croatians showed up and one by one cut in front of me, pushing me farther towards the back of the line. It looked like they were going to turn the tables and make me smell the glove, by making me late for my flight. I thought I was doomed and would miss the wedding, when a Lufthansa agent appeared behind one of the passport booths waving a sign, announcing "Lufthansa passengers. No waiting! Immediate service for those with Lufthansa boarding passes." I held up my boarding pass for the agent to see, and strutted past the miffed Croatians. Their angry faces were satisfying, but I didn't want to risk a false step. I held my tongue and waited until the passport checker turned on the green light that it was OK to pass through to the boarding area.

Yugoslavians were at war for most of the 1990s. The Serbs, Croatians, Macedonians and Bosnians that I worked with had taught me which buttons to press in order to make the other irate. The green light went on. Passing through the gate to the departures hall, I turned to the Croatians and flashed a

Belgrade salute, index and middle fingers out with an extended thumb, shouting "**Живела Србија!**" (Long live Serbia!) They'd seen my American passport and Lenin portrait. When they got slapped with Serbian on top of all that, they looked dejected and confused.

In most major cities people tend to avoid showing surprise at things that are out of the ordinary. Walking through Frankfurt airport, dressed in a suit and tie, carrying a framed portrait of Lenin elicited more gawking and rubbernecks than I would have expected. When I presented the "gift" to Juanjo and his bride with no explanation, they were stunned speechless and I left it that way.

Farther East

Clean airports with well-stocked bars and cafes had been a welcome respite. Immediately after Madrid, it was back to the Russian Far East. It was getting old fast, but more departments started doing business there. Coal, copper, lead, aluminum, zinc, iron and oil products were moving through several different ports constantly. There were also two oil refineries a couple hours north, Khabarovsk and Komsomolsk. Half my time or more was spent in the Far East.

The flight from Moscow to Vladivostok departed from Domodedovo, the worst of Moscow's four major airports. Passengers often got stranded there and couldn't bathe for days. Besides aromatic Caucasians, roaming bands of gypsies pickpocketed certain passengers unhindered, so long as they shared their spoils with the police. There were no sit down cafes or bars. Those with food and drink turned the departure hall into a makeshift picnic area. Domodedovo hadn't yet abandoned the Soviet tradition of shielding foreigners from reality. It had a separate departure hall for foreigners, located a couple hundred yards from the main terminal. Foreign passengers showed their passport to a guard at the top of a stairway that led to a bus stop below on the tarmac. The bus drove to the foreign departure hall and back non-stop.

After flying several times, I noticed that there was rarely an airport official below. I also noticed that the price of a ticket to Vladivostok was fifty or so dollars for citizens and almost nine hundred for foreigners.

A co-worker got me a domestic passport and named me Inokentii Makarovich Makeev. I only got to use it once to buy a cheap ticket to Vladivostok. A taxi driver stole it from my locked briefcase that I left in his car while I went into a store. I didn't notice it was missing until much later.

After showing my American passport to the Domodedovo gatekeeper, I went downstairs to the bus stop but instead of taking the bus to the departure hall, I hailed a baggage cart driver and offered him ten or twenty dollars to drop me off at the Vladivostok flight. I figured if a Russian ticket was fifty bucks, the crew would take a hundred to put me anywhere on the flight. I flew ticketless many times, but only to Vladivostok. The Russian expression for a ticketless passenger is "riding like a rabbit." The money wasn't important. It was just fun.

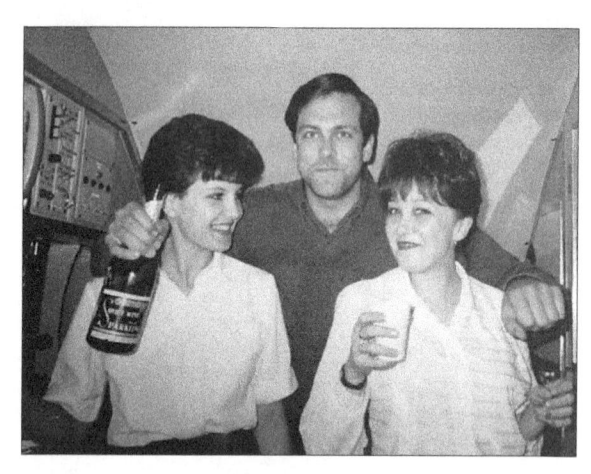

Flying ticketless to Vladivostok. Galley of an Il-62

There were no seats at all one day. I spent the entirety of the flight in the galley with three young, good-looking stewardesses. They told me they had never been anywhere in Vladivostok other than the airport hotel, so I invited them to my favorite nightclub, the Green Lamp, a cabaret with a variety show ranging from god awful to wonderful. After several visits, the doorman and I had developed a formal rapport, speaking to one another as if we were at a society soireé in 1840's St. Petersburg. His name was Anatolii Mikhailovich and he wore a black uniform with a black brimmed hat that had a white stripe around it. He also wore white gloves. His English mustache exuded an aura not from our era.

He stood at the entrance, nodding slowly and approvingly when he recognized me and the ladies' Aeroflot uniforms. Trying to make me look good, he announced that the best table in the house awaited us. A musical act performed a cover of a popular song at the time called "A Stewardess named Zhanna." One of the three in our group was named Yana. She joked that they should replay it with her name. I requested it and they played it for her.

The men's room was a floor lower. Not wanting to leave them alone for long, I hurried in and out. While exiting quickly, I accidentally stepped lightly on the foot of a Russian man who was smoking in the corridor. I apologized and kept walking. The guy yelled, "Hey! Get back here. We have to settle the score." I was confused, I had just barely touched his shoe. He was also confused. It's a Russian custom that if you step on someone's foot, the other person has to do the same back. Or maybe it's a superstition. Not knowing the shoe tradition revealed me as a foreigner. He tapped my foot with his and unleashed a slew of questions in English. Explaining that I had guests upstairs and didn't want to be rude to them, I told him to look me up at the Hotel Vladivostok. After the show, I put the ladies in a car to their hotel and walked up the hill to my hotel.

The hotel was on top of a hill near the end of a sixty-kilometer long peninsula. The Sea of Japan is on the east side and Amur Bay on the west. The rooftop panoramic view from the hotel would be about 300° of water. On the back side of the hotel facing east, a rock face cliff rose about five or six stories. On top of the cliff there was another small building. I had learned to request rooms in the back where there was shade, because without air conditioning the rooms exposed to sunlight got unbearably hot.

My room was right near the top of that cliff. The window was open as I fell asleep. The sounds of a woman being attacked were clearly audible. She started by desperately screaming, "Help. Help!. HELP!!!" It was impossible to tell if the sound came from below or across, on the top of the cliff. Her pleadings for help quickly turned to long loud moans of agony. Her voice got quieter and moans got softer. I could hear her almost whispering. "Help. Please. Help." I ran to the dezhurnaya and told her to call the police immediately. It sounded like a woman was just stabbed outside my window. Without any surprise, concern, or other emotion, the dezhurnaya replied, "What an idiot. That's what she deserves for going out at this time of night." I went down to investigate and saw nothing in the dark. The next day I saw a pool of dried blood, but no body.

I never went anywhere without a small cd player and a case of thirty cd's. While waiting for the car to take me to Nakhodka, I listened to John Prine's song, "Sam Stone," which was probably the saddest song in his greatest hits. It seemed a condign mood for what I'd heard the night before. When there was a knock on the door. I expected the dezhurnaya to have information about the attack. Instead, it was a professional looking American woman, who said, "There's no way you're not American. What are you doing here?" I asked her the same. She said she was doing research on the region's business climate. Assuming she was a professor, I offered her to ride along to Nakhodka with me, like soon. Without hesitation, she accepted.

She saw the port and city, and whatever else interested her. On the way back to Vladivostok, she was adventurous enough to stop for roadside shashlik (kebabs). Many Russians wouldn't. As we neared the final leg of the drive, the top of the peninsula, she handed me her business card. My heart sank. Her title was Editor, Wall Street Journal, Hong Kong. Marc Rich didn't have an employee manual, but there was an unwritten rule to never speak to the media and never attend trade shows. The thought of an employee rulebook, especially in 1990s Russia, is actually funny. I told her I'd be fired, beaten, and exiled if she wrote about our excursion. Claudia Rosett said she wouldn't, was honorable and mentioned nothing in her article about the Russian Far East.

The guy whose foot I'd stepped on at the Green Lamp was hovering around the hotel parking lot when we returned. He pitched himself as a problem solver deluxe. He made it clear that he'd take any job. For someone that lived in a country where they intentionally taught people to be non-functional in foreign languages, he spoke very good English. I don't remember what he said his job was, but he admitted that he was earning peanuts, as in less than $100/month. I thought if I could hire this guy as our Far East rep, I could save myself a lot of travel. I hired him, even though I didn't have the authority to. I also didn't know what I'd have him do. His nickname became Pubic, because it rhymed with his last name. After I hired him on a handshake, we sat in the hotel drinking until it was time to fly back to Moscow. I gave him a pen and paper. He wrote down the most ridiculous slang and insults that I could think of, which he memorized and became his trademark.

The emergency row, thirteen, on Ilyushin - 62s had double legroom. My seat was somewhere else, but there was one seat open in the emergency row that the crew said I could take. When I sat down, we found out why it was empty. It had a broken back that didn't support weight. When it fell backwards, the contents of a tray spilled onto the lap of the man sitting behind me. He punched the back of the seat and started yelling obscenities. I stood to see what had happened. Vodka had spilled on him and a piece of fish was on the floor. Apologizing, I explained that the seat was broken. It was not intentional. I sat back down without pushing back. He hit the back of my chair again. Without looking, I repeated that I did not know the chair was broken and I was sorry. When he hit me again, I told him, "Asshole. Shut your fuckhole!" (**Мудило, блядь. Залипи ебало!**) The guy sitting to my right started to shake with laughter, saying to me in English, "You just sayed veeery bad vords." The guy quit hitting my chair.

A few hours into the flight I went to the galley to have a drink or five with the crew and likely smoked a cigarette, which they allowed on non-smoking flights. As I was walking to the toilet I noticed the CPA from Indiana who'd briefly been my roommate at White Nights. We were both surprised. He told me he had fallen for Russia. After looking for somewhere to live with beautiful nature, but which was isolated from English speakers, he chose Vladivostok, where he opened a copy shop, like a mini-Kinko's. He handed me his card. After reading his name, I asked if he was serious or was it a joke. He didn't understand. He transliterated his last name, Wheeler, into Russian as **Хуйлер**, which in Russian sounds like "The Dicker." To learn Russian faster, he avoided English speakers. Out of politeness, no one had told him. He rented a room from an ultra-religious family, who likely accepted his unfortunate name.

Star City to W. Ukraine

It was rare for me to be in Moscow. The company rented an apartment for me near KGB headquarters on what was then called Big Communist Youth League Lane. It seemed like I spent about four days a month there. Anton smuggled me back into Star City. En route, we stopped at a currency store. I loaded up on foreign booze, hoping to get revenge on Marina for the Ukrainian moonshine.

Visits to Star City were a social highlight. The illegality of being in a closed city was a cool quirk, but it was about the people. No one was uptight. We did simple things like play charades. They called the feeling, "Shoulder." You could lean on the person next to you. Smolo had worked as a computer programmer for the Mir Space Station. He gave me my first tour of the space capsules. They were fascinating to look at, but I didn't understand much. Pavel Popovich said that the landing module could use more padding. Crashing into Earth in it had turned most of his body into a bruise. At the training center's centrifuge, Smolo goaded and prodded me to take a spin, literally. The device resembled something a villain in a James Bond movie would use to kill him. I vehemently declined to get in the thing.

Courteously offering to do some business networking, Smolo casually suggested I should meet his friend's father, whom he said was "some big shot." He wasn't sure what he did, but knew he was a heavyweight. He thought we could help each other. I agreed. Smolo set up the meeting.

The man had just recently retired from his position as deputy minister of railways. After becoming friends, his nickname became "Lip," because of his initials. Before Lip, transportation meant only ports. My first impressions of Lip were spot on. He was sincere, humble, and reliable. Previous interactions with the Soviet elite made me believe they were all self-important cruel bullies to be avoided. Lip struck me as someone to befriend, and not for the power he wielded,

After meeting him, I returned to the Marc Rich office, where I ran into ZNB and our co-worker, Zhompa. I told them I'd just met a high-level railway contact but didn't know how to use him. Zhompa's eyes lit up. He said, "Great! I've got a mission for you." Zhompa had just purchased 1.3 million tons of ore from a mine in Poland that needed to be shipped by rail to a smelter in Uzbekistan. The Polish seller preferred the Ukrainian border as the entry point. I called Lip for advice. He gave me the phone number of the regional director, Mr. Kishinets, whose office was in

Lvov. Lip didn't know him, but he said if I got tripped up, the national minister in Kiev was a good friend. Lip warned me that Ukrainians in the western part of the country have a "specific" character. I'd noticed that when I was there six years earlier.

Zhompa gave me a simple mission. Get the border station to switch the undercarriages of the Polish rail cars for less than $14 per ton. The two stations equipped to execute the operation were Chop and Uzhgorod, both managed by Lvov. The office manager gave me a round-trip ticket that clearly read: Moscow-Lvov – Moscow. I was looking forward to seeing what the city had changed since visiting it as a student.

After boarding the plane, the standard announcement came over the PA, "Destination: Lvov. Flight time: Two hours . . " After landing, they announced, "Welcome to Ivano-Frankovsk airport." I felt like I was in The Twilight Zone. I looked at the ticket and retraced my steps. The departure board at the Moscow airport definitely showed Lvov, Gate 7A. The sign at the gate showed 4:35 departure to Lvov. The takeoff announcement was destination Lvov. How did I land in Ivano-Frankovsk? I thought I'd solved the mystery, thinking that the crew flew so often, they mixed up the names of Western Ukraine's two major cities. As I was getting off the plane, I asked a crew member if they had noticed announcing the wrong arrival airport. "Oh no," she replied. "That was correct. We are in Ivano-Frankovsk" It made no sense. I asked how. She explained, "Everyone knows that the airport in Lvov is closed for reconstruction. We still operate this flight as Moscow-Lvov, but use the airport in Ivano-Frankovsk."

It was about a two-hour drive to Lvov. The taxi driver got lost on the outskirts of Ivano-Frankovsk. After driving around randomly for twenty minutes, we returned to an intersection I recognized from earlier.. He pulled up to a bus stop to ask for directions. I rolled down the window and pulled my head back to let him speak. Before he said anything, I heard a voice from the bus stop say, "Hey Kesha! Is that you?" Stunned, I looked to see who was at the bus stop. It was two of the geologists from the White Nights oil rig. I got out to shake hands and recited one of the x-rated cadences they'd taught me. They gave the driver real directions.

Ran into several of them at a bus stop
in Ivano-Frankovsk, Ukraine

Negotiating a deal with Lvov R/W should have been simple. After exchanging niceties, I told the director openly and honestly that there was a budget for 1,300,000 tons of cargo. I could pay him all cash, wire it to an account in Zimbabwe, or take him to Switzerland to set up his own account. I just wanted a contract and for them to do the job. He got out a tariff book, studied it, claimed the rates were in Swiss Francs, hit a calculator and told me the official rate was $29 per ton. Lip told me it was $11. Wanting to be done, I told him outright that $14 was the maximum and not one cent more. He said $29 was etched in stone and there was nothing he could do about it. I told him to think it over and that I'd return the next day for his final answer.

Curious what the border stations looked like, I took a driver in a Volga to the border, visiting Uzhgorod first. I found the stationmaster, who complained that there had been no traffic at all for over six months. Chop station said the same thing. I told them about 1.3 million tons. They begged for the business, promising to do it for $3/ton, but only Lvov could make that decision.

The terrain in Western Ukraine isn't mountainous, but there were plenty of hills. It was evening when we left the border and a heavy fog set in. In no time, visibility was next to nothing. A reasonable speed would have been 20 mph. The driver was going over 30 and had his bright lights on, which reduced visibility to about 5 meters. I told him he was driving too fast and that he should switch to low-beams to see better. He barked back, "You foreigners think you know better about everything. I grew up in these hills and have been driving them in every condition and I have never. . ." Before he could finish, we started rolling down a steep hill that could have been an intermediate level ski run. I regretted not having a seatbelt on. After jostling side to side for a minute os so, the car came to a stop. The brights were still on and all I could see was white.

A week or so before, I'd been stuck in a flood in Vanino, Russia's Far East, that wrecked my shoes. Not having time to shop, I bought replacements in the outrageously overpriced International Trade Center, where our office was, paying $600 for shoes that would cost $40 in America. I remember passing Mikhail Khodorkovsky in the lobby, who was walking with my co-worker, Igor Kotin. Khodorkovsky recognized me, but seemed to not know why.

In a blinding fog at the bottom of a hill next to the road to Lvov, I stepped out of the car, intending to go hitchhike back to my hotel. I stepped in mud that was halfway to my knee. That made me furious. As I slipped up the hill, I yelled at the driver, whom I couldn't see, every variation of dumbfuck I could think of. I could not believe the situation I was in. The driver ignored all the insults, and begged to be paid. I shouted back, "Get fucked. You owe me money." When I reached the side of the road, the driver continued hollering from below.

Traffic was almost non-existent. In thirty minutes, I'd seen a dump truck and a bus, both going in the direction of Uzhgorod. The fog lightened slightly. I waved down an approaching car, not like hailing a taxi, but by crossing my arms overhead to indicate an accident. It stopped. The driver was Italian. The car had Italian plates. He spoke some English and almost no Russian. Not certain he understood, I told him what had happened. He understood Lvov and agreed to take me there. I yelled "Goodbye " to the driver. He was still invisible in the fog.

The back seat of the Italian's BMW was full of boxes. The guy was a shoe salesman. He drove carloads of shoes back and forth. I showed him my mudded up feet. He sold me a better pair for fifty bucks when we got to Lvov.

The next day, I returned to the Lvov Railway headquarters, armed with the knowledge that the border stations had no income whatsoever. I asked the director if he had made a decision. He said that he was ready to compromise. The new rate was $21 and that was his final offer. I shook my head in disbelief and walked out. For failing to make a deal, I apologized to Zhompa, who said he understood, and repeated the phrase that people in western Ukraine have a "Specific" character.

Lip laughed as he listened to the story. He made a phone call to his friend in Brest, the border crossing from Poland into Belarus. The Brest station told Lip the rate was $6/ton. Brest faxed a contract and did everything they promised. When the job was over, they sent a thank you note for the opportunity to work for us. Chop and Uzhgorod remained idle.

Toolshed v. Tobacco Mafia

Toolshed quit Johnson & Johnson, moved to Moscow, and started selling cigarettes for British-American Tobacco. His main brand, Lucky Strike, was sold for slightly less than Marlboro and was marketed as "Real America." Lucky Strike kiosks and logos appeared all over Moscow and St. Petersburg. The Marlboro mafia threatened Shed, promising to take measures if he refused to pay them for protection. Toolshed told them to go fuck themselves. A week or so later, a dozen or so Lucky Strike kiosks exploded simultaneously all across Moscow. The Marlboro mafia let the operators evacuate before blowing them up. The racketeers returned to Shed and asked if his position had changed. He told them, "You've had it."

In the days of Tobacco Mafia.
Noviy Arbat. Moscow early 1990s

Betting Pool on Holy Hajj

There was some socializing among Marc Rich employees, but mostly the departments operated independently. To promote camaraderie, a Croatian in the Moscow office proposed a twist on a dead pool[1]. He suggested a Hajj pool. When he asked me to wager one hundred dollars on it, I had no idea what he was talking about. I knew he was obsessed with Muslims and Islam. One day he was reading a newspaper by himself and yelled, "Bullshit!" I asked him what he was on about. He said he was reading an article about a plane crash in an Arab country. On board were one hundred ten passengers, three of which were Europeans. He claimed that three people died and declared the larger number to be bullshit.

Explaining the betting pool, he pointed out that every year in Mecca, Saudi Arabia, the holy pilgrimage known as Hajj, dozens and sometimes hundreds of Muslim visitor are trampled to death. For comparison, he asked, "Can you imagine the outrage if one person was killed during the Easter Sunday service at The Vatican, and not once, but every year without fail?" Hajj deaths are widely ignored in the western press, so I'd never heard of it.

My grandparents had owned a casino[2] in Nevada. If it's an honest game, I'll bet on anything. It was the first I'd even heard of Mecca, let alone Hajj, so I picked a random number just to not miss out on a bet. Fifty or so of us kicked in and awaited reports on what the Croatian referred to as, "That year's harvest." The winning number was close to the high thirties. The organizer had guessed eighty-seven. Several of us had gathered in a conference room for the payout to the winner. The Croatian was inconsolable about his loss. For him, it wasn't about the money, He wanted higher numbers. He discussed with himself out loud ways to rig the results:

"Muslims are not big on pigs and dogs. If I could find a way to let them loose inside Mecca, it would certainly cause a more intense stampede. But the Saudi government would never allow an infidel near Mecca. Even if they did, they'd never let someone enter with forbidden animals." He pondered for a minute and announced, "Next year, I'm going to arrange for pigs to be airdropped from a helicopter!" His mood improved after saying it.

---

1 A dead pool is when betters submit a list of famous people that they predict will die within a calendar year. At the end of the year, the person with the most dead, wins all the money that was wagered.
2 https://en.wikipedia.org/wiki/Carson_Nugget #5 Chester H. Armstrong

The winner of the pool took the schtick up a notch. He commissioned an artist to create an image of pigs on parachutes falling from a helicopter over Mecca during Hajj. The painting started out as a gag gift, but spun out of control when every artist he asked was afraid or refused to take the commission. The idea was to commission a small artist's rendering for a bathroom wall. I heard that the artist who took the job did restorations for the Hermitage and Russian Museums, i.e. a world class painter named Vitya, who demanded the painting be "Museum-sized." It ended up as an oil on canvas with a size of something like 10 x 7 feet. When the finished painting was presented to the Croatian, he responded, "Are you crazy? I can't put something like that in my house. They'll kill me."

Izmailovo Park in Moscow is an outdoor bazaar, flea market, and art gallery with an array of random goods for sale over several acres. It includes permanent and pop-up vendors. One sold the dog tags and diaries of dead Nazi soldiers, that he claimed that he claimed to have dug up in the fields and swamps of Belarus. Others sold souvenir kickshaws for tourists, Soviet propaganda posters. Another section sold Persian and Islamic prayer rugs. Chechens, Tatars, Uzbeks, Azeris and Dagestanis sold slight variations of each. The Croatian spotted a small one, like two feet by three feet. He asked how much. The vendor replied, "Fifty dollars US." Without a word, he handed him the money. Once we got out of earshot, I asked why he hadn't haggled. They usually start with a price twenty times higher than what they expect to get. The Croatian explained, "I just fucked that guy's for at least a month. Every day he will be kicking himself for not having asked for a thousand."

The falling pig painting gag kept expanding. They wrote a biography in French about the artist, who was French Lebanese.

Jean Blique's painting "Last Day of Hadj"
Pushkin Square, Moscow

Jean «Bon» Blique
Né le 9 août 1946 a Beyrouth, Liban
Citoyen libanais et français
Etudes à l'Institut des Beaux Arts à Beyrouth
Studios à Coppet, Suisse et Bruxelles, Belgique
ean Blique est issu d'une famille de grands artistes. Il semble, à son tour, continuer la tradition familiale et devenir un artiste de grande renommée. Son oeuvre principale, "Mecca Fantasy" (ou le dernier jour du Hadj) et qui date de 2002 est un hommage à son arrière arrière-grand-père, Karl Brullov connu principalement pour son oeuvre "Le dernier jour de Pompéi".

L'histoire de la famille de Jean Blique est intéressante.

Remarquons en particulier les oeuvres de Karl Brullov (1799-1852) qui sont des pièces importantes de nombreux musées européens. "Le dernier jour de Pompéi" est exposé en permanence au musée de St Pétersbourg en Russie. Karl avait épousé Emelia Timm en 1839 mais divorça huit mois plus tard. Cependant, Emelia eut un fils de lui, Boris Nasralov qui vécut en Italie durant son jeune age. La fille de Nasralov qui plus tard s'installa en France épousa Luc Boitard, l'arrière-grand-père de Jean Blique. La soeur aînée de Luc, Clemence Boitard avait épousé Henri Rousseau en 1869.

Un siècle plus tard, durant les années soixante, Jean Blique, qui n'était encore qu'un jeune homme, se sentit attiré par l'Islam. A l'age de 30 ans, il se laissa tenter par un pèlerinage à la Mecque et Medina. L'idée lui avait été suggérée par la belle et envoûtante Badia Al-Banna dont le père avait fondé Abu Nidal. En fait, c'était plus la perspective de faire le pèlerinage avec Badia que son enthousiasme religieux qui motivait Jean Blique. Cependant, le Hadj lui fit une impression profonde et changea sa vie à jamais.

A son retour de la Mecque Jean dit a ses amis qu'il avait vécu une magnifique expérience religieuse qui n'était pas Hadj. Jean avait été fort déçu par ses contacts avec les pèlerins et, à l'époque, il considéra une conversion au judaïsme.

De 1970 à 1980 Jean Blique ne peint pas beaucoup. Il eut divers emplois et travailla pour la Cie d'aviation du Kuwait comme steward. En 1984 un avion de la compagnie avait été détourné sur l'Iran. Ce choc et les problèmes de son pays natal, le Liban lui firent dire "L'islam a toutes les vertus que je n'aime pas et aucun des vices que j'admire."

En 1988, Jean Blique s'installa a Strasbourg en France. C'est ici qu'il se remit en contact avec un membre éloigné de sa famille. Gérard était un passionné d'art et lui commanda une série de peintures que l'on nomma "Les Déesses arabes". La toile de la déesse Al-Uzza représentée comme une prostituée du Bois de Boulogne fut particulièrement remarquée par les critiques. L'interprétation de Jean Blique de la déesse Manat laisse apparaître une légère ressemblance avec son amie Badia. Sans qu'il le sache, Badia avait été victime d'une attaque suicide à Haifa contre un magasin de produits artistiques lorsque les explosifs qu'elle portait détonnèrent à son insu. Une des oeuvres de la série qui eut beaucoup de succès et obtint le prix "Frottis d'Or" du Ministère Français de la Culture est la représentation de la déesse Al-Lat, incarnation féminine de St François d'Assise en compagnie de cochons et chiens malades.

Malgré le succès de Jean Blique en France, les grandes galeries de Damas, Riyadh, Téhéran et Beyrouth refusaient d'exposer ses oeuvres.

Apres l'effondrement de l'Union Soviétique, Jean Blique voulut se rapprocher des origines de sa famille et en 1991 il se rendit en Russie, St Pétersbourg, Borodino et Moscou ainsi qu'en Ukraine où il visita

Kharkov, Kiev et Odessa. C'est en Ukraine qu'il découvrit une "delicatessen" typique de ce pays : le salo, produit de haute cuisine à base de graisse de porc.

De retour en France, Jean Blique essaya de promouvoir le salo au sein des communautés musulmanes. Il n'eut aucun succès. C'est a cette époque qu'il eut une vision qui allait constituer la base de son oeuvre importante "Mecca Fantasy- le dernier jour du Hadj".

Bien que Jean Blique ait été considéré faisant partie de l'école du Fauvisme, son art défie toute classification. Il semble que le choix du grand format pour ses peintures (2.4 par 3.3 mètres) soit un hommage a l'héritage de son arrière arrière-grand-père.

L'imagerie de symboles culturelles (islamiques et ukrainiens) que l'on trouve dans son oeuvre principale "Mecca Fantasy- The Last Day of Hadj" a certainement contribué a impressionner les critiques d'art du monde entier.

Mohammed McSharmout
Belfast, N. Irlande 2004
Il n'a été fait aucun mal aux cochons durant la production de "Mecca Fantasy."

The English Translation:
Jean Blique
Born: August 9, 1946 in Beirut, Lebanon
National Affiliations: Lebanon / France
Studied: Insitut des Beaux Arts Beirut
Studios: Coppet, Switzerland / Bruxelles, Belgium

Jean Blique was born into a family with a legacy of great artists. Heappears to be another artist from this clan destined for eternal fame. His main work to date, 2002's "**Mecca Fantasy**" (aka "**The Last Day of Hadj**") is a tribute to the legacy of his great great grandfather, Karl Brullov, who was the painter of "The Last Day Of Pompeii."

Jean Blique as a young man:
While most of the west was busy pursuing hippiedom in the 1960's, Jean was dabbling in Islam. At the age of 30, Jean accepted an offer to make the pilgrimage (Hajj) to Mecca and Medina. The suggestion to take a hajj was put forth by the beautiful and bewitching Badia Al-Banna, whose father was the founder of Abu Nidal. Jean's feigned strong desire to take a hajj, as he later confessed to Badia Al-Banna, was based solely on the assumption that she would be accompanying him to the holy kingdom. In short time Blique was confronted with a most unpleasant situation, namely that he had on one hand sworn to Abu Nidal his passion for the Hajj, yet on the other hand knew in his heart that his sole motivation in this matter was the prospect of a getaway with a sexy sidekick. When the severity of Blique's predicament became clear to him, encopresis occurred. The Hajj changed Jean forever.

After returning to Beirut from Mecca, Jean told friends that he had "had a wonderful religious experience, but Hajj wasn't it." In fact, Jean was so disillusioned by the reality of the hordes of mephitic muslim males he met at Mecca, vs. his fantasy hajj: a romantic skip down to Mecca with a pretty little Khadija, Jean Blique seriously considered converting to Judaism. To this day Jean eschews using the name Al-Hajji, preferring instead to remain simply Jean Blique, and never Jean Blique Al-Hajji.

Throughout the 1970's and 1980's Jean would paint only sporadically. Most of his time was dedicated to earning a living. While Jean was working as a flight attendant for Kuwait Airways, one of their planes was hijacked in 1984 and diverted to Iran. This event, combined with ongoing other numerous attacks in Blique's native Lebanon, prompted him to comment: "Islam has all the virtues I dislike and none of the vices I admire." So Jean saved up his money and in 1988 moved to Strasbourg, France.

In Strasbourg, Jean had access to genealogical records and quickly located his distant relative, Gerard Boitard, who, luckily for Blique was a sponsor of the arts. Boitard gladly commissioned from Blique a series of paintings, called "Arab Goddesses." Blique's presentation of Mecca goddess Al-Uzza as a beautiful Bois du Boulogne burqa-less streetwalker won him wide acclaim. His interpretation of the Medina goddess Manat clearly shows a striking similarity to his beloved Badia, who unbeknownst to Blique, had prematurely detonated en route to a planned suicide attack against an arts supply store in Haifa, Israel, blowing only herself to bits. Blique's finest work in the first of the Boitard commissions was the goddess Al-Lat, whom he depicted as a quasi female St. Francis of Assisi, nurturing sickly-looking pigs and dogs. Blique's Al-Lat was awarded the prestigious Frottis d'Or by the French Ministry of Culture. Yet despite Blique's many awards and wide acclaim in France, major galleries in Damascus, Riyadh, Tehran and Beirut refused to exhibit his works.

As a short family background, the works of Jean's debatable great great grandfather, Karl Brullov (1799 -1852), are the centerpieces of museums throughout Europe, including the famous "Last Day Of Pompeii" on permanent display at the Russian Museum in St. Petersburg. Karl Brullov was married for only two months in 1839 to his first wife, Emelia Timm. Eight months after the divorce from Brullov, Emelia gave birth to Boris Nasralov, who in early adulthood relocated to Italy. Nasralov's daughter then moved to France, where she met Jean's great grandfather, Luc Boitard, who was the older brother of Clemence Boitard, who married Henri Rousseau in 1869.

In 1991, right after the collapse of the Soviet Union, Blique set out to search for his roots. He visited Borodino, St. Petersburg and Moscow, as well as 3 Ukrainian cities. During his visit to Ukraine he discovered the local delicacy, "Salo." After dining on several variations of salo, Blique declared the food "Allah's pleasure and bountiful reward." Salo is an integral part of Ukrainian haute cuisine and is made mostly from salted pig fat.

When Blique returned to France he spent years trying in vain to promote Salo to the middle eastern communities of France. Blique became frustrated with the culinary intolerance of his middle eastern brothers and, remembering the experience of his first and last hajj, Jean claims to have had a vision. That vision is depicted in his best work to date, "Mecca Fantasy- The Last Day of Hajj."

Although Blique has been labeled a Primitive and Fauvist, his art defies categorising and makes strong statements through carefully selected subjects. Blique chose a museum-sized format for this painting as a tribute to his great great grandfather. The Last Day of Hajj's melding of cultural symbols is certain to make an impression on scores of art critics from all parts of the world.

- Mohammed McSharmout
Belfast, N. Ireland 2004

Notice / Disclaimer: **NO PIGS WERE HARMED OR MISTREATED DURING THE PRODUCTION OF "MECCA FANTASY" (aka THE LAST DAY OF HAJJ)**

One of Marik's art dealers bought the painting and hung it in an apartment on Moscow's Pushkin Square. He specifically chose that apartment, because it was a museum of a different kind. It belonged to an unseen die-hard communist, who evaporated after the USSR collapsed. His room was like a freeze-dried snippet of time. The bizarre thing about the owner was he continued to make regular payments for communal services. He rented the place through an agent on condition no one touches anything in his bedroom. If anyone ever leaked the location of the painting and a jihadist wanted to kill the owner, good luck finding him. It was a perfect place for it.

Several friends and I visited the apartment to admire the artwork. It was a hilarious twist on Karl Briullov's "Last Day of Pompeii." After smoking a couple joints, curiosity took over and we had to peek in the paranoid owner's abandoned room. Everything was covered in a thick layer of dust. There were stacks of yellowed propaganda newspapers and communist theory books from Marx to Dzerzhinskiy, all the way up to Andropov. Hanging on an exposed pipe there were two shirts and one pair of pants. Synthetic fabric, of course. There were a couple of primitive iron dumbbells on the floor. The invisible owner vowed to restore socialism and return. It was a surreal scene.

Attempted Communist Coup

The phantom landlord of Pushkin Square was not alone in his determination to bring back socialism. By 1993 Soviet central planners had become mostly irrelevant, simply by stripping them of funding and power via deregulation. Well-stocked stores, bars, restaurants, and nightclubs sprang up everywhere and regular people had more and more money to pay for them. Shoppers no longer had to ask, "What are they giving away?" They had choices and purchasing power. The ubiquitous abacus was replaced by a credit card machine. Remodeling apartments was a raging fad as well. Toolshed's wife decorated my small apartment. The before-and-after pictures appeared in an article of the first ever Russian-language issue of Cosmopolitan Magazine. Cindy Crawford appeared on the cover.

Where brick and mortar was unavailable for stores, aluminum kiosks popped up everywhere, on sidewalks, in and around metro stations, and in underpasses. A downside to the economic boom was hellacious traffic. Most everyone could afford a car now. There were almost no experienced drivers. Like diplomas, driving licenses could be purchased, as could traffic police. A German in the Marc Rich fertilizer department described Russian drivers as similar to drunken monkeys.

Siege Russian White House

For formerly elite overlords, widespread prosperity and a population whose entertainment they couldn't dictate was unbearable. In October, 1993 they attempted a coup, occupying the Russian Government House, which was about a half mile up the Moscow River embankment from the offices of Marc Rich. Muscovites mockingly referred to the occupied building as the "Bidet," which was a variation on the Russian initials for White House, Beliy Dom. With a slight change in pronunciation, B.D. became bidet. The incident to me was simple. Communists were throwing a fit because Yeltsin's laissez-faire policies revealed how not only useless they were, but shackling and detrimental, worse than the wizard behind the curtain.

On a balance sheet, privatization created more wealth in a month that central planning had in the entire history of the Soviet Union. That they chose to occupy the Bidet was symbolic. It had taken the Soviets sixteen years to build it. Yeltsin's forces shot up the Bidet just enough to run the reactionaries out. The socialists lost. The Yeltsin administration continued to let people make decisions for themselves. Some described what the socialists had attempted as "mutiny." I disagreed. Mutiny is when people band together to overthrow a tyrannical leader. The socialists' demands to reverse Yeltsin's policies of unraveling central power was the opposite of mutiny. They wanted tyranny restored.

During the showdown at the Bidet, one employee of Marc Rich got locked inside the office. We called him Georgian George. He reported being a little concerned when two anti-aircraft rounds punched inch-wide holes in the windows that faced the Bidet and went all the way through the building. He didn't seem concerned with the bullets zinging by, but claimed afterwards that the most unpleasant thing for him had been not being unable to find a razor. He hated being unshaven.

Mugged By Moscow Police

Georgian George had a reputation of deep mafia connections. The number of national bosses had held steady at twelve for years. They were called thieves-in-law, untouchables. Nearly all were Georgian or from Georgia. I wanted George to address an offense that happened to me when I walked out of a supermarket on Noviy Arbat[1].

Realizing that the smallest bill I had was fifty dollars, I decided to exchange it for rubles on the street. Even though businesses openly declared which currencies they accepted and at which rate, the Soviet law against foreign currency had still not been repealed. After I took rubles in exchange for fifty dollars, a much shorter man approached me and stood to my right. He put his left hand on my shoulder and reached inside his jacket with his right. I didn't know he was reaching for a police badge, so I elbowed him in the face and ran away.

Not far away, two large officers in uniform grabbed me and pushed me in the back of a Uazik, a Soviet Jeep. "Documents comrade," they demanded. I didn't have my passport, but told them I was an American citizen. He said, "We hear that one a lot." He cut to the chase. "Fifty for me, fifty for my partner, and you leave." I was livid. No one got arrested for currency trading anymore. It was a pure shakedown. Refusing to pay, they drove me to their local station and put me in what is called a monkey bench (Obyezannik). It's like a hockey penalty box, made of steel and about four feet tall. The latch for the door is a sliding lock on the outside bottom. An officer can unlock it with his foot. The monkey component comes from when someone tries to climb out, or hangs on the metal frame attempting to reach the latch. A policeman with a baton is always nearby, perhaps out of sight, but ready to beat anyone who tries to escape. It's a game.

One of my monkey bench cellmates was a foul-mouthed prostitute wearing a mini-skirt and mangy fur coat. After they threw her in, she went on a tirade, screaming "I hate all of you goddamned dickhead faggot motherfuckers. Die!" The guard listened calmly and said nothing. When it got too quiet, he'd liven things up by taunting her, saying in a com-

---

[1] One of the broadest streets in Moscow. There are four lanes of traffic in each direction. It starts at the Kremlin and ends at the Ring Road. It is just under a kilometer long. On either side there are four buildings approximately thirty stories tall. In Soviet times lights would be set to have each building show the letters CCCP. For the Soviets it was an impressive display of development. The same sight in lower Manhattan would look like a public tenement.

passionate voice, "Lenka." When she looked up, he'd say something like "Go suck a dick" and her rant started all over again. The experience was entertaining, but I couldn't believe that regular beat cops had the audacity to fuck with someone with my connections. They were dead and I knew it.

Sitting there irate, I imagined a hundred ways these petty shakedown turds were going to be steamrolled by team Marik or Georgian George. It was going to be a pleasure to watch them shiver in fear when I returned with overwhelming force.

After about two hours, they unlatched the door and motioned me to leave. After escorting me through a couple doors that we had to get buzzed through, I found myself standing in front of the poker-faced bully in charge of the place. He cited the statute for which I had been arrested. I countered that the statute did not apply to me because I was an American citizen. He pointed out that that was an assertion I failed to prove. He told an officer, "Search him." They emptied my pockets and put the contents on the boss's desk. He examined my cash, looked up and said, "I'm in a good mood tonight. I'll let you keep taxi fare," which was about the equivalent of ten dollars, "Or you can choose another option, which is to spend more time here. I guarantee you will not enjoy it." I searched his eyes for any sign of bluff. There was none. I took the ten.

As I left, the police station was already being burned to the ground in my mind. The little cop whose face I elbowed made me angrier by offering an apology. He said, "Please understand. Times are hard. We're just trying to make ends meet." I didn't say anything. I'd expected Georgian George to do my talking for me.

The next morning I explained to him what happened. He responded with a question. He asked, "Do you believe in destiny, or that a person walks a path of life?" I confirmed that I did. He continued, "Do you believe that wisdom is essential on one's path of life?" When I said yes, he revealed his meaning, "Last night on your path of life a bag of shit plopped down in front of you. Wisdom tells me the police are a bag of shit. What you are asking me to do is open that bag of shit, scoop it with my hands and make sure it is really shit. I'm not refusing to cause problems for the police, if you insist. But my advice is that you walk around this bag of shit. What did they get from you, $300 or $400? I will give you $1,000 to save us from wasting money on what I know for certain is shit." It wasn't satisfying, but I eventually accepted his point of view as superior. I walked around those bags of shit.

Transition: Soviet to Russia

Eventually the job gave me the chance to return to St. Petersburg, which was Leningrad no more. It felt strange to know no one there. Everyone I'd known had moved abroad, returned home, or was otherwise unreachable. The European hotel had been completely renovated. The second floor restaurant was converted into a world-class buffet. St. Petersburg was getting a massive facelift. The city was being restored to what it had been before socialism. I rode around in a taxi for at least an hour and videotaped everything. The transition was stunning and inspiring.

The commercial port in St. Pete was crucial for our business. Cargo ships to every major European port went in and out of there daily. We used it for almost every commodity. It was a coveted destination. Another employee worked the relationship, but Marc Rich management wanted me to know the port's operations as well. It was like a paid vacation for me to work in St. Pete.

Hoping to stay there for weeks, I got sent back to the Far East with even more to do. On a flight to Vladivostok, I had the good fortune to be seated next to a woman who introduced herself as Valeria. Her beauty was stunning. She exuded femininity. Pretty women in Russia tended to get instantly annoyed if a stranger tried to strike up a conversation. Once while riding the metro in Leningrad, a girl sitting next to me was reading James Joyce in English. I told her I was impressed and asked her if she really understood him. She snapped, "Like you'd know about reading English" and moved away.

After ordering a beer, the flight attendant replied that they had only champagne, which I don't drink. Valeria reached under her seat, pulled out a Heineken and handed it to me. In not good English, she told me, "I have more. Please take it." I thought she had to be a setup. What else could it be? Gorgeous women don't just hand out free beer on airplanes. We talked a lot, but I stayed guarded, wondering what she was really after.

Valeria K, suspicious for being too good-looking and generous.

Before I left Moscow, I'd remembered to call the Dicker. He told me about a new Canadian hotel that had just opened called the Vlad Motor Inn. They had North American staff, food, generators and water heaters. Its location near the top of the peninsula was more convenient for commuting to Nakhodka. More than anything, hot water was the selling point. Constant cold showers in Far Eastern hotels had led me to develop a technique so that the start wouldn't be so shocking. First, direct a stream of cold water on the femoral arteries of the inner thighs. Once you feel your body temperature drop, put your head under for a few seconds. After that it wasn't such a big shock to jump in.

The Vlad Motor Inn at the time was probably the highest rated hotel. I'd describe it as a trailer park mansion. It was two stories of what looked like well-built sea containers with windows that had been professionally stuck together. Each room had wall-mounted heaters and air conditioners. The location, though, was prime Vladivostok real estate. It was in a dense forest near the coast of the Amur Bay. The air was fresh. The governor's official residence was just up the street, as was the Negotiation's House, where a summit between Brezhnev and Ford had taken place. The owner/operators were a married couple from Vancouver.

The Dicker met me there for drinks. His big news was that a local radio station had given him a three-hour slot every Friday night for a music broadcast he called "Vladirockstock." Foreign music was a big deal in a city that had been closed to outsiders for forty years. Two years earlier his show would have been unimaginable. He told me he intended to play 100% American music. I tuned in. The first song he played was "Back in Black" by AC/DC. The second was "Black Dog" by Led Zeppelin. He followed that with Billy Idol. He looked stunned when I told him after\wards that nothing on his playlist was American.

Another upscale hotel opened in Vladivostok called the Versailles. It had an English-managed casino and bar stocked with foreign booze. We decided to check it out. Pubic and the Dicker were going to meet me there. I arrived first. There were no customers in the bar. I was surprised to see Guinness on sale and ordered one. The bartender poured it and said, "Fourteen dollars." That was outrageously expensive. I asked him, "What's cheap around here?" Without any irony, he thought for a second and replied dryly, "Human life." After the bar, Pubic and I popped our heads into the Dicker's place just to see how he lived. Afterwards, he reported that Pubic stole his cassette with the music for next week's show. There was no other candidate for the crime. He was mad about it, because the opening song was his favorite by Billy Idol.

At the Nakhodka clubhouse, the owners of Magdia and Prok introduced me to a thief-in-law, Mikho. Mikhail Osipov, Primorye's top mafia boss. I didn't know who he was, but I could tell by the way others acted around him that he was the authority. He was always extremely hospitable. He treated me like his pet American. The waitress in the clubhouse was the best I've ever seen. She never wrote anything down. A dozen guys would change their orders while she was taking another's. They'd announce, "Change mine from french fries to mashed potatoes," and someone else would ask for extra sour cream in their beef stroganoff. I never saw her make a mistake.

It was disheartening to hear the Nakhodka crew tell me Pubic had to be fired. We'd just bought him a car. I'd sent him to the Komsomolsk oil refinery with cases of beer and other gifts. The oil department had a contract to sell A-76 gasoline to Vietnam at a price way above market, because it was a violation of an embargo. The embargo wasn't a problem. It was that Russia had export quotas on refined products. Even corrupt lawmakers don't want to run out of gasoline for their cars, so they actually mostly adhered to the law. Only Komsomolsk could "legally" deliver A-76 for export. The refinery was holding out for the highest bidder.

Pubic wasn't without skills and resources, which made me reluctant to fire him. One of our main customers was a South Korean company, whom we suspected of falsifying discharge reports so that they could pay us less. We didn't have proof. Pubic knew that their representative loved to gamble, so they took him to a casino. Before entere\ing the gaming area, they forced him to check his briefcase. While he gambled, Pubic's friend snagged the briefcase, cracked the lock and copied all the contents. The operation saved us hundreds of thousands of dollars. On another occasion, a supplier shipped substandard coal to a Japanese power plant that could only function with the highest grade. We were contractually obligated to provide high grade replacement. Instead of trying to collect from a broke Russian entity, Pubic produced certified lab reports that confirmed the coal was a grade it was not. It was an internationally certified laboratory. The documents passed muster in an international arbitration court. I mentioned these things to the Nakhodka gang, in his defense. They remained adamant that he had to be fired, because he wouldn't shut up. He was yammering all over town, revealing connections of people who didn't want to be connected.

One of the Magdia employees drove me back to the Vlad Motor Inn. His real name was Chizov, but I gave the nickname Brinzanenko, because Brinza is a popular Russian cheese and the add-on made him sound Ukrainian. The real Ukrainian, Serdiuk, I turned into a Sicilian, naming him Serduccio. After a while it was shortened to just Dooch. I felt completely at home with their entire crew, but preferred staying in Vladivostok.

Russian Navy's Pacific Fleet

I'd become such a VMI regular that Zena the owner gave me the keys to the bar and told me to lock up whenever we were done. I'd just returned from Nakhodka and was starting to unwind with some usuals, when Vika the receptionist told me there was a call for me at the front desk. Noisy was on the line. Vitaliy had been arrested. They needed an additional five thousand dollars before the prosecutor's office opened the next morning or he might go to prison. Also, Noisy wanted me to deliver the money to the police by myself in case it was a sting. The police wouldn't want the headache of arresting a foreigner.

The time was close to midnight. There were no taxis and even if we called one, it might take a half hour from downtown. The only guy in the bar with a car refused to drive me, because he was drunk. I asked him for his keys. He told me it was too dangerous at night, and besides, I'd been drinking a bit too. Again, I told him to give me the keys. I knew the road and could pay for a replacement if something happened to his car. He said it wasn't my driving that he was worried about, but "Bandits" on the road. He said that at night criminals were ruthless. They'd dress up as policemen or military officers to get you to stop. If you stopped, they'd ambush you and leave you to freeze to death. Reluctantly handing me the keys, he made me promise that I would stop the car for no one until I reached Nakhodka.

It was a used Japanese car with a right-hand steering wheel. Every cargo ship that sailed to Japan from the Russian Far East returned loaded with used Japanese cars. The local government considered them a public safety threat, because in order for a driver to see if it was safe to pass, he'd have to almost completely enter the lane of oncoming traffic. The import of cars with right-hand steering wheels was banned. Almost everyone drove one and they continued to flow in through the ports daily.

It was cold when I left the VMI, like −25 C. The car had an annoying wimpy bell that sounded every time the speed exceeded 100 kmh. Somewhere near Tikheokeansk, a coastal city that the locals jokingly call Texas (**Тихас**) because it sounds like Texas in Russian, I spotted a Volga that had spun out. The car was stuck on a slope that it couldn't possibly drive out of on its power. The driver stood by his car, waving his hands for help. Looking for an ambush, I stopped. There was nowhere for someone else to hide. There were no people and no cars. Even if he was a gun-packing bandit, he was far enough away that I'd be able to escape before he got close.

I yelled to ask him what he needed. He said his girlfriend was badly injured. He asked for help to get her to the road. I surveyed the scene. It seemed impossible that it was a staged accident. To be semi-safe I hid the car keys before descending the hill to help. His girlfriend was barely conscious. She had hit the dashboard so hard that her sweater split open. The blood on her exposed breasts was viscous and thick. Her breathing was shallow. The driver lifted her from under her arms. I took her feet. We carried her to my car and placed her on the back seat. Expecting him to jump in, he started giving me directions to a hospital. I interrupted, "Just show me the way while you ride along." The suggestion surprised him. He didn't leave his car, because he feared everything would be stolen. I asked if he had lost his fucking mind, and bluffed that if he didn't get in my car, I'd leave the girl to die. He got in and we drove to the nearest hospital.

We arrived at the gates to the naval headquarters of the Russian Pacific fleet. I told the guard at the checkpoint we were carrying a woman, who had been injured in a car accident. He looked at her and opened the gate, telling us which turn to take to find the hospital. I parked in front of the entrance. The driver went inside to find help. Medics came out and carried her inside on a stretcher. I said goodbye and wished them well. Before I could get in the car, a voice warned, "You can't leave before the MP's write their report." I was driving someone else's car without a license or permission. I was slightly drunk, and was on a Russian military base, and was carrying an American passport.

Waiting for the MP's, I watched the medics clumsily cut off a clump of the girl's matted hair that was saturated with coagulated blood. I remember thinking that it's going to take her a year to grow it back, if she lives. The MP arrived. The first thing he said was "Documents." The driver handed him his and I sheepishly pulled out my U.S. passport and showed it to him. His eyes got wide. His look said, "We're gonna both be in deep shit." He separated me and the driver, interviewing the driver first in another room. After about 10 minutes he interviewed me. After concluding that our stories matched, he told me to wait until he wrote a report. After that, he had to clear my departure with an officer.

Shkotovo (pop. approx. 5,000) is on the Sea of Japan. Its population has steadily shrank since open travel was allowed in the early 1990s

The wait was more than an hour. Without saying a word, he returned and took his pistol out of the holster. I was about to crap myself. Instead, he dropped the magazine and took a bullet from it. Handing it to me, he said, "Thank you for rescuing our citizen. Not many would do that. Take this as a souvenir from me." The money got delivered to Nakhodka. No one went to jail. I stayed there all day.

The Dicker and some regulars were in the bar at VMI when I returned. They were making bets on what had happened to me and the car. None of their guesses were correct. The regulars were an Australian couple who represented M & M Mars, the candy company. Snickers hit Russia about as big as Marlboro cigarettes. An elderly Norwegian sea captain would sit in the bar all day, for days in a row, three sheets to the wind, annoying everyone with his acerbic comments. Then he'd hit the seas and be gone for a month or more. The American Consul General, Randy, lived there as well. I didn't know him, and just because of his title, I had no interest in interacting with him. He might have been a great person.

When I called the Komsomolsk refinery to find out if the gifts from Pubic had softened them up on the Vietnamese A-76, I was enraged to hear that he hadn't been there at all. It was doubly infuriating, because not only had he stolen from us, I now had to go to Komsomolsk. Pubic didn't deny it and offered no explanation. I fired him.

Embargo-Busting Gasoline

To get from Vladivostok to Komsomolsk, you've got to fly through Khabarovsk, the biggest city in the Far East with a population of more than 500,000. There was some time to kill before the flight. Up the street from the VMI there was an Australian restaurant called Captain Cook. After spending collectively weeks in one hotel, I had to mix it up. The road was a dead-end road with almost no traffic after passing the VMI. A woman walked towards me, holding what looked like a pitbull on a leash. As we approached each other, I recognized Valeria from the flight. She was walking her dog, Stinger. Her husband was the governor of Primorye and their official residence was behind a tall fence and located next to Captain Cook.

She invited me for tea, where I met her daughter Dasha, who was about ten years old and her friend, Lena, who worked as a pediatrician. A nice family with a dog and a beautiful home was highly irregular. I enjoyed being there. Valeria and I exchanged numbers and I left for Khabarovsk.

Komsomolsk then was a city of about 200,000. It is almost 9,000 kilometers from Moscow and most famous for manufacturing Sukhoi fighter jets. The powerful Amur River dominates the landscape. After telling the refinery representative in charge of quotas, Konda, that Marc Rich would provide him whatever he wanted within reason, he was more than willing to sell us A-76. He decided that because I was American, he wanted me to take him to New York and D.C. in exchange for the quota. Moscow greenlighted it immediately.

Because I was already so close to Vanino port, I made a courtesy call there. The trans-Siberian railroad splits in Khabarovsk, from where it goes south to Vladivostok and northeast to Vanino, which is about 175 miles from Komsomolsk. I chose to fly and landed in nearby Soviet Harbor. While passing through town, the driver pointed out a Soviet era gulag. He claimed that North Korean prisoners (slaves) were housed there. A year or so later, Claudia Rosett broke a story about North Korean prison labor being used all across the Russian Far East. She had a good nose, and eye for real and deep stories. Unlike Matthew Brzezinski, whose book "Casino Moscow" was given to me as a gift. I read it only to marvel at how someone with the insights of a first-day tourist could write an entire book. Then I remembered that his uncle had served in the Carter administration.

There was one restaurant in Vanino. I happened to be there on February 23, a major holiday: Defenders of the Fatherland Day. I wasn't aware of the holiday or the aura that surrounds it. February 23 is the day that any man can get laid if he wants to. I wanted to eat. But it's like it was a woman's duty to let you know she was available. The restaurant was full so I had to join someone else's table. Before I could even pick up a piece of bread, a woman invited me to dance. I do not like to dance. The woman insisted. It was February 23rd after all. I tried to use my citizenship as a reason to be exempt. She argued that America fought Hitler, too. For hours, repeatedly a woman, or group of women, would propose a toast to men. Drink a shot. Dance. Make a toast. Drink a shot.

There's a Russian phrase that a woman will chase a man until he catches her. On February 23rd they can stop at "A woman will chase a man." Another expression from Soviet times was that sex wasn't a question of with whom, but where. An empty room was extremely rare. To get out of the restaurant, I invited another couple, and a woman who'd been hounding me, back to my hotel room for cognac. I figured that having four of us in the room would stave off the advances of the woman I had no interest in. She and I sat on a cot bed, chatting about nothing when she motioned with her head to indicate I should look to my left. I turned my head and saw the other couple, standing up and fucking right next to us. I went out in the hall to finish the cognac.

The head of the oil department in Moscow was from London. He occasionally spoke with a bit of a cockney accent. I went to see him to report on Komsomolsk. His real name was Bernie, but I called him Perni, which is the imperative of the Russian verb to fart. It didn't sound flattering, but I knew his Russian was so primitive, he'd never know. Certain Brits like Perni add the letter "r" at the end of words that end in "a." One of them might say "I ate a pizzar when I flew viar Romar." When I asked Perni how his Russian was progressing, he replied that it was getting good. He told me that he'd picked up phrases like "Kak delar" and "Menyar zovut," which mean how are things and my name is. None of the words end in "r."

While discussing the trip with Konda, Perni called in his transportation team, who had a problem at the Volgograd refinery. Trainloads of diesel had been sitting idle for weeks because there was some kind of a ban on exports of rail cisterns. The customer was in Finland, the only European country that could take delivery of them without the extra cost of switching the undercarriages. If they had to cancel the contract, they'd lose hundreds of thousands of dollars in profits. The transport team said they had thrown their best offers at politicians and at the Volgograd railway, but no one would budge. I promised to see if I could help.

Lip was my only resource. I called him to explain the ban and the importance of circumventing it, which was meant to convey, "We will pay you and your friends." Lip called back within ten minutes and reported that a telex would be sent out from the deputy minister of railway's office (for oil products) within the hour, promising no more ban for us. He asked for the oil department's telex number and the Volgograd refinery's. I returned to Perni's office and repeated what Lip said. The transport guys scoffed. They told me that I hadn't understood. This was a serious issue that couldn't be fixed over the phone. All I could say was my contact's word had always been gold and there was no reason for him to lie.

As promised, the telex came through and the ban was lifted. Perni called me back down and gave a few notes of gratitude for Lip and Co. The company almost always had cars and drivers on standby. They served as taxis, couriers, and personal valets. I found a car and went to visit Lip, whose office I never left sober. He was retired and loved telling stories. Lip was born on a moving train in Kazakhstan, which made me think of him as a Soviet version of the lyrics from the song "Ramblin' Man" by the Allman Brothers, "I was born in the backseat of a Greyhound bus rollin' down highway 41."

He was reluctant to accept Perni's package. He told me, "I made a phone call and used a favor. Friends do that. I'm old. I have enough money. I don't need anything. Hire my son and you'll do me the best favor. Don't give him special treatment, and don't think you're hiring me. He is honest and will work hard. The best thing you can do for me is give him the chance to earn his keep. If you have to fire him, I won't take it personally." We finished our bottle of cognac and I left.

Lip's son, Pablo, arrived for a job interview the next day wearing black jeans, a black leather jacket, and a black collarless shirt. He had long black hair to about six inches beneath his shoulders. He was like a better looking Howard Stern. Most of the traders in the office wore custom suits from Milan or Savile Row. The office was strictly coat and tie, but there was no actual dress code. He knew enough about transportation to justify hiring him. Lip had told me to do no favors. $1,000 per month as a starting salary was normal. He looked disinterested, distant, and continued smoking his cigarette. I repeated the offer. Slowly, he got around to saying, "I accept," and "When do I start?"

Before we set a start date, ZNB staggered into our conference room. It was around 2 p.m. It was totally out of character for him to be drunk. His explanation was brief, "Chinese wisdom." I had no idea what he was talking about. Not sure if Pablo understood English, I told him Chinese wisdom in Russian. That meant nothing to Pablo either. I asked ZNB if he drank ginseng vodka? He expounded. As a negotiating tactic, when Chinese people conduct business in large groups and their counterpart is a single decision maker, they try to take advantage by getting the other party drunk. To do that, members of the Chinese contingency will make toasts individually. Each Chinese will have taken one shot of alcohol, whereas their counterpart might have had twenty. ZNB quipped, "I might be wasted, but I got the terms I wanted."

Miss Bust / Miss Legs

Returning to my rarely visited Moscow apartment, I listened to several messages on my answering machine. Cambo was back drilling oil in Siberia with another company. He was visiting Moscow on Saturday and wanted to meet up. My French roommate, J. Dog, from GWU asked me to help his friend navigate Moscow. His name was Strogy (strict in Russian). J. Dog and he had studied together at London Business School.

Around 11 a.m. on the Saturday I'd planned an outing with Cambo and Strogy, Smolo from Star City showed up at my apartment unannounced. It was unusual for him just to show up because Star City was an hour away when there was no traffic. Smolo told me to get dressed, saying he was doing me a great favor. "Trust me." The last time he'd told me to trust him, he tried to put me on a Soviet military flight to Berlin for a few days just because it was free and passports weren't required. I was leery, but went with him.

Smolo and I met Cambo at the Metropol Hotel in a small bar called Paradis that's no longer there. Smolo introduced a cocktail he'd created, which was straight gin with a splash of Tabasco. It did not sound enticing. He insisted, claiming it was both a cure and preventative. It actually went down smoothly. Smolo revealed what he had up his sleeve for the afternoon. Without asking me, he got me hired as a judge in the Miss Bust / Miss Legs pageant that was being put on by the newspaper "Komsomolskaya Pravda." Why not? Cambo was down for anything. It came about that morning when Smolo was talking to his friend, the organizer, who thought adding a foreign judge would make the competition more credible. Smolo's friend sort of sighed that he didn't know any Russian speaking foreigners when Smolo told him, "I got you covered. I know a guy."

Sipping cocktails and rating a stream of attractive women seemed like a good way to start a Saturday. The MC kept the crowd laughing by making me field embarrassing questions and taking goodhearted jabs at American stereotypes. Every time one of my top picks failed to advance, Cambo and Smolo raucously mocked my taste in women from the stands behind. The judges did three rounds of paring down the entrants, until there were only three left in each category. After that it was up to the audience to decide.

Champions were announced and the results were published in the paper Monday morning. As a resumé filler, I liked that I could add: "Judge in Moscow's Miss Bust / Miss Legs Competition."

We hadn't eaten anything and were floating a little when we left. Strogy's apartment was two blocks from the biggest, and first, McDonald's in Moscow on Pushkin Square. I suggested to Smolo that we get a snack before going out. He refused to "Eat that shit." When we got to Strogy's, he poured us enormous glasses of whiskey and set out a bowl of nuts. As we discussed dining options, he smiled mysteriously and pulled out several joints that he'd picked up in Amsterdam. Quality herb was almost impossible to find back then and highly illegal. Strogy had, and still has, a cynical sort of "Don't give a fuck" attitude about everything, which included cross-border marijuana.

He lit a joint that we passed around. When we downed our whisky, ready for dinner, Strogy refilled our glasses without asking and taunted with a second joint, "One more?"

We said, "No! We haven't eaten all day and . . .aw fuck it." He lit it and refilled the bowl of nuts. Smolo stumbled to his feet and made his way to the toilet. It was a small flat and we could clearly hear him puking. He emerged refreshed and returned to his seat at the kitchen table. Pointing at the snack bowl and shaking his head, he uttered a legendary quote, "Fucking peanuts!"

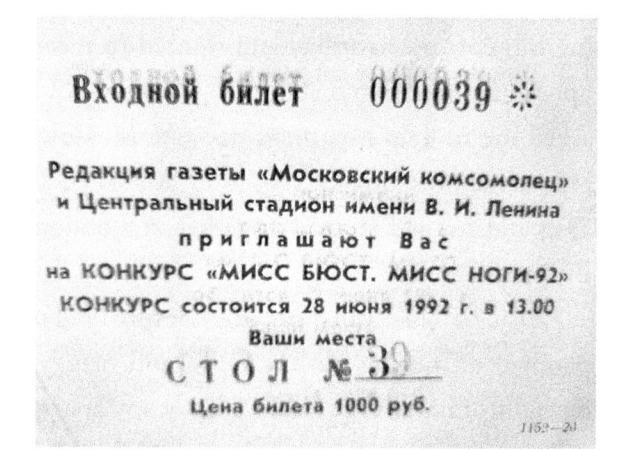

Входной билет 000039

Редакция газеты «Московский комсомолец» и Центральный стадион имени В. И. Ленина приглашают Вас на КОНКУРС «МИСС БЮСТ. МИСС НОГИ-92» КОНКУРС состоится 28 июня 1992 г. в 13.00
Ваши места
СТОЛ № 3
Цена билета 1000 руб.

Tequila!

Pablo showed up for work in the same clothes as he wore to the interview. A lot of people in the office asked me, "Who in the hell is that?" or "What were you thinking?" I said very little. On the Friday at the end of the first month, I gave him $1,000 USD cash as agreed. The following Monday by noon he hadn't shown up for work. He didn't necessarily need to be there, but I thought it unusual for someone not to report they weren't coming.

Pablo called right about 1 p.m. I asked him where he was. He replied, "I am Russian." I repeated the question. His second answer was slightly different, "I am a Russian person." I told him to knock it off. Tell me where you are. After a slight pause, he said, "I'm in St. Petersburg." I pointed out that we had no cargo going through St. Petersburg and also, our relations with the port were excellent. There was no need for him to be in St. Petersburg. Again, "I am Russian."

I just wanted an explanation and said, "Pablo. What the fuck?!" After another pause, he asked, "Have you ever tried tequila?" I started laughing.

Pablo eventually revealed the story. Before I hired him, he had worked for a Polish trucking company that hadn't paid him for seven months. His salary was $80/month. He didn't believe we'd actually pay him, either. The $1,000 was the most cash he'd ever had at one time. Santa Fe restaurant was a five minute walk from the Marc Rich office. He got looped there and took a taxi 400 miles to St. Pete. Instead of being mad, I was impressed. That showed the kind of "spirit(s)" we expected in an employee. Now, whenever I hear the song by The Champs, I imagine Pablo slurring in the back of a taxi en route to St. Pete.

Ukrainian Wheat Thieves

As I was preparing to leave for New York with Konda from Komsomolsk, our grain trader approached me and casually said, "I need you to sort something out in Ukraine, mate." I did not like Ukraine. Tens of thousands of tons of Hungarian wheat that he had purchased for delivery to Uzbekistan had gone missing. After it crossed the border into Ukraine, it disappeared. The grain trader's Russian was, and is, excellent. He was savvy in local business. That he was asking me meant it was a shit sandwich. To get out of the job, I told him I was on assignment for the oil department. His grain would have to wait.

He had also experienced unpleasantries in Ukraine, like contracting scabies in a hotel somewhere near the Sea of Azov. His ranting about it afterwards prompted me to give him a Ukrainian-sounding nickname, "Voronchuk." Voron is "Raven" and 'Chuk is a common suffix in Ukrainian last names. I referred to him in three ways, Voronchuk, Voron, or just Chuk.

He told me about contracting scabies to one up me on bad port visits. After I once got stranded for days in a flood in the Ukrainian port of Nikolaev, water on the streets was up to your knees. Everything shut down. The hotel sold one type of beer and had one TV channel, which ran a marathon of Mexican soap operas. One was "Simply Maria" and the other "The Rich Also Cry." Chuk wasn't impressed by the Mexican soap operas. He repeated, "Scabies. Fucking scabies!"

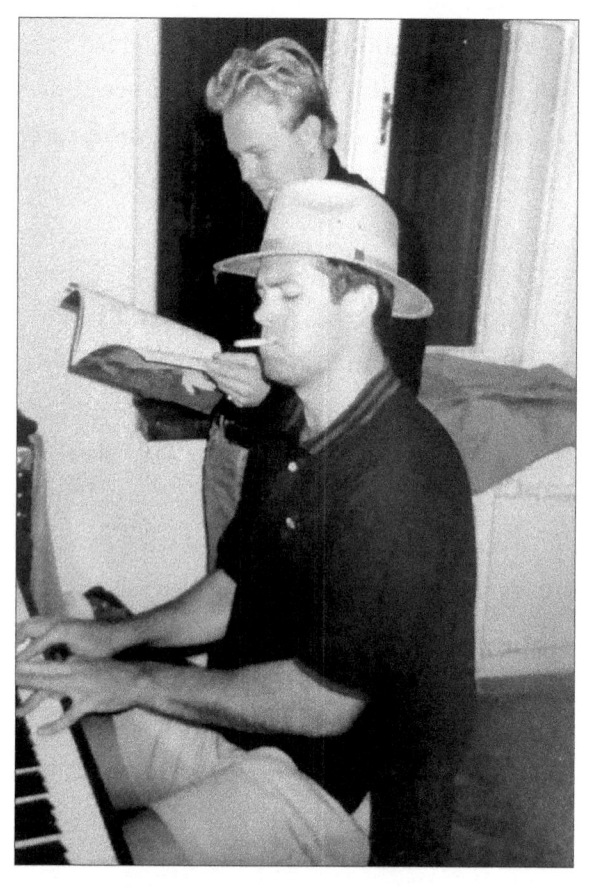

Besides getting his grain stolen,
Voron can also sing

My position about the missing Hungarian grain was that I hadn't arranged any shipments through Ukraine, nor would I have, so fuck you, fix it yourself. The threat of having to travel in rural Ukraine likely scared him into using heavy handed tactics. He told the Moscow boss, Daniel, that I refused to fulfill my duties as transportation manager. The boss walked out of his office, pointed at me and said, "Hey mick. Get the whiskey out of your blood and come talk to me for a minute."

Voronchuk was already sitting in Daniel's office. I was at a disadvantage. Daniel had hired me specifically for transportation. I couldn't see a way to get out of it, but I intended to drag Chuk with me. This was his fault.

The boss started with, "You have access to the railway's tracking system, right? Find out where the train is, and then we'll figure it out."

Near a place called "Three Train Stations Square" in Moscow there's a building with a sign that reads simply: Information Center. Inside it is a supercomputer that tracked all rail movements in the Soviet Union. If a cistern arrived somewhere empty that was supposed to be full, they could pinpoint where it had been discharged. They claimed it was the 2nd largest computer in the world, after NASA's. Lip had access to everyone there. I faxed a list of railcar numbers to him. Within twenty minutes, he called back, reporting that all our rail cars were located, empty, in Strabychovo, Ukraine. I asked, "What's Strabychovo? There was a pause, followed by laughter, "Grain elevators."

I protested that I shouldn't be punished for Voron's bad decision. The oil deal with Komsomolsk was worth more. Perni was depending on me. . . .Daniel told us, "Both of you fuckers hit the road. Bye."

There were no flights to Ukraine at all. The country had pissed off Russia and in retaliation Russia cut off their petroleum. A train to Strabychovo would take a minimum of thirty hours one way. Neither of us was pleased. The task was surreal. We had to go on a mission to recover trainloads of stolen Hungarian wheat bound for Uzbekistan in a Ukrainian village?! We decided to fly to the closest major city, Budapest, rent a car, and drive from there.

We mapped out a route the night before, calculating that on shitty roads, 300 km from Budapest to Strabichovo would take 4 hours. Voronchuk offered to drive there if I'd drive back. I agreed. Chuk drove like a professional driving instructor, especially compared to drivers in the Far East with right-hand steering wheels. I recall him performing a courtesy I saw for the first time. After he passed, he remained in the left lane with his left blinker on. I asked why. He said he did it to show the cars behind that it was safe to pass. I liked it. It also must have been an ingrained habit for him, because there was no one else on the road except for the car he had passed.

We arrived at the border. The checkpoint was a small two-story brick building. We were the only people trying to get in or out of Ukraine. It looked deserted and appeared to have no electricity. All the gates in front of the four or five inspection stations were padlocked. Neither of us had Ukrainian visas. The country had only very recently started selling visas at the border. After waiting several minutes, Voronchuk started to rant about where we were, and why. The scene was quintessentially East Bloc, splotchy cement on an uneven brick façade. Everything was gray, drab and dilapidated. Along the building were rows of stainless-steel inspection tables that were covered in a thin layer of dried mud. Chuk took it in and shook his head.

After unleashing a stream of obscenities in English and Russian, he laid on the horn for at least a minute until an agent emerged from the building. The nonchalant look on the customs officer's face indicated that he had absolutely no idea that some Englishman was livid. He assumed the honking must have been a horn malfunction. His mood changed instantly when Voron rolled down his window and asked, "What the fuck kind of shithole is this?" (Что за хуйня тут блядь?) The officer's expression changed from disinterested to hostile. Without asking for our passports or visas, he instructed us to place our luggage on the table and to open the trunk. We only had gifts, booze and cigarettes. Chuk's demeanor remained confrontational. I asked if I could use the restroom. The guy pointed to an open door.

Inside, the station master was sitting at his desk doing nothing. I didn't need to go, but wanted to leave Chuk alone. I looked out the window for progress. Judging by the body language of the officer, Voronchuk was not succeeding. The agent had started emptying the contents of the bags onto one of the mud-covered tables.

Knocking on the director's door, I ran with the stupid tourist ruse. I showed him my passport and in Russian with a heavy American accent, said, "Good day sir. My friend and I would like visas to Strobychova. The man outside didn't let us go for a hundred dollars. Maybe you'll let us go for a hundred dollars? My friend will pay too." When his eyes lit up, I knew it was a done deal. He promptly put visas in our passports. I gave him a couple bucks. He escorted me outside and instructed his underling to put all our stuff back. They lifted the gate and we were off to have a chat with wheat thieves.

In Hungary we passed several cars, but in Ukraine there was no automobile traffic at all, only an occasional horse and carriage, (a kibitka), or horse and cart. Voronchuk continued to rant. I suggested he pull over and vent so that he might continue in a better mood. I had a video cassette recorder with me and filmed his opinion on Western Ukraine, while capturing on video the surrounding area. It had taken us five hours from Budapest, but the grain silos of Strabychovo were visible. Now we had to locate the office that managed them. It wasn't easy.

The office was inside a railyard. There were trains standing on all the tracks that blocked our view. We rolled up to four or five workers who were smoking and drinking on top of a pile of burlap sacks. That part of Western Ukraine, Zakarpattia, is famous for despising Russians and for locals that refuse to speak it. The only way we could ask was in Russian. There was no chance they knew English. Chuk asked them where to find the office. Each gave a different answer. One told us to go right. The next said we needed to make a U-turn, no, a left and then a U-turn. We got the message. The office was somewhere nearby, but they weren't going to tell us. They were bumfuzzlers.

Entering the admin building of a grain elevator in Zakarpattia, Ukraine

Armed with a carton of Marlboro Reds for the records department, I asked Chuk to give me fifteen minutes to confirm that they'd discharged his grain. Two people were more likely to scare whomever worked there and they might not give us any information. He took the carton of cigarettes, opened his log book and quickly identified the exact dates on which all of our cargo had been discharged. He wrote the dates and corresponding silo numbers directly on my list. I thanked him and told him that he would soon be entering into his records how they were dispatched to Uzbekistan.

The station master's office was upstairs. Every Soviet boss had the same setup all over the country, a reception area, with a few chairs. Those without access had to sit and wait. There was always a gatekeeper. I stormed right past the secretary and entered the stationmaster's office. He was sitting at his desk with a stunned look. His secretary was right behind me, saying that I came out of nowhere and barged in. I placed the list of cars on his desk and handed him my Marc Rich + Co AG business card. Pointing at the card, I told him, "Before you steal something, you should find out who owns it. If it isn't dispatched to Uzbekistan exactly as consigned, you will be visited again, but not by me." Stealing the line from the Moscow Arbat police chief, I added, "I guarantee that you will not enjoy it. Goodbye."

The man's expression of pure fear told me there would be no further shenanigans. He never expected anyone to even know that the wheat was in his silos, let alone show up in his office.

It had taken ten minutes. I knew that I didn't want to drive back to Budapest. Dodging horse-drawn carriages and potholes was not alluring. This whole thing was Chuk's fault anyway. I devised a simple plan to get out of driving. Whiskey. I had a bottle as backup, in case the carton of cigarettes failed. I returned to the records department, showed him the bottle, and asked if he had glasses. He not only had glasses, but black bread croutons as chasers. After downing several shots with him fast, I walked out of the building. Chuk got out of the car to ask how the visit went. I said, "Perfect. The records department told us everything and I told the fucker upstairs to ship it, or else. We will not need to come back."

Voron started walking towards the passenger door when I told him that I was drunk and shouldn't drive. I told him it was necessary to get info from the records department. He started ranting again, directing all manner of uncomplimentary terminology at me. Throughout the drive back, he switched back and forth from laughter to rage. He giggled when I described the stationmaster's expression when he heard, "You have fucked with the wrong company!" About an hour outside of Budapest, I admitted that I did the whiskey trick on purpose. Chuk was furious all over again. Then we got lost trying to find our hotel. We spent at least an hour haphazardly seeking landmarks in a city neither of us knew.

We had only both visited it once before. The grain was delivered to Uzbekistan. All future shipments went through Poland and Belarus.

Twenty years later, Voronchuk landed in Kiev to film an episode of a long-time popular TV show he hosted on Russia's NTV, which was similar to Anthony Bourdain's food travel series. It was called "Поедем Поедим" or "Let's go there, let's eat there." Ukraine wouldn't let him into the country, even though he has both an English and American passport. They barred him because of his employer. When I read about his border problems for his TV show, I dug up Voron's video rant from outside of Strobychovo and sent it to him.

Oil Equipment Thieves

When the Uzbeks got their grain, I was certain that the schmooze cruise to New York City and Washington would go forward, Expecting to get an itinerary with Konda, the oil department instead asked me if I might be able to help them solve an issue in Nizhnevartovsk. Someone remembered that I'd worked at the railyard there. The situation was similar to Chuk's wheat. An organization called 21st Century had taken several containers of drilling equipment that belonged to our partner, Total. They said no matter who or how they asked, 21st Century refused to admit they had them. They already had an airline ticket for me.

When I arrived in Nizhnevartovsk, it was amazing to see how quickly things had changed. Ford trucks were no longer technological exhibits on wheels. They'd graduated to parking lots of Range Rovers, Lincoln Navigators and Land Cruisers. The only people I knew there were Gennady and the ladies I worked with at the railyard. They were still there and in the same office. I presented them with a bottle of XO cognac, which they promptly opened and we enjoyed the reunion. I asked about Gennady. They said he had become a bigwig at a private freight forwarder called 21st Century. They called him and told him I was visiting. He said he'd be waiting for me in his office nearby. I had a bottle for him too.

We rehashed a few stories. Then he asked why I was there. I explained that his company seemed to be refusing to deliver some containers to Total. He looked surprised and asked, "Those are yours?" Putting emphasis on "Yours." When I told him I sort of worked with Total, he said he would release them right away. Just send trucks to pick them up. He gave me the address of the warehouse. I asked why he hadn't done it before. He said he knew from the customs declarations that the contents were very expensive and that it was a French company. He figured the owners were roofless foreign pussies. He wanted to find out how much they'd pay to get them back. He didn't expect any recourse for holding or stealing them. What could Total do, call the police? He was the police. Call customs? He owned them too.

When I told the story about 21st Century to Toolshed, it turned out that they had held his cargo hostage as well. When he met with them as a hostile outsider, Shed dropped the names of some of his mafia boss friends. He told 21st Century that unless they released his property immediately, they will have had it. It worked.

Beretta 9mm for Gasoline

Konda from the Komsomolsk oil refinery was in Moscow. We had plane tickets to New York. The morning of our flight, The guys from Nakhokda called me. They were angry and asked if Marc Rich + Co. was stupid. Pubic had been re-hired and was running coal through nearby Vostochny port, about a half hour's drive from Nakhodka. Pubic had found a way to get an interview with the Californian, aka serial urinator. The English slang lessons I'd given Pubic in the Hotel Vladivostok paid off for him.

The Moscow coal director was a Frenchman named Willy. I called him to ask how Pubic had surfaced in their world and why they hired him. Willy told me that during the interview with Pubic, the Californian couldn't stop laughing hysterically. Pubic wanted to display his deep knowledge of English and responded to interview questions with rude and ridiculous words and phrases, oblivious to what he sounded like. In today's hyper-sensitive politically correct environment, any human resources department would have thrown him out instantly. Willy didn't remember verbatim what was said, but he recalled hearing things like, "Some other cumguzzlers or pillow-biters might, but I'm a swinging dick. If you're looking for a felch-breathed shirt-lifter, that's not me. I'm no fudgepacker, or buttstabbing turd burglar."

Konda got his chance to experience Marc Rich's hospitality. It was my first time in the U.S.A. as a tourist. I'd been to New York dozens of times, but never went to Windows on the World or the observation deck in the Empire State Building. I didn't like it. We used to visit NY and do things like go to amateur night at the Apollo every couple months. That was better than any tourist attraction.

We took a train to D.C. and stayed at the Carlton. One of the doormen, J.T. or Luther, gave me an extra warm greeting, giving Konda the impression that I was a regular guest there. I was a regular. Just never a regular guest. It was a strange feeling to check in where I had worked, and to pay more per night than I had earned in a week. I took him to dinner at the Powerscourt. Seamus the manager remembered me and comp'ed our meal. Even though I was on an expense account and didn't need his generosity, I certainly appreciated the gesture.

Like most Russian tourists, Konda thought the Capitol was the Whte House. They're surprised when they see how small the White House really is. It was October and the weather was colder than usual. In South

Carolina temperatures were near record highs. I asked Konda if he'd like to road trip south to somewhere warm. We drove to Hilton Head for a few days, where even though it was late in the season we both got sunburned. Driving back to D.C., I saw a billboard for a gun shop off the Interstate in North Carolina. Foreigners seem fascinated by American gun stores. Konda was no different. He spent almost two hours in it, falling in love with a Beretta 9mm. He stared at it in his hand and made me an offer. If I delivered that Beretta to him in Russia, he'd give us double what we wanted. I had no idea how I would do it, but I told him on the spot that I would deliver the gun.

Perni didn't like the plan much. As a Brit, he was a bedwetter about guns. He didn't say no, but he didn't know how to discuss it over the phone. I asked him to put Yarmo, the trader, on the line. Yarmo was a Russian we hired from Cargill, where he had been a little frustrated like I had been at White Knights.. I told him what Konda's proposal was. Yarmo was on board, but the "how" of the operation still needed to be figured out.

Permits to buy guns are issued federally, but a person can only purchase a gun in their home state. Konda went back to Russia and I flew home to Minneapolis to buy a Beretta. I'm sure I could have found one on the street, but I imagined that if I was caught with it flying internationally, the charges would be worse if I wasn't the legal owner. The Frontiersman gun shop on 394 had exactly what Konda wanted. For myself, I threw in a 357 revolver. I was expensing the purchase to Perni anyway. He wouldn't know what the cost of a Beretta was.

I had flown in and out of Moscow at least a hundred times. I thought I knew how they searched and what they were looking for. A plane arrives and the baggage is offloaded onto one of those little land trains. They take the bags into the back room, where, out of sight, I imagined dogs sniffing for drugs and explosives, but not guns. After getting past the dogs in the back room, bags were put on a conveyor belt for retrieval by the passenger. The last step was presenting your passport and customs declaration. An agent sat behind an X-ray machine and could request to place your suitcase on the belt for inspection. Not once had they ever patted me down or even asked if I was carrying anything. My plan was to put the gun in my suitcase and take it out right away at the baggage conveyor belt. I'd put it in my pocket and walk out the door, because no one was going to frisk me.

I let Yarmo know to be on standby. Legal entanglements are cheaper when they're resolved right away. Instead of the usual Minneapolis - Amsterdam - Moscow route, I booked a flight through Chicago, assuming that if the gun was discovered, I could say, "Oops. I forgot to declare it. But it's legally mine and in a locked case." A decent lawyer could wiggle out of that easily. The likelihood of Amsterdam x-raying a bag that just got off a flight from Chicago and was routed to Moscow seemed miniscule.

I put on a Burberry raincoat with pockets big enough to conceal the Beretta and drove to MSP to make a delivery for Konda. The curbside baggage handler told me he was not allowed to accept bags for international flights. I pulled out a fifty dollar bill, telling him it was worth it so spare me the headache of standing in line inside. He checked the bag through to Moscow and gave me the claim ticket.

Waiting for the flight to Amsterdam in Chicago, I worried that the police or customs would call me aside for questioning. Boarding made me nervous. When the plane lifted off, I was relieved.

The layover in Amsterdam was about three hours. If the airport's official policy is to ignore kilos of cocaine, I didn't expect them to search for other contraband. I was right. A KLM flight to Moscow had a 9mm in its cargo hold that only Yarmo and I knew about.

Despite having run through the script in my mind, it was much more difficult to casually execute than I had expected. Imagining is different than doing. When my bag came out, any calmness I had felt turned to fear and thoughts of "What if?" Standing over the suitcase and using the tan Burberry raincoat to cover up what I was doing, I unlocked the gun case, extracted the gun and quickly put it in my pocket. The coat had a slit for the pocket inside as well, so the gun could not have been seen when the transfer happened.

Remembering a story about a Dutch woman who'd been caught at Sheremetyevo with a false bottom suitcase full of cocaine, I started to second-guess myself. The woman's ten-year sentence was reduced to one year. The Russian government explained their decision by stating that one year in Russian prison is equivalent to ten years in a European one. I thought it over so long, the baggage claim area was emptying out. To avoid suspicion, I had to move. Filling out the customs form, I decided at the last second to not initial the "I have no weapons" declaration. I thought maybe the agent wouldn't notice. I also thought that if they found the gun, I could claim that I never said I didn't have one. The panic was real.

The agent instructed me to put my suitcase on the x-ray belt. He looked at the scan emotionlessly and took my declaration, which he quickly placed on top of the x-ray machine with a pen. Pointing to the line, "No guns," he ordered me to initial it. My hand was trembling when I picked up the pen, which caught his attention. Focusing on the paper, I could feel him staring at me. He knew something wasn't right. After putting my initials on the form, I attributed the trembling to shivering, telling him I had just come from 85˚ F weather and it was freezing inside Sheremetyevo. The tan from South Carolina supported my statement. He stamped the declaration and waved me through.

As I walked to the awaiting company car, my sweat turned to swagger. I pictured how I was going to strut into the oil department, deliverer of gasoline to Vietnam, and show that I was a man willing to go the extra mile. I kept the Beretta in my coat pocket and took it out when I was standing in front of Perni.

Standing in front of him, I noisily pulled back the slide, locked it, and set the Beretta on his desk. He stared at the gun for a few seconds and yelled to Yarmo across the hall, "He did it!!" Yarmo came in, saw it sitting there and started beaming from ear to ear.

Konda was a man of his word and did what he said he would as well. It was a bittersweet deal, though. He found out that 9mm NATO and 9mm Russian are not the same caliber. He couldn't get ammo for it in Russia, at least not right away. Yarmo arranged for me a Tula Tokarev pistol, that had never been fired, and a box of armor-piercing ammo. At the time, you could buy a Tokarev in the U.S. for $150, but on the black market in Moscow a new untraceable one was worth up to $4,000. Bullets for it were $10 each.

The first time we needed to use Nakhodka's oil products port was for Komsomolsk's A-76 shipments to Vietnam. It was a different entity and managed by a Chechen named Imar. Arranging delivery of the A-76 to Vietnam was not a telephone conversation. I was back at the Vlad Motor Inn and commuted daily to Nakhodka. In the Soviet mafia world, Georgians had a reputation like gentlemen Sicilians, whose code didn't allow women and children to be harmed. Chechens had the reputation of being ruthless and without moral boundaries. I had no idea what to expect from Imar or how to approach him. I didn't want to get the "schmuck off the street" treatment like I had, when I first tried to make a deal with the commercial director.

Schmoozing at Hilton Head, S.C.

En route to the oil port, I stopped at Mikho's clubhouse. There were several brand new Mazda 929s in the parking lot, with left-hand steering wheels. That was like really showing off. The car was like a precursor to a Lexus, one of Japan's top luxury vehicles. They had purchased about fifty of them. There had been some big score. I asked if I should be concerned about the oil port. They told me that Imar was a sweetheart, a great guy. After insisting that one of the underlings drive me to the oil port in a 929, Mikho invited me to a party Friday night at the city's only night club, Bay of America. They were celebrating whatever the big score was that paid for the fleet of cars.

One of the regulars at VMI, Shura, was a low-level mafia type, whom I knew fairly well. When I mentioned to him that I intended to go to a party at Bay of America on Friday night, he looked terrified, telling me to absolutely stay away. He went to the hotel's front desk and found a recent newspaper article about how the week before someone threw a grenade into a crowd of people outside Bay of America. "You have no idea how dangerous that place is. Do not go!" When I told him that I was Mikho's guest, he blanched even more. It seemed overdramatic, but he said, "If you're stupid enough to go there, I will drive you and sit outside with my gun, in case someone tries to kidnap you." The free ride was nice.

After a few drinks at Bay of America, I told Slava about Shura and his gun outside to protect me. He laughed and laughed. When he finished laughing, he said "Bring him in," and laughed some more. Shura was too scared to say no. We were seated at a banquet table for about 24 people. They opened a seat to my left for Shura, my self-appointed bodyguard. He couldn't hide the fact that he was very frightened. His eyes darted across the room, checking the faces of people who didn't appear to be Mensa members.

Two or three guards stood with their backs to the wall, watching the entrance and guests. The top of Shura's gun was visible, sticking out of the holster on his right hip. I tapped Slava on the shoulder and pointed it out to him. He convulsed with laughter. He whispered to me, "That's not even a real gun. It's a gas gun," and laughed some more.

Enforcers in Vladivostok

After a few more drinks, he told me to try taking the gun without Shura noticing. I pretended to tell Shura an animated story and kept bumping him with my shoulder. After a few times doing that, I timed the shoulder bump with a holster grab. He hadn't noticed. I passed his gun to Slava, who had devised a gag to scare the shit out of Shura.

He made sure there was no gas ammunition in it and whispered something in the ear of one of the guards standing behind Mikho. The scene was set and everyone in the room knew about Slava's gag, except Shura and me. Slava reached over and pressed on the empty holster, and acted like he had just taken Shura's gun. Instead of pointing it at Shura, he pretended to threaten Mikho with it. Shura almost fainted and was trembling visibly. Trying to explain why he had the gas gun in the first place, he started stuttering and stammering. Slava clicked the trigger over and over and fell apart cracking up. He pointed the gun at the ceiling and continued pulling the trigger. With each click, Slava laughed harder. It was pointless and cruel, but when the shock wore off, I thought it was pretty funny. I never felt in danger around them.

The equivalent of a made man (not me), Mr. No Sir, who carried a "get out of jail free" pass.

Border with North Korea

When we returned to VMI, the receptionist at the Vlad Motor Inn handed me a message from someone named Andrew, who claimed to work for Marc Rich oil in Moscow. I'd never seen him or heard of him before. I called Perni to verify. Andrew was a new hire. He was English, but spoke very good Russian. I invited him to Captain Cook to meet Valeria and the governor. At dinner, Valeria couldn't get over the fact that an Englishman and American were carrying on a conversation, in Russian, and in Vladivostok, something that until a year or so ago could never have happened. Valeria's friend hosted a local morning TV showed called "Cup of Coffee." She was convinced her friend would love to put us on the show. We agreed, as long as business wasn't discussed.

Andrew was in the region to investigate possible movements of oil products into North Korea. Our fertilizer trader had also asked me to sniff around, if I got the chance. We booked a helicopter and flew to Khasan, a village of less than a thousand people located where the borders of Russia, North Korea, and China converge. Driving, it's a little more than one hundred miles from Vladivostok. By air, it's around fifty.

The coastline and islands on the Sea of Japan there are mostly pristine. The only structures appeared to be military installations and there were not many of them. could be seen. I don't remember seeing any villages. The region is also home to one of the world's only colored glass beaches.

As we descended into Khasan, the pilot hadn't noticed overhead wires. To prevent us from getting entangled, he threw the helicopter backwards and up so violently, it felt like we were going to flip over and crash upside down. Andrew, noticing that I was terrified, asked, with typical British reserve, "Did you notice that?" We both had on dark woolen overcoats, dark suits, and were wearing sunglasses. People came out to stare at us. When we asked where the railway office was, they just pointed.

We presented the records department with some gifts. After collecting information about which commodities were moving in and out of North Korea, we flew back to Vladivostok where we appeared the next morning on live local TV.

The conversation quickly veered from citing quotes by Chekhov and Pushkin, to hurling insults at each other's country. Andrew started with the tired English observation,

"You can never find out what an American knows by talking to him." I countered with, "If you want to keep your money safe from an Englishman, put it under toothpaste." The show's host seemed a little uncomfortable and tried to steer us away from the cultural jabs. We kept going. I recall getting the last dig in, but will wait to see if Andrew is still out there and what his recollection is. Maybe the recording still exists?

Khasan, Russia / East of China

From Infidelity to Khanka

A tense situation arose at VMI. We were in the bar when a small-time thug named Albert walked up to Vika, the hotel's receptionist, and slapped her so hard her earring flew across the room. As she sat there sobbing in pain, several of us got up to investigate. Before we even spoke, a Canadian chef named Allan stormed out of the kitchen, dragged Albert outside where he kicked and punched him until he fell to the ground. Allan choked him and bounced his head off the sidewalk, stating rhythmically with the head hits off the sidewalk, "You do not hit women. Understand?" Allan looked up and saw me standing there. I was stunned speechless. As Allan walked away, with Albert semi-conscious on the ground, he told me "Translate that for him, will you?"

Albert was jealous that Vika was surrounded by foreigners. He constantly accused her of cheating. He slapped her when he saw a regular guest give her an innocuous present he'd brought from abroad. We knew Allan as a goofy Canadian from a small town in Alberta, who stereotypically ended everything he said with "eh?" None of us knew he had been a contender for kickboxing champion of North America. He was in Vladivostok on self-imposed exile, trying to shed his cocaine habit that had killed his career as a fighter. Albert picked the wrong guy to aggravate.

By pummeling Albert, even though it was justifiable, Allan upset a hornet's nest. Albert returned to the hotel with mob soldiers. Their leader was Gera. He was built like Mike Tyson. His team looked seasoned and hard. They were calm, except for Albert, who was agitated and hungry for revenge. They asked for an explanation. I translated. They accepted that Albert had been out of line, but indicated that maybe one should refrain from using physical force before first finding out who the target is. When Gera alluded to Albert being connected, as in mafia ties, I played the Mikho card, not only dropping his name but that I'd just been at a party with him at Bay of America. Mikho's name got Allan off the hook, and gained me an invitation to go pheasant hunting with Gera and his crew at Lake Khanka, which is four thousand square kilometers of freshwater. The Western shore is in China. The Eastern shore is in Russia.

Driving on a remote road through a field with no trees, a pheasant crossed in front of the Land Cruiser I was riding in the back seat of. Gera, who was in the front passenger seat, urged the driver to stop. Before I knew what was happening, Gera's window was down and he rapid fired a Mossberg twelve gauge shotgun, blasting the bird. When my ears stopped ringing, Gera was telling us that the cookout at the lakeshore just got better. The second car in our group passed us and drove off road through the flat, treeless field. We bounced around slowly for about ten minutes and stopped in front of what was a slight mound, on the side of which was a grass covered door that opened into a tunnel.

One of Gera's partners yelled out a name. A short time later, an army soldier in uniform emerged. They started discussing weed, marijuana, herb, ganja, and hash. Gera asked me if I preferred bud or hash. I told him whatever was natural. I felt I had to say that because an Armenian in Vladivostok offered me a joint that he said was laced with acetone. The soldier went back inside and returned with about fifty grams of weed and I'd guess about a ten gram ball of hash. I didn't go inside, but evidently defenders of the border have a system of tunnels, some of which are equipped with grow lights.

We drove to the lakeshore and set up for a picnic. There was no road and no people. Two guys left with shotguns to hunt pheasants. A definite former convict with tattooed knuckles, hands and neck and whose right side of his face was dented, packed several papirosas[1]. They opened a bottle of vodka to pass around. There was a raging bonfire. The scenery was amazing. It was genuine wilderness. The lake was huge, yet there were no visible structures or boats and no other people. It was serene. As I strained to see if the Chinese shore was visible, dented face started shooting an AK on automatic into the fire. He was dancing and laughing as he unleashed short bullet bursts. When the gun went off, it seemed to surprise him. I looked to the others for their reaction. They shrugged and showed no surprise. For a final blast, he pointed the barrel towards China. As he unleashed into the air another twenty or so rounds, he shouted "Die! You yellow-skinned motherfuckers." He laughed, put the gun down and didn't shoot it again.

Chinese – Russian border, Lake Hanka.

---

1 Papirosa is a Russian cigarette. It is standard length but only has about an inch and a half of tobacco. The rest is a tube of thick paper. By pushing the paper tube forward while holding the outside thin rolled paper, one can expel the tobacco. Without tobacco, one can reload it with whatever. To prevent ashes from getting into the smoker's mouth, they bend the thick tube at a forty-five degree angle, which is a substitute filter. The most famous brand, Belomorkanal, was said to have been the favorite of Soviet workers forced to labor in frigid cold.Unlike a regular cigarette, the long tube allowed them to smoke without burning their gloves

Rabbit Gets Caught

Ready to return to Moscow ticketless, I ran into an Australian, Karl. He worked for an air cargo freight forwarder called Petra, so he had a badge to walk freely past the airport gates. Karl and I met on a beach the previous Summer where we got into a serious debate over which of two girls was better looking. They were identical twins.

There were five or six flights daily to Moscow. Karl offered to show me his company's operations. It was a long walk in the opposite direction of the passenger planes, so I decided to just get on board. Waiting in the galley, pre-takeoff, to see what the seating situation would be, a stewardess suddenly told me to hide quickly in a bathroom. Through the door, I could hear a woman repeatedly saying, "Where is he? I saw him? I know I saw him." The crew pretended to not understand her. She said, "That tall foreigner. I watched him board the plane." The crew almost had her convinced that they hadn't seen me, when she spotted my foldover Tumi bag. After she made a bunch of noise and promised to not leave until I was off, they knocked on the bathroom door and apologized that I had to leave.

I was a little miffed that I'd have to wait a few more hours for the next flight, but who knew? Maybe that one would crash and it would turn out to be a blessing. The separate departure hall in Vladivostok was called VIP and it served foreigners and government officials. I'd been through it so many times, the lady on duty recognized me, which is how she knew that I didn't have a boarding pass. She was the only person who could have issued it. Getting on board without her permission had really gotten her goat. She was irate and let me know it all the way back to the VIP hall. She told me things like I had committed an effrontery against the protocols of air travel, and she scolded me for egregiously disturbing an orderly seating chart.

Alone in the VIP lounge, the woman told me to not bother waiting around for the next flights. She declared it her mission to make sure I didn't leave that day, and if she could fix it, the next day too. She was steamed. I offered her to make a bet, for any amount she wanted, that she would escort me to the next flight with a boarding pass in row 13. After some prodding, she made a symbolic wager for something like twenty-five cents.

From a payphone in the main terminal, I called the governor and told him that I urgently needed to return to Moscow and that I was already at the airport, adding that for some reason the lady in VIP wouldn't sell me a ticket. Could he please help? I returned to the departure lounge and waited for the phone to rang at the VIP desk. The woman answered. Listening to the governor's instructions, she glared at me like I'd insulted her mother. Right before hanging up, she said, "It will be done" and hung up. As she wrote out my boarding pass, I told her that I'd forgive her gambling debt.

The governor, by the way, struck me as patriotic and someone who genuinely wanted life in the region to improve. After he returned from an official trip to Australia, he asked me why everyone had called him "Govno," which is the Russian word for shit. No one told him that 'guvna' is the Australian pronunciation of governor.

Police Escort

Back in Moscow, Shit King drove us around barhopping. We had just walked out of a bar called Marika, which had been one of the first private enterprises in Soviet times. Marika had a reputation as a gathering place for those who like to fly the middle finger at authority. As soon as we got into Shit King's car, a policeman appeared next to the driver's door and started knocking lightly on the window with his baton. Shit King told us to stay put, saying "I've got this," which meant he had money. Anton, Smolo, and I were in the back seat. There was a female passenger in the front.

Paying off a DWI shouldn't take too long. Anton and I both had cash and decided to offer assistance. As soon as we stepped out of the car, Shit King angrily waved us to go sit down again. We did, telling Smolo that we didn't understand what was happening. We sat for another five minutes or so when flashing police lights appeared behind us. We wondered how he could fuck up a simple operation like paying off the police. Shit King jumped in the car and started it up. We asked what the lights were about. He replied nonchalantly, "I got us an escort to the next club. I didn't want to get stopped again."

Amateur proctologist Tatiana V and Shit King

We arrived with a police escort at MS Max. The owner's name was Oleg, but everyone called him by an ambiguous nickname, "Buck," which could be slang for a dollar, or it could mean Бак, the Russian word for gas tank. When I felt comfortable enough, which was right away, I asked him which of those terms his name meant. He replied, "Neither. Bak is short for Baklazhan," eggplant in Russian. Bak gave me his card and told me his club was open for us any time. Shit King told me afterwards that Baklazhan, eggplant, stemmed from how a woman once described his unit.

A week after meeting Bak, a group gathered at my apartment on the river across from Gorky Park. From there it was a short walk to a water taxi station. Like tourist boats in Paris on the Seine, double decker passenger boats run back and forth between terminal stations on the Moscow river, making numerous stops on both sides of the river during their route. It was a good way to spend a sunny afternoon, drinking on the water with friends while sightseeing.

About twenty of us jumped on a river boat mid-afternoon, after getting primed at my place. We rode all day. The sun was giving off light, but it would soon be dark. As the boat was about to pass the Kremlin, Jarveikin, a drunk English aluminum trader, noticed that the ladder to the roof was unlocked and could be unfolded. We climbed on to the roof and looked at the spires of the Kremlin that we were nearing. Jarveikin declared the Kremlin a perfect backdrop to take a "Moon" shot. He yelled down for someone to grab a camera and to snap the photo. As we stood on the boat's roof with trousers dropped and our exposed butts pointed at the back of the boat, an identical type of boat passed in the other direction. The captain of that boat radioed the captain of ours, informing him that there were two bare-assed morons standing on top of his roof.

One of the mates ran up the ladder and angrily told us to get off the boat immediately. They pulled directly to the shore, telling us to jump off where there wasn't even a dock. The captain was so furious, he refused reconciliation money. The entire group jumped off. We were stranded on the Kremlin Embankment, where there were no traffic lights. The road is sort of a main thoroughfare and not a likely place someone would try to hail a taxi.

We tried to hail taxis and private cars, but no one stopped. Eventually, a rickety bus approached with unaligned tires that appeared to be crabbing down the road. The driver didn't care about the amount of passengers, but asked, "How far?" I decided to take everyone to Bak's club, MS Max, which was far away in the Southwest region. He said he couldn't go that far, because the bus was for the Kremlin guards, whom he needed to return to their barracks. He was about to drive away when I offered fifty dollars. Without hesitation, he told us to get in. Fifty dollars compared to the military salary he earned was likely about six weeks' pay.

The parking lot at the club was by permit only. Armed guards stood watch. There was a checkpoint at the entrance. As soon as our bus approached the gate, the attendant vigorously waved us away. I told the driver to pull up to the gate. The driver opened the door. The guard blurted out, "This is a private club. You can't come in here." I slurred, "I know. We're here to see Bak. Tell him Kesha's outside." The guard radioed to the bouncer. A minute or so later, Bak emerged and waved us in.

McHugh Construction

Katya, a friend from work, called me at home around 10 p.m. on a weekday. She was panicking. After some kind of seminar, she and another co-worker, Anya, went to the apartment of an American, who she said dosed them with something. Anya was crawling on the floor. I could hear her howling gibberish. Katya said she was losing control as well. I asked where she was. She told me they were in a 4th floor apartment that faced the street, somewhere near Patriarch's Ponds. She didn't know the street name, only that there was a blue ford with yellow 004 license plates[1] parked in front of the building.

It was very unusual in many ways. For me to be at home relatively early in the evening, in Moscow, didn't happen. There was so much to do every night, it felt like you were wasting your life by staying in. I considered Katya among my best friends, but why had she called me? The company employed problem solvers. Her grandfather was the Red Army general who liberated Auschwitz. She had connections. Were it not for the fact that numerous men in the office advised me to absolutely shun her romantically, I could have easily considered her forever. I should have asked them why they held that opinion, but never did. I knew she was in trouble and would do anything to help. Loading the Tokarev that I'd received as a bonus for the Beretta, I started jogging towards the section of old Moscow where Katya said she and Anya were. It wasn't far from my apartment.

The first street I guessed was the right one. The Ford was parked out front. I was sure the residents of the building all knew there was an American on the 4th floor, so I ratcheted up the accent, pretending to be a friend. Someone gladly let me in. I knocked on the apartment door and the owner let me in. Katya was not herself, but Anya was delirious and incoherent. The apartment was clean, spacious, renovated, and well-furnished. The guy said he worked for McHugh Construction from Chicago. He claimed that he had not dosed the girls, but instead offered them psilocybin mushrooms, which they ate voluntarily. I called for company cars to pick up the girls and take them home.

Jim, the American, offered to buy a few drinks at a café a few blocks away. I agreed to meet him there in thirty minutes. I wanted to leave the gun. Jim was sitting by himself at a table when I arrived. The bar was counter service only. He went to get us drinks and disap-

---

1 Russia issued three colors of license plates for cars. White was for locals. Red for diplomats. Yellow for foreign company cars. 004 was the designation for USA.

peared. I was about to leave when I heard what sounded like a gunshot behind the building. The back door was open, which made it sound louder. When I stood to go peek around the corner to see if someone had actually been shot or was it fireworks, a gorilla pushed me back down into my seat by my shoulders. I looked up to see prison tattoos on his fists and a rack of gold teeth.

Apartment building on the left, where the mushroom-roofie server lived

I asked what he wanted. He slurred, "We're celebrating. I just got out after eight years." He mentioned some prison I'd never heard of. His rage at the new society was understandable. He could have been sent up for engaging in capitalism, and then he was released into a capitalist society. Kamala Harris did the same type of thing. She put over two thousand people in prison on marijuana violations, bragged about it, admitted to smoking it herself. I can only imagine the emotions her victims felt when they got out of jail to see legal marijuana stores all over town, with people like Kamala pilfering the tax money that those stores generate.

Gold teeth pointed towards another table, where a similar character was looking at me. He looked a bit like Brock Lesnar. Gold teeth told me, "His nickname is 'War.' If he likes you, he likes you. If he doesn't, he will snap your spine." My heart was pounding. There was no reason for these two to target me. It was a case of the wrong place at the wrong time. For a second I thought maybe they worked for Jim. After all, he said he was from Chicago, but there was no benefit to him either.

"You just got out of jail?" I asked, without waiting for an answer, I suggested that I should buy a round of drinks. The convicts were seated between the bar and the exit. When I ordered, I stared the bartender in the eyes, trying to ask with my face, "Are those two worth worrying about?" He conveyed that they were dangerous. I ordered double shots of vodka for them, and water for myself. I did that three times. Once they showed signs of sufficient impairment, I ran. A friend from South Africa often cited the phrase, "Once you're over the wall, keep running," except he usually used it as an excuse to have another drink at the end of the night. That night I kept running until I reached my apartment.

Moscow homicide rates in the early 1990s were said to average around one hundred per day, but they weren't random. People murdered each other over property ownership issues, or to get revenge against power abusers. I couldn't stop thinking about Jim. The Golden Rule compelled me to return and investigate, just not alone. I imagined myself being shot behind a bar and no one seeking justice.

There were several Embassies near my apartment, all of which had diplomatic police posted 24/7. The guard across the street directed me to a police station about a block away, saying most people can't find it. It was in a courtyard with only a mall sign. He drew me a little map. The two officers there said they wouldn't even talk to me about anything until they had my passport info, home address, and phone number. Protocol is protocol, they said. They seemed completely disinterested in my story. They offered me to ride with them back to the scene of the possible crime. I accepted.

En route, they stopped a person, who was just walking on the sidewalk alone. They opened his backpack and took from it whatever they wanted, threatening that if he dared to file a complaint, they would do worse. Georgian George's bag of shit was open. It stank. They parked on the Ring Road (Sadovoe Koltso[2]) about ten feet away from the curb. Gold Teeth and War were still sitting there, drunker than when I left them. War stared at me with glazed eyes. He looked angry, but he probably always did.

My stomach knotted up when one of the cops shook War's hand and asked, "What's up, War? Did you hear any gunshots?" War shook his head no. The police said to me, "See you later." Gold teeth stared at me as I walked with one of the policemen back to their jeep. They told me to have a good night. I asked for a ride back to the station. One of them mockingly asked, "What, do you think we're a taxi service? We're not a taxi service. For $100, we can give you a ride. If you don't have cash, we can even give you credit. We know where you live and have your passport details." I paid.

When I got to my apartment, I loaded the Tokarev and slept with it on a couch, which offered the best angle to shoot anyone trying to enter. I called my friend Gnida (The Louse) whom I knew had a Tommy gun with a round high-capacity magazine. He summarized the evening's adventure as, "Not fun." He told me to stay put, doubting that anyone would show up right away. He predicted that they'd study me for at least a week or two, before pursuing robbery and extortion. In conclusion, he said, "You're either going to have to live somewhere else, pay extortion, or employ bodyguards."

---

2 One of central Moscow's busiest thoroughfares. There are five lanes of traffic in each direction.

The next day in the office, the girls told me their version. They were adamant that the McHugh rep. had not warned them at all that the mushrooms were hallucinogenic. Jim was out of line. He told them only to have a "snack." Because it was a large American company, I decided that before retaliating locally, a letter of complaint should be sent to McHugh's headquarters in Chicago. In the letter I pointed out that our firm was the number one business in the former USSR. I wouldn't find out the other side of the story for fifteen years. It is an understatement that he was lucky Katya didn't use her contacts to pursue justice.

Katya could have requested her stepfather, retired KGB officer Vadim Biryukov, to make life quite unpleasant for the man, who roofied her. I talked her out of it.

Train From Odessa

Marc Rich also had a sugar department. Two Brits worked it in Moscow. They asked me to sign a port agreement for them in Odessa. We had an office there in the semi-circle shaped facade at the top of the "Potemkin" steps on the right. The woman who ran the office there didn't have the authority to sign contracts. It was supposed to be just a formality. We already had a faxed copy of the agreement with rates that the port manager had agreed to.

At the signing, the port handed me an agreement with a rate that was sixty percent higher than what they'd put in the fax. I asked him why they were trying to pull a fast one. He started bullshitting about increased traffic, blah, blah. I told him to get fucked and walked out. Novorossiysk port, also on the Black Sea, handled the sugar for cheaper and without any games. The local rep begged me to placate the guy, claiming, "I have to work with him." I told her, "No. You don't."

When I called Moscow to report what happened, they told me my father was in the hospital after a heart attack. I asked Daniel for an early vacation. When I told him why, he said, "Of course. No brainer. Get going."

They still didn't have any jet fuel. There were no flights. I had to take about a thirty hour train ride to get to Moscow, so I could fly home. On the leg from Odessa to Kiev I shared a berth with two card hustlers who had terrible skills. I kept switching the position of one card, which changed the entire rotation. It was hilarious to watch how they looked at each other when they picked up their cards. Their expressions said, "That's not the way we stacked them." After a few tries, they gave up.

The only thing available from Kiev to Moscow was the equivalent of steerage on a ship. It looked like sailor's stacked horizontally four high to the ceiling on a submarine. Each car was completely cluttered. Dozens of eyes watched as you walked through to make sure nothing was stolen. I had my cd player with me and spent the entire trip listening to music in the bar car with a Bulgarian champagne merchant. I bought and shared a couple cases of beer with several people there. I remember that the Bulgarian really liked Van Morrison's cd "Hymns to the Silence." A couple weeks later he dropped off a case of champagne for me at the Marc Rich office with a nice thank you note.

Before entering my dad's hospital room, a doctor warned me that he might not be the same person. Cautiously opening the door, I heard him on the phone placing a football bet, complaining to the bookie that the spread wasn't fair. He was fine. When he was playing blackjack at a casino about ninety miles north of the city, he had a heart attack, but drove himself home to avoid surgery in a country hospital. He said that when a nurse saw him reading the book, "Inside Spinal Tap" by Peter Ochiogrosso, she commented that maybe he should cut back on pain medication.

Rigged Casino

When dad got discharged from the hospital, I went straight back to the Far East. The Dicker didn't gamble but he started playing blackjack after making friends with the casino staff at the Versailles. It was show gambling, a rigged game. I went to a casino with Gera and overheard him tell the roulette croupier about his wife, "Let her win a couple and then cut her off." The Dicker's Versailles game was no different, except it was blackjack. The place had six blackjack tables, two roulette tables, and some games I didn't know. There were no cameras. Roulette had permanent eyes on it, but blackjack was mostly up to the dealer.

The first time I sat down to play there was at third base on a blackjack table, I gave the dealer $200 and received between $350 and $550 in chips. The randomness came from the need to quickly convert before a pit boss could see. The game would be mostly straight, but the payouts were erratic. If no one was watching, he'd pay a 22. Or the dealer would take a quick peek at the next card, but not flip it. He'd then signal to us whether we wanted it or not. Sometimes it was lose - lose, even with the fix.

A Mafioso type sat between us. As our stacks grew, he was losing steadily. I was at third base and did something normally stupid like ask for a card on a fifteen against the dealer's six. The Russian was properly livid and told me, "Do not take a fucking card." I knew what card was coming, but obviously couldn't tell him that.

I told him, "When you put your money on my spot, then you can play my cards." That made him madder.

He told me, "If you take a card, I will cut off your head and shit down your throat." The Finnish bouncer overheard the man and took position right behind him. I told the dealer, "Hit."

Before even seeing the card, the man shouted, "I will bury you right here" (Я тебя похороню на месте, блядь). I looked at him and saw that he was cross-eyed. I hit twenty-one and laughed at him as the bouncer hauled him out. After cashing out, Dicker and I would go to the 24-hour floating disco, permanently docked in Vladivostok harbor, where we could divvy up the earnings.

I remember being on the boat at five a.m. when they played Neil Diamond's, "Forever in Blue Jeans." I asked out loud to no one, "Why would Russians play Neil Diamond in a dance club?" A younger Irish kid from the Versailles staff couldn't believe my question. "Why? Why?!" he enthusiastically explained: "Because Neil Diamond is the fucking man! I requested this."

Dogfights

After spending more time at the governor's residence, I confessed to Valeria my sincerest affection and admiration for her dog, Stinger. He was an American Staffordshire. When I first saw him, he scared me. I'd never been afraid of a dog. He looked menacing. Valeria knew that I genuinely adored him and tried to force me to get one of Stinger's relatives for myself. She called Stinger's breeder to schedule a meeting with him for me. I knew it would go nowhere. I wasn't going to buy a dog in Vladivostok, but nonetheless agreed to meet him, just to be polite. I doubt Valeria knew it, but the breeder sold dogs to dogfighters. Thinking it was enticing advertising, he showed me a video of a brutal bloody fight between a Pitbull and Staffordshire. To me it was nauseating, needless evil.

Hunting Ussuriysk Tigers

After telling the Nakhodka crew about pheasants at Lake Khanka with the Vladivostok gang, they misunderstood that I enjoyed hunting and forced me to go on what they called a "nature excursion." We drove about 40 miles inland and arrived at a cramped observation post that was in a forest at the base of substantial hills and bluffs, but not mountains. The structure appeared designed for three people. There were five of us, plus a guide, who was the manager of the Ussuriysk Tiger Reserve, commonly referred to as Siberian Tigers.

Hunting was forbidden there. The people in our group intended to go tiger hunting. A tiger skin on the black market was worth up to $100,000. Well-meaning, but naive, people donate money for causes like saving tigers from extinction. I'd guess that tiger saving funds from organizations like the WWF were partially spent on accountants, who certified that all expenditures were compliant with whatever agreement was made before getting the funds from donors.

When I found out that we were going on a tiger hunt I asked if they'd lost their minds. "Not at all," Slava replied. "We brought snow pants for you and an extra gun." I couldn't believe I was where I was. I wondered what would happen if an honest game warden caught me walking the tiger reserve with a loaded gun. I'd have to speak like Al Gore when he was caught taking bribes from Asians, telling investigators, "I didn't realize I was in a Buddhist Temple." If there was a tiger police, I doubted they'd be as corrupt as those who ignored Al Gore's blatant misdeeds. "I didn't realize I was walking around a Siberian tiger reserve with a loaded gun," was probably not going to be a convincing alibi.

The night before the hunt, we drank vodka in the shack. The Jaeger "Meister" (Hunt master) demonstrated a rifle. He pulled the trigger and a bullet went through the ceiling and roof. When my ears stopped ringing, I let loose, regretting my words as I spoke them. "Look at you, huddled in a tiny house, the fucking door of which can't be opened without three people standing up. The "master" hunter here can't handle his gun. He shot a goddamned hole through the roof. This place is supposed to be a sanctuary and you assholes use it like it's an aquarium to go fishing in. Are you for real?" They listened, smirked, and shrugged their shoulders, as if I had said nothing. The drinking continued.

I dreaded the hunt. First, I did not want to shoot a tiger. I also did not want to get attacked by one. When they gave me a Makarov pistol, I asked if they expected me to shoot the tiger in the eye for protection, because a body shot from a Makarov would do little more than irritate a 600 pound animal. The forest and hills there were pristine and beautiful. Snow was occasionally waist-deep. When it was, it required a lot of energy to trudge forward. After a mile or so my heart was pounding out of my chest like I'd never experienced. I was sweating inside the snow suit. I gave up and turned around. There were no other tracks in the snow besides mine so I couldn't get lost.

I sat in the hut alone for seven or so hours. The group returned after dark and announced that they had shot an izzubr. I didn't know what that was. A zubr is a European bison, but there weren't any of those near the Pacific coast. I knew what a zubr was from the Polish vodka, Zubrovka, which was banned in the U.S. because it had a piece of grass in the bottle. It used to be like Cuban cigars, coveted because it was forbidden. I loved Zubrovka vodka because of their advertising slogan, "Flavored with the herb most beloved by the European bison." Who wouldn't love it? If it's good enough for the European bison, who else needs to endorse it?

They waited for the izzubr meat to be frozen enough for shaving to make Stroganina. I was confused. I knew Stroganina is a Siberian fish dish. Izzubr was a local species of deer. While it was still warm they skinned and gutted it, leaving outside to freeze. They shaved raw venison into a bowl and poured boiling vinegar over it. After sprinkling a little salt and pepper on it, they handed me some on a fork. I thought they were trying to haze me, or pull a prank. After some convincing, I tasted it. It was excellent. I ate a lot of it. I'd gladly eat it again.

Cynical political theater for profit is rampant the world over. Bilking the budget and abusing peoples' goodwill in Primorye to "save" tigers is just one example. Protecting the environment has to be the world's number one con. Raising money to keep the world clean and healthy is sacrosanct for political profiteers. How many people actually investigate what good is done to accomplish stated goals. The combination of a cash cow and a chicken that lays golden eggs turns a lot of people "green." When a politician claims their opponent is opposed to clean air, water, etc. hide your wallet. You can be certain there's cash flowing based on bogus goals.

It could be an urban myth, but many people in the Russian Far East repeated this scenario to me. It seems believable. The Russian nuclear naval fleet stationed in Primorye was rumored to sink barrels of depleted uranium into the Sea of Japan in the Pacific Ocean. Japanese scientists, monitoring the safety of their fishing territories, supposedly determined the source of the radiation was the Russian Navy. The Japanese government requested Russia to stop dumping. Russia replied that they didn't have a budget to build a storage facility for nuclear waste, but for two hundred or so million dollars they would build one. Japan provided the funds. Russia continued to dump, using a tiny portion of Japan's two hundred million dollars, to buy more barrels for dumping.

Marc Rich Ousted

Having been away for almost three weeks, I returned for work at Marc Rich Moscow and saw that the office was unrecognizable. There had been a mass mutiny. The company splintered into three main new entities, Glencore, Trafigura, and Xtrata. I knew nothing about internal politics. I was happy fixing problems and happier that I never had to attend corporate meetings. It was a great gig. I'd built relationships from Kamachatka to Kaliningrad and everywhere in between. Now, it seemed there was no one who needed them.

An older Englishman had taken over Daniel's office. I'd never heard of him. He claimed to be interim CEO of the new configuration of Marc Rich + Co. He knew about me. He told me, "First thing I need from you is a port agreement in Ventspils for crude." Perni's oil department managed that in the past. I jumped on a plane to Ventspils and went to see my friends in the dry cargo port, hoping they'd open doors for me.

They explained that crude throughput was run 100% by the company Transneft in Moscow. The Soviet national pipeline for all oil belonged to them. Nobody in Ventspils had any authority to make a crude deal. Considering that I'd taken Vladimir Lenin off their hands, there was no reason for them to deceive me. They warned me that if Transneft even heard that I was sniffing around their port and thought I was trying to procure crude, they might kill me. Their advice was to leave town without even speaking to anyone at the oil port.

I returned to Moscow and reported to the interim CEO what reliable and trusted people had told me in Ventspils, i.e. that we needed to soften up Moscow. His reply was straightforward. "Are you gonna be a pussy or are you gonna do your job? Go the fuck back to Ventspils and get me a crude agrement." That was an easy decision.

I had never tested the limits of the Marc Rich corporate American Express card. That day was a good day for doing so. I left the office and rounded up as many friends as were still around. One of the top restaurants at the time was Le Chalet. I don't remember all who attended the farewell dinner, but Voronchuk and Strogy were definitely there. Chuk had jumped ship from Marc Rich to a grain venture near Rostov, where he didn't have to rely on Ukrainian transportation anymore.

We started with a $28,000 bottle of 1969 Domaine de la Romaneé-Conti and then drank the second and only other one of it they had. We then worked our way down the captain's list until we emptied it. Le Chalet prepared steak tartare tableside. The server's command of English was not strong. We all took turns commending the staff's ability to beat meat. There was a point in the dinner where I experienced a little bun-clenching fear the moment I thought that maybe the card could have been canceled, but then remembered that I had used it earlier that day to buy a plane ticket in Riga. At the end of the evening, the table was covered in open bottles and stemware. It was the first time I remember noticing that the price and enjoyability of a wine are not connected. There was an "inexpensive" Pomerol for about $700 that was my favorite.

I used the Amex one last time to buy airline tickets, a visit to Klempner in Istanbul and a return ticket to Minneapolis. I regret not using the opportunity to fly the Concorde before it was decommissioned. I only thought of it afterwards.

For me it had been a dream job. No corporate meetings. No employee rule book. People told me what they wanted done and I did it. It was like working for General George Patton, who said, "Never tell people how to do things. Tell them what to do and they will surprise you with their ingenuity."

"Best Bar In America"

When I was in Russia, friends stayed in my house with reduced rent with the understanding that I could come back, or move back, whenever I wanted. After Marc Rich + Co evaporated, Nitz was staying in my house. His nickname was "Stormy" because he and his woman would get engaged, split, get back together, and then split again more than any other couple. When I left him the key to my house, he and his girlfriend were living together, but I knew for certain he would move into my house, which he did. I'd known Nitz since we were about six years old, but I never knew he was adopted. After he watched a TV show about an agency that connected adoptees with biological parents, he hired them.

Our favorite destination bar in Minneapolis was Nye's Polonaise. It was launched by an immigrant from Poland in 1950, a block from the east bank of the Mississippi River. There were two separate music rooms, the piano bar and the polka lounge. There was a large dining room next to the piano bar that had a row of gold speckled vinyl booths shaped sort of like baby grand pianos over which, hanging from the ceiling, were light fixtures that appeared to be made of stone and filled with translucent crystals of red, blue, yellow, and orange. We liked to wash down the pork knuckle and sauerkraut with Zywiec or Okocim. On the wall behind the piano player an oil painting of Frederic Chopin wearing a black tuxedo on a red background lent an air of sophistication. The carpet was burgundy red. The coat check was always attended, even in Summer. In the basement below the piano bar there was a banquet hall. Above the landing of the split staircase leading down to restrooms and the banquet hall, a three foot by four foot black and white photo blow up of Al Nye's daughter was framed. She was wearing a bikini and had been superimposed into a martini glass, or maybe she'd posed in a really large one. The bar's motto was "Home of the jumbo cocktail."

The entrance to the polka lounge was a set of swinging doors over which two ornate accordions sat in a glass case with the words "Polka Lounge" written underneath. When you walked in, you were on the dance floor. The front of the small stage was maybe twenty-five feet away. It was always a three piece band, led by Ruth Adams, who sat on the right. She didn't have a lot of teeth, was overweight and wore sleeveless shirts, but was a virtuoso on the accordion. Her long-time drummer, Al Ophus, played until he was almost ninety years old. The trumpet player liked to blow what he called "BRT's," belly-rubbing tunes.

The main piano player for decades was "Sweet" Lou Snider. Nye's baby grand had a ledge for cocktails around it that could fit seven or eight people. They were coveted seats. Lou kept a tip jar next to the stack of song requests. She was an expert at knowing who'd tipped what and requested which song, even if she hadn't been looking when it was placed there. Esquire Magazine declared Nye's, "America's Best Bar[1]. Every type of person went to Nye's. Many of the people who worked there were in their seventies and had never worked anywhere else, nor wanted to.

On a Friday night it wouldn't be uncommon for someone to have to wait through fifteen songs to have Lou play their request.

From Ruth with love

Since opening in 1950, Nye's never advertised. It didn't need to. In the early 1990s an investment consortium spent millions of dollars to open a nightclub across the street from Nye's called Mississippi Live. They advertised multiple stages of live music in several genres. Mississippi Live lasted about two years. Hard Rock Cafe also opened and closed in Minneapolis. Its location was across the street from Minneapolis' long-standing premier music club, First Avenue, which is still there.

Nitz sold ads for a local newspaper, the publisher of which got a new nickname when

---

1 https://www.esquire.com/food-drink/bars/reviews/a255/esq1006bestbars-147/

I once got stranded in Frankfurt overnight after missing a connecting flight. I called to check on the state of my house and told Nitz I was in Germany. He said the publisher had a German intern and suggested I send him a postcard written in German just to confuse them both. The postcard was delivered during a staff meeting. Not able to read German, the boss handed the card to the intern. When he read out the translated salutation, "Liebe Süße Hosen" and spoke it in English with an astonished look, all present thought the moniker fitting. From that moment on, his nickname was "Sweet Pants."

Nitz hadn't been able to sell an ad to Nye's, but had convinced them to do a promotion with the paper. His feat was envied by colleagues in the ad biz. His success probably stemmed from the fact that he had developed an incredible bond with "Sweet" Lou. Nitz could walk in on a Friday night, and when Lou spotted him, she'd stop to recognize Nitz's entrance by playing the first fifteen seconds or so of his all-time favorite song, "The Girl From Ipanema," and then go back to what she was playing. With Lou, Nitz had what we called "Jay You Ice," Juice.

On the night of Nitz's promotional event, the phone rang just as he was about to walk out the door. It was the parent locating agency. They'd just spoken with his mother and grandmother, reporting that they were both beyond impatient to speak to him. He tried to postpone the call until the next day. The agency told him that he probably didn't understand how desperate they were just to hear his voice if even briefly. They were insane with anticipation. I never use the word, but the agency beseeched him to at least say hello to his grandmother, whom he called.

She responded to his introduction by saying, "We have been looking forward to this call all of your life." He apologized that he had to continue the conversation the next day because he worked in advertising, and she probably wouldn't understand, but he'd scored a new client called Nye's Polonaise. His grandmother said, "Are you kidding? Lou Snider has been my best friend for decades."

When Stormy and his gal finally got married, they hired the Ruth Adams band to play at their wedding. He gave them a banner for the event that they kept behind the stage until their last day at Nye's, "The World's Most Dangerous Polka Band."

The producer of the Jon Stewart show was a Minneapolis native and Ruth Adams fan. She invited them to New York, all expenses paid and with pay. Ruth brushed off the offer immediately, saying curtly, "Not interested." Al and Dick had to lobby her to agree to perform on national television. I have original video footage of the band performing at Nye's that I took during a snowstorm. During several songs there is no one on the dance floor.

After a day or two of being home, word got out I was in Minneapolis doing nothing. A friend named Dap called me on a weekday around lunch, asking if I wanted to day drink. He worked at a radio station called Cities

97. When digital recording first hit the music industry, the station he worked at started recording and releasing compilation CDs of popular songs. Famous acts would record different versions of their hits in the station's studio, like a precursor to NPR's Tiny Desk but without video. Dap used the station's equipment to record a cd called "Live at Nye's." It contains ten songs by Lou and ten by the Ruth Adams Band. Because I funded the pressing, they listed me as "Executive Mixologist" in the credits.

Dap said the reason he wanted to go drinking was because he'd been fired. A competitor of Cities 97 had hired him as program director for more money and more flexibility. He went with the competitor. As soon as the other station's numbers rose, they fired Dap. Checking my schedule to confirm I had nothing to do, I met him in a bar.

Once, and only once, I had the honor to play a duet of "Misty" on Nye's piano with Lou Snider.

Nitz and I with a Nye's waitress in front of a poster of Al Nye, founder and owner of "America's Best Bar."

Lou and Nitz

Road Trip Across America

After a couple drinks, Dap and I decided that a road trip to Mount Rushmore for photographs was in order. Neither of us had been there. The place is in South Dakota, which borders Minnesota, so we assumed we could go there and back, lickety split. After drinking a bit in the bar, we had beers in the car and were headed west. Before even reaching the interstate beltway, I got stopped by the police for speeding. We weren't even ten miles from downtown. We felt like we'd dodged a bullet, though, because the officer hadn't noticed the open beer cans and we were in a convertible with its top down.

After entering South Dakota, we assumed we'd be at Mount Rushmore within an hour or so. In reality it was 400 miles away. We stopped at several local bars on the way to check out the characters. In the first one, a man at the end of the bar announced loudly to the bartender, "You oughta open up a barber shop so you can get that long hair outta here." Dap's hair was below his shoulders.

We stopped at Wall Drug where I bought several stuffed jackalopes. We took pictures with Mt. Rushmore behind and a helicopter ride over the Black Hills. We already crossed about a quarter of the country, so why not keep going? We weren't over the wall, but we were going to keep running. We went to the Great Salt Lake. Because of Utah's liquor laws, we high-tailed it to Arizona and the Grand Canyon. On a perfectly straight, empty downhill highway with maximum visibility, I decided to find out what the car's top speed was. I was driving a two-door Mercedes. Going about 115 mph, a Trooper appeared on our tail with his light flashing. There were no trees, rocks or vegetation for him to have hid behind. It was baffling where he could have come from.

Jackalope. Native to western S. Dakota, Wyoming and Montana. Rarely seen in the wild

The officer offered me a gentleman's agreement. In exchange for giving me a citation that showed my speed at 14 mph over the limit, I had to promise him to not contest it and just pay the fine. I agreed. When we drove off, Dap noticed that the lid of our beer cooler had blown off. Crushed empty beer cans and full ones were visible. He could have ticketed us for that as well. We went North up through the Grand Tetons in Idaho and through Yellowstone Park in Montana. We were thinking of listening to some music in New Orleans and headed south. From a hotel in Colorado Springs, I checked my answering machine. There was a fresh message from Mountain Hebe, telling me to get to Switzerland ASAP.

He had worked in the aluminum department at Marc Rich Moscow. When the upheaval happened, he jumped ship to Gerald Metals, which was at the time the world's number one copper trading company. Mountain was running their Moscow office. For reasons that White Nights found out about, Gerald's Moscow office operated under a division based in Lausanne, Switzerland. Minneapolis based commodity company, Cargill, also operates internationally from a branch office in Switzerland.

I called the Hebe to ask what's up. He said, "We need you in Russia. Fly to Geneva as soon as possible. There will be a formality of an interview at our office in nearby Lausanne. You're hired. You will be working for me in Moscow." It's similar work to what we were doing at Rich" I questioned the urgency. He just said, "Please. Be on a flight tomorrow."

Figuring I'd be away from the U.S. for at least three years, which is how long speeding tickets stay on driving records, and I already had two on that trip, I resolved to drive as fast as I could from Colorado Springs to Minneapolis, which was just under a thousand miles. I told Dap my plan. He said, "Do it."

I didn't see one police car in Colorado and only one in Nebraska. We averaged almost 110 mph for the first six hundred miles. We stopped for gas twice. In central Nebraska on I-80 I passed a trooper parked in his car going about 130 mph. He was stopped in the middle of eastbound and westbound lanes, which were about one hundred yards apart. I detected his head turn as it followed us blowing past. I remained committed to not slowing down. The trooper did not chase us.

Outside of Des Moines, Iowa, when there was only about 250 miles left, or what should have been a maximum of a three hours drive, I felt certain that the goal of a thousand miles in less than ten hours was a fait accompli. Then we ran into a parade of assholes, driving the speed limit side by side, making it impossible to pass. These people have no idea that there are places like the German Autobahn, with no speed limits, where people adhere to the motto, "Links gehen. Rechts stehen," which I'd translate as, "Left lane go. Right lane slow." I doubt many of them know that the rearview mirror can also be looked into while going forward. Ever since the Iowa letdown, whenever I see an emergency vehicle that has its siren blazing and flashing lights on, but is stuck behind an oblivious driver who won't let it pass, I automatically think the car in front has a driver from Iowa. Dap and I arrived in Minneapolis about ten hours and twenty minutes after leaving Colorado Springs, without a speeding ticket.

Road Trip

Gerald Metals

Responding to Mountain Hebe's distress signal, I made my way to Lausanne for what had to be among the shortest successful job interviews ever. A petite Indian woman ran Gerald Trade, a Swiss subsidiary of Gerald Metals, which was based in Stamford, Connecticut, about forty miles from New York City. I flew home to pack as many things as I could. On the way to Moscow, I stopped for a brief meeting with Gerald Lennard, owner of the company.

Marc Rich was the king of oil. Gerald was the king of copper. He had twenty offices worldwide. We referred to the company as Gerald and the man as Gerry. He looked to me a bit like the nuclear plant director from the cartoon series, "The Simpsons." The topic of our conversation was his only obsession, copper, purchasing more copper and the transportation of copper. The company traded numerous other commodities. For Gerry those were only relevant activities because they generated revenue to support the copper business. Because he spoke in a New York dialect, Gerry pronounced the metal as coppa.

Mountain Hebe ran Gerald's Moscow and Almaty offices. Before Marc Rich he worked for Marvin Davis at 20th Century Fox. Marvin and Marc were friends through oil. The Hebe's way of doing business was a deviation from the haphazard, unpredictable style that was prevalent in Russia. He had an MBA from Wharton. The Gerald manager in Almaty was also a former Marc Rich Moscow employee. He was the Serb who'd vacated the apartment that I took over. The one that Toolshed's wife designed. We made up a Kazakh-sounding name for the Almaty office manager, calling him Zoranbaev.

The Hebe and his wife, whom I called Linty, had just moved out of an apartment on the Moscow River across from Gorky Park. Their first child, Drewshska was just born and they needed a more child friendly place. It was perfect timing. I didn't have to go apartment hunting. Russians are into custom license plates and easy phone numbers. The phone number of my new apartment was 245-2000. When I gave it out as my home number, most people didn't believe me. After writing that number on a piece of paper and handing it to a woman, she sneered at me and said, "Yea right. And my number is one hundred twenty-three, forty-five, sixty-seven."

Gerald's aluminum trader in Moscow had a last name that meant "Juices" in Russian. Mr. Juices was eternally mopey. If you asked him how things were, he had two answers: bad and very bad. His demeanor reminded me of

Ben Stein's teacher role in the movie "Ferris Bueller's Day Off." The urgent problem that Mountain had called about was in Nakhodka port. Juices had purchased something like 5,000 tons of aluminum scrap and sold it to a customer in South Korea. The supplier sent the cargo to port with a customs classification of aluminum ingots. Because it was scrap, customs refused to allow the port to load it for export. The port was heaping on daily storage fees and likely sharing the proceeds with their friends in the customs office. The metal had been stuck in port for over a month. Juices told me that he visited Nakhodka customs, offered them cash, but they pretended to operate in accordance with the law. He said they derisively called the lot of metal, "Frying pans," because of its shape.

I called a contact in Nakhodka and asked if he knew anything about frying pans. He said, "Of course. Buttstick's been bragging about bilking some company over them for a month." When I told him I'd joined Gerald, he laughed and asked, "Does that mean those are **your** frying pans?" A day or so later they were declared ingots and shipped to Busan, South Korea. On Marc Rich's dime, I'd accompanied the man who arranged the release of the frying pans to the 1992 World Cup match between Russia and Brazil, in San Francisco. There were a few others in the group, too. On the way to the World Cup, we stopped in Minneapolis where I got us 10th row seats for Pink Floyd's Division Bell concert. He and his friends were huge fans of the band. Back then, the concert culture was that guards ignored smoking and concertgoers passed around lit joints to one another. When the first song was over, I looked at my Russian entourage to see how they'd liked it. Every one of them was slit eyed and smirking. They gave the act a big thumbs up. I took him fishing on Leech Lake. After that, we went to Las Vegas. I mention those things, because favors earn favors. Marc Rich's backing deserved the credit for the good will they showed Gerald and its frying pans.

Hiring a Roof

The mid-1990s Russia was likely the peak of the "Wild Wild East" era. Gerald Moscow employed a couple former KGB officers, but had no formal roof, aka paid protectors. The entire country was a criminal enterprise. Small time hustlers and big time syndicates sized each other up and shook each other down all day every day. If you didn't have a roof, you would soon be paying someone to be yours. Smaller businesses like shops and restaurants were hit especially hard.

A lot of bluff and bluster was involved. Someone seeking protection payments would hand their card to a business and request that the owner's roof make contact. The two would then discuss who was tougher. If the roof was weak, there'd be a new, more expensive roof. You couldn't go to the police. If you told them you were roofless and someone was shaking you down, you'd be paying for police protection.

There was no Dun & Bradstreet or roof rating system. You had to know a guy who knew a guy. Mountain let me handle finding a roof. A couple trusted friends referred me to a "Trading" company, run by Mikhail Golovatov, whom they claimed had created and commanded Alpha Group, KGB specialists in hostage rescue and anti-terrorism. His credentials, they bragged, included leading the team that assassinated Afghan President Amin in 1979. His organization sounded promising.

A friend gave me Mr. Golovatov's business card, whom I called to arrange a meeting. His office was between the Kremlin and TASS in an average looking apartment building that had been converted to offices. I walked up a few flights of stairs until I saw a GTL plaque in front of me. The roof was called Gorandel Trading Ltd. I rang the buzzer of the door in front of me where the GTL sign was. The door to my right opened. The person looked me over and asked what I wanted. I said that I might be in the wrong place, but was looking for Mikhail Golovatov. Then the door behind me opened. A well-dressed young lady said she would escort me to the general.

GTL
Gorandel Trading Limited

Michael Golovatov
DIRECTOR

22 Gertsena Street
Moscow
Russia

Lithuania convicted in absentia the former KGB officer of committing in 1991 war crimes and crimes against humanity. Mr. Golovatov passed away August 1, 2022

We spoke for about two minutes, when his phone rang. Right away, he apologized that something urgent had just popped up. He had to go to a quick meeting near Moscow State U. He offered for me to ride along with him. I accepted. En route to his meeting, I told him we were looking for extraction capabilities and a general roof. Basically, a number to call when lawyers and money weren't sufficient. Yes, of course, was his answer.

A traffic policeman stuck out his baton and motioned for the general to pull his car over. Not slowing for one second, Mikhail stared at the cop, and waved his finger slowly. The policeman looked at his license plate and saluted. Russian license plates were coded. The Kremlin's bodyguards and hitmen were said to drive cars with EKX on their plates. EKX on the streets was said to stand for **Ебу Кого Хочу** (I fuck whom I want).

Riding around Moscow with Slava, one of Mikho's deputies, the police stopped him in Moscow. I was in the passenger seat and pulled out some cash that I showed to Slava. That made him mad. He waved his open hand down, gesturing to put the money away. He told me, "I've got this." He started digging in the glove compartment and took out a small bi-fold cardboard ID. The policeman looked at it and motioned for him to drive away. Jokingly, I asked if he had shown a "Get out of jail free" card. He handed it to me. It read: "DO NOT ARREST," and was signed and stamped by the minister of internal affairs.

The slang for that type of ID in Russian is an "All-terrain pass." (**Вездеход**.)

Gen. Golovatov drove us back to his office. We signed a service agreement. He assigned two Alpha soldiers, Oleg and Borya, to Gerald's contacts. No last names. No address. No office. Just phone numbers. They were supposed to be ready twenty-four hours a day. I never saw Mikhail Golovatov again, but we continued to pay him for many years. Oleg had the build of a bowling ball. He was very muscular and round. Borya's appearance and temperament were reminded me of characters played by Vinnie Jones in Guy Ritchie movies.

The first time I made a service request, it wasn't business related. The Dicker took Vika, the receptionist at the Vlad Motor Inn, for a romantic getaway in Moscow. Albert was enraged beyond words when Vika teased him about it. She was perhaps drunk, evil, or both but she even told Albert the address of the apartment where they were staying. Albert flew to Moscow. The Dicker answered the intercom at the apartment, wondering who could be calling him. Albert angrily announced that he was on his way up to kill them both.

The Dicker called me in a panic. I promised to help. Oleg answered. It was embarrassing to ask him to intervene in a love triangle. Oleg did not want to take the job. I offered a bonus that I'd make the Dicker pay. Oleg promised he would promptly take care of Albert. By the time Oleg showed up, Albert had backup. Oleg described the two of them as Far East rednecks. They hadn't even been able to get inside the building. They all went upstairs and started talking to the Dicker through the door. Oleg assessed the situation and asked, "What in the fuck are two idiots fighting over? This woman is obviously a run-of-the-mill slut? You'd both be better off without her. She's cheating on you both." The scene reminded me of the classic Little Milton blues song, "Your Wife Is Cheating On us." Albert and the Dicker made peace and sent the girl packing. Toolshed should have been there to tell her she'd had it.

Gerald Moscow Expands

Our Moscow staff doubled and we moved to a new space that was a block away from Lip's office. His son Pablo was working for Gerald as well. One of the new hires, Denis, was the son of a Soviet diplomat. He used a cigarette holder, wore gold chains and darkened eyeglasses. He replied to just about every suggestion that there might be a competitor or obstacle by saying "Fuck'em in the mouth." When he got his first bonus of $50k he spent it all on a Volvo, even though he lived with his parents. The Hebe suggested he insure the car, Denis said "Fuck insurance in the mouth!" Ten days later he totaled the car, but wasn't hurt physically.

Walking past the conference room, Denis motioned me in and shut the door. His look suggested he had mafia or financial trouble, like he was struggling to say what was bothering him. He asked me if it was customary in America for a person to fart without remorse or apologizing. "Excuse me?" I asked. His question was completely unexpected.

He said, "I will not fly with the Hebe ever again. We just returned from Tashkent. He farted the entire flight. Denis said that Uzbek shepherds were looking around in horror, trying to determine the source of the malodorous wafts. Denis pretended to sleep, making sure he breathed through his mouth. As Denis sat with his eyes shut, Mountain continued dropping air bombs without mercy. Angry passengers glared in every direction. Mountain said of the flight that when passengers made eye contact with him, pleading with their expressions to quelch the source of the stench, he pointed with disgust at sleeping Denis. When they landed in Moscow, Denis said numerous passengers scolded him for his bad manners and lack of bowel control.

Jackalope In St. Petersburg

I brought with me to Russia a couple of the stuffed Jackalopes I'd bought at Wall Drug, while on the road trip with Dap. I presented one to the export manager, whom we called Uncle Vic, during St. Petersburg's Port's daily planning session held in the dispatcher's conference room. The planning session was the only time of day all the department heads were together in one place. I walked in without saying anything and set the jackalope in front of Uncle Vic. I told him it was a present from the American west and walked out. A few people were laughing. Others examined it inquisitively with their eyes.

Later in the day, I ran into several people who'd been at the planning meeting. Almost all shook their heads and laughed, saying "That was a funny gift. Well done." And then after a short pause, ask "Do they really exist?"

An exceedingly rare flying jackalope being inspected by a native of Tblisi.

Kazakh Zinc

Gerald entered into a "Management" agreement for two zinc smelters in Eastern Kazakhstan, Leninogorsk and Ust-Kamenogorsk. The Soviet Union's major assets had only been private for two or three years. Ownership battles were often deadly. Political uncertainty meant that even those ventures with no legal disputes had to worry about nationalization, i.e. the return of socialism and the preventable economic misery it always results in. Another threat to profit projections was the mafia component. Whose crystal ball could predict how long one's roof could stave off suitors. Those in control wanted to monetize their position of power quickly. Long-term development and reinvestment plans were generally not considered wise strategies, except by people like Mikhail Khodorkovsky, who was the country's richest person.

After 75 years of non-stop government strangulation, former Soviet citizens were testing the boundaries of societal structures. The elimination of government controls had unleashed a flood of wealth. That was an undeniable fact. In a short time, Moscow became home to more billionaires than any other city. Lawmakers had no business experience. Corrupt courts were expected to make rulings about scenarios that hadn't yet been fully codified, or were poorly thought out in the first place. The paucity of impartial law enforcement created a widespread get rich quick mentality.

The Hebe and I flew to Almaty to negotiate the zinc deal. We ran into ZNB at the airport, who unusually didn't have a driver that day. We offered him to ride with us. The road into the city wasn't a full-fledged highway, but a three lane boulevard each way with an island of trees down the middle. The flight from Moscow arrived around six a.m. Car traffic was mostly non-existent. Almaty is at the base of a mountain. The ride from the airport is a constant upward slope. In the middle of our conversation and for no apparent reason, our driver stopped in the left lane and accelerated as fast as I'd ever seen anyone go in reverse. I looked at ZNB, confused. He pointed ahead. There was a canvas sided panel truck, with "Bread" written on it that had intentionally bumped a shiny new Audi sedan. When the Audi stopped, masked men with AKs jumped out of the back and emptied their magazines into the car. The likelihood of survivors was zero. None of us, including the driver, reported witnessing anything.

Gerald bought the right to profit from the two zinc smelters for two years. Projections indicated they'd generate $1.5 billion in revenue and we could expect to earn between 8% and 10%. Gerry didn't care. It was a zinc deal. His focus was copper, Coppa! Gerry was famous for a short attention span about non-copper related topics and butchering foreign names. Ust-Kamenogorsk and Leninogorsk were comingled in his mind. He referred to both as Lemonogorsk. Kazakhstan was Kekostan. Uzbekistan was part of Kekostan. Kazakhstan's main copper smelter was called Dzhezkazgan. He called it Jack-o-stan. The other copper factory, Balkhash, he called "Ball-scratch."

Taking phone calls from Gerry was a source of fear and entertainment. He tended to explode in anger easily. Whenever Gerry was on the phone, Mountain put him on speaker and summoned us in to listen. It didn't matter if there were 20,000 tons of zinc en route to port and 2,500 of copper. If you told him about any other metal or factory name first, his reaction would be a rage-filled variation of, "Jack-o-stan. Crapostan. I don't give a fuck-o-stan. Where's my COPPA?!"

The unwritten deal we made to get the zinc smelters was we'd deliver three million USD cash. We agreed to be three separate bag men, taking one million each. We weren't worried, but it was a precaution in case someone got robbed. When my turn came up, a guy in Lausanne we called Whorewhacker was supposed to deliver the money to me in Moscow. I had promised a top Kazakh government official I would be in his office Monday morning with the cash. Whorewhacker called me in Moscow about 2 p.m. on the Friday he was supposed to be there. He reported a problem. Banks in Lausanne and Geneva had run out of cash USD. The only place he could grab a million was Zurich. Going to Zurich meant he couldn't deliver to Moscow. He told me I had to come pick it up at his house near Geneva.

Whorewhacker greeted me as I exited customs. He validated his parking at the automated system. We jumped in his Porsche 911 and set off for his house. He took the car up to about 50 mph in the parking lot and was headed straight through the crossbar at the payment booth. "Dude. Stop!!" I yelled. "What the fuck? This is a parking lot." He slammed on the brakes and skidded right up to the cross arm, stopping just in time. It was like a staged stunt. He inserted the ticket. As the gate opened, he looked at me and slightly slurred, "I thought we were on the highway on-ramp. I forgot." I could see in his eyes that he'd consumed more than drinks. It was Saturday, after all, and he'd been at the Montreux Jazz Festival.

His house was in Switzerland, but the nearest village to him was in France, the small town of Divonne. I relaxed a little when we turned off the main highway by Coppet and more slowly headed uphill on a winding road. The slope to the right was becoming increasingly steep. Fenced in fields of crops and animal pastures were on the left. Traffic was very light. The deep slope on the right was substantial and made me nervous with an impaired driver. We went around a right curve. A car pulled out from a road on the left and entered our lane. It stopped in front of us. As Whorewhacker drove into the left lane to pass the stopped car, it suddenly turned left again to get back on the road it had just exited. They hit our car and knocked us off the road to the left. We went through a fence and stopped in a pasture. Luckily there was no mud. The ground was hard enough that we could drive out, but the others yelled to us to not move the car until the police arrived. Waiting for the police, a lot of finger pointing went on. In my opinion Whorewhacker had driven perfectly.

He guided me away from the others and told me, "You have to say you were driving." I couldn't believe my ears. I told him I had been drinking all day and didn't want to experience Swiss strictness. He repeated it again, adding, "I am wasted. I already have a Swiss DWI. If I get another, like right now, they will take me to jail. The million dollars you need is at home in my safe. I give that combination to nobody. So, back to square one. You have to say you were driving." I was not pleased, but agreed to take the charge.

The police didn't show up for over 30 minutes. By then I hadn't drunk anything for a couple hours. The police exited their car and asked for Les conducteurs (the drivers). "Oui! C'est moi," I answered. The three people in the other car protested and said "No no no. The other was the driver." I repeated, "J'etais le conducteur." The police interviewed us separately. I don't know French well. It strained my language skills to explain what happened. When the policeman was satisfied with my statement, he summarized it in English, "You were driving up the hill. A car came out and stopped in your lane. You went around. They made a u-turn and hit your car. Is that correct?" I was cursing him in my mind for having forced me to sound like Jen Psaki in French. I forgave him when he let us go without any citations.

It surprised me to see that Whorewhacker had other types of green in his safe room, four or so pounds of marijuana. He claimed that weed was not a crime in Switzerland, which was not true. The next day he drove me back to the Geneva airport, sober. I flew through Frankfurt with a million dollars in cash, aka "Nothing to declare." It never entered my mind that it was a really bad idea to let someone know where and when you'd be with a lot of cash. There could be a bad actor anywhere. But deliveries were so common, I didn't even think about getting robbed, or killed. You could order someone whacked for peanuts, like ten thousand dollars. But the thought that someone might kill me for the million I was carrying never entered my mind. In retrospect it was a blatant failure of logic. I fell asleep on the flight, leaving the bag in the overhead compartment.

Privatization, Sort Of

To mask enormous profits from the zinc smelters, those in control issued press releases about Gerald's expertise in international marketing and how the company added value to the long ago already operational smelters. They held a Q & A session at Ust-Kamenogorsk. There was a panel of twelve from the new "Management," sitting at a microphone. The panel was composed of factory managers, a lawyer, and government ministers. The panel took scripted questions from department heads and union leaders, and responded with scripted answers. The only people taking the event seriously were low-level local newspaper reporters.

Family and clan affiliation are extremely important in Kazakhstan, as in most of Central Asia. Let's call Gerald's man in Almaty, "Sultan." His father was cabinet level in the national government and his cousin a director of one of the enterprises. We had to employ him. Sultan had more than an affinity for alcoholic beverages. During the Q & A session, a lady announced her question as leader of the factory's Women's Collective. The assigned actor was about to answer her question, when Sultan started slurring an unscripted reply, "Allow me to speak on behalf of our foreign partners. As an integral part of their team, I can unequivocally assure you that the desires of the Women's Collective will always remain a top priority for us."

I felt a kick on my leg under the table. A panel member passed me a note, which read: "If you let that idiot say one more word, I will kill this deal." Sultan didn't even have a microphone, but carried on about our intentions to address all women's needs. I handed the note to the person next to him, who promptly pulled him down and kept him silent.

To celebrate the deal, something on the lines of a state reception was held in a former retreat for Communist Party elites. It was in the foothills of the Altai Mountains that cross from Kazakhstan into Russia, home to some of the most pristine wilderness in the world.

The dinner hall could seat several hundred, but that day there was one table with approximately 20 seats per side. A head table that was elevated two or so feet had twelve seats all facing the long table. The company told me I was at the head table. I protested that it would be disrespectful. The likes of the governor, deputy prime minister, export minister, factory president, etc. were there. I wasn't senior enough. They claimed it was because my Russian was the strongest.

The real reason they put me there was revealed almost right away. In Kazakh culture, guests are served a boiled ram's head. Everyone knew about the tradition but me. The highest-ranking member, whose parents must not be alive, slices off pieces of it and explains why he chose which part of the head and for whom. He sliced off an ear that still had connective tissue hanging off of it and hair like a wire brush. He put it on my plate, saying the significance of the ear was that I was wise and should be listened to. I was supposed to eat it. With a grin, Mountain Hebe motioned me to start chewing. All eyes were watching and waiting for me to nibble on the ear. I was trying to find a way out of it. Sultan stood up and proposed a toast.

Everyone in the room was incredulous. He was wobbly drunk, but jubilant. His cousin, two seats over, stared in disbelief. After the women's collective calamity, he couldn't imagine Sultan dared speak again. With shot glass in hand, Sultan rambled on about history and nationalities and the women's collective and . . . then he forgot what he was saying. He requested permission to interrupt himself (Alaverdi[1]). While everyone was slack-jawed and staring at Sultan, I stuffed the ram's ear inside my shirt collar.

After the reception we went up to Mountain's presidential suite and smoked a couple joints of my uncle Doug's farm grown weed. Before lighting up, Mountain asked Denis if he thought it was safe to stink up an elite resort with the smell of marijuana. Denis said, "Fuck 'em in the mouth" and lit it. Baked, the Hebe started singing "Rocky Mountain High," repeating the word "high" several times and taking it up an octave each time he said.

The task of analyzing rail and port tariffs fell on me. There were two transportation managers at KME, which was a clearing house for metal produced in Kazakhstan, including all that came from the two smelters, known to Gerry as Lemonogorsk. KME was paying about double the real rates. After not much coercion, they admitted they took a 3% kickback from rail tariffs. They were wasting about $1,500,000 per month. I offered to reduce their rates and give them an 8% kickback.

KME transport didn't trust banks, local or foreign, so we hand delivered cash to them all the time. Bank of New York flew plane loads of cash flights into Moscow weekly. They supplied uncirculated sequential crisp $100 bills. The USD we got in Switzerland was almost always covered in Arabic stamps. Kazakhs and Russians quickly started demanding the fresh U.S. bills.

Gerald's core group in Moscow and Lip took a cut from the rail game. We incorporated an offshore company to act as railway agent. For example, KME paid us $80 per ton for delivery to St. Petersburg, and we paid the railway $40. KME took $6.40 cash and our

---

[1] A Georgian toastmaster is called a Tamada. The culture of making toasts all across the Soviet Union shows deference to the superior Georgians. Alaverdi is a request by someone not making a toast to interject a short aside about whatever topic was at hand. For example if someone was toasting a golfer, someone might request Alaverdi to add, "I saw him make a hole-in-one at Pebble Beach."

team divided up the rest. I advised KME's transportation department to keep our arrangement discreet.

KME's general director and I never interacted one on one. Walking past his office one day, he summoned me in. He told me to sit down and opened the blinds. Pointing out the window, he asked, "Do you see that?"

I replied, "Yes, I see a parking lot."

"No. That!!" It was difficult to ignore the only bright red car in the city at the time. There was a brand new 5 series BMW in the parking lot. He asked me if I had any guesses who had exited that car. Before I could even think about how to deflect, he made a declaration, "I want my share. I've thought about this for days. You are the only person he knows capable of providing him the money to buy that. I don't need any details. Don't say anything. Just know I expect my cut. That's all. Dismissed"

I went to the transport department and asked them if they were fucking stupid. When they heard that the boss wanted a cut, they told me they were going to shop around for lower rates. I was confused. Lower rates meant everyone would earn less. Their "Logic" was that the boss made enough money already, so they wanted to trim him back. From that moment I started calling those two, Khokhli, which is the plural derogatory term in Russian for a vindictive type of Ukrainian. The stereotype is that out of spite a khokhol (singular) will do things that are detrimental even to himself. The Soviet joke about their spiteful nature is that if you asked a khokhol what he would do if he came across a truckload of apples, he'd reply, "I'd eat as many as I could and take a bite out of all the rest." I bought custom made baseball caps at the Mall of America with ХОХОЛ (Khokhol) stitched in and gave them to KME transport. We incorporated another offshore company in a different jurisdiction with a new name. To spite their boss, the KME khokhli signed a rail tariff agreement with our new entity. To make sure the boss got less, they reduced their own take.

Everyday piece of kit

Real Wife

Changing the timeline of a Robert Frost quote, but not the sentiment, "A mother will invest thirty years to make a man. It will take another woman thirty minutes to make a fool of him." For my 30th birthday, we shut down a small nightclub called Marika for the night. A friend from Star City, who was born on the same day, was there as well with many mutual friends. Since high school, I'd imagined that thirty was the age to get married and start a family.

ETM Anton arrived at the party without his wife, but not alone. He was accompanied by Matilda. She was attractive and atypically for Moscow, dressed modestly. Because it seemed Anton and she were cheating, my interest in her evaporated. After enough drinks, I stopped being non-judgemental and asked Anton how he could blatantly cheat on his wife in public in front of mutual friends. He laughed and explained that he chose to come to the party with Matilda specifically because going out with her wouldn't raise any suspicions. He claimed her reputation was that she was "unfuckable." I considered that encouraging. He added that Matilda was part of the Star City scene. It was strange our paths had never crossed.

"Matilda"

In Russia it is customary for the person whose birthday it is to pay for their own party. It doesn't make sense to me, but that's the way it is. In a violation of protocol, I ghosted out of my own party and left the Dicker to cover the bill. Bak gave me rollerblades (which ironically were invented in Minneapolis) that I put on when I got home. I don't know how to skate. Scuff marks from the rollerblades were on the walls the next day. While wearing them, a house guest and I were reported to have tried Sumo wrestling. Matilda called around 2 p.m. She was surprised that I was home at that time on a weekday. She said she was calling to leave a message of thanks for allowing her to attend the party.

Her voice, her manners, and her looks tweaked my interest. Out for dinner with Shit King, I mentioned that I was interested in Matilda and even considered inviting her on a date, which was something I hadn't done since college. Because of Leningrad, I reacted to any indication of potential romantic relations with extreme suspicion. Shit King's advice was to drop the idea of dating Matilda immediately. He told me he had thrown his A-grade material at her and got nowhere. Like Anton, he used the term, "unfuckable." For me, it was like they were her promoters.

Oksana in Star City and Matilda were best friends. I considered Oksana a close friend as well, and still do. Oksana told me Matilda was an opera fan and worked for Mitsui, one of Japan's largest companies. Oksana added that she thought Matilda and I would make an excellent couple. When I found out that Milan's La Scala had an upcoming production of Verdi's opera Aida in St. Petersburg to commemorate 150 years of cooperation with the Mariinsky Theater, I broke protocol and invited Matilda on a date. I called her at Mitsui from Almaty. She started laughing when she heard my voice. I asked why she was laughing. Matilda said that when the receptionist connected my call to her, she said "There's some guy named Kevin on the line. He's obviously a Russian, pretending to be a foreigner."

When I told her I wanted to invite her to Aida, she knew enough about opera to know there was no Verdi in all of Moscow at the time. If she agreed, I would send a car to take her to the airport, give her a plane ticket and meet her in St. Pete.

I arrived in St. Pete two days before the opera. The day before Matilda's flight, a group of drunken friends called me from my own apartment. Anton had a spare key. Shit King and some people from Star City were teasing me about my first date with a woman they knew well. As they drained my bar, they joked that I should change my mind about Matilda. Their comments made me want to roll out the red carpet. Sasha from St. Pete port admin arranged a Mercedes with an airport pass for me that allowed me to greet Matilda at the bottom of the stairs when she got off the plane. Arrival gates weren't yet common. I took an ice bucket and bottle of champagne from the Grand Hotel Europe and picked up a bouquet of flowers on the way to the airport.

There is a certain rivalry between Moscow and St. Pete. As we drove into the city, Matilda insulted what I considered my second home town by saying, "I never knew St. Petersburg was nice." Nice? It's much more beautiful than Moscow and I had to show her. I booked a boat and took her for a tour of the canals, which remains a favorite thing to do. When we passed the Mariinsky, we got out of the boat to pose for a photo on the bridge (and take a pee break at the Irish pub across the street). By the time we hit the opera, Matilda dozed off from too much champagne. The production of Aida had a cast of hundreds, including live camels and elephants. It was described as historic, but neither of us can remember much of it.

After the show, I offered to get a room for Matilda, which she misunderstood as an invitation to spend the night. She refused, so we set off to Moscow on the overnight train in a sleeper car with two beds. We talked and talked, sleeping maybe for an hour or two. A company driver greeted us at the train station. He looked at Matilda approvingly and when she wasn't looking made a gesture to ask how many times we'd done it on the train. I didn't know how to convey that I was thrilled that we hadn't.

The next weekend we went to Istanbul together, where we met up with Klempner and his girlfriend. The next weekend was Prague, where we met up with Detroit Ellen and another friend from GWU. The two jokingly referred to Matilda as my "Love bunny," but said they liked her. The next weekend we visited J. Dog and his wife in London. After four weekends traveling together in a row, Matilda told an incredulous Oksana where we'd been and how I'd acted towards her. Oksana explained that in the five or six years she'd known me, it was rare for me to turn my head to look at a woman. Now Matilda was encouraged.

After London, I was summoned into the conference room where most of the men in the office were waiting for me. It shocked me when they said the agenda was me. I couldn't think of anything I'd done wrong. A seasoned metals trader looked accusatory when he told me, "These people tell me that your DFR has gotten out of control." The others nodded in agreement. The term meant nothing to me. One by one, they went around the room, berating me for either a ridiculously high DFR or a skyrocketing DFR. A maladjusted DFR was unacceptable and they wanted me to know it. I didn't want to admit that I was ignorant about the meaning of DFR, but had to because it was impossible to infer it by context. "What the hell is DFR?!" I finally blurted out. In a deadpan tone, someone stated, "Your Dollar:Fuck Ratio." It's simple economics, they explained. If a man's DFR exceeds the prevailing price of a prostitute, he must either cease the expenditures or marry the woman. I chose the latter.

COPPA

Gerry was the world's top copper trader, but he wanted more. Two Kazakh factories, Jack-o-stan (Dzhezkazgan) and Ball Scratch (Bakash) were his targets. The Hebe and I went to Jack-o-stan. Pablo and Zoranbaev took Ballscratch. The commercial director we met was named Yelkair Kabdularimovich Syzdykov. When I read his business card, my very first thought was that Gerry can never meet this man, because he will butcher his name so badly it might sound like a mother insult. Gerry's ability to stumble over pronunciations was unmatched. We worked with a man whose last name was Dzhanisbaev. Gerry referred to him as Jism boy.

Gerry decided to host a world copper summit in Almaty. An Argentinian named Jaime represented South America. When I went to meet him at the airport, our company car was a Mitsubishi Pajero. Approaching the car, Jaime noticed the name and fell over laughing. He could barely breathe, he was laughing so hard. "You've got to be kidding?!?" He continued laughing uncontrollably for minutes, repeating, "Pajero. Pajero!" When he regained the ability to speak, he asked "Do you know what the word means?" Nope. He said it was an insult, like a husband whose wife everyone bangs. "No one in South America would be caught dead buying this car." Google Translate says the English for "Pajero," is "Wanker."

An unsubstantiated article in a trade magazine about Turkish copper caught Gerry's attention. Instead of investing in minimal due diligence, he hired two traders on the belief they dominated the copper market in the Middle East. The article said so. They met the Gerald team for the first time at the Rahat Palace hotel that had just opened in Almaty. It attracted the who's who of Kazakhstan when it first opened. We referred to it as the Racket Palace (as in criminal racket).

We gathered in Mountain Hebe's suite for an informal get to know one another session. Pablo, Sultan and I were impressed that for the first time in Kazakhstan Jack Daniels was available from room service. We ordered a bottle. The two Turks, Ahmet and Mustafa, were both from Istanbul. Jaime's South American contribution was to ensure everyone was aware that our company cars were called "Wankers." We had to explain the term to Mustafa. Once he understood, he excitedly announced that his nickname was "Mister 27." There seemed to be no correlation. We asked, "What's with the 27, are you an isotope?" Everyone present and paying attention was more than dumbstruck and speechless by Mustafa's clarification. His sobriquet, he elucidated, stemmed from his ability to ejaculate in 27 strokes. His braggadocio cooled when people from all over the world uniformly asserted that masturbation contests were not part of their mainstream culture.

Ahmet played down Mustafa's record, steering the conversation to his useful skill, which was a technique to produce hashish from low-grade ditchweed. Sultan put Ahmet to the test, ordering a bag of marijuana for delivery to the hotel. Ahmet had room service send up an ironing board, iron, and cheesecloth. Since the marijuana topic had been broached, one of our Kazakh employees went to his room and returned with a "special" drink. He brought kumys, which is fermented mare's milk. His was infused with marijuana. Kumys also contains about 4% alcohol. Kazakh and other central Asian Muslims consider it Halal, or Sharia compliant, as is marijuana. I did not find the taste pleasant at all, but as an intoxicant it was effective.

Kazakhs I found to be not entirely sharia-compliant. Jism boy once invited me to drink cognac, chasing it with Spam on crackers. He said the cognac was to "Cleanse" on the first evening of Ramadan. He waited until after sundown to start drinking.

Ahmet made good on his boast. He turned Kazakh schwag into hash right there in our hotel room. After smoking up, Jaime put a napkin on his head and pretended it was a helmet. He announced that he was going to jump on a motorcycle and ride, ride, ride across the world.

Within a month, "27" was fired and Gerry began to refer to Ahmet only as "Asshole." When Ahmet asked why, Gerry said, "Because you are one."

Gerry was in heaven in Almaty. During local daylight hours it was possible for him to terrorize employees worldwide. Twelve hours ahead of New York, and 5 hours behind much of Asia, he could reach most anyone during their office hours. Moscow was nine hours ahead of New York, so we were somewhat insulated from his telephonic tirades. Eavesdropping on his conversations could cause convulsive laughter, "No. I'm not in Jack-o-stan yet. We just got another fifteen thousand tons from Ballscratch. Lemonogorpsk will be shipping through Nakodakka by the end of next week." After a while, The Hebe instructed us to never tell Gerry during phone calls anything other than "Everything's on schedule."

For Gerry's visit to Dzhezkazgan, we chartered a larger than necessary plane to ensure it had enough fuel for a roundtrip. The airport was known to run out of fuel. We toured acres of sulphuric acid baths and watched several hundred tons of copper cathodes get strapped onto pallets. Gerry lovingly stroked a copper cathode that was about to be put in a rail car. He looked so uncharacteristically blissful and rapt, I took video of him.

The airport outsmarted us. We had jet fuel, but our plane was grounded because there was no electricity. The tower was unable to announce our flight plan. As we waited, we ran into an Italian copper trader and former colleague who was flying commercial. He was stranded too. We offered him a seat on our plane. While we waited, he suggested getting something to eat. We were leery.

The Italian said he was going to try a chicken sandwich. It wasn't quite green yet, but there was a visible dubious film on the skin. About 20 minutes after eating the chicken, the Italian started doing the head back, spine straight, kind of strut one does while your butt cheeks stay together. We pointed to a free-standing toilet shack at the edge of the parking lot. He made it there without leaking. We watched him enter backwards. He emerged not long after with his arms flapping and calling for help. Without electricity, the toilet was dark. The Italian had sprayed a man who was squatting on a toilet built-in to the floor.

Governor Crosses the Pacific

After forty years of being a closed city, the brief window of benevolent governance in the Vladivostok region (Primorye) came to an almost instant end when governor Vladimir Kuznetsov[1] was promoted to the post of Russia's Consul General in San Francisco. Local politics were of no interest to me other than if a new law would create the need to bribe in order to circumvent it. During Kuznetsov's tenure, I noticed improvements all over the region. He attracted investors from Japan, Australia, South Korea and to a smaller extent U.S.A.

For a sendoff dinner, we went to the Australian restaurant, Captain Cook. Its owner, Eric, dated Valeria's good friend, Elena, who was a doctor at a maternity hospital. That evening was the first time I'd tasted Penfolds Grange wine. The restaurant didn't sell it, but Vladimir had received it as a gift in Australia. All of us walked out of the restaurant long after closing time. There was a path from the restaurant through a small forest that led to the governor's residence. Vladimir suggested we walk to his house for a last call. They thought it was dangerous to walk the road at night.

Governor of Primorye, Vladimir Kuznetsov, near N. Korea on the Sea of Japan

---

1 https://www.vgoswamilaw.com/vladimir-kuznetsov.html

Stinger the dog leaving Vladivostok to his new home in the residence of the Russian consul general in San Francisco.

North Korea is just a few miles to the right

Valeria went to bed right away, and Vladimir put a case of 22 oz. Sapporo beers on the table. We sat in the kitchen and drank several. When I started to ask about something potentially financially sensitive, he swung his index finger in a circle, which is the signal that the room was bugged. That topic was shelved.

After finishing the beer, he pointed me in the direction of a guest room and told me to spend the night. He was proud to have an untranslated movie in English, which was "Backdraft." He turned it on and left me alone. I was tired and paid no attention to the movie. Every half hour or less, I woke up to pee. I drank way too much beer and got up to pee several times. The movie ended and automatically rewinded. I started it again as background noise. The next time I awoke it was in a panic. That time I didn't get up to pee. My clothes, the bedding, and the couch were soaked in cold urine. It felt like I'd pissed out a gallon.

The washer and dryer were far enough away from their bedroom, that I could use them without fear of the noise waking them up. It was still dark outside. There was a handheld hair dryer in the guest bathroom. I pointed at the cushions on high until it overheated and automatically turned off. To restore a cool temperature faster, I put it in the freezer for ten minutes at a time. I continued doing that until past sunrise. My clothes, the blankets and sheets were dry. I patted the couch with my hand and was unable to feel any moisture, managing to leave before they got up.

I was going to miss them, especially Valeria and Stinger. But when friends move away you don't lose a friend. You gain a destination. For some reason, I remember seeing them off at the train station and not the airport.

Kuznetsov's Kremlin-appointed replacement was Yevgeniy Nazdratenko. He demanded control, was anti-foreigner (except North Korea and China), attacked any business he couldn't collect from, and suppressed media that portrayed him negatively. His administration intentionally cut off utilities like electricity, running water, and heat in regions where he wanted to force compliance. Noisy's boutique hotel in Nakhodka put buckets in the guests' rooms so that the staff could collect water during the intermittent half hours or so when Nazdratenko's team turned it on. And forget about hot water. It was cold only.

It didn't take long for an anti-Nazdratenko consortium to form. To send a message they burned down the governor's mansion. Afterwards, the region started to needlessly spiral downward. Nazdratenko struck me as a classic despot, blaming what he inflicted on his opponents. A frightened media reported none of his misdeeds. When I read the news about the governor's mansion burning down, I called the residence of the Russian Consulate in San Francisco to express my sadness.

Valeria answered. I told her I thought it was truly tragic. It saddened me to see the region fall into preventable poverty and conflict. I honestly considered the brief time I spent with them as good as Russian life could be. I thought of them as an ideal family and sent my regards to Stinger. When I lamented the burning of the governor's residence, Valeria sliced to the quick, saying "What do you care? You pissed on our couch and left."

Charity / Moiseev Dance

CNN's Moscow bureau chief, Eileen O'Connor, held a fundraiser to benefit Operation Smile. Any charity should be scrutinized, but more so in Russia. The fact that there was a "name" associated with the event lent it credibility. Russians are exceedingly leery of organized charities and with good reason. Operation Smile, however, has verifiably performed hundreds of thousands of cleft palate repair surgeries for free all over the world. Most of the attendees of the Moscow event were wealthy "New" Russians. I was on a double date, accompanied by pregnant Matilda and an American couple.

The items for auction fetched tens of thousands of dollars. Things like a bottle of 75 year old cognac, or a supersonic flight in a MiG fighter jet elicited lots of competing bids. When a performance of the Igor Moiseev Ballet at Tchaikovsky Hall was put on the auction block, my friend and I had no idea what it was. Matilda assured us the troupe was excellent, world class, and on par or better than the Bolshoi. We agreed to bid up to five thousand dollars each. The starting bid was $3,000. We bid and the room remained uncomfortably silent. The auctioneer couldn't goad anyone into going even a hundred dollars more. We couldn't believe we bought an entire 1,500 seat venue with a performance by what we'd just heard was arguably the greatest dance troupe in the world.

Igor Moiseyev's Dance Troop

presents:

Charity Night

at the

Tchaikovsky Hall

March 5, 1996

7:00 p.m.

All ticket proceeds go to the following charities:

* Action for Russia's Children
* Operation Smile
* World Wide Fund for Nature

Igor Moiseyev is the "Patriarch of Russian choreography".
— The Moscow Times

It would be fun to brag about having been the smallest audience in the history of Tchaikovsky Hall, but that was too gauche even for 1990s Moscow. We decided to sell tickets to raise more money for other charities. After the performance, Moiseev himself came out on stage. I had the honor of shaking the maestro's hand. The show was absolutely stellar and I've seen it a dozen times since, including a performance at the Bolshoi to commemorate 100 years since Igor Moiseev's birth. One of my co-donors chose World Wide Fund for Nature. I held my tongue. I gave my portion to an orphanage.

False Narrative In USA

On April 19, 1995 Timothy McVeigh bombed the federal building in Oklahoma City, killing 168 people and injuring almost 700. I was in Moscow when I saw the news. Most people falsely assumed Islamists did it. When it was announced that it was an act of domestic terrorism, the Clinton administration couldn't let an opportunity to scaremonger go to waste. They created a narrative that domestic extremist groups were rampant. The media stirred the frenzy without evidence.

At that time, the Saint from GWU was living near San Jose, CA, where he ran an import/export company that traded guns and ammunition. The Clinton machine exploited the Saint's company to bolster their narrative about militias. It didn't matter that everything he bought and sold was licensed and legal. I was home in Minneapolis, hoping to close on a house. The Saint invited me to the Bay Area. It would be great to catch up with him. After I bid on a house, I flew to San Francisco. The Saint showed me his warehouse and described the operation. Among other items, he imported Tokarevs and Makarovs from Eastern Europe. They weren't popular so he didn't have many. He also paid for them about 5% of what they cost in Moscow. The stronger the ban, the more you can charge for them. California's State Senator, Leland Yee knew that.

I called the Russian consulate. The Kuznetsovs invited me to see their new government residence. It was a large home in the city's "Pacific Heights" area, approximately 8,000 sq. feet with views of Alcatraz. When the guard buzzed open the gate, I was happy to be greeted by Stinger who was walking in the yard. As we ate lunch in the dining room, my real estate agent in Minneapolis called to report that I was a homeowner. How did she find me there, was my main question. The Saint had told her. Vladimir went for champagne and we toasted my new home that was on Cedar Lake. The consul's residence seemed more like an event center. It wasn't homey. I preferred the feel of their place in Vladivostok.

On the same evening I was planning a farewell dinner with the Saint, they invited me to an official soireé at the Russian residence. They told me to bring him along too. It's customary in Russia to give people in authority gifts when you first meet. I thought it would be a pleasant surprise if I attributed this custom to my friend. After filling out legally compliant paperwork, his manager grabbed me a Taurus pistol, which was presented inside the Russian Consulate as a gift for Vladimir.

A few days after the party at the Consulate, the Clinton Administration seized most of the merchandise and records from the Saint's warehouse. They brought the media along to bolster the fake narrative that feds were doing something useful about mostly non-existent domestic militia terrorists. They seized legally imported property: pistols, rifles, shotguns and ammunition. The USSR is famous for show trials. The US federal government stages arrests. In violation of the 4th Amendment federal agents seized inventory and records. Complicit "journalists" cranked out stories about how the Clinton Administration was cracking down on suppliers to domestic terrorists. Never mind that McVeigh had used explosives, the narrative against the Saint played well with fools and other consumers of mainstream news.

For a political stunt, U.S. federal agencies halted the operations of a fully compliant corporation. To put a third-world cherry on top of their corruption cake, I recall the Saint telling me they offered to return his inventory and drop the case in exchange for a fifty-thousand dollar donation to an organization with irrefutable ties to President Clinton. The abuse of power was nauseating but not surprising.

At the same time, nearly sixty heads of state were expected in Moscow to mark the 50th anniversary of the defeat of Nazi Germany. May 9, 1995. I knew that Vladimir Kuznetsov and Andrei Kozyrev, who was Russia's Minister of Foreign Affairs in 1995, had studied together and graduated from МГИМО (Moscow State Institute for International Relations). Andrei Kozyrev was among the most senior members of the Russian welcoming delegation. I explained to Mr. Kuznetsov what the Clinton administration was doing to the Saint, i.e. my friend who had just been in his home and gave him a gun as a gift. I requested to have Kozyrev relay a message to team Clinton that their illegal shenanigans against the Saint were not appreciated.

There is no evidence that Kozyrev relayed the message, but soon after Clinton's visit to Moscow, the Saint's property was returned and no charges were brought against him or his company. The event led him to start a new business in China. He remained outside the U.S. for at least twenty years. The government never apologized for their actions nor retracted any of their unfounded statements to the media.

Kazakhstan with Lip

Lip was happy to be back in the game in his native Kazakhstan. He invented a reason to visit and insisted I join him at the Almaty passenger train station. I sensed from his voice that he'd arranged something special, but could not guess what. He met me out front and proudly walked the station, out the back door, and through a zigzag of hedges. Hidden by greenery, there were two rail cars on the tracks. We entered. It was the VIP wagon of the Kazakh minister of railways. The interior melded opulence and authority. No Soviet muckety-muck could even feign importance if there wasn't at least one phone on his desk with no dials or buttons. There were three. Lip had one in his office, too, even after retirement.

The minister invited us to ride along for a meeting he had about an hour away. En route, we sat in velour armchairs and downed a bottle of cognac. Lip was beaming. His smile revealed he felt at home again. When we arrived at the next train station, we parked behind a tall green metal wall. While they conducted official business, I was relocated to the guest car, which was arguably more opulent than the main office. It just didn't have any hotline phones. A half hour or so later, we returned to Almaty. I regret that we never had any need to do business with Kazakh rail. That was the coolest way to travel I'd seen. Lip knew it too.

Solntsevo Mafia

When we returned to Moscow, the mood in the office was sullen. It was as if Mr. Juices had infected the entire staff with gloom. We had a (retired?) KGB seductress on the payroll named the Grape, or if you were close enough like I was, Grape-ochka. Grape took her job as KGB seductress so seriously she had a child with a foreign military attaché in order to extract state secrets from him. She told me that the Solntsevo mafia had come calling and wanted an audience with our roof. Solntsevo was as big a name as there was. I took them seriously. False claims of affiliation can cause broken bones and death. Sonny Barger's Hell's Angels set that standard with a reputation for zero tolerance for bogus name dropping. Most any gang will pummel a person for lying about being a member.

I called Golovatov's team, Alpha, to report the Solntsevo inquiry. Alpha was not concerned. Golovatov offered a reduced service fee in exchange for me helping them find out exactly which crew was behind the shakedown attempt. Alpha was formed under the KGB. Collecting intelligence was very much part of their M.O. They asked to arrange a meeting with Solntsevo in any public place, but they preferred the Radisson Slavyanskaya. President Clinton and Al Gore stayed there when they visited Moscow. It was completely infiltrated by state security. Its business center was run by a Solntsevo rival Chechen.

Solntsevo agreed to meet me at the Slavyanskaya. I believe they thought I chose the Radisson because I'm American and didn't know another hotel. They definitely didn't appear to expect a set up. They introduced themselves by nicknames like 'The Axe" and "The Grater." There were five of them at the table. Only two asked detailed questions about Gerald's business, trying to determine how much to demand for protection. They left and said they would call me the next day at noon for a final answer. I saw no one from Alpha, who assured me not to worry, saying that even if I couldn't see them, they would be there.

I left the hotel and rode the metro home. The Radisson was one stop away from my apartment at Park Kultury. I was convinced that Alpha had abandoned me. After ten p.m. one of the intel officers called and asked if I had a VCR. He wanted me to watch what they had recorded. The officer entered my apartment and laid out an organizational chart, asking me about everyone I'd met. He was most interested in one of the younger guys, whom he thought was the head of that group. He asked things like, "Did the others seem to show him more reverence or act afraid of him?" It looked to me that Alpha had the power rankings nailed.

Then he popped in the video cassette. The first thing I saw was a closeup of my face, looking around the lobby of the Radisson. From the angle of the footage, it looked like the waitress had a camera in her tray. The table was bugged. They also had footage from the front door and from the parking lot. They took video driving 130 kmh in downtown Moscow, chasing Solntsevo back to their office. It was impressive. To get ears inside the Solnstevo office, Alpha claimed to have deployed a cat that was trained to chase fish pellets. The cat crawled through the bars on their windows and transmitted their conversation. The intel officer was one of the shortest men I'd met and had a face with no memorable features. My coworkers told me that a forgettable face is a component of an ideal agent.

The agent was proud of what they had done. The operation was fascinating and video entertaining, but my question was, "When are you going to tell them to fuck off?" To my great surprise and dread, he replied, "We're not. You are." He handed me a list of their nicknames, followed by their legal full names. He told me that all I had to do was to ask, "Who's speaking?" When they say their nickname, call him by his full name. It seemed like we were getting scammed, i.e. paying for faux protection. I protested the plan, saying,

"Alpha employs special forces and intelligence agents. You're telling me that I can make gangsters go away by confronting them with their names?"

Confidently, he replied, "Yes," and convinced me I could handle it from there.

The next day exactly at noon the call came in. I asked who was on the line. "This is Axe. $250,000 per month. What about it?" I found his real name on the list and replied, "I think we will not be working together, Sergei Ivanovich Petrov." There was silence for several seconds. He finally responded by saying one word in a deflated voice, "Understood." He hung up.

U.N. Oil for Food — Mogilevich

About the same time as Solntsevo was trying to extract protection money from Gerald, Claudia Rosett unleashed what should have been the leading scandal of the year. Abusing the goodwill of kind people for cynical self-enrichment should be the United Nations' motto. The oil-for-food program to allegedly provide humanitarian aid to the people of Iraq was a perfect ruse. Around the same time, Claudia released another well-researched story about North Koreans and Chinese citizens who essentially worked as slaves in Russian labor camps.

The Iraq oil-for-food scam was attributed to Semion Mogilevich, whom Wikipedia claims is the "boss of bosses," and the FBI described as "the most dangerous mobster in the world." His resumé is perfect for a U.N. "humanitarian" program. Claudia's revelations and irrefutable evidence of the Iraq scam garnered about as much attention as the information on Hunter Biden's laptop. Marik from the art gallery worked with Mogilevich. Marik operated automotive service stations where Mogilevich took his fleet of cars.

The cynical application of embargos to drive prices up is rampant. Milton Friedman observed, "One of the great mistakes is to judge policies and programs by their intentions rather than their results." The Yugoslavians in the Marc Rich oil department supported sanctions against their country, because skirting them meant higher profits. A few trainloads of gasoline was chump change compared to a master like Mogilevich, whose oil-for-food scheme bilked billions from world governments.

California's State Senator Leland Yee[1] claimed publicly he wanted to ban guns, because privately he sold them. A ban would drive prices higher. Yee struck me as an embarrassment to political hustlers. Yee's model was correct, i.e. maintain a public persona and do the opposite off stage. People will say anything, but what they do is always the truth.

The U.N. pretended to feed suffering Iraqis. Al Gore's global warming scam enriched millions of people by purporting with zero supporting evidence to improve the environment. Obama's idea was to siphon one sixth of the U.S. economy through bogus healthcare shenanigans. Yee's gun ban was Fischer-Price politics. Mogilevich's scam was grand and successful enough. Why didn't he get a peace prize like for Gore and Obama?

---

1 Leland Yee was a Democrat politician who was sentenced to 5 years for racketeering.

Fabrik spoke with reverence about how Seva Mogilevich and Marik negotiated. In the 1980s, aka the mafia's incubation period, Marik operated and collected from automotive repair shops around Moscow. Mogilevich's fleet was serviced at Marik's shops. When it came time to pay, sentiments and words flew, similar to. . .

Marik: "You are a despicable lowlife. I can't believe you'd even think about shortchanging me like this after you broke bread in my home and enjoyed a meal cooked by my mother."

Mogilevich: "You have some nerve. When your sister was in the hospital and couldn't get food, I rode a bus all over town to make sure every item on her shopping list was purchased. That means nothing to you?"

Marik

False Medical Alarm

One of our most important Kazakh business partners confided that his doctor diagnosed him with late-stage cirrhosis of the liver. It seemed odd. He didn't drink much and the skin color of ethnic Kazakhs could be described as yellow. Gerald's Swiss office arranged for him to get a second opinion at one of the world's leading diagnostic clinics near Geneva. I accompanied him in case he needed a translator. The clinic had a Russian speaker and he stayed overnight. I had free time.

With a VIP guest, I could justify renting a Porsche 911 turbo. While doctors were checking him over, I drove to Montreux. On the way back there were three lanes of perfect open downhill highway. I could see miles and miles ahead. There was not one car in front of me. As the speedometer neared 300 Kmh (186 mph) a red flash went off. The camera generated the most expensive speeding ticket I ever had, in the fifty thousand dollar range.

The Kazakh was ready to be released. I looked forward to hearing the test results. The doctor was exceedingly diplomatic. Without saying that the doctor in Kazakhstan was a useless buffoon, the Swiss professional said, "When we see test results like these, we can state with confidence that not only are you in no danger of liver failure, we would go so far as to suggest that you safely celebrate tonight with a bottle of wine, or several. Whatever methodology was applied in your country, we assure you that our tests are accurate and you have no health concerns at this time."

Our office booked a table for us in a 19th century manor just off Lac Leman, South of Geneva. Our VIP guest invited three friends to celebrate his good medical report. Whorewacker was the only local rep. All through the dinner they drank vodka shots and chased them with vintage Bordeaux. At the end, they asked the sommelier what was available from our main man's birth year, which I recall was 1936. Some ten minutes later the sommelier returned pushing a service cart atop which were 6 or 7 bottles from his year. Whorewacker whispered, "Do you have any idea how much this is going to cost?" Our guest looked over each bottle and chose an Armagnac that was still sealed. The sommelier put a crystal in front of each guest and poured everyone a sliver. He was about to walk away, when the Kazakh asked to see the bottle, which he took in hand and proceeded to fill everyone's glass. Onlookers from nearby tables and the sommelier couldn't disguise their shock as they gulped down in large swigs of vintage Armagnac from full crystal snifters.

We guessed the Armagnac would cost $25k, but it was closer to $8k.

The Swiss government delivered by certified mail a speeding ticket to my Moscow address. I was impressed they were able to locate me. The fine was around fifty thousand dollars. The ticket got misplaced and never returned to Switzerland to request a duplicate. I researched fines for speeding in Switzerland. Fifty thousand dollars meant I got off light. In 2000, a driver from Sweden was fined nearly one million dollars for going about the same speed, 290 kmh.

Razzle Dazzle Documents

KME transport decided that less income wasn't desirable after all. When Gerald purchased spot lots of copper by FOB[1] contract, the khokhli arranged port operations on their own. They made a deal in Nakhodka to pay $18 per ton in order to get a $4 kickback. Gerald paid less than $6 per ton. Paying triple for a fifth in return, told me that at the negotiating table, Buttstick got the better of the khokhli.

On December 5, 1995 a vessel chartered by Gerald sailed from Nakhodka to Busan, South Korea. It was carrying approximately 2,500 metric tons of copper. The terms of the contract were that Gerald would pay based on the price of copper as declared by the London Metal Exchange at the end of the trading day as dated in the bill of lading.

KME's port agent faxed them a copy of the bill of lading as soon as the vessel sailed. Based on the December 5th closing price on the London Metal Exchange, KME prepared an invoice for approximately $3,000 per ton or a total of $7,500,000. The next day the price of copper fell $186 per ton, a difference of nearly $500,000. The vessel had already sailed and per the terms of our buy/sell agreement, four original copies of the bill of lading had been issued: one was on board with the captain, one each by DHL to the seller, buyer, and bank.

After New York saw the closing copper price on December 6, they called me in Moscow and instructed me to absolutely, under no circumstances, allow the vessel to sail from Nakhodka. They wanted the date on the bill of lading changed and offered a success fee of half of the difference, in cash. Half of $186 x 3,500 = $465,000. I doubted anything could be done because the ship was already halfway to S. Korea. There were four original bills of lading and three with in envelopes with DHL tracking numbers. And who knew where they were?

I love a good challenge and a two hundred thousand dollar budget for forged documents buys a lot of talent, not just in Russia, but especially so there. It was difficult to explain what needed to be done over the phone, but we'd worked together so much that some things were understood without saying them. When Noisy caught on exactly what needed to be done, the team went to work.

The job was 1) create four identical original bills of lading, replacing December fifth with sixth. 2) get on board to replace the Captain's

---

[1] Free On Board. Ownership of the cargo is transferred from seller to buyer once the cargo is on board.

original. 3) get to the DHL station and switch out all the envelopes. The DHL "office" was a room in the Vlad Motor Inn. The Norwegian, who operated it, personally drove DHL packages twice a week to the VVO airport. 4) change the Nakhokda port dispatcher and customs logs to show she sailed Dec. 6.

Few things better motivate Russians than payouts for forgeries. If you promise to pay for an official document, they'll ask what color paper and ink you want. Within four or five hours of explaining the task, Noisy called back with a one-word message, "Done" (Есть). I was celebrating inside, but also refused to believe that they could have been so efficient. He ended the call with "We look forward to seeing you soon."

Four or five days later the originals arrived by DHL. The khokhli immediately called me and asked something on the lines of, "What kind of shit did you pull?" I pretended to not understand. They explained that they had already invoiced us based on December 5th, and the faxed copy from their port agent clearly showed December 5th. The fax had a time stamp from December 5th. I told them they probably had an incompetent port agent. After all, I was seven time zones away in Moscow. How could I influence anybody from that distance? This was a credible defense. Operations like that were almost impossible to pull off by phone. To discuss an operation like that, we'd usually say only that the topic wasn't a phone conversation. Sensitive issues were spoken about face to face.

Fax copies weren't contractual. The date on the "original" was December 6th. KME smelled the glove, but the khokhli got $4 back per ton on port fees. I flew to Vladivostok a week later with a couple hundred thousand dollars. I didn't tell anyone I was on my way. I took a taxi and made sure to haggle over a few dollars in case someone was sizing me up. I figured that would-be thieves would never target a cheap bastard, who was arguing over nickels to save on taxi fare. Rich people rode in expensive cars, not Volgas.

We met at Mikho's clubhouse to decide who had earned what. Slava easily got the shipowner to order the Captain to divert back towards Vladivostok, keeping no record of it in the ship's log. They sent a speedboat offshore to courier the replacement bill of lading. Toker handled the port's records, changing the dispatcher's log and customs registry. The DHL part had been a little trickier. The Norwegian at The Vlad Motor Inn refused to play ball. Sasha K didn't tell him specifics, but he would not give access.

Sasha K waited in the parking lot for the Norwegian to go out. When he did, Sasha paid or persuaded the front desk to give him a master key. Inside the DHL room, he skillfully opened the envelopes and replaced the bills of lading with the changed date. He never revealed how he got the envelopes opened and resealed, but they went out with the same tracking numbers, exactly as written by the port agent. All said, they asked for around $165,000. The money was nice, but that wasn't the motivation. Playing and winning a fun game was.

We all got drunk and I took a taxi back to The Vlad Motor Inn. It happened to be the last night of the hotel's controller. He was a Canadian who'd been working for months without pay. The owners, Ray and Zina, had left him in charge of the hotel's cash while on a trip to Singapore. They returned to find an empty safe. While they were away, the accountant got swindled with a get rich quick scheme. After his "partners" had the cash, they vanished. The controller was forced to work off his debt. After a few months of not being paid, he looked defeated and slowly moped the halls of the hotel. On his last night, he wouldn't even come out of his room for free farewell drinks.

Zina often gave me the keys to the bar and told me to lock up when we were done. It was mid-December and the expats were getting ready to fly home for Christmas. After settling up in Nakhokda, I had $35,000 in funny money and was buying drinks for everyone. We were having a great time and couldn't believe the accountant wouldn't join us. It was his last night, after all. Someone suggested sending hookers to his room. I agreed to pay if someone arranged it. That was probably around 11 p.m. My memory from the time between when I agreed to pay and 6 a.m. was at best blurry.

The prostitutes arrived while I was bartending. We gave them a master key in case he wouldn't open the door for them. At some point I remember thinking to myself, "You dumbfuck. You gave a master key to prostitutes in a port city and you've got $35,000 cash." The next thing I remember was waking up to the increasingly louder knocking of the pimp, who wanted to collect. The accountant was gone. He slipped a note under my door that read, "Thank you. I rose to the occasion." The pimp wanted five or six hundred bucks.

I went to where I thought the money was. It wasn't there. I checked a compartment in my suitcase, where I stashed money. It was empty. I lifted the mattress. I checked the bathroom, closet, etc. Nothing. I told the pimp that he and his girls had written their obituaries if they stole from me. "You might think I'm a helpless foreigner, but I'm friends with Mikho and Vladivostok bratva. You're fucked! Absolutely fucked! Do you understand?" Without any emotion or reaction, he repeated what I owed and said, "I will be waiting for you in the lobby. No one stole from you." I picked up the phone and called Gera. After he answered my call, I yelled down the hall to the departing pimp, "You are FUCKED!"

Gera and his crew were on their way. I got dressed and intended to confront the pimp as soon as I found my second shoe. I pulled open the curtains for some light and felt resistance on the right side. The shoe was dangling from the curtain rod by its laces. Inside was about $35,000. Oh shit!! False alarm. I ran to the lobby and gave the pimp $1,000. He left before Gera and his team arrived.

I told Gera that the hotel manager saw I was drunk, so he put my money in a safe without telling me. Inside, I felt proud that I remained aware enough, drunk, to hide my money and not remember it. When I started writing about this incident, I called Allan the Canadian chef to see if he remembered the accountant and the shoe the same way. Allan blurted out, "You asshole. I hid it for you in your shoe. You were stupid drunk, waving that cash like you wanted to get robbed. I hid it. Not you."

Pablo's Chechen Fax

The Khokhli were upset they'd smelled the glove over the copper bill of lading, so they withheld around $200k of payments for rail shipments of zinc. We had them on speakerphone with Gerald Moscow. Those of us who were in on the rail scheme, took turns threatening them. Denis told them he'd fuck them in the mouth if they didn't pay. Mountain Hebe threatened to give their bosses more money. I maintained innocence because I could prove I was in Moscow when the date switch occurred. Pablo said nothing and left the room. Thirty minutes later the lead khokhol called me to report he'd wired the payment to us. He added, "You didn't need to press us that hard." I had no idea what he was referring to.

Pablo smiled and laughed when I told him what the Kazakh khokhol had said. He placed on my desk the fax, which he'd sent to Almaty. We had an arsenal of letterheads that we used as templates to make fake faxes, mostly for comedy. Pablo chose to use the Chechen Cabinet of Ministers onto which he added text that was so ridiculous, I refused to believe that someone could consider it a threat. It was full of bad grammar and stereotypical innuendo. It read, "Azot[1] hasn't shaved for days. You know what that means. If the crates of oranges turn out to have mandarins in them, he will visit you. What good is fruit if you can't make juice? Allah akhbar!" Signed and stamped by Mr. Mamodaev. Pablo reminded me that he grew up in Kazakhstan. He knew what buttons to push.

---

1 Azot could conceivably be a real name, but means Nitrogen in Russian.

Honor Fight In Minneapolis

Home for the holidays in Minneapolis, I invited about 75 people to a pre New Year eve party at my house. Unexpectedly, Gera called from San Francisco. He was with his wife and her twin sister. He never mentioned they planned to visit America. He told me they were flying to New York next and asked if Minneapolis was on the way. I told them to please stop by, join the party, and that they could stay with me. Not long after speaking with Gera, there was another unexpected call. It was Pubic, who was in New York. He said he knew no one in the United States but me. Stating that he didn't want to spend New Year's alone, he invited himself to visit me. I reluctantly agreed.

The theme of the party was everyone had to try at least one random cocktail. Someone had given me a book of drink recipes, which we copied and cut. Attendees were expected to take a recipe from a hat and drink whatever cocktail they drew. Dap and I had spent hours at several liquor stores, sourcing all the ingredients. There were hundreds of cocktails in the hat, but Hopper, who's known to not have the best luck sometimes, drew the worst cocktail recipe I'd ever seen, twice. The recipe called for equal parts Wild Turkey, Sambuca, and tequila.

The bar that I was tending was on a walk-out lower level. Most of the party was upstairs on the main floor. Someone indicated that I should urgently go upstairs and check on things. One of the first people I encountered was my angry mother, who said something to me like, "I didn't raise a bigot." I was confused. The crowd of friends was made up of people that could be at one of Auntie Mame's soirées. Walking deeper into the crowd, several people motioned me towards the master bathroom.

After cautiously sliding the door open, I saw Pubic on the floor, writhing in pain, with Gera standing next to him. Gera saw me and said with a smile, "One of your guests is leaving." When Pubic attempted to explain himself, Gera kicked him on the side of his ribcage so hard that Pubic lifted off the floor. Gera was calm. He told me to call a taxi for Pubic. In an agonized voice, Pubic asked, "What the fuck was that for?" Gera didn't ask me if Pubic could stay. He was hellbent on throwing him out and I intended to do nothing about it. I told Pubic to leave, for now, and that maybe we could figure something out the next day. The taxi arrived. Pubic sat with his suitcase, in the car, in front of the house for fifteen minutes. Gera got annoyed and walked out. The taxi immediately sped off. Gera didn't speak English. Curious what he said to make the taxi leave so fast, I asked Gera what he told the driver, which was, "Go!"

What sparked the beating was drunk Pubic told my mom that Russians hated me because I derided them and mocked their culture. That could have been true of my opinion of their government, but not the people. Gera didn't understand the conversation, but noticed the look of revulsion on my mom's face. Gera asked for a translation. As soon as he heard Pubic's lie, Gera took it upon himself to defend my name.

After everyone left the party, Gera emphasized that for Pubic to slander the man in whose house he was a guest was bad enough. But to upset the man's mother was outrageously egregious. Gera hammered home his point that what Pubic had done was unforgivable. Gera made sense. I didn't speak to Pubic again for at least twenty years.

Aluminum Wars

Almost no one with legislative authority in the new post-Soviet Russia had any business experience. Instead, they had been indoctrinated that the West, and America in particular, wanted to invade and conquer. It was a classic case of psychological projection, when someone accuses another of their own guilt. A comparison of the Soviet narrative that the U.S. intended to invade and conquer the USSR was logically akin to a Russian country girl's acute fear that Johnny Depp was waiting at the bus stop to rape her on her way home.

In a leap of faith, the Yeltsin administration engaged Harvard economist, Jeffrey Sachs, to advise ways to transition from control to freedom. Uncharacteristically for someone from Harvard, he presented a plan that wasn't drenched in socialism. Mr. Sachs advised Russia to privatize as much of the Soviet economy as possible as fast as possible via vouchers, which could be used to acquire shares in enterprises that the government was releasing into private hands.

For the simplest of analogies, the Sachs plan represented the difference between public housing and a private home. If the resident of a public dwelling thinks that the government is going to take care of fixing what's broken, how likely is that person to fix something himself? What is likely is that the person is going to incessantly complain about what a bad job the government is doing, while still taking no action to improve the situation. Apply that to everything.

French economist Frederic Bastiat noted, "Every time we object to a thing being done by the government, socialists conclude we object to it being done at all." Anatoliy Chubais was the privatization minister who oversaw much dispensation of State assets. Mayor Luzhkov took a small cut from every building privatized in Moscow and became a multi-billionaire. When the political optics about his wealth soured public opinion, the mayor's wife also became a billionaire. Most people in America didn't know anything about Elena Baturina until she wired millions of dollars to Hunter Biden for unknown reasons.

The holy grails in Soviet metals producers were two enormous aluminum factories in Siberia, Krasnoyarsk and Bratsk. A reasonable expectation of revenues from the two factories was two hundred and fifty million dollars ($250,000,000) per month. Even though Gerry was all about coppa, Gerald pursued a contract with the recently privatized

Krasnoyarsk[1] Aluminum, mostly referred to as Kraz. The other massive smelter, Bratsk, is only 450 miles away from Kraz. The output of those two factories alone equaled the entire aluminum production of the USA.

The privatization plan for massive state enterprises like Kraz and Bratsk was crucial to understanding the mafia battles that raged in the 1990s. Shares in these companies were valuable, especially a controlling interest. But the reality was that workers and other minority shareholders were being issued what they perceived to be worthless paper. It was very difficult to convince someone who'd just lost their life's savings in rubles, that their tenure in a Soviet enterprise now had value in the form of a voucher. Being told something by the same Soviet government that had collapsed and made their life's savings worthless did not instill a lot of confidence about the future. Mikhail Khodorkovsky had demonstrated to others the value of equity. By investing in shares of oil companies, he had allegedly become the country's richest man. Few people dared to risk cash to pay for vouchers or buy shares.

Initially, when the privatization process started at Kraz, rumor was that a majority of shares, around 60%, belonged to four thousand workers. In order for someone to be issued shares, they had to prove they worked at the factory for a minimum number of years. Russians had no faith in paper already, and then a story broke about a man named Sergei Mavrodi whose pyramid scheme called MMM famously collapsed in 1994. Mavrodi should have been prosecuted for fraud, but instead he was considered untouchable because he had become a member of the State Duma, a position for which he paid using money stolen from "investors." Legally, he could not be prosecuted. Yesterday's ruble millionaires gathered in front of Mavrodi's office, throwing their shares in MMM like confetti or burning them. I was there and picked up a mint condition MMM certificate as a memento.

If someone was committed to purchasing shares, it was very easy to buy small lots of stock for cash below market. While most imagined shares as worthless, people who were paying attention would notice meteoric rises in net worth by those who acquired large amounts of shares in productive entities. More and more groups wanted a piece of the action. Serious contenders started jostling for control of every major venture in all of Russia's eleven time zones. Al Capone noted, "You can get more with a kind word and a gun, than you can get with a kind word alone." In that environment, regular shareholders were not going to stand up or unify. They were going to jump at the chance to sell at the first offer of tangible cash.

Anatoly Bykov became chairman of Kraz with the financial backing of a New York based trading company, AIOC, whose initial con-

---

1   The Krasnoyarsk region, similar to a U.S. State, is triple the size of Texas and about four times the size of France.

tract was for approximately half of the plant's annual capacity, 500,000 metric tons. Gerry paid attention, not because of aluminum but because a New York firm was involved. Gerald had been offered to purchase aluminum from the Pavlodar factory in Kazakhstan at below market prices. Gerry didn't even reply.

"Tolling[2]" was an emerging trend in the metals game. Because most former Soviet ventures were cash-strapped and didn't have the international reach to source foreign raw materials, smelters had excess capacity. To factories all across the former Soviet Union, multinational trading companies delivered raw materials like iron ore, zinc and copper concentrates, or bauxite, for no up front cash. In exchange for the raw materials, factories charged a fee to convert them into cash commodities.

Ores and concentrates were easy to transport. Transporting alumina posed a challenge. Alumina is the main material used to produce aluminum metal. Alumina is very fine and dusty. It penetrates everything and is toxic if inhaled. In most ports worldwide, dock workers and ship crews need to wear protective suits to handle it. Expensive offloading equipment is required to prevent environmental damage.

Gerald had a source for alumina in India. Kraz was willing to toll it, but there was no port in Russia willing to discharge it. When the obvious Far Eastern choices, Nakhodka, Vladivostok, and Vanino all refused to take the cargo, I figured the topic was not a telephone conversation and flew there to discuss.

Supplying bauxite and alumina to smelters is a $250 billion annual business worldwide. Nakhodka agreed to discharge alumina, but only on condition we invested tens of millions of dollars in specialized equipment. Vladivostok's port was in an even more densely populated area. They too refused. It surprised me that the same people who allegedly dumped radioactive waste into the sea were ecologically conscious about toxic dust.

Not willing to give up, I mean we're talking Russia, where everything is possible, except reform, continued inquiries eventually led to a potential solution. A company called Dalso in Vladivostok managed a port in nearby Rajin, North Korea. Ever since Pyongyang pulled off the biggest car theft in history[3], no one would do business with North Korea. But Dalso was run almost entirely by retired Russian military officers. The likelihood of theft was low. Also, in order for North Korea to convert alumina into cash, i.e. metal, massive amounts of electricity and a smelter were required, neither of which they have. I reported the potential solution to Mountain Hebe, who joined me in Vladivostok to sign a transportation service agreement to deliver Indian alumina to Kraz via Rajin, North Korea[4].

The operation went surprisingly smoothly. When Dalso reported the rail cars had crossed

---

2   Tolling was the term used for the fee charged by a factory to convert raw materials into commodity grade metal.
3   The North Korean government ordered and received at least one thousand Volvo cars from Sweden and never paid for them.
4   https://koryogroup.com/travel-guide/rajin-port-rason-north-korea-travel-guide

into Russia at Khasan, I applied the Russian adage that Reagan used to butcher, "Doveryai, no proveryai." (Trust, but verify). I asked Lip to run the wagon numbers through the Information Center to see if Dalso was telling the truth. They were. Kraz did the tolling and delivered the metal.

We soon had Rajin port working at full capacity, which was pretty feeble. I went out for dinner in Moscow with Serduccio (aka Dooch) from Nakhokda, mentioning the need for alumina capacity in any port. He had somehow gotten involved in Murmansk port, which is almost 7,000 miles away, about as far apart as possible within Russia. Murmansk is the world's largest city inside the Arctic Circle, but the port remains mostly ice free all year. Dooch said he guaranteed we could discharge alumina there.

It seemed like a ridiculous proposal to add more than ten thousand miles and almost two months sailing time from India, but the numbers worked. I flew to Murmansk, where Dooch introduced me to his allies. The port had only one berth that was equipped to handle alumina. They tested me and told me that the port would only reserve the berth for me if I paid for the operation immediately. I trusted Dooch completely and sent wiring instructions for $1,000,070 to the account that Murmansk provided. It wasn't in Murmansk, or even Russia, but in Monaco. I remember the specific amount because it was the first time I committed a million dollars of the company's money on a handshake. To initiate the wire, I provided the details of a contract that had yet to be drafted.

Gerry noticed the profits from tolling and gave Mountain Hebe fifty million dollars to get more metal from Kraz. Gerry wasn't interested in pursuing Bratsk. They didn't have any connections with New York. With his Wharton pedigree, Mountain insisted that contracts be thorough. To apply the fifty million at Kraz, he brought in Deutsche Bank. One of the bankers on the deal claimed to be the first Kazakh-born graduate of Harvard.

Kraz agreed to every term of the delivery schedule and numerous caveats about the use of funds. As soon as Gerald's fifty million dollars hit Kraz's account, they violated nearly every term of the agreement. One of the first things they did was overpay for about seventy-five Toyota Land Cruisers, equipped with every accessory imaginable. Management handed the keys to friends and family. Chairman Bykov and corporate officer Ratnikov created a side venture called Sibalco, which claimed a large percentage of Kraz's metal production. Sibalco supposedly owned no shares in Kraz, but had a substantial claim on its output.

Kraz was a uniquely ultra-profitable smelter. The city of Krasnoyarsk enjoyed essentially free electricity, provided by a 6,000 megawatt hydroelectric dam. The dam is such a feat of engineering that an image of it is featured on Russia's Ten-Ruble note. Electricity is the main cost component in the production of aluminum. The rates Kraz paid for electricity were likely around 5% what the rest of the world was charged. This made Kraz the most profitable metal factory by far. Anyone who could read a balance sheet, even in a country with cooked books, quickly concluded that Kraz was worth many billions of dollars and was worth fighting for, to the death.

Besides Bykov and Ratnikov, two infamous brothers joined in the pursuit of Kraz, Lev and Mikhail Cherney (sometimes Chernoy). In 1994 a government investigation was launched into the theft of $100 million from Russia's Central Bank. The investigation concluded that a criminal consortium had pulled off the heist and also that a portion of the funds ended up in accounts controlled by the Cherney brothers. The investigators somehow found no evidence of wrongdoing. They maintained it was impossible for the Cherney brothers to have known the funds were stolen. Mikhail's street name was "Misha Krisha," aka Micky the Roof.

To make the group even more formidable, Kraz teamed up with a wealthy brother duo from London, the Reubens, David and Simon. Their group amassed a majority of shares in Kraz and Bratsk. They pooled their funds to form Trans-World Group (TWG) in 1994. By 1995 TWG was the number one exporter in dollar amounts from Russia. As Shakespeare wrote in Julius Caesar, "There is a tide in the affairs of men, which, taken at the flood, leads on to fortune." As recently as 2020, the Reuben brothers remained England's richest non-royal family. It strikes me as symbolic that the common Russian word for mafia, or an affiliation of gangsters, is "Bratva," stemming from the word for brother, "Brat." Bratva is not the word for brotherhood, but a variation with one meaning. In English I'd call it brotherdom.

When Gerald decided to jump into the Kraz game, approximately thirty people so far had been murdered over ownership disputes. We stopped delivering alumina via Rajin. Murmansk did everything they said they would, and more. Because alumina is bulk, the tonnage delivered is determined by analyzing the ship's draft at arrival and then again after discharge. By calculating the ship's weight and the salinity of the water, a surveyor can determine how many tons were on board.

Having shown them good faith by wiring a million on a handshake, Dooch's friends at the port wanted to show their appreciation by performing a little unrequested maritime razzle dazzle. To measure the ship's weight, they didn't use the salinity of the White Sea, but instead some other distant port's. This reduced our obligation to the seller by almost 1,500 tons. Then they claimed a loss of 4,4% on wind, which freed us from paying for another 1,000 tons. Kraz took delivery by rail of just over 26,000 tons. Because of the port's tricks, we had to pay for approximately 22,500.

The Moscow office could have made another $30 per ton by running the rail freight through one of our off-shore companies. A man who worked in Lausanne transportation had tried to step on my toes and made a deal with a freight forwarder to pay $67 per ton, when Lip could get us $37. I decided to use the opportunity to politically bash the guy. I made sure Gerry knew that Lausanne had almost needlessly cost us a half million dollars, how and why. The overreaching employee was fired.

If cash had motivated or interested me, I'm certain I could have made at least a hundred million dollars. An operator of a rail freight company called Transrail operated in a similar manner as our offshore. He bought freight from the Ministry of Railways and sold it to those who needed it at a substantial markup. I heard Transrail made billions.

Internal politics at Gerald was the Hebe's purview. He tried to talk me out of bashing Lausanne, but two of the employees there aggravated me. To sway Mountain to my point of view, I reminded him about the time one of the transport guys went into the Hebe's hotel room in London, drained his mini-bar, passed out on a train and woke up the next morning in Scotland. We had been in London specifically to work a deal with a major shipping company and the missing hungover guy on the train in Scotland was supposed to be our lead negotiator.

Another reason for me to want to drop a bomb on Lausanne transport was for a vessel they'd chartered to Nakhodka to pick up a couple thousand tons of zinc. I took a call at 3 a.m. in Moscow from Nakhokda port, who was screaming at me, "Are you stupid? Have you lost your mind? How am I supposed to load this? What the fuck is wrong with you?" Lausanne had booked a Chinese rust bucket passenger ship.

By the time Kraz delivered the metal from the tolling operation, media was reporting around seventy-five murders related to the ownership dispute over Bratsk and Krasnoyarsk. News outlets were calling it "The Aluminum Wars[5]." Taking delivery from the fifty million dollar purchase agreement, which amounted to approximately 22,500 tons, was problematic. Mr. Juices, who headed our Moscow aluminum department, returned from Kraz and declared the situation there "worse than very bad."

Gerald gave me the go ahead to incentivize our roof. We offered $500,000 to get our aluminum on rail and $500,000 once it had been loaded onto our ship. Mr. Golovatov said he would send an active service FSB (formerly KGB) general. The general returned from Kraz and summarized his visit thusly: "My country no longer exists. Imagine that a general from the Pentagon went to a military

---

5 https://freerepublic.com/focus/f-news/2089206/posts

base in California and the colonel there told the general to get fucked, because authority is no longer recognized. That's how I was greeted at Kraz."

I remained convinced that something can always be done. I naively thought that I could fix things by going there myself. By the time I got on the plane to Krasnoyarsk, the murder tally stood at a little over one hundred dead. The real bone chiller for me was the report that Felix Lvov had been found dead sixty miles outside of Moscow. Felix was the representative of AIOC, Kraz's joint venture "partner." The assassination of Felix Lvov demonstrated a new level of brazenness, even for 1990s Russia. After passing through security, customs and passport control at an international airport in Moscow, They extracted him from the boarding gate. Airport security cameras recorded nothing.

Paul Tatum's Assassination

About the same time as the Kraz kerfuffle, our Moscow employees started another cynical betting pool. We wagered on the date Paul Tatum would be killed. I never met Paul Tatum and don't want to rub salt in the wounds of his family. To outsiders, his business decisions seemed insanely reckless. Intentionally using the media as a megaphone to talk about the situation was unlikely to help.

Paul Tatum was an Oklahoman who claimed a stake in the Slavyanskaya Hotel, operated by Radisson. I speculate that Mr. Tatum got his start by getting an "exclusive" from the mayor's office, just like B.A.S.E. Corporation had a few years earlier. The difference was Tatum succeeded in bringing in a partner. What seems likely was that Taum was unable to come up with the venture's capital requirements when prices and costs skyrocketed in 1990s Russia. Word on the street was that he partnered with Chechens to build Americom Business Center, which were offices for rent inside the Radisson. Their expectations of rental income reminded me of a $35 glass pint of bottled water I'd seen in a Moscow hotel. The pool of people willing to pay that kind of price was limited.

I didn't know the rates at Americom, but knew that when Marc Rich + Co was looking for a new office, the manager responsible for finding one told me that she basically had a blank check to find a secure space. Money was barely a consideration. Then she mentioned looking at Americom and finding their rates ridiculously high, insulting even. If Marc Rich + Co deemed something stupidly expensive, they might struggle.

It was no surprise then that Americom and Tatum generated little or no revenue for the venture. Likely it was suggested that he exit quietly. It wouldn't be a surprise if they even offered compensation. Instead of bowing out, Paul Tatum started placing full-page ads in Moscow business papers, like Wall Street Europe, The Moscow Times, The Financial Times, and Kommersant.

The ads accused Mayor Luzhkov of corruption. They claimed that Russian courts were rigged. They offered "Freedom bonds," that promised a stake in the hotel and a piece of the settlement, in case Tatum's lawsuits prevailed. The outcome of the conflict was so obvious that even the U.S. Embassy issued a warning. Paul Tatum was shot to death just outside the fence of the Radisson. The location was near Kiev Train Station, which is also a transfer station on the Moscow metro. It is always teeming with people. It's one of the busiest parts of the city for foot traffic. There were no witnesses. The winning guess to the date of the assassination for the office lottery was nine weeks earlier. We concluded that all the publicity delayed the inevitable.

Visit to Kraz

I arrived in Krasnoyarsk unannounced. Juices had told me that a Mr. Kharlamov managed exports, but didn't really have control over anything. I delivered him a customary bottle of XO cognac. He laughed at the gesture, without being rude. He advised me to leave undisturbed the forces that were in play. No one could influence anything, he commented. He asked where I was staying, which was in an independent hotel. He strongly urged me to stay in a hotel that was owned by the smelter. Then he insisted. His plea seemed genuine.

The Kraz hotel was like a fortress. I was not free to go in and out without an escort. In the parking lot there were about 25 of those Land Cruisers that Deutsche Bank had complained about. Judging by the menu in the hotel restaurant, automobiles weren't the only luxury items that Kraz bought. They were demonstrating the Russian phrase: **Любой каприз на Ваши деньги**, which to sound good in English I'd say is "No whim is too small, if you're paying for it." The Kraz hotel had Kobe beef, Kamchatka crab, Burgundy and Bordeaux wines, 25-year scotch, etc. Their in-house gourmet pelmeni (traditional Siberian dumplings) were as good as any I've ever tasted since.

There was nothing for me to do business-wise. I didn't expect to accomplish anything by staying, but wanted to kill a couple days to give the appearance that I'd given it my best effort. Sightseeing seemed in order. I tricked the gate guard into letting me off the compound on foot, claiming I was just going to get cigarettes at a kiosk a short walk away. When he let me out, I immediately stopped a gypsy cab[1], jumped in and told the driver to not let anyone follow us. He was surprised to hear I had no idea where to go.

Krasnoyarsk Hydroelectric
Dam on the Yenisei River

He suggested the hydroelectric dam. It was a very impressive structure, 400 feet tall. We descended sixty or so feet below the surface of the world's fifth largest river, the Yenisei. A damp coldness permeated everything. I imagined how a crack in the dam would turn into

---

1 In Russia it is commonplace to stop any car as a taxi.

a Biblically sized flood of ice cold water. The driver suggested the next stop should be a national park called "Stolby" or The Poles.

Stolby is a nature reserve with unique rock formations across the river from downtown Krasnoyarsk. The park attracts climbers from all over the world. "Stolby" are rock towers that seem foreign to the region. They are not part of any geological trend. We arrived to find the park's main entrance gate locked. The parking lot was empty. In Russia, never trust a "Closed" sign. The driver jumped the fence and went to see if he could find anyone, and if he couldn't, he would show me the pole monuments anyway. The driver returned with the park director. He said he couldn't let us drive in, because he didn't have the key to the gate, but offered to guide me up one of the poles, if I was interested. I asked what kind of gear I needed. The park manager, Andrei Rogovsky, looked me over and replied, 'You look strong enough. Just use your feet." I was wearing leather-soled wingtips and I have an uncontrollable fear of heights.

The park manager announced we'd climb ropeless and gave me a pair of climbing shoes to wear. The soles were so flimsy it felt like they were made of raw rubber. On rock, though, they gripped like glue. As we climbed onto the first rock, the driver blurted, "Fuck that! Don't do it. An Italian fell to his death not long ago." The park manager brushed off the dead Italian by saying, "He wasn't with me. I know every step to take on every hill." About that, he wasn't lying.

I followed the guide's every instruction and in what seemed like two minutes we were 60 feet up, looking at a rock face. I had absolutely no panic, yet. The driver was watching from below, probably worried he was going to lose a fare, he yelled for me to turn around and come back. When I looked down, I got vertigo and felt acute terror like never in my life. I felt myself about to start pissing my pants, but controlled it with the thought that urine running down my leg and onto the rock would cause me to slip. As a reflex, I must have yelled something like, "Oh Shit!" out loud. The driver yelled up, "I told you to fuck it." In my mind, I was apologizing to my family, who I hoped would forgive me for trying such an idiotic stunt.

Without doubt, the guide's calm confidence saved me. Several times, he stopped in a safe spot, of which there weren't many. Before taking a dangerous next step, he would repeatedly demonstrate its execution. In the hairier spots, it took up to ten times of him showing the step before I'd attempt it. To prevent the thought that any misstep meant death from taking hold, the guide used a hypnotic technique, repeating, "See. It is not difficult. Step with confidence." The first part of the climb had gone by so quickly it was like riding an elevator. The last part seemed like it took hours. I have no idea. Just before reaching the peak, a few light snowflakes hit my face. They motivated me to hurry to the top, which was a flat surface wide enough to sit on without fear of sliding off. When we got there, I pretended to be calm and took a selfie with a film camera. The expression on my face looked as naturally fear-free as did that of the little boy, whom Saddam Hussein patted on the head in a press conference right before the start of a war.

Dread about the descent prevented me from enjoying the spectacular Siberian panorama. I asked the guide to take several more photos, which I promised to enlarge and send to him, if I made it back to Moscow alive. Going down was mercifully much easier and the snow stopped. When we reached the bottom, the driver was as jubilant and relieved as I was. The guide asked for something like $20. I gave him $50 and took his name and address so I could send him the photos. That's how I remembered his name, or at least the one he gave me. When I got the film developed, I mailed him everything as promised.

Stolby National Park

When I returned to the hotel, the export manager excoriated security for allowing me off premise. He asked where I had been. I told him I had just climbed whatever number (7?) pole. He asked where my climbing gear came from. When I told him we climbed without ropes, he declared my story bullshit and asked, "Where did you really go?" Throughout dinner and drinks he repeated my claim about climbing a "Pole" ropeless to others. Not many believed me. Without the guide, I'd be dead. But then again, without the guide, I would have never tried.

Bykov and Ratnikov showed up at the hotel. I was encouraged when they invited me to their table. They quickly revealed that I was there not because they gave a shit about fifty million dollars, but because a Russian-speaking American was a novelty in Central Siberia. The one they had before, their partner Felix Lvov, was dead. They asked my opinion about American universities. Their children were likely going to study in the USA. I thought that helping them park their kids in American colleges would be a great way to get preferential treatment. I promised them, "I will make it happen," without having any idea how.

Park manager Rogovksy: Thank you!

Who Has a Spare Key

The flight time from Krasnoyarsk to Moscow is about the same as the time difference. You can depart at 9 a.m. and arrive around 10 a.m. When I flew back, I stopped by my apartment for a change of clothes before going to the office. A driver waited downstairs. I couldn't tell what was different, but something seemed amiss. There was a cabinet above the toilet that housed an on demand gas water heater. As I peed, I opened it. Wrapped in a newspaper there was a hand drill with some bits and wires. Hmm, that's unusual, I thought. I looked at the newspaper. It was dated that day. I searched the apartment. There was no one inside. There were no signs of drill holes. All the windows were shut. The door was locked. Nothing was missing. I locked up and headed to the office.

The first call I made was to the intelligence officer from our roof. I complained that they were doing a shitty job and told him about the drill in the bathroom. He promised to investigate. He called back not long after, saying, "This is beyond our control. You've got some fucked up friends. You're going to have to move to another apartment if you don't want to be bugged." I had no idea what he was talking about, and he didn't tell me.

After work, I met some friends at the sports bar on Noviy Arbat which had dozens of closed-captioned TVs. It might have been on CNN, but I noticed a headline, "Americans detained in the Russian Far East after entering the country from North Korea." It seemed likely that the Dicker had to be involved in that story.

The tools in the water heater cabinet were gone when I got home. I did an inventory of my small bar in the kitchen and noticed that Van Winkle and Booker's bourbon had been replaced with Johnny Walker red and blue, which are whiskies I would serve only when I wanted people to leave. The Dicker had a spare key to my apartment. He also had terrible taste in whisky. Even the FBI might have been able to conclude who was behind the whiskey switch.

I found the Dicker at his home in the U.S. I asked him WTF. He admitted that he had stayed at my place, drank my good whiskey and replaced it with perfume. Yes, Russian border guards had detained him after he and two friends videotaped one another pissing on North Korea. Alcohol was involved. The Russian government didn't eject him, but suggested he should take a break from Russia for a while.

The Dicker reported that being ordered by armed border patrol agents to "Get the fuck out" (**Уёбивай**) was a joke. He asked the border patrol, "How much?" It was a holiday. The agents wanted only bottles of vodka. The Dicker and his friends had almost none left. They stood by their Jeep, drinking the last bottle when more border patrol agents arrived. They assumed it was a show to negotiate a higher price. Their mood was casual and jovial until one of the Russian agents started speaking impeccable English legalese, saying things like, "You are not being accused of a crime and are not detained. However, you are not free to leave." They asked to examine their camcorder. One of the guards removed the cassette and violently smashed it, calmly saying, "You will be reimbursed for the value of that cassette." The Dicker returned to Russia a year or so later, but stayed in Moscow.

U.S. Detainees Released After Far East Incident

COMBINED REPORTS

Three U.S. citizens detained by Russian authorities near the Chinese border on suspicion of espionage have been released, the Federal Security Service said.

Security Service officials in the Far Eastern city of Vladivostok denied Tuesday an earlier report that the trio had been turned over to them after being taken into custody near the border town of Khasan, Itar-Tass said.

The town, 140 kilometers southwest of Vladivostok, is on the Sea of Japan and also sits on Russia's tiny border with North Korea.

The agency cited border authorities Monday as saying the Americans were caught Sunday carrying video footage of a section of the Russian border, the Khasan checkpoint and an electrical alarm system.

The videotapes had been confiscated, the agency said, citing security officials.

Gregory Elftmann, the U.S. Consulate spokesman in Vladivostok, confirmed that the three had been freed but gave no details on what they were doing near Russia's sensitive borders with China and Korea.

"They were within very short distance of the Russian-Chinese border. They weren't supposed to be there," he said in a telephone interview.

"To our understanding, they were questioned and released. As far as we know, there are no charges standing against them."

The report said the Americans worked for foreign companies in Vladivostok.

A spokesman at the U.S. Embassy in Moscow said Tuesday that American officials were trying to check the incident, but had no information beyond the Itar-Tass reports.

They didn't report the Dicker's name in the Moscow Times article

U.S. Embassy In Moscow

In an attempt to ingratiate myself with Kraz, I arranged the paperwork and personally escorted Ratnikov's daughter to the U.S. Embassy in Moscow to get a student visa, which might have been at the University of Virginia. I dreaded interacting with the staff at the Embassy. They're a combination of self-important, stupid, and tyrannical. Before they started processing visas online, applicants would be interviewed in person. Visa applications were pushed through pass trays. The embassy staff stood behind security glass with no speaker, making it necessary to speak loudly. The comments and questions from the Embassy staff were like an uncomfortable comedy script, whose author wanted the audience to cringe. There were only four or five windows. Not wanting to raise the noise, the fifty or sixty people in the visa waiting room made gestures to one another like they were reacting to surreal comments made by bureaucrats in a scene from a Kafka novel. Unless you had earplugs, it was difficult to not listen.

State Department official policy claimed that red flags to reject a visa applicant were: 1) Criminal background 2) No assets in Russia (either property or a high-paying job), 3) No immediate family, and 4) never traveled before. It was beyond infuriating to overhear conversations like a successful banker presenting meticulous verifiable papers, showing a diagnosis and treatment plan for his ten-year old daughter at St. Jude's hospital, and her disease was untreatable in Russia. He'd show them irrefutable proof of tens of millions of dollars in liquid assets, i.e. the ability to pay any and all medical costs. Without explanation, they'd say "Denied," and walk away.

People in the room would look at each other with mouths agape. There was no possibility of appeal. The dumbfounded and irate applicant would politely request to discuss further. The person who'd rejected the application stood silently behind the security glass, shaking their head no, announcing the name of the next applicant. Anyone who complained too appropriately would be threatened with having a U.S. Marine throw them out. No wonder they stood behind security glass and rarely went outside the compound, where they might learn something first-hand about where they lived.

Mikho's predecessor as thief-in-law of the Far East was a man known to most as Yaponchik (The little Jap-anese). Like most leading mobsters in the USSR, he grew up in Georgia. His real name was Viacheslav Ivankov. In Yaponchik's early career he was pretty creative. His team forged search warrants and used them to rob rich peoples' houses. They also presented bogus documents to gain access to police evidence warehouses. Later on he earned another nickname, "Father of extortion." He'd done ten years of a 15-year sentence, which was the maximum. Ivankovand was arguably the most famous crime boss in all of Russia. He was definitely as infamous in Russia as Al Capone was in 1930s Chicago. In 1992 The U.S. Embassy in Moscow issued him a three-year business visa. Their Russian expert background checkers had never heard of him.

Yaponchik left for New York right at the same time Vladivostok opened to foreigners. I would have likely crossed paths with him, instead of Mikho, were it not for the mind-boggling incompetence of the U.S. State Department. Yaponchik hit the U.S. where his first racket was shaking down Russian NHL players, whose salaries were considered astronomical. I imagine his conversations with NHL players were brief, i.e. "Does your mother live alone in Saratov?" To demonstrate seriousness, it was widely believed that he ordered the father of an NHL player murdered. Russian NHL players were never going to ask for help from the same government that gave Yaponchik a visa.

The FBI opened a Moscow office in the U.S. Embassy at the beginning of the Yeltsin administration. As a gesture of openness, the G.W.H. Bush administration presented to Vadim Bakatin, the last chairman of the KGB, photographs and video of a top-secret U.S. operation called Project Azorian. They showed a proper burial at sea of six Soviet sailors who had been secretly lifted off the floor of the Pacific Ocean inside their sunken nuclear submarine.

To reciprocate, Mr. Bakatin gave U.S. Ambassador to Russia, Robert Strauss, blueprints to the U.S. Embassy that showed where all the KGB listening devices had been planted all over the U.S. Embassy building. Bakatin's gift may have been an empty one, because I suspect that Russian intelligence had found better ways to listen in on conversation, but it was a nice gesture. I have to believe that the same State Department employee(s) who allowed the building to be bugged with impunity were promoted and granted even more authority. Soviet spy Robert Hanssen leaked information undetected from the FBI in Washington for 22 years. If a Russian NHL player contacted the FBI, I bet Yaponchik would have found out about it within hours.

While on the topic of crime bosses, this seems as good a place as any to place an online article in Russian about Mikho, aka Mikhail Osipov[1]. There are a few photos.

Because we had fifty million dollars at stake, I subjected myself to interact with U.S. Embassy staff and escorted Ms. Ratnikov into the benchless waiting room of the visa section. The room was full of people and stuffy.

---
1 https://www.mzk1.ru/2021/03/avtoritet-mixail-osipov-mixo/

The young lady reacted like a "pea in the mattress[2]" type. She fainted after a short time. I wasn't too concerned about her health, but thought, "Now we're never getting that metal" A U.S. Marine guard saw her faint and got us a visa processor without waiting. I explained that she was Mr. Oligarch's daughter and that I represented an international company with headquarters in the New York area. She got the visa. After doing the same for Bykov's son, I honestly expected Kraz to release our metal. Instead, as the blues lyrics go, I got a pocketful of thank you and a handful of much obliged. Bykov and Ratnikov released not one ton.

While we scrambled to find a way to pressure Kraz, a German bank called West LB was hungry to enter the Russian market. They begged to participate in the riskiest deal of the decade. The Swiss office cynically let them take over Deutsche Bank's loan to Kraz and agreed to force majeure clauses that held Gerald harmless if Kraz was revealed to be as lawless as we knew they were. To placate the new bank's demand for updates, I forged shipment reports on the Ministry of Railways letterhead. Facing potential criminal forgery charges seemed preferable to risking assassination in aluminum crossfire.

Lip called me to his office, which was in the former Voronstov Mansion on Petrovka Street, barely two blocks away from Gerald. He was the most honest and genuine high-ranking official I ever interacted with. I never left his office sober. After a few drinks, he liked to retell the story of how Siemens had tried to bribe him and failed. I recall reading an article that made the observation that the same passenger trains by Siemens were purchased by Russia and China. China paid $7 million for them. Russia paid $26 million. Lip asked what I'd been up to. I mentioned that it seemed Krasnoyarsk would be our first major defeat.

Lip said he had read about it. The body count from the Aluminum Wars had gone over one hundred twenty. It was news outside of Russia. Lip and I changed topics for a while. After a few more beverages, it was unavoidable to get away without hearing his story about a delegation from China who had never eaten shrimp. They asked what it was. When they heard shrimp, they repeated it, replacing the "r" with and "L" because they can't pronounce "r." Lip would laugh and say "shlimp!"

I got up to leave and Lip announced, "I've got you covered!" There was no context. I asked what he meant. He said, "I will turn off the railway for Kraz unless the metal they ship is consigned to you." That sounded great, but I didn't want him to become the 125th victim. He laughed at my concern and said, "I'm retired. I have enough money. I know how to stay alive. If you want proof that I know how to stay alive, I'm old. I have been through worse." He said it sounded like a fun challenge.

---

2 From the Hans Christian Andersen fairy tale, "The Princess and the pea," about a young woman whose royal ancestry is established by a test of her sensitivity by placing a single pea under her mattress.

All shipments by rail to were subject to interdepartmental approvals between the receiving port, railways, and ministry of marine transportation. To rail 22,500 tons, we'd need seven of what were called "Marshroutes," sets of 50 railcars. The two best ports for a single vessel to pick up a cargo of that size were St. Petersburg and Novorossiisk. I chose St. Pete because I love the place, and besides, the port had a jackalope for a mascot. They agreed to accept 350 cars of metal for us. With the port's agreement, Lip got the 350 cars approved within a day.

When Kraz received a telex that railcars had been approved for Gerald, the export director finally remembered our phone number. He called me to ask what the fuck I was thinking. I explained that they had promised to ship our metal several months ago, so they must be ready by now. I was helping them keep their word.

Lip reported that the first 50 rail cars had arrived at Krasnoyarsk and that metal was being loaded. It wasn't clear for whom, though. I didn't dare speak directly with Kraz and risk revealing I was part of the rail blockage scheme. They dispatched the first fifty and Kraz even sent us a fax copy showing "Gerald Metals" as consignee, destination Saint Petersburg commercial sea port. It seemed so easy. It made me wonder why they hadn't put up a bigger fight.

It takes six to eight days for rail freight from Krasnoyarsk to reach St. Petersburg. With seven trainloads, the shipments would be staggered over a week. Then it would take the port a few days to unload the cargo and prepare a berth for loading. The fastest we could expect to take clear ownership after the first train left was two weeks. Kraz continued to dispatch metal consigned to us.

With Uncle Vic, somewhere on the coast of the Baltic Sea

A former co-worker gave me a courtesy call from Krasnoyarsk. He had jumped ship from Marc Rich and was working for a competitor that had also dumped money into chaotic Kraz. He said he overheard Kraz discussing Gerald. They intended to readdress the metal to Transworld. Their plan was to send a customs arrest before the cargo reached port. They'd claim that our metal had been erroneously consigned. My colleague/informant believed that the telex had already been sent. I thanked him for the information and told him, "I owe you a chip."

Gennady was the point man at St. Pete port customs. I knew him fairly well, even though there wasn't much reason for me to deal with his office, he was always around socially. I felt I could trust him. I described the situation to him by phone. He assured me he had all the facts he needed and that the cargo, consigned to Gerald, would be loaded onto the vessel chartered by Gerald. I kept asking him about the telex. He repeated, "We have NOT seen any telexes. No such telex was received." What I couldn't see over the phone was that he was trying to wink as he spoke of the "Non-telex." They had received it and ignored it. He ended the conversation by reassuring me that all was under control. "Uncle Vic" was aware too.

Gerry called for an update. I reported that the aluminum situation appeared to be under control. He asked when I was scheduled to arrive in St. Petersburg. When I said I didn't think it was necessary, his reaction ran something on the lines of, "You fucking nitwit. Have you read the papers lately? There is a war on." I replied that my contacts were honorable and highly reputable. They had never hung me out to dry even when they had a hundred chances to. I told him I considered many of the people there more than business partners. It would be rude to second guess them by showing up in person. Nothing I said dissuaded Gerry. His instructions were explicit: "Go to St. Petersburg now. Do not leave there until you have an original bill of lading,"

Most of the port's management knew who I was, the dude with jackalopes. It was not possible for me to walk around without being recognized. To be seen would send a message that I didn't trust them. I decided to go straight to the ship we'd chartered to verify that aluminum was being loaded. The Nakhodka crew had given me a badge and I.D. from the Ministry of Marine Transportation that allowed me to enter seaports and customs zones. I used it to enter the territory of St. Petersburg port.

The dry cargo terminal is over 5km long. It took nearly an hour to locate the crane lifting pallets of aluminum and placing them in the ship's hold. The site of that Kraz aluminum being loaded excited me. All of the shit around the Aluminum Wars was a game to me. They tried to make me smell the glove and failed. The sight of our ship being loaded meant they were going to smell the glove instead and it made me euphoric. As I neared the gangplank, hoping to board and say hello to the captain, a Volvo with dark tinted windows drove towards me. There was only one car like that and it belonged to Sasha, the director's son-in-law. He got out of the car. We shook hands and he asked "What in the fuck do you think you're doing out here? Do you want to insult us? We told you everything's under control. It's under control. Victor and Anatoly (export department) want to see you.

"Kesha!? Why do you insult us?" the port's export director asked, offended by my show of distrust. His mustache made him look a little bit like the cartoon character Wally Walrus, but without the fangs. I blamed my visit on the New York office, explaining that they forced me to monitor loading. Victor listened and replied, "Well, New York doesn't handle relations with this port. You do. So, what you are going to do is leave now and go find out if Nevsky Prospekt is still there. We will bring your bill of lading to the Grand Hotel Europe. What room are you in?" The order to go see if Nevsky was still there was like telling a New Yorker to make sure 5th Avenue hadn't moved, or telling a Parisian to go find out if the Champs-Elysees was missing. I got the message. My choices were to anger the port's management, or to follow Gerry's orders. I left.

Entrance to the St. Petersburg Commercial Port Authority, home of a stuffed jackalope

It wouldn't be the first time that baseless information was reported to Gerry. I knew the port's load rate was about 800 tons per hour, so if all went well, it would take two to three days for the ship to be loaded and sail. To kill the first day, I rented a tour boat and invited guitar-playing friends. We rode the canals and rivers while singing Russian ballads. We shot champagne corks at passersby on the embankments. It was like a St. Petersburgian twist on bologna throwing. We didn't hit anyone, but those who noticed us shooting corks gave a thumbs-up. Every four hours or so, I'd report to Gerry on the progress about which I had no information.

Each time I called in with an unverified update, or to use diplomatic terminology "I bullshitted him," I expected to hear, "What are you talking about? The captain reported an entirely different situation. You're fired." On day two I decided to visit Tsarskoe Selo, a place I hadn't been since I was a student. There are several palaces there and the area gives a sense of what Russia in the 1700s was like. Even the distance markers on the highway to there are still shown not in kilometers or miles, but in Versts[3]. The first stop was Catherine the Great's Summer Palace, famous for the Amber room. After touring palaces all day, I made a final report, bluffing that "We should have the bill of lading tomorrow." I hit the hotel bar and got sloppy drunk with friends.

An increasingly louder knocking on my hotel door got my eyes open around 11 a.m.

---

3 A Verst is an obsolete Russian measurement of distance. One Verst is 3,500 feet or 1.0668 kilometers. In Tsarist era Russia a Verst's length was described as 500 Sazhen.

A Finnish friend, who was a world traveler, described the feeling one has when waking up in a hotel, post blackout, and having to examine unfamiliar surroundings, with no recollection of how you got where you are as: "What country? What currency?" Those were my questions before I went to answer the door. I opened up to see a courier with an envelope. I asked how much. He handed me the bill of lading, saluted, and said, "No charge." Every ton was en route to a warehouse in Rotterdam. I faxed a copy to Moscow, NY and Lausanne, doing a happy dance.

Real Wedding

In May 1996 my pregnant bride (to be) arrived in Minneapolis two weeks before her due date. She told me she wanted a church wedding and wanted to wait until her shape returned so that she could wear a nice dress after our child was born. My mother had a different plan. When I arrived within a week of the due date, Mom immediately unleashed a tirade like she never had, on me at least. The short version of what she said was, "I've studied over three hundred years of our family's history. Not one child has been born out of wedlock. Yours will not be the first. I don't care what Matilda says about wearing a dress." I got the message.

My grandfather and middle namesake had started as a stock boy and ended up running a company called Butler and Sons, which was a warehouse and distribution hub for Ben Franklin stores. After grandfather's death in the mid 1970's the space was converted to an office building in downtown Minneapolis called Butler Square. In 1996 the restaurant D'Amico Cucina was on the first floor of Butler Square. It seemed like an historically appropriate location for carrying on the family tradition. We met the manager on a Tuesday afternoon to discuss a wedding party for about seventy people. Things turned bleak when he asked us which month we were planning on. When we told him, "This Friday or Saturday," He told us that it was impossible on such short notice. He changed his mind when I told him we wanted three cases of Barolo, and Cinque Terre for dessert.

I called my mom to tell her that we had the wedding space booked three days from then, but no one to perform the ceremony. She said, "You can't do this. I need more time."

I replied, "You started it."

Mom found an available judge friend to perform the ceremony. It wasn't a Las Vegas wedding, but with seventy-two hours of planning it was close. J.P. wasn't born until June 9. It turned out we had a little over two weeks to spare.

Mom considered herself an Irish Catholic. She always spoke with reverence about spending time there. Ireland was sort of halfway between Moscow and Minneapolis. so I expected her to show up at J.P.'s baptism in a church inside Cong Abbey. The Abbey was established in the 7th century. Over the centuries, the British burned it down one less time than the Irish rebuilt it. Besides its symbolic location between the hometowns of the parents, I liked the tenacity represented by the fact the place was still there.

Leonid Chizhik and his wife joined us. Leonid composed and dedicated a song that he called J.P.'s Lullaby. He performed it in the basement bar of nearby Ashford Castle, where a piano accompanist had been playing for a singer. We asked if Leonid could perform one song and explained why. They agreed. Before he started playing, the bar ignored the cue to quiet down and the noise was too much to play over. To get the room's attention, Leonid reworked the melody of an Irish folk song that the singer had just been performing and turned it into a Rachmaninov-style power concerto. The room went silent.

After Leonid finished, the other piano player refused to play again. The song is here, but titled differently: Leonid Chizhik - Spirit of moon | Roque d'Antheron (2002) - YouTube

Whorewacker Does Russia

After St. Petersburg port had "somehow" misplaced the customs arrest, Whorewhacker insisted he personally deliver thank you envelopes for me to relay. I tried to explain to him the Russian logic that a reward for something personal could be insulting. The aluminum loading was a matter of principle, so they refused payment. I once encountered the same kind of gap in logic with the police. When I opened the outer door to my apartment, I saw that the second pushed outwards from the inside. It opened the other way. As soon as I noticed, I locked the outer steel door with a key-only deadbolt and went for the police.

The police examined the steel bars on the apartment's windows and found everything safe. We entered the apartment and found nothing missing. When I offered them payment for their time, they refused. The police told me that they only took money if something was wrong. It made no sense to me, but that's what they said.

Whorewhacker didn't really care about his relations with the port. He wanted a justification to take a trip to a beautiful city. He said that the perception in Lausanne and New York was that St. Pete was a lawless mafia town, and by going there he would prove them wrong. I told him I'd greet him at the airport. Before hanging up, he asked, "Should I bring some weed?" I advised him not to, but if he insisted, it should be vacuum sealed and worn in his clothes. The main thing was to not put it in a checked bag.

We got in the back seat of a waiting car outside the exit of Pulkovo airport. Whorewhacker's bag was between us. He opened it and revealed about a half pound of marijuana, unsealed, as well as fifty thousand USD cash. He truly qualified for the "green" channel. I was flabbergasted that the bag made it past the baggage check.

We went for dinner at a Russian restaurant called Adamant on The Moika Canal. At the time it was one of the best restaurants in Russia for local cuisine. The fad in the 1990s was all things foreign. Good Russian restaurants were surprisingly hard to find. The layout of Adamant was like a manor with several rooms. That night, nearly all the rooms were empty. In fact, I'd never seen it so empty. In the room where the bar was, a single couple was seated, doing vodka shots and zakuski. We sat near them. I taught Whorewhacker about toasts and the food. The man at the next table insisted we join him and his girlfriend. This wasn't uncommon. When the man started to speak, his words were smattered with Feni,

Russian prison slang. He ordered another half-liter of vodka. The waiter and waitress behind him looked nervous, afraid even.

The mafia in the Far East had taught me phrases and gestures, some of which I had shown to Whorewhacker. He wanted to ask me discreetly if we were in the presence of a convict, but instead he used the gesture for "I will fuck you." Before I could react, the convict noticed. Considering it a threat, he jumped to his feet, knocked his chair over backwards and pulled a Makarov out from behind his back. He wasn't really pointing it at us, but held it in his hand.

Backpedaling away from the gesture, I told the man with the gun that he had completely misunderstood. "In his country," I explained, "that gesture means you're a great guy." He put the gun away. I hoped to just go back to our table when the guy's phone rang. He told whomever was on the other end,

"Yes. They're all the way live. Easy pickings. Chicken in a pot. Appear to have some coin. There'll be no pushback. Stop by." I must have had a bad poker face. Whorewhacker was clutching a steak knife by the side of his leg and staring at me as if to ask permission to start stabbing. I announced that I needed the restroom. "Your friend stays," the guy told me. Whorewacker's eyes were begging me to not leave. I said, "I'll be right back." I locked the bathroom door and called Sasha from the port. Luckily, he was not far away and said he would get us out.

Sasha said he would enter first to not raise suspicion. Once I noticed him, he would nod to confirm that a car was outside waiting for us. Once we got the signal, we were to run out as fast as we could. I relayed the plan to Whorewacker in serious slang, in case the girlfriend understood English. "My homey's gonna swoop us. When he peeps and drops a nod. Scoot. I mean GTFO ASAP. Ya dig?"

Sasha popped his head in and gave the signal. Whorewhacker and I bolted out the door and jumped into his Volvo with the dark windows. Sasha had a tail car with muscle, just in case. Sasha asked what the hell happened. He too was baffled. It made no sense. Things like that were exceedingly rare, especially in a nice restaurant. It was the wrong place at the wrong time. That's all. I thanked Sasha for the rescue and suggested we walk back to the hotel, so the city could show off its beauty. Neither Sasha nor I thought there was any chance of similar trouble.

We had walked almost all the way back to our hotel. As we crossed the bridge on Nevsky over the Griboedov Canal, two police officers jumped out of their car and demanded documents. I had intentionally told Whorewhacker to leave his passport and weed in the hotel. He looked terrified and the cops sensed it. As I was protesting in Russian, they threw the scared obvious tourist into their car and sped off. Nevsky is the city's main street, so I got a tail car instantly. There were two guys in their 20's in the front seat. I told them, "Those cops took my friend. Don't let them get away."

My guys were driving about a 15-year old Mercedes. The police had a Soviet-era Lada. They knew we were following them and couldn't outpace us. They turned on their emergency lights and started driving the wrong way down a one-way canal embankment. We followed them. When we got close to the Neva River, the Mercedes guys parked, because they knew which police station Whorewacker was going to. They pointed it out to the entrance and said they'd wait there for us.

When I entered the police station, the officers hadn't even started to shake Whorewacker down. He was standing behind a see-through door, convinced the police had lost me. He expected to go to jail. Not because of a lack of passport, but because the dumbass had stuffed an ounce of herb down the front of his pants. They didn't even pat him down. I explained to the police that the Grand Hotel Europe had his passport, but to save time offered them some cash. They let him go right away.

The driver and passenger were happy to see that the police lost. There was a Russian reality show on TV in the 1990s where car thieves would get ten minutes to steal a vehicle that had a tracking device in it. Then the police chased the stolen car. Almost the whole country cheered for the criminals. Whorewhacker asked if these people were cool. When I asked why, he pulled the bag out of his crotch. I asked our new friends if they enjoyed "Shmal," slang for marijuana. They showed me a reworked pack of Marlboro, which was labeled "Shmal-boro." Instead of red, the Shmalboro had a green leaf on it. They drove to a store. We bought some papers and rolled several for them, in lieu of taxi fare.

Exit Sultan

There came a point when Sultan's penchant for potent potables crossed paths with dollar and tenge accounting. After a visit from the CFO of Gerald's New York office, political and family connections were no longer a sufficient buffer. Sultan's budget overruns consistently hovered around triple what they should have been. Gerald's curious accountant casually suggested dinner and a drink with him to witness in person the frugality of our political employee. Sultan misread the situation and thought it was an opportunity to garner favor from the CFO, so he rolled out the red carpet.

There was a club in Almaty with several special purpose rooms. It had casino table games, elegant dining, a supper club with live music, a beer bar, and the "Smiles" room. "Smiles" was played by male participants, who sat across from each other at a wide table, while underneath the table prostitutes serviced their manhood with their hands and mouths. The first man to crack a smile loses the game and has to pay for everyone. The situation about the CFO learning what the Smiles table was made me imagine Sultan as Travis Bickle in the movie "Taxi Driver" and his date, Betsy's reaction to him bringing her to a pornographic movie theater. As the saying goes, never test a river's depth with both feet.

Sultan buried himself by trying to make up for the smiles fiasco by bidding on and winning a gourmet cake that was auctioned in the club. He paid a thousand dollars for it. That was the end of his career at Gerald.

Exit Pablo

Pablo walked up to my desk and threw a business card down, announcing, "I will start using my new title when you tell me it's OK." It had his real full name, but his new job description was, "Born not to earn. Retiree." (Не для денег родившийся. Пенсионер.) He was as unpretentious and loyal as his father. He explained that he felt obligated to me for having given him the chance to prove his worth, but he had enough money to survive as an artist in St. Petersburg. He wanted out of corporate life. I loved everything about his gesture. It validated my trust in him and proved his abilities. It confirmed he was an honorable artist.

Before quitting, Pablo suggested sending a gay Russian, who worked at Balkhash copper (Ball-scratch, to Gerry) to the Moulin Rouge in Paris. Pablo considered it a cruel twist of fate to place a cultured gay man to work at a metallurgical factory in the middle of the Kazakh steppe on the shores of one of the world's largest and oddest lakes, Balkhash. It has freshwater in the West and saltwater in the East. Pablo devised a scheme to justify sending him at Gerald's expense. It was a win-win proposition. Balkhash would look at Gerald favorably, and Pablo got to use his position in the company to provide what might be a once in a lifetime opportunity for someone he'd enjoyed working with.

Crimea

The Kazakh khokhli continued to search for ever more ridiculous ways to generate kickbacks. They routed a small lot of zinc through a port called Kerch, which is at the western end of Crimea. Kerch was Ukrainian then. Even if the khokhli could collect $10 per ton from the port, the extra money they had to pay for rail guaranteed the deal would cost more money for their company than using a traditional port. They got a little revenge by forcing me to travel to Kerch to get a port agreement.

The port manager met me at Simferopol airport and drove me to his apartment. His wife had prepared borscht and pierogi for me. The food was very good, but the real reason he stopped by his home was to bring along his dog, "Bug" (Жук), who accompanied us to my hotel room. It was a nice second-floor suite with an office area. It had a long balcony, from which the Azov seashore was close enough to be visible but not heard. The port rep. closed the curtains and started writing down numbers, i.e. an official fees and kickback schedule. "Bug" started growling by the balcony door. The port guy threw open the curtains and jumped onto the balcony. I was close behind. There was a man standing below on the grass, pointing a directional mic at our window. The port rep. praised his dog, "Good boy Bug!!" The man holding the mic scurried away into the darkness.

His price was acceptable. For a one time lot of 1,500 tons, no one cared. The trip was an annoyance. The man drove me back to the airport in Simferopol. Despite his protest, I assured him that I needed no help to buy an airline ticket. The place was full of people, but not many of them were going through security or passport control. When it was my turn, the woman at the ticket counter said that she had no tickets left. "Only the airport director on the second floor could issue tickets," she said, which I understood to mean, "You need to bribe someone other than me."

In front of the director's office, there was a line of about fifty people. I took out my blue U.S. passport and left a fifty dollar bill protruding from it. An assistant was monitoring the scene and motioned me to the head of the line. The director agreed to sell me a ticket at the foreigner price, plus the fifty dollar bill I had shown. I felt like I had pulled one over on everyone waiting in line. That was, until I boarded the Il 62 to Moscow, a plane that seats about 200. There were exactly two passengers on board besides me. Both were from India. I asked if they two had bribed to get tickets. They had. "How Soviet," I thought. The airport director preferred the plane to fly empty, rather than not collect a bribe.

Bolshoi Ballet

A favorite perk of working at Gerald Moscow was not only the geographical proximity of our office (less than five minutes walking) to the Bolshoi Theater, but the fact that one of our managers was best friends with the theater's projectionist, Nelli Ivanovna. My co-worker, "The Grape," took me to the Bolshoi ballet so often, it became almost ordinary. Almost. Not once did I regret going to ballet at The Bolshoi.

The projection booth of Grape's friend, Nelli, was on the right side of the stage. In it she had a mini refrigerator, wine glasses, corkscrews, and extra chairs. I felt sorry for the saps who had to sit in the center orchestra, or in a V.I.P. loge. We had an open bar and no neighbors to "Shush" us for speaking. What fascinated me most was Nelli's and Grape's commentary. I would be rapt by the lithe, effortless, grace of some dancer, while those two would be harping, "Look at that hippopotamus! Shameful." Their high standards made me hesitant to admit what I thought about a performance.

I recall the first time I saw Svetlana Zakharova. She was visiting from the Mariinsky in St. Petersburg. I didn't want to again get slammed for my terrible skills at critiquing ballet, but when they asked me what I thought of her, I couldn't refrain from stating that I thought we just witnessed perfection. Nelli corroborated, saying "Svetochka dances on air." She also hoped Ms. Zakharova would leave St. Pete and join the Bolshoi.

Nelli Ivanovna Tyurina,
legend of the Bolshoi Theater

A Message from Kraz

Toolshed was visiting Moscow. He was still with the tobacco company but had temporarily relocated his family to their headquarters in Louisville, Kentucky while his daughter successfully went through medical treatment. Toolshed's godson, my five month-old baby was in the apartment. I suggested we walk half a block to a bar called Direktor so he could smoke without worrying about the baby. The place was a bit of a dump. It was one floor below street level on Komsomolsky Prospekt. There was a railing around the stairs, except for where they started. Above the landing at the bottom, on top the railing, a camera was pointed at the stairs leading down.

The place was empty. It had one pool table and a limited bar. Toolshed and I ordered a beer and a shot and started shooting pool. After fifteen minutes or so, two Chechens and a Russian thug came in and started talking to us. When one of them called me "Aluminum boy," I told Shed in English that we needed to leave immediately. I went to the exit and pulled on the steel door. It was locked and could only be unlocked with a key. A few feet from the door, a guard sat at a desk, watching the feed from the outside camera on a monitor. I animatedly gestured to him to unlock the door, as in right now. He was indifferent.

One of the Chechens walked up to me at the exit and announced, "We are playing a game, called 'Who gets out of here alive?' tonight'. I bet on myself. What about you?" I pretended to not understand, spoke with a heavy accent and asked if we could bet on a game of pool instead. Toolshed told him, "I will fuck your mother." Shed's glasses flew across the room after the Chechen smacked him in the face. They promised Shed that he would regret having said that.

We offered to play a game of pool for $100 and buy more drinks. It seemed they were waiting for a van or someone else to haul us away to somewhere else. They didn't notice or didn't care that I had a cellphone and let me go to the bathroom with it. Catching a signal in a basement seemed a longshot, but I managed to reach the Alpha team. I explained that we were locked in the basement bar, Direktor, and told them to hurry. They seemed hesitant, like it was a false alarm. I assured them it was not. I pleaded for them to get there immediately, or it might be too late.

Then I called Matilda, who was a half block away upstairs with baby J.P. I told her we'd managed to get into a bit of a spot, but it was OK. Alpha was on their way. The last thing I told her was, "Do not call the police."

I think she sensed panic, and decided to do the unthinkable, which was to leave the baby alone and try to rescue us herself. Before leaving the apartment, she called the baby's godmother who lived across town, telling her, "If you don't hear back from me in 20 minutes, call the police and come get the baby."

Expecting the extraction team any minute, I felt more comfortable in the pool room. Shed didn't know help was on the way. After several minutes, the guy, watching the camera feed, announced that there's someone outside the door. One of the Chechens said to me, "If you called the police, start writing your obituary. Police won't touch me." I assured him that if anyone was there for me, it would not be the police. The Chechen asked the camera watcher who was at the door. He replied, "Some chick." The Chechen instructed him to unlock the steel door. There stood Matilda. She thought she had come up with a cover story to get us out. She pretended to be an angry young mother, feigning anger that I was out drinking when I should be upstairs with her and the baby. The Chechen listened to her faux rant and asked, "Are you done?" He shut the door in her face. They locked it again.

After locking the door, the Chechen commented, "If I had a wife yell at me like that, I'd punch her fucking kidneys out." The godmother was dumb enough to call the police. Thankfully, they told her that they only handled regular kidnappings. Kidnapped foreigners were covered by a separate police force, but they didn't have the number for it.

Shed and I beat them at pool again, challenging them to higher stakes. We all knew no one was going to pay anyway, so we bet a thousand. When Alpha arrived, carrying compact machine guns, the guy who was monitoring the camera got wide-eyed and summoned the Chechen, who repeated his threat, "If those are police, I will cut your head off in front of them and they will let me walk." I assured him that they were not police, but I bet he wished they were.

After what seemed to be a twenty minute standoff, they unlocked the exit. Oleg's body filled the doorway, AK drawn. He looked a bit like the boxer, Butterbean, but after he'd been on a diet. He stuck his left finger out, pointed it up the stairs and said, "Run!" I ran past him at full speed up the stairs and started zigzagging down the sidewalk, thinking that it would make it harder to hit me if someone started shooting. The entryway to my apartment's staircase was around the back. I waited for Shed in the archway. He meandered casually to where I was waiting for him. He didn't even look back to see if someone was following.

We sat in my kitchen and recapped the sequence of events. Matilda said that when the door opened and she saw the severity of the vicious visage with injurious intentions staring at her like a hungry pitbull would at a porterhouse, she immediately regretted going on stage. With baby J.P. asleep in the next room, I wondered if the consequences of making Soviets smell the glove for a profession was worth the risk. Toolshed said that he had thought our captors and would-be killers were scared of him, because he had told them the name of his Chechen boss friend. When the doorbell rang, my heart sank. Had Alpha lost the fight?

I turned off the lights and looked out the peephole. It was an FSB officer, Pavel Gerasimov. Oleg and Borya had sent him to collect statements while our memories were still fresh. Toolshed loved to tweak Gerasimov by innuendo that only one of the two was a superior spy. Shed's Russian was and is impeccable. His ability to glibly quote verbatim classic quotes from Russian literature that were germane to the discussion exacerbated Gerasimov's suspicions of Shed as a spy. Only one of them lost sleep trying to solve the mystery. For Toolshed, it was like sending an adult on a snipe hunt more than once.

The next morning Alpha placed a guard in the stairwell of my apartment. Another was parked outside. At the office, I told my co-workers about the incident. Denis suggested to "fuck Chechens in the mouth." When I told Mountain that I was leaning towards quitting, he advised me to stick around a little longer, because Gerry was about to announce bonuses.

When I got home, Alpha insisted that they escort me to Direktor right away. They didn't expect me to see any familiar faces, but said that by just walking in, it would show the other side that we were hunting them. The guy who watched the monitor was there. Alpha said that he would definitely relay that I had stopped by and wasn't alone. It seemed like a waste of time.

When Gerry announced bonuses, I thought it was a joke. There had been more fruitful days with the railway tariffs. Maybe he knew about that. Either way, it was insulting. Solving problems had been a lot of fun, but after just two days of living with guards around the apartment with our child in it, Matilda and I decided to take a break from Russia and returned to Minneapolis.

About the same time I exited the Siberian aluminum wars and Russia altogether, the Reuben Brothers hired a U.S. law firm to advise how to take the company public with a maximum valuation. After doing background checks on the venture's key personnel, the law firm concluded that the public information on Misha Krisha, aka Michael Cherney, was so detrimental that they advised that someone should pay him just to go away. Some time around 1997 they paid him $400,000,000 (four hundred million dollars). By the end of 2021 the net worth of the Reubens was estimated at twenty-five billion dollars. They are the second richest family in the U.K. after the royals.

Hitlerina

After mentioning to the Saint that the weather was around twenty below in Minneapolis, he suggested a get together in Maui to bring in the New Year. My mother-in-law flew over to babysit. I thought the nickname I'd given her was pretty inventive, Hitlerina. My wife's friends, who knew her from Star City, were not that impressed by the moniker I'd created for her. They already referred to her as "Saddam Husseinka." At a crowded new year's eve party in Star City a man had gotten down on his knees to propose to Matilda. Saddam Husseinka took off her shoe and beat the man on his head with the wooden heel. She chased him out of the room. He scrambled so hard to get away, he fell down the stairs. He left the party unbetrothed and with a severe concussion.

I learned about the marriage-proposal beating after we went on our date to Istanbul. On the way to the airport, I had to pick up Matilda, who lived with Hitlerina. The kind folks from Star City said afterwards they were very curious what kind of reception I'd get from Hitlerina, when she heard I was there to take her daughter to Turkey. Our friends from Star City didn't think it was appropriate to warn me about the potential for Hitlerina to react violently.

Holder of a world record parachute jump and my mother-in-law, Valentina Rybalka

Valentina Rybalka (Hitlerina) set a world record parachute jump in the late 1950s for the USSR. They dressed her in double mink coats to protect her from the high altitude frigid temperatures. She missed the landing zone and found herself in a field of collective farmers. Military helicopters flew back and forth at low altitude searching for her. She said that when one landed to pick her up, none of the farmers dared even raise their heads to look. She parachuted from a plane that flew over Moscow's (now defunct) Tushino airfield. After landing, she delivered a bouquet of flowers to the new Soviet leader, Leonid Brezhnev, at his swearing in ceremony, after succeeding Nikita Khruschev.

With J.P. safe with two grandmothers, we took off for Hawaiii, stopping in Las Vegas to meet friends from the Moscow scene. One was a Lezgin. I mention his ethnicity only because most Lezgins live in the Republic of Dagestan, which is part of Russia. It is the only region in the former Soviet Union with no ethnic majority. Everyone's a minority and they all seem to live mostly peacefully.

We stayed at the Luxor, because it was the newest. The building is a pyramid. We were curious what it would feel like to ride an elevator that moves at a thirty-nine degree angle. Before going to see the Blue Man Group show, we agreed to meet at a video poker bar. Almost immediately, Matilda announced that her machine quit working. She'd hit a jackpot. The Blue man Group's cover of Donna Summer's song "I Feel Love" caused the Russians to act like teenage girls watching the Beatles in 1965. I asked what the big deal was. They informed me that Donna Summer was one of few American acts allowed in the USSR and she was considered a goddess and widely loved.

Off the coast of Maui the Lezgin and I had a close encounter with a humpback whale. We were in a two-seat kayak. The whale surfaced for air about fifteen feet from us. We looked at each other with our jaws dropped, gawking in silence as its massive black tail rose above the surface in front of us, and then slowly disappeared back into the deep. When we returned to shore, waves had gotten much bigger. Anyone on the beach who was paying attention to us, got a genuine belly laugh watching us flip and get pounded into the sand. Matilda said she laughed so hard her stomach muscles were sore.

We returned from Hawaii to find that Hitlerina had used an abrasive bleach powder to strip the varnish off the parquet floor in the kitchen. She said she thought initially it was soap, but she didn't stop until the job was done. Baby J.P. was fine and there was another on the way. Our house was built by an architect who had designed it for himself and his wife, with no children. For the future new baby's room, we decided to convert a bathroom into a small bedroom. After tearing out all the fixtures, I decided it was the wrong house for a family. The original design was a 1960s party house. There was a tree growing through a hole in the twenty foot overhang at the entrance. The house sat on a hill overlooking a lake with one of the best views in the city of the skyline behind the other shore. The view was such that the entire wall was floor to ceiling windows. Out of respect for the original design, we wanted to put the bathroom back as was.

I knew nothing about contractors. I'd only ever rented. After asking for advice, a friend recommended a plumber. I showed him the job. He gave me an estimate. I said yes. He said he would start the job in a couple of days. He asked for $5,000 to buy materials. I gave him cash. Weeks went by and he had done nothing. When he stopped answering his phone, I got a little angrier. The guy who recommended him said that he worked for a plumber's union and was a regular at a bar called Mac's Industrial. I went to look for him. Sure enough, there was Tony the plumber at Mac's.

Giving him the benefit of the doubt, I asked when he was going to show up to do what he said he would. My brain couldn't process his words when he asked, smirking, "What are you going to do, sue me over a transaction that doesn't exist? There are no documents." That was an incredible declaration. Saying something that brazen in Russia could get you maimed in a hurry. To make certain I understood him correctly, I gave him two options: Return the cash, or do what he said he would. He replied by telling me about his gun collection, repeating that there was no contract, so also no way to file a court claim. In Moscow, a booger like that would be immediately flicked. Tony had shown me the type of American scumbag who abuses the law. I walked out of Mac's livid.

It was economically unjustifiable to fly someone like Gera to do a small job, but the principle of the matter required action. I flipped through the rolodex in my head and recalled a Finnish heavyweight wrestler who lived in Minneapolis on and off. I met him briefly in Moscow. The two had become friends when my father, Roger McKinney, was president of the men's club at Greenhaven Golf Course in Anoka, MN. The golf course had arranged a visa for Rantu the Finn by using an employment loophole. If an American company advertises a skilled position and no American candidates come forward, they can hire a foreigner. The golf course placed ads for the all-in-one position of executive chef, greenskeeper, and head of security. They were flabbergasted when a black man from Chicago applied for the job and he had expert credentials. They paid him to withdraw his application.

When Rantu and I went out for drinks in Moscow, he wore bulletproof vests and stab proof clothes. He said that some man had tried to stab him while he was sitting at a bar. With the special clothes on, he said it felt like someone was poking him with their finger. When Rantu saw it was a blade, he grabbed the stabber's wrist and smashed his hand on the bar. When the knife came loose, Rantu grabbed it and rammed it through the back of the man's hand, leaving the blade deep in the wood. He laughed about it, adding, "I bet he don't use that hand to stab no one no more."

He and my father became friends after an incident at the golf course's bar/restaurant when a few members of a local biker gang called the Grim Reapers showed up. They harassed a waitress, who warned them she would call the chef if they didn't stop. They laughed and threw food on the floor. Rantu emerged with a baseball bat and ran them out. They waited in the parking lot to ambush him when he got off work, which was a decision they regretted. Rantu inflicted severe physical harm on the attackers, which was self defense. But he had also put dents in several car doors by ramming the bikers' heads into them. The owners demanded that someone had to pay to get them fixed. My dad took up a collection, which was an act Rantu didn't forget. When he told me about it in Moscow, he ended by saying, "Your dad is good people. You can cash in a chip with me some time."

It was embarrassing to cash in a chip to collect a debt from a rogue, chump-change plumber, but the principle of it was infuriating. I got Rantu's number from my dad, explaining to him why. Dad told me that the Finn had been collecting gambling debts on the side for an illegal bookmaker friend named Barry. Rantu was the right man for my job. When he answered the phone, I asked if he remembered telling me I could cash in a chip. He confirmed, and added that his word is always good. Reluctantly, I explained the situation. Rantu told me, "No problem! Once you locate him, you come with me to make sure I don't get the wrong guy." He hung up.

Whoever answered the phone at the union had no qualms telling me Tony the plumber's schedule. He was supposed to be working in an office building not far from Rantu's house the next day. As soon as the Finn sat down in the passenger seat, my car tilted right. It was at that moment I changed his name to BiFF, the abbreviation for Big Fucking Finn. He liked it and the name stuck. I started doubting whether the visit was worth it. If BiFF broke legs, etc. it could spiral into criminal charges and medical expenses. I told him about all my concerns. BiFF brushed them aside with a simple phrase, "Old fox don't eat no poison."

We arrived at the building. BiFF sent me in to identify Tony. He was working on an overhead pipe in the basement with a large wrench in his hand. I warned BiFF about the wrench. He didn't care at all. BiFF asked only if I was sure that was the right guy. As soon as I affirmed it was, he told me to stay out of sight. From around the corner I heard, "Tony, Tony, Tony." Five seconds later, Tony's stressed voice shouted, "I don't have a check. I will bring you the cash tonight." BiFF strutted out with a grin and we got back in my car.

It happened so fast that I couldn't believe it worked. BiFF summed up Tony as, "puppy dog." I asked how he could be so sure he'd pay. BiFF explained what he'd done, "I put my hand on his shoulder and I tink my tumb was touching his heart. Then he wet himself. He'll pay."

Later that evening I met Tony alone in a parking lot at a national chain restaurant on Central Avenue. He asked me if I'd arrived alone. I answered his question with a question, "Did I need to?" Tony gave me $5,800. After counting the payment, Tony had the nerve to say, "You didn't need to do it like that." I reminded him that he had started it. If Toolshed had been there, he would have told Tony that he had now had it. BiFF refused to take any money for the job, hinting that maybe someday I'd owe him a chip, but we were even then. The extra $800 was a convenience fee that BiFF tacked on, because that's how he worked.

Stops Bullets / Shoot Back

A commercial airline pilot had seen a product demonstration in California. It sounded impossible. It was a one-way bullet-resistant transparency. Bullets shot at one side were stopped, while those shot from the other side passed and could still be lethal. The pilot lived next door to one of my dad's employees. Through the grapevine, or as they call it in Russian, a broken telephone[1], he thought I was in the personal security business and threw my name into the hat as a potential investor. It wasn't a proven product, was pre-revenue and with no serious production.

A serial huckster named Dom Culver contacted me and claimed to own the technology. The concept was intriguing. I knew nothing about "bullet-proof" glass (there is no such thing). I called Moscow to ask if anyone had ever heard of such a product. They hadn't. They asked for samples, which they would have evaluated by the Steel Institute[2] (Институт Стали). After a few weeks of me demanding to see where the product was made, Culver abandoned his fantasy of being a middleman and gave me the inventor's telephone number.

Production was in San Bernardino County, California (the largest county in the USA, by the way). The place was more like a laboratory for prototypes. The other half of the building belonged to a motorcycle restoration garage. All I wanted to know was whether there was a market and did the product fit in. I purchased a few thousand dollars of samples and shipped them to Moscow.

The cover letter from my contact that accompanied the Steel Institute's official report piqued my interest more than the lab results. They wrote, "You have removed all doubt that you work for the CIA." The lab technicians observed that the product stopped bullets with a thinner, lighter, and clearer material than they'd ever seen. They observed that the shoot back aspect functioned, but they did not test for loss of velocity or accuracy. The man who arranged the testing told me to find out what it'd take to get it going. If it wasn't too big a lift, he offered to put in half a million dollars.

Someone recommended the Minneapolis law firm, Larkin Hoffman as good business lawyers. I engaged them. With input from

---

1 Игра Сломанный Телефон. Broken telephone is a Russian parlor game where a simple sentence is repeated ear to ear around a room. The final player announces what he/she heard. The starting player then recites what the original statement was. The two almost never match.
2 http://www.niistali.ru/ Russia's main testing laboratory for armor and personal protective equipment.

the inventor, I wrote a business plan that we agreed on. I knew nothing about American corporate law. The lead lawyer's first question was, "C or S Corp, or LLC?" When I replied that those terms meant nothing to me, he asked if I was certain that I could cover the likely fifty thousand dollars of legal fees I was going to incur. I reacted to that by asking him if they needed a check right then. I told him to go print an invoice and I'd pay it. Taken aback, he told me, "That's not how business is done." We were both confused.

The introduction to the product had come through Dom the scammer's company called "Ballistic Technologies." When we agreed to launch a venture, I knew there would be Russian inventors, so I wanted a name that sounded good in English and Russian. I called Matilda to ask her how she would creatively translate ballistic technologies so that it would sound different. She didn't understand the question and asked, "Ballistica?" That became the company name. Return-fire would become Ballistica's trademark for one-way transparencies.

A lawyer drafted a private placement memorandum. Stock certificate number one was issued to the inventor in exchange for his know-how. His title was president, with oversight of production. I put in seed capital and was issued the second stock certificate in Ballistica, Inc. a Minnesota corporation. My position was CEO.

The president found an empty warehouse on the recently decommissioned Norton U.S. Air Force Base in San Bernardino. He thought it would be perfect. I'd opened a business office in Minneapolis' River Place, which was no good for throwing bologna. The windows didn't even open. One of the politicians in D.C. who pushed the buttons for Norton AFB was Minneapolis' representative, Martin Sabo. He visited Balltica's office, looked at the product, and what we wanted to do with the building. His lobbyist spoke a language I understood. He told me in private that I should write a check in the amount of whatever the maximum campaign contribution was. We got the building, for below market prices.

Mike Crotch (Stage Name)

As the factory in California was getting put together, I got to know some of the Russians in Minneapolis. A guy named Misha worked at a swanky hair salon in Calhoun Beach Club. He moonlighted as a taxi driver. Originally a tailor and hustler from Leningrad, he asked me to suggest a name that sounded appealing and was easy for Americans to pronounce. I suggested that Mikhail Karacharov should change his name to Mike Crotch. He liked it. With a substantial accent, he pronounced it out loud several times in different tones to see how it sounded. It took control for me to not burst out laughing.

Crotch ran with it. Like the Dicker in Vladivostok, the citizens of Minneapolis did not tell Mike Crotch that his name had a meaning. He had a Thai ladyboy passenger in his taxi, who asked him for his name. When he told "her" Mike Crotch, she invited Misha to her apartment. Without shame, Crotch told the story of how they kissed and he ran his hand up "her" legs to find more than he expected. I say without shame, because Crotch insisted you would never know he was a dude and he was a beautiful woman.

Another time his taxi fare was a gay man whose affectations were so exaggerated as to leave no doubt about his sexual orientation. The passeneger became sexually aggressive when Crotch used his new stage name. The passenger reached over the back of the seat and started rubbing Crotch's shoulders and chest. Mike smacked his hand away and told him to stop. The passenger continued. Crotch stopped the car right there and ordered the man to get out of the car. The passenger got out on an empty road, where there was no chance of hailing a taxi late at night, pleading, "You can't leave me here." When Crotch rolled down his window to say something, the man put his hand inside the car and tried to grab the driver's genitalia. The infuriated Crotch reacted by quickly putting a switchblade knife to the supremely gay man's neck. Expecting to elicit fear, the man reacted to the blade on his throat by erotically cooing, "Oooh! You're aggressive too. I love that."

Mike Crotch went to court to officially change his name. Hearing his accent, an alert clerk sensed that a prank might be afoot and asked if Mikhail knew the meaning of his new name. When he admitted that he didn't, she pointed with both hands at her private parts, gesturing "Now do you understand?" He changed his name to Kara, but still today if someone yells "Crotch" in a crowd, he will turn around to look.

Crotch created another piece of legendary local lore after getting tested for AIDS. He and a female doctor were engaged to be married and went through one of those "be honest with me" sessions and she asked how many women he'd had. After hearing his answer, she insisted he be tested for diseases. When the test results came in the mail, Crotch didn't show up for work and went on a weeklong epic blackout bender. He told no one what he was up to. When a friend finally cornered him and asked, "what the hell are you doing?" He admitted what he thought was terrible news: his AIDS test had come back and the result was: Negative.

We produced a promotional video in Minneapolis about Ballistica[1]. The filmmaker was a guy named Joe Brandmeier. Again, I was not entirely accustomed to local business practices in my native town, so I called a friend and asked her in Russian to deliver twenty-five thousand in cash that I intended to give Joe when he requested a retainer for the video project. Local Russians had plenty of cash that they wanted to send globally. I could send whatever from offshore. It was a win-win. No fees to Western Union or red flags at a bank for making a reportable deposit. After I set the cash on Brandmeier's desk, he looked a little wary and asked, "Am I going to be safe in the parking lot when I go outside for lunch?" For 1990s Moscow, $25,000 cash was like pocket change. I thought he was joking. He wasn't.

Once the plant in San Bernardino was able to produce small orders, we were ready to hire sales staff. As David St. Hubbins of Spinal Tap wisely observed, "It's hard to sell something that doesn't exist." Dom had made the initial connection, so we gave him a chance at Ballistica. When BiFF stopped by to check out my new digs, he mistakenly walked into Culver's office. BiFF inferred from Culver's reaction that my employee was, "A bad one. He has the eyes of a thief." I thought that maybe the unannounced appearance of a 6'8" bearded mean-looking heavyweight Finnish wrestler might startle anyone, but BiFF was adamant that his ability to read peoples' eyes was expert. He always told me to read a person's eyes.

While BiFF read eyes, a potential investor told me the reason he would not invest was because the president wore a toupee. The man was a doctor at the Mayo Clinic. After spending hours discussing the project and business, the doctor had given only positive signals. I fully expected that he would invest enough to deserve a seat on the board. That was until he noticed the president's rug in a photograph. He announced that it was a personal inviolable rule to never trust a man with a toupee. I appreciated his honesty, but had to ask, "Really?!" He replied with the same word, but without the question mark.

A contractor for the British Army in Northern Ireland was Ballistica's first high-

---

1 https://www.youtube.com/watch?v=4vc8a1YcGE4&t=305s&ab_channel=KeshaMpls

profile customer. Before they ordered, I flew to Belfast with samples that I took to the Royal Ulster Constabulary (R.U.C.), which had its own ballistics lab. The lab technician measured the light transmission, turned on a chronograph which measures bullet velocity, and set the first transparency in a frame. He smiled as he showed me a Russian AK-47. He said, "We nabbed this shooter off of one of Qadaffi's boats that was bound for the IRA. Now they're ours."

He fired several shots until the product stopped enough bullets to satisfy the specification. I encouraged him to shoot a few more, which rounds were also stopped. When I mentioned the Return-fire feature, he said, "I've seen that stuff before. It doesn't work. Forget it." After a little convincing, he turned the sample around, put a phone book behind the exit side and shot. He picked up the pierced phone book and said, "You've impressed me." He gave me a business card for a Mr. Robert B. who worked for a construction company called Henry Brothers.

The Royal Ulster Constabulary decided what protective materials they wanted, and the Henry Brothers built with them. A glowing review from the R.U.C. lab opened the door. I kept up the Russian tradition of giving a bottle of booze. As we sipped Booker's Bourbon, Robert told me how Henry Brothers started as a small contractor for British Army projects. The company morphed into a security focused conglomerate when the IRA[2] started killing their workers. As an example, a cement truck driver would be assassinated, so the cement company refused to deliver more cement. Henry Brothers had to start a cement business. And so on. Eventually, their entire construction supply chain was armored.

According to Robert, the R.U.C. and British Army maintained impeccable real time intelligence about the location of every IRA member, of which there were a little over one hundred. Even though each could be pinpointed, the IRA continued to invent new methods to murder, like converting a manure spreader into a flame thrower, which drove across a field to the border where it started spraying fire on unsuspecting British soldiers on the other side. It was a revelation to learn about automated license plate readers. The R.U.C. had placed them all over the region and could monitor the movements of any car they chose. For the time, that was cutting edge technology.

On the way back to my hotel, Robert drove past a home that had been shot at from an automatic weapon. He laughed when he showed me the bullet pattern on the bricks of the house. It was an upward forty-five degree angle from left to right that showed the shooter couldn't handle his gun, which they considered an insult to be shot by someone with a sophomoric skillset. Robert's opinion was that IRA members just wanted to feel

---

2 Irish Republican Army, a named by various paramilitary groups, considered by some to be freedom fighters, by others terrorists.

important. He thought that instead of armoring everything it would be far cheaper to pay them and tell them they won. It seems that is eventually what happened. The final terror attack was in 1998, done by a group who called themselves "Real IRA." They killed 29 and injured 200. After peace was declared, the Royal Ulster Constabulary was eliminated in 2001. Its closing really impressed me. Government agencies never declare success or admit they need to be dissolved.

Even though we attended trade shows, had top-notch media coverage, and did live demonstrations across the country, orders were scarce. I was unaware that contractors and architects specify only established products, as in items that have been in use for a minimum of seven years. When the White House's Secret Service detail put out a bid to retrofit guard shack windows, it struck me as an opportunity to sell the Return-fire feature. Also, the fact that we had won a contract in Northern Ireland should be a selling point, I thought.

A Secret Service agent showed me the windows on the guard shacks located near all gates on the White House grounds. I'd walked by on the other side of that fence a thousand times. The pedestrian passersby on the Pennsylvania Avenue sidewalk look more menacing from inside the fence. When I mentioned that our product would allow an agent to shoot from inside the guardhouse, he reacted like I'd suggested injecting trespassers with cyanide. Confused, I asked "What do you do if someone jumps the fence? Wouldn't you want to shoot them?"

"No," he explained, "There are too many people around." Pointing to little circular plates in the yard, he said "We instead prefer to microwave them." Evidently in reaction to a dose from HPM, high-powered pulse microwaves, any living being will react by projectile vomiting and losing control of their bowels. If not entirely knocked out, the best they could hope for was to become so disoriented they wouldn't be able to act. Also rooftop snipers at undisclosed locations were readily available to assist with eliminating intruders. I realized we had no chance of winning the bid, but wanted to not miss the opportunity to wander the grounds of the White House with a Secret Service agent.

On the South lawn we walked past the Clinton's cat, Socks, who was leashed up to a tree. The agent confided that they hated that Socks was kept on a long leash, because every time Marine One (the president's helicopter) landed or took off, and that was often, the cat would panic and get tangled. It was their job to get the cat down from the tree. It was no surprise that Ballistica didn't get the order, but the photographs from the White House lawn and Socks the cat boosted credibility.

Another high profile opportunity requiring high-level protection arose in Chicago. When the Housing Authority started demolition of the infamous Cabrini-Green projects, angry resident gangbangers reacted by shooting at the demolition offices. It had been an interesting meeting, to which I drove in a new Cadillac STS with Minnesota plates. In urban myth, a white person in the Chicago ghetto was supposed to be attacked on sight. I cruised in and out unscathed, without anyone leering at me, and they left my car alone.

We couldn't sell transparencies to them in good conscience. All they needed was high-grade steel that cost a small fraction of glass. When we still thought a deal might be afoot, the way Chicago discussed contractual terms reminded me of Russia.

Sitting at my desk in Minneapolis, I took a call from a man who claimed to be an irate investor. His name was Dan, from Central Minnesota. He claimed that I had cashed his $100,000 check months ago but never issued a stock certificate. When I guaranteed him that no such transaction took place, he announced menacingly that he and an associate would discuss it with me within an hour. I told him I'd be waiting for him.

A recently retired ATF agent, Rogy, had been helping Ballistica in numerous ways. I called him about the hostile phantom investor and asked if he could stop by the office to provide backup. He arrived quickly. Then I called BiFF, who also arrived before the investor and his friend showed up. I didn't know what to expect, but I felt sufficiently prepared to meet and greet.

Dan and his sidekick arrived. They both were stocky and solid. Their faces were serious. Rogy and BiFF stayed focused on every move they made. We sat down around a conference table. Tension permeated the room. BiFF was reading eyes. Rogy's hand was close to his holster. We were about to introduce ourselves when the front door of the office opened. A friend known as Carpet Guy came strolling in. He was stoned to the bejeezus.

Before moving back to Minneapolis, Carpet Guy lived on the big island of Hawaii for many years, where he developed a penchant for powerful marijuana. He had just finished a job near my office and smoked himself silly. All he wanted to do was stop by and say hello. He stood in the doorway of the conference room, baked out of his brain. Examining the blank stares on the faces of those seated, he quickly surmised that perhaps it was not an optimal time for an unscheduled visit. I insisted he sit down and join us. The introductions went like this:

"I'm a retired ATF agent."

"I'm head of security, former heavyweight wrestler."

"I'm a criminal attorney."

"I'm president of a construction company."

"I'm CEO of Ballistica, Inc."

The others waited for my high-flying friend to introduce himself. He stayed silent. Rogy knew he was stoned and goaded him with a smile to tell us who he was. Realizing that he'd plopped himself down in the middle of a razborka, like a Russian mafia showdown, he shrugged, "I'm the carpet guy."

Dan's canceled check for a hundred thousand dollars was made out to "Ballistic Technologies." BiFF's first impression of Culver was spot on. He lied to Dan, claiming that Ballistic Technologies was the parent company of Ballistica. I was infinitely angrier at Culver than Dan was. I indicated to Dan that BiFF was an effective collection caller, who would gladly help. Dan reacted by saying, "Shame on me. I should have done some research."

Minnesota elected Jesse Ventura governor in 1999. It was a hilarious pie in the face to both major political parties. His opponents could never admit that it was their shitty policies that attracted voters to Jesse, so they reacted to his win the way they always do. They created lies and paid bogus news outlets, commonly known as mainstream media, to parrot the lies. Once one of the lies was accepted by the public as truth, the media ramped up their hype of the fake narrative. If you give the people what they want, it will not be honest facts for analysis. It will be a story that bolsters the fantasy already predetermined in the "news" consumer's mind.

Before Ventura's election, Rogy zealously touted Jesse for governor for over a year. I didn't think he had any chance, but attended rallies and made donations to his campaign. The political world was shocked when he won, but not Rogy, who triumphantly declared, "I told you. I kept telling you, and I'm telling you now."

One of the manufactured scandals that the bottom-feeding press tried to slap on governor Ventura was that he tried to pilfer from the State's treasury for personal use. Their evidence was that he had requested the state to pay for armoring his car, after receiving death threats from the losers he defeated. The same people who complained about Ventura wanting to be safe were the same ones riling people up with fake narratives to incite death threats against Jesse. If safety for an elected official's car at the gubernatorial level is theft, what is Air Force One, a decoy, and an escort with fighter jets? Never let thinking or logic interfere with an emotional narrative is the motto of those clamoring for power, so Jesse openly dropped the idea of getting an armored car.

As a makeshift fix, I offered to give bullet-resistant shields to the governor's security team, off the books, of course. Rogy relayed the offer and Jesse accepted, but on condition that I go to his home and shake his hand. He was courteous enough to allow a photo with him, while we held Ballistica shields. I promised I would not leak, or allow to be leaked, the photos we took. He's long gone from office and smart enough to not want to repeat, so I don't feel like I'm violating our handshake. The shields were rated to stop up to a .44 magnum. They wouldn't have stopped a sniper's bullet.

The local NBC TV Station did about a 5-minute news feature on Ballistica during sweeps week. An actress from The Philippines, living in Minneapolis, saw the piece and reached out to become the product's ambassador. I didn't know anything about Lotis Key's career in movies, but when we met, she spoke an understandable language. The country is corrupt and she has connections. I flew with her to Manila. On the flight she warned me to expect horrific traffic. What she considered terrible made me laugh. Drivers in Manila behaved like English butlers serving afternoon tea compared to those in Moscow.

When Lotis was out in public, there were surprised faces everywhere and hushed finger pointing. I heard many people say, "That's Lotis Key!" She arranged a meeting with one of her actor colleagues, the country's president Estrada. After doing a live demonstration of Return-fire in front of officers and soldiers from the Philippine Army, we went to the president's office. Lotis standing before President Estrada reminded me of the same uneasy eeriness conveyed at the end of the movie, "Apocalypse Now," when Capt. Willard meets Col. Kurtz. President Estrada was visibly very drunk. The dark bags under his unfocused bloodshot eyes showed more than fatigue. It was early afternoon. He had wet his pants and was sitting behind the presidential desk of a nation. It was not shocking, just surreal. I'd encountered plenty of powerful people with equal or stronger quirks. Lotis was embarrassed and tried to deflect by telling me, "Don't forget that we are simple peddlers and have an audience with the president." She was right. We sold nothing.

Mike Crotch

Bullets Shot at BiFF

Before leaving on a trip to Finland and Russia, BiFF asked if we could mold bullet resistant plastic and attach it to a helmet. He wanted it rated to stop 9mm NATO and .357 Magnum. Ballistica San Bernardino created a prototype faceshield for him. He took some flat samples as well and flew off to Helsinki.

A few days later, BiFF called me at the office to tell me he had arranged a "promotion" for Ballistica the next day. A friend was going to shoot him in the face with live ammunition in front of a group of reporters. He sounded drunk. The local time in Helsinki was close to midnight. His plan didn't sound like it had much upside. If the faceshield stopped the bullet, we'd look reckless and insane. If it didn't work, BiFF would be dead and Ballistica would have an unenviable reputation worldwide. When I told him to call it off, he hung up on me.

I called the engineer who designed the mold. He adamantly insisted that no person should ever live test anything, especially with lethal bullets. He stressed too that the bends had never been tested. There was no guarantee or even indication that the material could stop bullets after being altered. I called BiFF back at the Four Seasons to tell him the engineer's warning. The hotel operator said that BiFF had checked out.

Then I called our law firm. After explaining the situation, Paul the lawyer dictated in fluent legalese Ballistica's new company policy that banned every employee and representative from intentionally placing themselves in front of a gun barrel. Anyone who violated the rule would be immediately and permanently terminated. I faxed the warning to BiFF's last known location.

The next day BiFF sent a fax. There was no cover letter. It was a newspaper article in Finnish that showed him wearing the helmet. The faceshield had a bullet mark on it just under his left eye. A little later, he called and asked, "Am I really fired?" He told me he had done the "testing" in Tampere and that it wasn't dangerous, because his friend the shooter was an expert marksman, who never missed. That was great, but what if there had been a product failure? BiFF told me he also made a video of him holding a two foot by three foot piece of bullet resistant plastic while taking seven bullets. I asked why he couldn't have just put in a frame and done the same demonstration. He said he did it because he wanted us to have a genuine motto, "If we don't stand behind it, why should we ask someone else to?"

headed to The SHOT (Shooting Hunting and Outdoor Trade) Show in Las Vegas. I called the S. African to ask if he'd be there too. He said yes. Without ambivalence, but also without saying anything explicitly threatening, I indicated that my Finnish friend was looking forward to discussing the outstanding balance with him. The S. African replied by reciting his kickboxing stats. He claimed to have held the title of continental champion. He said the chances of collecting were nil. I ended the conversation, stating, "If you and the Finn get locked in a room, the Finn will walk out."

BFF, calm after watching a .357 get shot at his face

In reaction to the seven bullets, I told him he was insane. Even though it had been laboratory certified, the standard was to stop five bullets, not seven. BiFF told me not to worry about that, because he claimed he "cheated." I asked how he could cheat when a sharpshooter pointed his firearm at your body and discharged it seven times/ He explained that the gun was a .357 but was loaded with 38 special bullets. 38s are weaker than 357s, but still lethal. The motto was never spoken and the video was shown only to insider VIPs.

San Bernardino Ballistica reported that a contractor originally from South Africa, but in Southern California, had a delinquent debt of around $25,000. BiFF and I were

BFF, aka Randolph Koivisto He wanted us to run with slogan, "If we won't stand behind it, why should expect you to?"

We went for dinner at whatever the top restaurant was in one of the enormous casinos. BiFF and S. African sat directly across from each other. They sized each other up during small talk. When lobster bisque was served, the S. African took a spoonful and spit it out. BiFF asked, "You don't think I poisoned it, do you?"

"No!" The S. African explained, "It has cognac in it and I cannot drink alcohol."

"Why not?" asked BiFF.

"I'll go crazy and do something like start a fight in public," said the concerned S. African. BiFF jumped up and threw his chair over backwards, staring at the S. African, saying, "Why wait for alcohol? Let's fight now." As BiFF always said, "Look in their eyes." Ballistica collected a check that didn't bounce.

BiFF took his portion of the take to Binion's casino to play blackjack. What made the session memorable wasn't that BiFF won quite a bit, but that every time he took he card he mimicked the sounds made by Chevy Chase's character, Ty Webb, in the movie, "Caddyshack" while he was on the practice putting green. After several minutes of BiFF jovially blurting in a decrescendo, "Nuh-nuh-nuh-nuh-nuh-nuh-nuh-nuh, and Noo-nah-noo-nah noo-nah noo-nah," half of the players in the casino started doing the same thing. Every time he heard that sound from another table, BiFF laughed goodheartedly.

On Bill Clinton's last day in office 2001 he pardoned Marc Rich. I've read probably 100 explanations by people who claim to know why Clinton did it. Almost every article omits the obvious, which was that Clitnon's pardon was based on cogent and well-researched legal analyses by Bernard Wolfman of Harvard Law School and Martin Ginsburg of Georgetown University Law Center, who both concluded that Marc Rich + Co had complied with U.S. Law. People will read what they want to hear, which is generally not facts. For me it was an interesting opportunity to see how the left and right, and opportunists like Giuliani, manipulate a story.

As I was waiting to pick up my sons from the International School one day, I listened to Sean Hannity speak out of his ass about Marc Rich and why Clinton pardoned him. For the only time in my life, I called a talk show. I got through to the screener quickly. I presented myself as solidly not Democrat, an American patriot, and someone who had worked for Marc Rich. She seemed enthusiastic. When she asked what I intended to say, I told her I wanted to refute almost everything Hannity was saying about my former employer. She told me to stay on the line. After about three minutes of waiting on hold, she curtly told me, "We have enough callers. Goodbye," and hung up. The lynch mob left hated the pardon too. Nothing irritates them more than freedom.

After two or so years of Ballistica manufacturing hiccups, it became evident that production capabilities and quality control were nowhere near consistent with the representations that went into the business plan. Material costs were almost identical to the price of the finished product. I asked Ken, the plant manager, straight up if they were stealing. He reported that it wasn't theft, but it might take three runs to get a quality finished product. I admired Ken's street skills. Trash removal was charged by weight. Glass is heavy. We had to throw out a lot of bad products. To keep costs down, Ken would put the defects on the loading dock, tape an invoice to them, like they were going to a customer, and leave them out overnight. Product was always gone in the morning.

Ken once mentioned taking a call from a man, who claimed to be a security advisor for Bill Gates. This "architect" asked which type of pistol rating would we advise to protect against snipers at a lakefront property. From what I've read about Gates and his position on guns (anti), it might not be too far-fetched to believe that he hired a ballistics imbecile for protection advice.

Even though sales increased substantially, inconsistent production kept the company solidly in the red. We needed to raise more money. Someone recommended to me a law firm that worked closely with merchant bankers and private investors. Ballistica engaged that firm. One of the first people they introduced me to was Holt. He lived in Minneapolis and was chairman of a holding company that owned hundreds of entities in Canada. As my grandfather said, "Never trust a man you can't sit down and have a drink with," Holt agreed with that. His first test to gauge whether we were investment worthy was to invite me to his favorite bar.

After a dozen or more vodka martinis, each, I may have been starting to teeter. Thinking that he might want a reason to stop, I warned him that I had extensive Russian training in excessive drinking. He replied with something like, "That's cute. I'm schizophrenic and the medications I take make me mostly impervious to the effects of alcohol." We drank some more. The story he told that I remember most was about a car he had driven into a lake. After he got his car out and running again, he said that whenever he drove it over a pothole or railroad crossing, sand would seep from the dashboard. He sold the car at a price above market. I asked, "How could you knowingly sell a defective car?" He replied, "There's an ass for every seat."

Holt's assessment was that our shares were overpriced, but the product was stellar. He vowed to become a shareholder, but at a discount. Holt reached out to a company called Armor Holdings, which was a genius corporate pairing. Armor marketed and sold protection products across America. Holt set up a meeting for me with Armor's president, Steve Croskrey. I'll never forget when Steve started his car as I sat in the passenger seat in Jacksonville. One of my favorite Iggy Pop songs was on his stereo at near full volume. I asked if his son had been driving his car. "Fuck no," said Steve, "This is my music." When I left Armor's headquarters in Florida, some kind of deal seemed likely. We agreed to meet next at the plant in California.

In the interim Holt called me to triumphantly announce that he had purchased

100,000 shares of Ballistica for about a third of the offering price. The stock wasn't transferrable and I personally signed every certificate. His name was not on the list of shareholders. After he read me the certificate number, I had to tell him it was a forgery. Holt asked me to stay on the line while he three-way called the lawyer, Ugen, who had sold him the shares. When Ugen thought only Holt was on the line, his voice sounded lovey-dovey and ebullient. As soon as Holt said, "The CEO of Ballistica is on the line with us," the lawyer's voice dropped to a near whisper. Holt told me to hang up so that he could share some words in private.

Stock forgery was an act I'd anticipate in Russia, but not from an American attorney with an office that had lots of copy machines and a conference room in a modern building. I reeled from the blindside slap upside the head that the situation represented. The forgery had to be reported, but to what agency? I had become friends with an extremely competent attorney, the Yooper (from Michigan's Upper Peninsula). I met him when our sons were in Kindergarten together in Ms. Kamsheh's class at the International School. She was an attractive woman from Syria and all the fathers went out of their way to personally escort their children to her classroom to say hello.

The Yooper's a real estate expert, but he follows every quirky case imaginable. We bonded when he told me about leaving San Francisco to avoid being murdered by a raging Nigerian landlord, whose tenants and their lawyers went missing after they filed suits against him. Two dead tenants were discovered at remote beaches. They had been weighted down and left to drown when high tide came in. The Yooper won a case against him, which made him want to split town. He and his wife rated aspects of American cities and chose Minneapolis.

Regarding the stock fraud, the Yooper told me it was imperative to report the facts to the Lawyers Professional Responsibility Board. He suggested that as a courtesy to Ugen's partners, I should forewarn the principal at the law firm about the pending action. D.W. was the principal. I told him what was done and what was going to happen. D.W. not only seemed to ignore his employee's forgery, but he billed me for our conversation. That made me more than livid. My disbelief was taken to eleven, when Ugen sent me a message that I remember as unprofessional. After receiving a copy of the case details I'd sent to the Ethics Board, he wrote something like, "Dude! How about a little heads up if you're gonna send heat rounds my way?" After the case was reviewed, Ugen's law license was suspended indefinitely.

Mr. Croskrey's comments after visiting the plant were encouraging. Ballistica had also taken and filled its first major (for us) order from a contractor in Las Vegas. It was for approximately $300,000 of Return-fire windows that they claimed were going into the office of Steve Wynn. I didn't see any payments for about sixty days. I called the contractor to ask when we might expect a check. They informed me they'd paid in full over a month ago. I asked them to fax me the front and back of the cleared check. The front was made out to Ballistica, Inc. but it had been deposited into an account in a bank that was unrelated to our company. I searched the California Secretary of State and found a Ballistica, Inc. registered to the president of Minnesota's Ballistica, Inc. They were legally separate entities. Ballistica was a registered trademark, but that didn't help with financial matters.

After speaking with the president on a Friday to ask about the rogue bank account, I knew I had to be there in person. On the evening of September 9, 2001 I landed at the Ontario, California, airport. Our lawyers prepared demand letters for the bank in Redlands, showing the paper trail of ownership to the funds that had been deposited in the erroneous account. As I was about to leave for the bank on the morning of the 10th, Heidi, our office manager at the plant called, reporting, "Things are bad. Really bad." I asked what she meant. Casually, she stated that almost all the production line equipment was gone, files were gone, computers were gone, and the guns from the ballistics lab were gone. I was speechless.

I called our lawyers in Minneapolis, who claimed the only quick recourse was to call the police and report a theft. The police caught up with Monsieur Toupeé while he and his team were still unloading some of the equipment, but because he was able to show that he was president of both Ballisticas, the police could do nothing. The lawyers filed a quick motion for injunctive relief to freeze the account and stop any more assets from going out the factory door. They faxed me the documents and service affidavit. I was ready to serve papers on him and the bank first thing the next morning, September 11, 2001.

September 11, 2001

Staying in some chain like Motel 6 off of I-10 near San Bernardino, I'd fallen asleep with the TV on. The hotel's default station was a Spanish language news network. When I woke up it was still dark outside. The live feed of what appeared to be a smoldering world trade center building tweaked my curiosity. I did not think it was real, but instead thought that Mexicans had taken plot twists to ridiculous heights. I watched for several minutes, expecting a break like in the soap operas, "Simply Maria" and "The Rich Also Cry."

I never studied Spanish but was determined to discern what this unrealistic low budget Mexican thriller was about. When the second plane smashed into the south tower, it occurred to me that maybe it wasn't a soap opera after all. I switched to news in English and watched in utter disbelief the first tower crumble in real time on live TV. When coverage switched to the Pentagon, my phone rang. Heidi called to let me know "He" was there.

From my perspective, everything was collapsing. The World Trade Center and Pentagon seemed more pressing, as if I could do anything to change what was happening by watching it. It didn't seem proper to be serving legal papers during one of the deadliest days in American history, or to take video and photo inventory of everything that remained in the Ballistica plant. After a lot of hesitation, I got in the car to go confront the problem.

The damage to production was complete. Almost everything of value was gone, except the waterjet. It was either too heavy for them to remove, or he knew that I had personally guaranteed it and stealing it could mean criminal charges. Without equipment, the workers had to all be let go. The question was which Ballistica had employed them. Minnesota made sure that they received their wages.

With all flights grounded and Ballistica with a shell of a factory, there was nothing more to be done. I went to visit a friend, Gregot from Philadelphia, in Los Angeles. I knew him from GWU. When Gregot visited me in Minneapolis, I had taken him to Nye's. In Los Angeles, he thought that a similar vibe was the Dresden Room, which is where we tied one on. Gregot spoke French, spent a year or so in Thailand, was gay, and had a sense of humor that reminded me of Paul Lynde. We became pretty close friends when we were neighbors in a dormitory. He was an excellent relief from the situation and his choice of bar was spot-on.

I barely remember walking back to his apartment, but distinctly remember invoking

BiFF's question, "What country? What currency?" when I opened my hungover eyes on Gregot's couch. There were photos of obviously gay men on the walls and Gregot had gone to work. It took me a minute to remember where I was.

The airlines announced that the emergency grounding had been lifted. The security presence at LAX was more than enhanced. Expecting chaos, I arrived six hours early for my flight, and waited ten hours for it, only to hear an announcement that all flights were canceled. The reinstatement of flights was staged. They pretended in order to see if any more hijackers could be netted.

With at least one more day to kill, Oksana L was next in my Los Angeles rolodex. Oksana was part of the Star City children of cosmonauts club. Her father, Alexei, was the first person in history to conduct a spacewalk. She and her husband lived near Mulholland drive in Beverly Hills. The neighborhood was full of expensive residences. One building stood out to me. It was a little market just down the street that looked like a mom and pop 7-11 that you'd expect to see in rural Mississippi. I asked how a building like that could be zoned for such an opulent area. Oksana assured me that their local "Deli" had a better wine selection than almost anywhere in Los Angeles. It did.

Over several bottles of burgundy and bordeaux, I was kicked under the table for the second time in my life. The first was when Sultan addressed the women's collective at the press conference in Kazakhstan. This time I was kicked by Oksana's husband. After she mentioned that he had been trading naked options, I commented that options trading was extremely risky. After being kicked, he clarified, "But I trade renewable options, Not the ones that expire."

I got the message and said, "You must be trading on the Denver exchange." We left the topic alone from there.

Brian May – Oksana and Alexei Leonov

After the 9/11 attacks the markets plummeted. When the third Friday of the month came around, his substantial options positions were poised to be obliterated. After suffering an economic catastrophe stemming from September 11, Oksana and her husband returned to Moscow. Years later I saw a photo of her, with her father and Brian May, the guitarist from the rock band Queen. I snidely asked her what the riff from "We Will Rock You" had in common with a spacewalker. She derisively pointed out that Brian May has a

Ph.D. in astrophysics from London's Imperial College and had plenty to talk about with her father.

Flights resumed September 14. I returned to Minneapolis where I spent about a year and $300,000 in federal court. We got a piece of paper that said we were right, but recovered none of the equipment. We found a glassmaker near Pittsburgh, who did successful test runs of the configurations. It appeared possible to revive the project, but as Holt and Croskrey summed it up, "No one invests in litigation." The potential for litigation from Ballistica shareholders was undeniably high, if we launched a successful new entity. And after what happened on the first go around, not many were interested in reinvesting. The investor from the Mayo Clinic's credo of zero tolerance for toupees was validated.

BiFF took the loss of Ballistica personally. When he read details of the lawsuit, his summary was inimitable, "It sounds like that fokker has poured himself a pool of cyanide and he wants to go swimming." BiFF was fond of saying, "A Russian is a Russian even if you fry it in butter," so I asked him what his opinion was of Moscow Matilda. He said, "She has clear eyes. She is good people."

Cursed Prescription Pills

On August 16, 2001 I got a message that BiFF was dead. A twenty gauge slug from under his mouth went into his brain. BiFF often joked that he'd been shot so many times that cats envied him. I initially concluded that an enemy must have finally caught up with him. The questions were, "Was it suicide?" or "Was he suicided?" Matilda and I went to visit his widow immediately. The police report concluded suicide. An officer commented that the selection of weapon and ammunition was an excellent choice to guarantee death, but not blow his head all the way off. What was baffling, though, was that just before dying, BiFF had dropped off his son at a karate lesson and planned to pick him up afterwards. Wisely, Matilda asked his widow if he had recently been prescribed any new medicines. He had. She retrieved his release papers from a visit to an emergency room. He went in for a bleeding stomach ulcer and walked out with a prescription for Ativan[1].

After a cursory review of Ativan's side effects and contraindications, BiFF's prescription was unconscionable. His ulcer was from drinking alcohol. Ativan and alcohol do not mix. The first side effect I read was: Suicidal ideation. Avenging BiFF's poisoning became a crusade for me. I contacted a woman named Dr. Heather Ashton at Newcastle-upon-Tyne University in England, who was considered the world's expert on benzodiazepines. Her words were guarded to outright attribute Ativan as the cause of BiFF's decision to commit suicide, but she also clearly could not and would not rule it out.

Dr. Ashton kindly referred me to an organization in the Netherlands called "The Centre for Monitoring of Adverse Reactions to (prescription) Drugs." They provided me the results of a large case study, whose author concluded that as many as ten percent of people who take Ativan experience an "Almost irresistible urge to commit suicide." BiFF probably had a hundred guns in his house and enough ammunition for a battalion. To me it was crystal clear that Ativan had compelled him to take his own life.

I intended to make an example of the doctor, whom I considered guilty of BiFF's death, as a warning to others. During my research, a woman gave me a copy of her brother's death certificate which listed "Ativan" only as the cause of death. I sent a copy of it to Dr. Ashton, who commented that she wasn't sur-

---

1 Lorazepam, which is from a class of powerful anti-anxiety drugs called benzodiazepines.

prised by the coroner's conclusion, but that it was unusual for a coroner to write a drug's trade name.

For months I searched for law firms willing to take on the case against the prescribing doctor, which hopefully would lead to a class action suit against Ativan's producer. Everywhere, I ran into a stone wall. Those in the know said that my only option was to send a complaint to the medical ethics board, who everyone predicted would do nothing.

I tried to engage Dr. Peter Breggin, who has been referred to as the "Conscience of American Psychiatry." He authored the book, "Talking Back to Prozac," as well as many others on the topic, like "Toxic Psychiatry." I was deflated for BiFF when I read how Dr. Breggin had been run over in court by a freight train of corruption. He provided a list of fifty expert questions for plaintiff's lawyers to ask Eli Lilly, the manufacturer of Prozac, during a class action suit. Not one of Dr. Breggin's questions was posed during the hearing. After the case was settled, it was revealed that the plaintiff's counsel had been paid to remain silent.

A stock broker who had raised money for Ballistica also told me to abandon the concept of medical justice. He had been prescribed and consumed a medicine that was known to cause irreversible liver damage, which was his diagnosis. The drug he was given was banned in Canada years prior, specifically due to adverse side effects. The doctor who prescribed it to him was legally untouchable. During my research into benzodiazepines and psychotropic drugs, I read a lot about a natural compound called Sam-e. In addition to treating depression, it was claimed to restore liver function. I suggested Sam-e to the broker.

Sam-e was too expensive for him, so he showed clinical research about it to the doctor, who had given him the prescription that damaged his liver "irreversibly." The doctor agreed to pay for it, if the broker let him monitor his progress, if any, once a week. After taking Sam-e daily for several months, his doctor was so incredulous about the restorations of the broker's liver function, he concluded there had to have been a misdiagnosis.

Dr. Ashton relentlessly pushed a campaign called "Beat the benzos." Her efforts were focused on preventing addiction, aiding withdrawal, and successfully bringing about a change in British law. A summary stated that because of Heather Ashton's efforts, benzodiazepines were classified as more dangerous than heroin. Dr. Breggin has also never abandoned the fight against deaths caused by drugs for profit. The consensus conclusion by many doctors is that a lot of prescription drugs are associated with causing and exacerbating the symptoms they're intended to treat. If someone taking an inappropriately prescribed psychotropic 'medication' commits suicide, the default position of the producer and provider is, "They were crazy to begin with. Otherwise they wouldn't be given the drug."

Job Lead from London

BiFF and Ballistica were dead. I had two young sons, a Russian wife in Minneapolis, and no job. My resumé meant little to cookie cutter human resources interviewers who are trained to check boxes. Out of the blue, Strogy called, the Englishman who served "Fucking peanuts" to Star City Smolo. He said a gold mining company with operations in Russia and Kazakhstan could use my help. He recommended me to the company's managing director and suggested I send a resumé asap. In short order, I was on my way to London for an interview with Celtic Resources Holdings, Plc.

As is usual when I'm in London, I stayed at J. Dog's. Strogy was visiting London from his home in Bath, staying at the Hyde Park Hotel (the Royal Mandarin today). I went for a couple drinks at the hotel bar where he was entertaining some English upper class types. For humor and possibly to show off, he bashed Americans and railed on their general lack of culture. I didn't disagree, but wondered what I had done to spark his tirade. I asked if I could use his room to make a quick private call. Strogy gave me his key.

As I spoke on the phone in Strogy's room, I noticed chocolate in his mini bar. I took the chocolate bar, melted it in its foil wrapper under hot water, and squirted it into the bidet. To add to the visual, I left a little chocolate-stained toilet paper next to it. I wasn't halfway across Hyde Park on the way back to J. Dog's when Strogy called, excoriating me with colorful expletives for not knowing the difference between a toilet and a bidet. He fell for the hoax completely. I laughed and told him that Europeans should try washing their whole bodies some time. They'd smell better. When I told him I'd done it on purpose, as a prank, he appreciated it and wished me luck at the interview the next day.

London Lodgings courteously, consistently and sometimes constantly provided by GWU roommate, Stophely J. Dog

The Celtic interview was Monday at 10 a.m. It was late October. Every year The London Metal Exchange hosts an annual worldwide get-together. It is a week of more debauchery than business. Before I left Minneapolis, I told ZNB I would be in London. He called about nine p.m. from a Chinese restaurant in nearby Mayfair, saying he was with mutual friends and insisted I join them. I declined, saying that I was jet lagged and had to go to an interview the next morning. ZNB was persistent. He would not reveal who was there, only that we had much in common and guaranteed that I would not be disappointed at the opportunity to reconnect. I took the bait and went for "one."

Seated at the table was a sort of who's who of Kazakhstan. All were familiar faces. Vodka was poured, and spilled. Toasts and memories started flying, like when we smuggled Slurpy the healthy liver patient into France without a visa and won big at the Casino in Divonne. The khokhli's subtle bright red BMW came up. Neither ZNB nor I mentioned the bread truck assassination. After serially rescheduling the restaurant's closing time, the staff was getting testy. It was past midnight Sunday into Monday and we were the only table. Just as I was about to walk out, the copper supplier from "Jackostan" pulled me aside and whispered, "I'm not mad, but tell me how you got that bill of lading switched." I told him I had no idea what he was talking about and left.

Jetlagged and hungover, I descended into the kitchen where J. Dog told me I looked like shit and reeked of alcohol. I tried to mask my condition with coffee and fragrances, and headed to the office of Celtic Resources for an interview with the managing director, an Australian miner named Foo. He rattled off a list of issues that he said needed fixing. It seemed that Celtic had cultural issues and not business problems. Within a couple hours, I was hired and ready to move back to Moscow. I didn't want to put my family in danger, so we agreed on a six-month trial period.

The Dicker had purchased an apartment in central Moscow and offered me to stay there while deciding whether it was safe to bring the family. The very first morning back, someone was pounding on the door and ringing the doorbell incessantly. WTF?! I hadn't done anything yet. We looked through the peephole and saw two men in black leather coats. They looked like Buryats or Mongols, ethnicities that tend not usually to be associated with hitmen. I asked the Dicker if this was common. He said it had never happened before. I was stunned when he said he had no weapons. I was deflated when he said he had no roof, or any physical support. We had no one to call. The two kept ringing the doorbell.

I found a meat tenderizer hammer in a kitchen drawer. Studying the two more carefully through the peephole, it became obvious they weren't hitmen. They were comatose wasted on something other than alcohol. With the spiked meat hammer in hand, I opened the door and told them to get the fuck out of the building. They reacted without emotion to someone threatening to split their heads open. Realizing they were in the wrong building, they stumbled down to the elevator and left.

The building's elevator, by the way, was an afterthought, a retrofit. The building was built before elevators existed. They added a shaft on the outside of the building. The elevator stopped between floors. It protruded onto the sidewalk of Pechatnikov Lane. If someone wasn't paying attention and walked along the side of the building, the bottom of the elevator shaft was about face level for people of average height. I lived there, and still hit my forehead on it many times.

The Dicker owned successful businesses. Not having a roof was like running a taxi business without car insurance. He also had a New Orleans themed bar under construction that he planned to call "Bourbon Street." Bars and restaurants were prime shakedown targets.

The next night we stayed home at Dicker's apartment and downed a bottle of Booker's bourbon. We were standing on the balcony, listening to music and looking at the street below when a police car pulled up. The Dicker looked a little deflated, complaining, "I bet that asshole called the cops again." Answering the question, "Which asshole?" before I asked it, he explained, "Nikolai, my neighbor below, is a member of LDPR[1]. He loves to call the police."

The LDPR party's leader, Vladimir Zhirinovsky, spewed anti-everyone rhetoric. His adherents were among the dregs of Russian society. Zhiriniovsky claimed to be exclusively pro-Russia. I attended and videotaped one of his rallies. He whipped the crowd into frenzy when he angrily declared that after taking control of Russia, he would make America return Alaska to him. When he was asked during a live interview, "How can you spew such hate when neither of your parents are Russian?" His response became a national joke, much like he himself was. He said, "My mother is Ukrainian and my father's a lawyer," Zhirinovsky's father was Jewish. His entire persona was a clownish caricature, like a white Al Sharpton. If the Dicker's neighbor, Nikolai, was an LDPR member, I knew what to do. For inspiration, I thought of the character Joliet Jake in the movie 'The Blues Brothers" and the reverence he showed to an Illinois Nazis rally.

Two Moscow policemen came to the Dicker's apartment. I requested that he let me handle them alone. I suggested to the officers we should discuss things outside on the street. On our way down, I saw Nikolai standing in the staircase, shaking his fist in a menacing way. He looked like a feeble nobody, which might explain his affinity for racist political buffoons. Mentioning to the cops how busy they must be in central Moscow, it seemed that responding to noise complaints was not a good use of their valuable time. I told them I'd pay for the disturbance, but offered double if they agreed to a deal. I warned them that Nikolai would summon the police back because I intended to

---

[1] Liberal Democratic Party of Russia, a jingoistic political party. .

crank the music up again. However, for extra pay, the police could (A) tell the dispatcher to ignore him, or (B) return and demand money from Nikolai for making a false report. I said we'd be watching from above. If they returned, we would turn the music off as soon as they arrived, so they could accuse Nikolai of a false alarm and charge him for it. They understood perfectly and drove off.

I didn't tell the Dicker about the deal with the police. Instead, I cranked up a song by Metallica and started hopping across the floor. The Dicker went to the balcony to watch for the police. He signaled me to turn the music off when the police returned. Berating me with a "nice job asshole" kind of look, he announced that the police were in the elevator, on their way up again. Ten minutes went by and they didn't knock. I told the Dicker to turn the music back on and jump if he wanted to. I explained the deal I'd made with the cops. We both stomped on the floor until our feet were sore. The next morning when we went out, Nikolai was standing in his doorway wearing only underwear, and angrily shaking his fist in the air.

Celtic Resources PLC

Celtic's Moscow office was inside a branch of The Ministry of Natural Resources, the very agency empowered to regulate the company's activities. Similar set-ups were not uncommon. For example, on the first floor of the police division responsible for fighting prostitution there was a French-owned brothel called Shandra. It was like a crack dealer running a shop in the DEA. Someone had been connected to get Celtic their office, but it certainly wasn't anyone on their payroll when I joined. Celtic employed an army of useless consultants and connectionless lawyers. It was unclear what needed fixing.

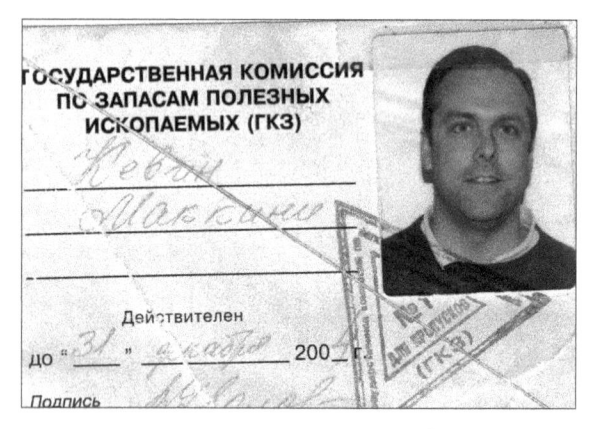

Russian State Committee for
Natural Resources ID

Celtic's main asset was a 50% stake in SVMC, South Verkhoyansk Mining Company, which owned the license to one of Russia's largest gold mines in The Sakha Republic (Yakutia). The other 50% belonged to The Committee of Precious Metals (KDM) of The Sakha Republic (Yakutia). The gold deposit was discovered in 1775, but it is in such a remote location in one of Earth's coldest climates that it was prohibitively expensive to support mining operations there. SVMC had a license issued by the Russian government to develop the mine and extract resources from it for 25 years. Celtic's second biggest asset was a gold mine near Semipalatinsk, home to the Soviet Union's nuclear testing site. It is probably the most nuked place on Earth.

Foo asked me to arrange a meeting with the governor of Eastern Kazakhstan, Mr. Mette. I did not ask what the agenda was. I had interacted with him in the 1990's when he was deputy prime minister. He said we could pop in any time. When I landed in Almaty there was no car or other sign that I was expected. I called Foo to ask what his plan was. He claimed that there weren't any airline tickets available, so we should postpone. What do you mean you can't get a ticket for a flight in Kazakhstan?! I called a friend to pull strings with the airline. Instead, he offered us his plane, which was parked at the Almaty airport. He said to just let him know what time and he'd have the crew ready for us.

With a private plane at no cost and the governor expecting his visit, Foo had to meet the governor. It was an embarrassment. He had nothing to say other than "We operate a mine in your region and thought we should meet." We didn't even deliver an obligatory bottle of XO, or some other expensive drink.

The mining operations in Semipalatinsk were managed by a Polish man. A Geiger counter measured radiation in the air. On rare occasions, strong winds shifted over the nuclear testing site and made radiation levels unsafe. He then showed me the cyanide pool for heap leaching. As I asked if breathing cyanide fumes was potentially harmful, two workers dove into the pool, which seemed to ignorant me a suicidal decision. He saw my stunned reaction and toyed with me a little before explaining that the concentration levels of cyanide were miniscule and the water was safe.

When I got back to Moscow, I mentioned to a co-worker the odd episode with the governor. He posited that Foo used the governor's meeting as a ruse to get me out of town while Peter the Chairman visited Moscow. It made no sense. I couldn't discern what either were trying to accomplish. The co-worker believed that Peter Hennen, Celtic's chairman, was second-guessing Foo. He claimed that the Hennen family had owned Christie's Auction House and after selling it had some money to invest. Russia was a hot asset. Foo had genuine gold mines. My predecessor likely had a story to tell, but I couldn't find him.

Celtic's operations in Russia lost money. Two things needed to occur for it to become profitable. The price of gold needed to rise above $325 per ounce and Celtic's metallurgists needed to find a way to get recovery rates[1] over 80%. At the end of 2003 the price of gold hit $415 per ounce. The team at the mine took the recovery rate to 83%. At that point, I determined that the position was safe enough to move my family to Moscow.

An agent found me a very nice apartment in a section of Moscow called Clean Ponds (Chistiye Prudi), a historic and prestigious section of the city. After agreeing to take the place, the agent informed me that the landlord was the Kremlin's Chief of Staff, Aleksandr Stalyevich Voloshin.

My mission became to buy out the shares in SVMC that belonged to KDM, the Committee for Precious Metals. With information that prospects for a profitable 2004 could be substantiated, Celtic's share price rose quickly on London's AIM exchange. Operations at Nezhdaninskoye, "Nezh," were run by an Australian named Wilson. Digging rock out of remote Sakha mountains and Moscow politics had little in common. The closest Wilson had come to Russian reality was a fist fight with a village drunk in Khandyga, population 6,000. I took him to

---

1 Recovery rate defines the quantity of metal that remains after processing ore.

dinner with someone high up in the federal tax authority, who openly and matter-of-factly discussed methods to compel KDM to sell us their shares. Wilson listened attentively, but didn't know what to say. As I remember it, he summarized the dinner conversation thusly: "We are such fucking babies in this country."

Dan Rapoport and Mikhail Khodorkovsky. Two victims of Vladmir Putin's lawless regime.

The Dicker's adversaries miscalculated that a ransacking would make me run. It annoyed me.

While The Dicker was away on a bender in Amsterdam, I moved into Voloshin's apartment. When I went back to pick up my things, the Dicker's apartment had been ransacked by professionals. The floor was completely cluttered. All the closets and cabinets were open. He was in a battle with dirtball partners, so I knew it wasn't targeted at me. I took it personally anyway. Dicker had two American partners. One was Paul Panitz in the D.C. area. He could be dealt with simply via good lawyers. I'd befriended a future lawyer at Leningrad U we called Zhenya. She was a rare native of D.C. Most Washingtonians are transplants. Zhenya grew up in a family of lawyers. Dicker hired her. When he eventually won his case against Panitz, he claimed, "Zhenya could not have found a more perfect and powerful attorney for me." Thank you Zhenya!

The Dicker's other partner, Patrick Snodgrass, was in Moscow and likely the one who hired the ransackers for scare tactics. Nothing was missing from the apartment. The Dicker didn't know that I'd moved out and also that I was planning to unleash some gloves for Snodgrass to smell, without asking permission.

Snodgrass's weaknesses were women and discounts. He had recently been married in Washington State and his wife was in the USA. I ordered a kompromat (compromising material) DVD on him, which was delivered within weeks to me in the Celtic office. A team had placed a camera in a prostitute's apartment. They filmed him cheating on the wife he'd just wed. That wasn't the devastating part.

It was a set up, but Snodgrass and his friend negotiated the price to two for one. His friend fucked her first. I fast-forwarded through that footage until I saw fat boy Snodgrass get on the bed with the prostitute. He looked around to make sure no one was watching and went down on the hooker that his friend had just fucked. I reeled in horror and involuntarily screamed "Nooo" so loud that the rest of the office came running to see what was wrong. I turned off the vid. When they asked why I'd screamed, I couldn't speak. Disgusted beyond words at what I'd just seen, all I could say was I'll explain later.

The Dicker missed his flight from Amsterdam three days in a row. I had someone on the payroll to get him home safely from the airport. His bender was beginning to annoy. Finally, he called from Schipol airport, and guaranteed he'd be on that day's KLM flight to Moscow. I rode with the driver to inspect the Dicker's apartment one more time before his arrival. His cleaning lady had put everything mostly back to normal. My new place wasn't far, so I let the driver go to the airport and stayed behind, intending to walk home.

A stray dog had been sleeping in the staircase of Dicker's building for months. Russians like to give English names to dogs, so we called the stray Richard. As I was leaving Dicker's apartment I heard a woman downstairs calling for Richard to come eat. At the spur of the moment, I got the idea to leave Richard as a welcoming committee for the Dicker. I lured Richard into the apartment with a piece of salami and locked him in. As soon as the Dicker got off the elevator, Richard started barking. Before opening the door, the Dicker thought, "I need to drink less. It sounds like there's a dog barking in my apartment." After opening the door, he said that Richard shot daggers with his eyes as he strutted out.

A geologist from Seattle worked in Celtic's Moscow office. I asked if he knew anyone named Snodgrass. He didn't. The geologist was headed home on break and he said he'd be glad to leave the video at the Snodgrass residence with no postage or marks. When I offered to execute the scheme, Dicker declined, saying it was too dirty a tactic. I thought it was too mild. To me it seemed the more time Snodgrass spent dealing with the backlash from the video, the less he'd have to arrange things like ransackings. It would have been a glorious bodyslam, but I had to respect the decision of the combatant.

Small World of Lawyers

When Celtic's lead London lawyer, an Irishman called D.O., visited Moscow, he mentioned to me that he'd worked in Washington, D.C. To make it a small world, D.O. worked at the same firm as Zhenya, who had helped the Dicker. D.O. knew Zhenya well.

Putin Chokes Liberty

Few people recognized at the time that the Putin regime was unleashing an army of boa constrictors that would coil around every profitable enterprise in Russia. I expected the laissez-faire life of the 1990s to continue, hoping mostly for reform in the courts, which required legislators who were capable of defining clear rules for business. Instead, one of the first major policy changes implemented by Putin was to remove regional autonomy by nullifying elections. Putin installed whatever governor or president[1] he chose. In Sakha where Celtic was mining gold, Vyacheslav Shtyrov was installed as president. Mr. Shtyrov previously served as the director of ALROSA, Russia's diamond producing cartel, largest in the world by output. South Africa's DeBeers sells more, but doesn't produce more. To get an idea of the size of Alrosa's production, just one of their mines, the Mirniy diamond pit in Sakha, produced as much as 10,000,000 carats per year. In 2002 the pie of Alrosa was sliced up and served to friends of Putin via an IPO. To placate the newly appointed president Shtyrov, a not so subtly named venture was launched called Investment Group Alrosa (IGA).

The purpose of IGA was clear, to swallow up profitable ventures in Sakha. As the price of gold continued to rise and production at SVMC ramped up, Celtic's stake was an obvious target. The CEO of IGA, Sergei Vybornov, considered it a foregone conclusion that he would steamroll an underfunded junior miner like Celtic Resources and take from them their stake in SVMC. After all, the other 50% owner, KDM, was a state-run entity and IGA had federal backing. But Putin's tentacles hadn't yet come close to infiltrating everywhere.

It is said that when starting a gang fight it is wise to take out the strongest opponent first. In 2003, Mikhail Khodorkovsky was considered Russia's richest person. He was also an outspoken proponent of financial transparency, which was a policy that meant financial and political death to the kleptocratic Putin administration. To prevent Khodorkovsky from using his resources and intellect to propel Russia towards liberty and openness, Putin had Khodorkovsky arrested on October 25, 2003 by sending federal troops to surround his airplane on the tarmac of Novosibirsk airport. On October 29, 2003, Aleksandr Voloshin, Kremlin chief of staff (and my landlord), resigned in protest. Team Putin also arrested Khodorkovsky's partner, Platon Lebedev, who was in a Moscow hospital receiving treatment.

---

1 The Russian Federation consists of administrative territorial divisions designated as Oblasts, Krais, or Republics. Regions like CHechnya, Dagestan, and Sakha are republics whose leaders carry the title of president. ALl others are governors.

Anyone paying attention should have noticed that Putin's actions were completely inconsistent with his rhetoric, but as Hitler observed, "If you tell a big enough lie and tell it frequently enough, it will be believed." The lie was that Vladimir Putin was acting to benefit Russia. To prevent any refutation of that lie from reaching a wide audience, in August, 2003 Putin arrested the owner of open television and radio stations, Vladimir Gusinsky. Human rights activist and well-researched journalist, Anna Politkovskaya, didn't reach as wide an audience, but she continued to criticize Putin. She was murdered in her apartment's elevator in 2006.

One of the KDM shareholders met me on a noisy Moscow street, in order to not be overheard. He offered to take one million in cash to transfer to Celtic a one percent stake, which would give the company control over SVMC. I called Foo and as cryptically as I could, relayed the offer. Celtic didn't have the cash. Foo countered with two million dollars worth of shares. The offer was rejected instantly and was taken as an insult. In retrospect, the declined offer was prescient. In Putin's unfolding lawless Russia, legally registered shares meant nothing if the Kremlin wanted them. Cash is king. As the Russian saying goes, a dollar is a dollar even in Africa.

IGA agreed to meet. Their address, which was on Posledniy Pereulok (The Final Lane), sounded ominous. It was a bit of a fortress behind a tall iron fence and with bulletproof glass. It indicated they had enemies, or expected them. When I entered their conference room I was stunned and pleased to recognize Alexei. He had previously worked for Leucadia. His former boss was my co-bidder when we bought the Moiseev dance concert at Tchaikovsky Hall. He was also a friend of Strogy. Alexei knew I was capable of dropping bombs, so there was no need to size each other up. We quickly determined that there was no way either of us could influence our higher-ups. Some type of war over the SVMC gold mine was a certainty. Our goal was to keep things gentlemanly.

ZNB called to advise he was in Moscow and invited me to dinner at a Siberian-themed restaurant called "Ekspeditsiya." I recall seeing a promo piece that CNN had declared it the most exotic restaurant in the world. Aside from the body of a helicopter in the middle of the main dining room, it was a cool restaurant, but not a world-beater. ZNB had Kazakh governor Mette with him and thought I should stay connected. We had a double sit down. First we dined with the governor in a private room, and then with a Russian friend, Boris. Mr. Mette passed away unexpectedly a few months later. That was the last time I saw him. R.I.P.

Boris was married to Matilda's best friend from Star City. He had also grown up in Kazakhstan with Pablo. When Russia opened up to Western investments, MacKenzie Consulting announced they would hire two Russians, one for their Stockholm office and one for London. Boris got the position in London. ZNB had a brother in London.

Bad Contract / Worse Language

We started our casual dinner conversation in English. ZNB's brother noticed the substantial financial benefits that seemed to be associated with commodity trading in the former Soviet Union and announced that he too intended to participate. ZNB explained that it was a terrible idea to attempt it without serious financial backing and connections. The brother ignored his advice with calamitous results.

He entered into a contract with a Russian supplier of pig iron, which was supposed to be delivered to a customer in China. The buyer and seller were contractual amateurs. In their agreement there were no Incoterms, i.e. which events trigger payments. There was also no force majeure clause, aka "Acts of God." After the pig iron was loaded in Vladivostok, the ship sank en route to China. London expected to pay the supplier after the Chinese customer paid him. The Russian expected payment after loading. The cargo wasn't insured.

The phone calls from the Russian supplier to London became increasingly threatening. The brother was extremely scared. He did not want to let ZNB know that he had ignored his advice and found himself in what seemed like a deadly predicament. Desperate to find a way out, the brother called their father, who had also been a commodities trader. He repeated as much of the threatening phone call as he could remember to his father, telling him to absolutely not mention it to ZNB.

The brother claimed a Russian mafioso told him, "Listen me, bitch prostitute. We know where you live. If you do not want sportsmens to give your wife a torpedo, slut mother, you fucking pay fast, bitch prostitute. We know where you daughter goes school, bitch prostitute." As Boris listened, he got a quizzical look on his face and interrupted, "Wait a minute. Your brother was working with Vitalii Ivanovich?" It was indeed the same person. Vitalii was famous like the Greek mobster in the movie "Johnny Dangerously" for butchering the English language. Bitch prostitute was his signature phrase.

The father listened to the story and promised to keep it secret from ZNB. He told the brother, "I know a guy." After hanging up, the father called ZNB, who interpreted the graphic threat as a sign of weakness. Attack dogs don't bark. The father called London and without naming sources reported that there wasn't anything to worry about from the Russian. A few days later, Vitalii called London again, this time to ask for help to get a visa into the UK. "These bitch prostitutes at UK Embassy don't give me visa. It's fucking dickness, slut! Will you send letter to them?" The brother had to check his ears to confirm that he heard what he just heard.

He said to the Russian, "Let me get this straight. You threatened to have my wife gang-raped and children kidnapped. Yes? Now you're asking for my help to get a visa so that you can come do these things?!?" He understood correctly. No attack happened.

To Produce Gold

Boris had substantial experience working mergers and acquisitions in London. He was a graduate of Moscow State Institute of International Relations (MGIMO), considered Russia's most prestigious university. I'd know him for over ten years and our wives were best friends. He seemed the ideal candidate to structure a peaceful agreement between the parties. Alexei from IGA was also an MBA type. He agreed to use Boris as a mediator. The first meeting revealed nothing unexpected. There was a massive gulf in expectations and evaluations, but at least there was dialogue.

Foo directed me to arrange a meeting with the president of the Russian division of a London-based bank that finances mining operations worldwide. She was originally from Wales. Her name was Cerys. When we agreed to lunch, she mentioned that her bank's gold expert would also be with her. I knew little about the mining operation and brought along our lead geologist to field any technical questions. Foo told me the agenda was to demonstrate being Russia savvy.

It was a warm summer day. I proposed we meet at a restaurant called Accenti on a small side street with outdoor veranda seating, which was a rarity in Moscow. The owner and general manager were both named Igor. Igor Masiagin was Accenti's financial backer. Masiagin's ex-wife, Tatyana, was another cosmonaut's daughter, whom they claim to be the first Jew in space, even though he was never religious.

Tatyana said that Masiagin paid for the restaurant with winnings from a casino in Odessa. He had a friend who was a roulette croupier, who figured out a way to spin the ball and precisely predict within three numbers where it would land. Their system nearly bankrupted the casino. Masiagin took the cash from the Odessa casino and threw it behind chef Igor, making Accenti one of the most storied restaurants.

The bank's gold expert and Celtic's geologist discussed the plan to extract ore and produce metal. Cerys and I discussed random pleasantries. I recall avoiding the topic of business with her altogether. After the geologist left, the gold expert started peppering me with questions about Russia. After twenty or so minutes, he said "I think you're the component that was missing from this company. I recommend we do the deal." He left.

It was an unusually perfect warm sunny day, so I proposed to Cerys that maybe we should have another bottle of Ugni Blanc, which turned into another three. I confided that I knew next to nothing about mining, but I knew Russia. Cerys countered, "I don't know much about finance, but I know people." Celtic got their money and Cerys and I remained friends ever since.

Armed with cash, Celtic was able to be a little more aggressive and creative. Joe Pitch, a friend from Marc Rich days ran a Swiss-based metals trading company. He agreed to get me cash in Moscow for any wires Celtic sent from London. The transactions would look legitimate to any stock auditors. Boris had an attorney friend whose father was deputy director level of the FSB (successor organization to KGB). They arranged to visit president Shtyrov in Yakutsk and convey to IGA that we too had support at the federal level.

The attorney returned from the trip irate. Shtyrov had given him a copy of a letter of intent, signed by Foo and Shtyrov, that Celtic would transfer 30% of their shares. It was a non-binding agreement, but nonetheless an aggravating document. It was unthinkable to put in writing a promise to the president of a republic where you had operations and then refuse to honor it. That seemed to explain why the previous Russian representative of Celtic had evaporated. The honorable thing would have been to keep his word, but Foo wasn't honorable. One might also suspect that a pledge by a managing director of a publicly traded company to transfer a majority of its assets would be a required material disclosure. The market knew nothing about it.

Powerful Landlord Perks

Even though he resigned, Mr. Voloshin as landlord had benefits. Across the street from was a real estate development fund called Rosbilding. The apartment at Mashkova Street 16 had windows both on the street side and in the back of the building, where there was a small parking lot and courtyard. To enter the parking lot, cars passed through an archway that had a padlocked thick metal chain to keep non-residents out. Rosbilding's employees often parked their cars in front of the archway, making it impossible for residents to reach the parking lot.

On a nice summer evening, family and friends were over. The kitchen window to the courtyard was open, as well as the bay windows in the living room that looked out onto the street. We'd had several bottles of wine and were enjoying a home cooked meal by Hitlerina when a car's horn started honking in front of the archway. It blasted so long it sounded like Chuk at the Ukrainian border when we were on the mission to recover his stolen grain. People were screaming at each other. The mood sounded plenty hostile. I popped my head out the window and saw a shiny black Audi TT blocking the entrance. One of my neighbors was yelling obscenities at Rosbilding's guard, who was standing in the street with one of those security earpieces, pretending to be talking to backup.

Bolstered by liquid courage and sick of Rosbilding treating our parking lot as their own, I went to the street with a screwdriver and removed the Audi's license plates. The guard advised me to put them back on, threatening that the owner would not be kind. I pointed to my open window above and told the guard, "That's my apartment. If the owner is brave enough, tell him to come see me. I want to teach that asshole some manners about how to park." I returned to the dinner with a couple of license plates. About a half hour later the doorbell rang. I expected to see AK-toting goons or the driver with bodyguards. It was a relief to see two uniformed regular policemen.

When the first thing the officer asked was, "How is Alexander Stalevich (Voloshin)?" I knew the plates were staying with me.

I had and have never met Mr. Voloshin, but I bluffed, "He's fine. Do you want me to call him?"

"No! No! No need," the police nervously responded. But, they explained, there was the delicate issue that I had committed a theft and admitted to it. They proposed it was fair to ignore the crime and just let me return the plates.

That was not happening. I wanted to set an example for would-be inconsiderate car parkers from Rosbilding. I told them that I would not return the license plates. They abandoned getting the plates back and swerved into cash negotiations. To finish the chat quickly, I offered them $100 each. They countered with $200, pointing out that replacing the plates would cost a lot and the likely fines from driving without them would also lead to multiple fees, blah, blah blah,

Hitlerina emerged from the kitchen and walked to the front door. She went full verbal diarrhea on them, dropping names of generals in this and that agency, cosmonaut friends, professors, etc. After less than a minute of her excoriating them non-stop they agreed to $100 each and couldn't get away fast enough. I took the license plates home as a sort of war trophy. One of them is nailed to the back wall of a friend's burger joint called Cuzzy's. It's a couple blocks from the Minnesota Twins Baseball Stadium and not far from the U.S. Federal Reserve Bank. The other plate is on a bar wall somewhere in Indiana. If the Audi TT owner from Rosbilding is reading this, your license plate has been a bar decoration in Minneapolis, Minnesota, USA for about fifteen years.

Cuzzy's Bar N. Washington Ave. Minneapolis

Bourbon Street Bar Moscow

When construction started on Dicker's bar, Bourbon Street, the owners of a rave club next door called Propaganda called for a conversation to determine whether Bourbon Street would siphon business from the club. They weren't threatening, but Anton and I were there for backup just in case. Anton diffused any tension by telling a new version of the fairy tale, "The Three Little Pigs." In Russian, the pigs are named Nif Nif, Naf Naf, and Nuf Nuf. Anton said that there was a fourth little pig named Nach Nach (Нах Нах), which to a Russian ear sounds like "I don't give a fuck about anything." That's what Nach Nach did in Anton's revised fairy tale. When they warned him about the wolf, the pig replied "Nach Nach" and he didn't even seek shelter. After that evening, Anton's nickname became Nach Nach.

The Dicker put me in charge of the bar's playlist, with instructions to stay focused on artists with Louisiana connections. The place had a 100 cd player to fill. I'd become friends with O.P., a man from Gorbushka, Moscow's pirated movies and music market. I drew a circle around New Orleans and told him to get me as many songs as he could find from the region. He came back with about twenty thousand songs on DVDs full of MP3s. The titles of songs by someone named Johnny Rebel caught my attention. He recorded classics like "Niggerhatin' Me," "Some Niggers Never Die (they just smell that way)," "Jigaboo," and "Move Them Niggers North." I called O.P. and asked what was wrong with him. He told me he was just following instructions and he hadn't reviewed one song.

I listened to every Johnny Rebel song. They were recorded during the segregation and civil rights turmoil. The lyrics were textbook demonization propaganda. If his lyrics were switched to target Jews, his songs could be mistaken for compositions by Joseph Goebbels. If Johnny Rebel is still alive, I wonder if Daryl Davis could work his magic on him.

O.P. was a drug dealer, art broker, and music guru. He didn't look like Karl Lagerfeld, but reminded me of him somehow. I met O.P. at a place called Disco Banya (Bathhouse) that was in the backyard of a friend's property in the opulent Rublevka region, Moscow's version of The Hamptons or Bel Air. O.P. proudly showed me a German marijuana smoking device that resembled a thick credit card. It used magnets, was reversible and could store a small amount of weed inside. He declared it modern technology. I yawned at it and showed him an old American smoking device, a dugout[1]. Every time I went home I'd buy all the dugouts

---

[1] A small wooden box with two storage compartments. One is for marijuana. The other contains a metal cigarette that has a small bowl at the end.

from Minneapolis' old school head shop, The Electric Fetus. O.P. filled them and we handed them out all over town. Dugouts were a great gift and a door opener on the night club scene.

Gorbushka always seemed expert at stealing foreign music and selling it for cheap, but there were some pretty serious gaps when it came to New Orleans. I filled in the playlist by spending a few thousand dollars on CDs at the Electric Fetus, which sold music for less than half the prices at London's Virgin Superstore. Nach Nach specifically requested the song, "Hello Brother" by Louis Armstrong. It wasn't available in Russia anywhere at the time. I'm not sure where Nach Nach heard it, but it is definitely one of Satchmo's best. If I ever run a political campaign, it has to be the theme song.

Every time I traveled to London for Celtic, which was often, I bought rare whiskies at Selfridge's and the World of Whiskey near Tottenham Court Road. By the time Bourbon Street opened, it had the best selection of whiskey in Russia. Legally, the bar could only sell what it purchased from licensed distributors, but it was less than a kilometer from Lyubanka, home to KGB headquarters. It was a certainty that laws would be broken there.

By opening day, I thought I had crafted a stellar New Orleans playlist. None of Johnny Rebel's songs made the cut. The bar was open 24/7. The music played continually on random. After three days, I asked the staff what they thought worked and what didn't. They initially complained that there were too many Louis Armstrong songs. They suggested I mix it up. Because one hundred cds wasn't really that many songs, I told them to give it another week before deciding how to rework the playlist. When I asked them again, the staff's consensus was, "You can change anything you want, but do not get rid of any Louis Armstrong songs." They declared his music mood brightening.

For Bourbon Street's opening day, Masiagin showed up with Petya, the keyboardist from a famous Russian pop band called "Time Machine." The Dicker had started dating Masiagin's ex-wife. She was there too. A KGB officer referred to her as a slut, to Masiagin, for dating a foreigner. Masiagin knocked him out with one punch. The Dicker thought it meant his bar would be short-lived. When the KGB agent regained consciousness, he wasn't angry and offered to buy Masiagin a drink.

I chatted with Petya, whom I didn't know. He told me he had traveled a lot around the U.S. and had never encountered a whiskey he liked. I intended to shock him by pouring barrel strength Blanton's which was around 147 proof (73.5% alcohol). I handed him a double. He chugged it. Expecting him to reel from the powerful hooch, he instead extended his hand to shake mine. He declared it a lovely beverage and drank the whole bottle. Masiagin invited me to join them at the next bar. I declined, but was surprised to see Petya walk out of Bourbon Street unfazed.

Celtic Hits Bumps

The 30% share transfer document was a political catastrophe. An analogy I'd use is that Foo had alleged rape. When a team was dispatched to confront the rapist, he not only denied it, but showed video evidence that Foo tried to seduce him. Celtic issued shares to Boris and me, with incentives for more. Otherwise there would have been no reason to defend it.

Celtic London exacerbated their SVMC woes by broadcasting their Russian ineptness. Whenever they crossed paths with someone who claimed to be connected and powerful in the former Soviet Union, it seemed they tried to enlist their services. That statement applies to me as well, I guess, because they hired me too. But putting their naivete on display made life difficult for us in Russia.

The first "you've got to be kidding" moment was when London flailed in front of a power group known on the street as the (Eurasian) Trinity. Their reputation was a trio of criminal billionaires. Telling these guys about an ownership dispute in one of Russia's largest gold mines was not a bright maneuver. Without warning or consulting me, London advised Alexander Mashkevich to coordinate an attack on KDM with me. I didn't know who Mashkevich was. He called me out of the blue to announce that he was on his way to see me, because London had asked him to. Before he entered, a security crew of three armed guards swept the rooms to make sure it was safe.

When I shook hands with Mr. Mashkevich, I noticed that his middle and ring finger were fused together. His security team made it obvious that he was a serious figure, but I had never heard of him. We dropped a few names. He seemed a little light in Russia and I said so. He explained that another member ran their affairs in Moscow, while a third was in Uzbekistan. Mashkevich's turf was Kazakhstan. Upon hearing that, I asked if he knew ZNB. He said that he knew him very well and asked whether I should call him or should he. I understood that he wanted to see if ZNB would answer my call.

When ZNB answered, I explained that I'd crossed paths with a mutual acquaintance and passed the phone. They spoke for a couple minutes and Mashkevich handed the phone back to me. ZNB said, "Congratulations. You're in the presence of the second most powerful man in Kazakhstan after the president." Mashkevich suggested I meet his Moscow associates and left.

Within a day or two a lawyer for the Trinity called to arrange a meeting. Outside the group's Moscow office on Tsvetnoi Bulvar there were two white marble lion statues on each side of the entrance. They looked like three-foot high bookends. I remembered seeing gold lion statues about twice as big across town on Ostozhenka. My first thought was that I had to find a way to switch lions simply as a prank to cause confusion.

Roman the lawyer escorted me into the office of Dmitry Yakubovksy. His name was familiar, as was his nickname, "General Dima." He'd been in the news in the 1990s after a conviction for stealing ancient manuscripts from the Russian National Library estimated to be worth $150 million. It was interesting to be face to face with him, but I would have preferred to be at a party and not discussing the fate of my employer. London had let Mashkevich know that I had a complete power of attorney to conduct all of the company's business in Russia. General Dima placed a document in front of me. I read it. It was vague and clear at the same time.

It stated that Celtic would pay his company $5,000,000 for "Services." There was no enumeration of services or reference to an appendix that listed services, just "Services." I asked if it was a joke. A Chechen lawyer answered for Yakubovsky, "Dima is serious."

I refused to sign and that was my final answer. Dima countered with, "How about we finger wrestle for $1 million?" I looked at his hand extended out to me and saw thick and muscular fingers. I declined that offer as well. As I got up to leave, the lawyer told me it was a smart move to not finger wrestle. Dmitry was the prison champion at it. Yakubovsky gave me a short tour of his mini Christian Orthodox shrine adjacent to his office. On the way out the door, they told me I had to meet Potakh (the P is pronounced as an F) Shodiev. He was the principal member of the Trinity. The second I hit the sidewalk and was out of earshot, I called London and begged them to please stop advertising weakness to the powerful.

Edibles from Night Flight

Moscow's arguably best known prostitution bar was Night Flight. It was managed mostly by Swedes. On the second floor there was a good hooker-free restaurant. The women for sale stayed in the street level bar and dance room. Night Flight and their affiliated restaurant, Skandinavia, constantly had fresh food trucked in from Sweden. Because of that, they served the best never frozen steak in all of Russia. My wife and elementary school aged sons would eat there as a family. The chef took them in the kitchen and showed them how to prepare a few dishes.

It was a full-service restaurant. The chef made excellent steak tartare that wasn't on the menu. When I ate there without the family, with friends like O.P., I'd ask the waiter to send the chef out. I'd do the Las Vegas handshake, but instead of cash, his palm would receive a 5 gram bag of marijuana in my palm, which by the end of our meal he turned into an infused molten lava cake. He read that the enzymes in pineapple made edible THC stronger, so he made a pineapple sorbet to go with the chocolate.

The first time we tried the cake, I was there with the Louse. O.P. and Liosha were supposed to join us, so we ordered four cakes. The other two never arrived. Neither of us felt any effect from the first cake, so we ate the other two as well and went home. It was the first time in my life I woke up more wasted than when I went to bed. Matilda shook me awake and told me I had to get moving. When I opened my eyes, she looked frightened and asked what was wrong with me. I asked why she told me to get moving. She said, "Foo called several times last night and needs to make a presentation to a group of potential investors at a mining forum. I was baked, unprepared, and didn't know the material.

On the way to make the presentation, I called the Louse to ask him if he'd been wolloped as well. He said he drove home without incident. All the way on the forty-five minute or so drive, he reported really enjoying the soundtrack he was listening to. When he parked in his driveway, he noticed that the faceplate of his car stereo wasn't plugged in. There had been no music.

I stumbled through the presentation and only occasionally laughed awkwardly, I think. It could have served as a training film for Jen Psaki. Combining drug induced stupidity with poor preparation and an overall ignorance about most of the topics that were discussed is he bailiwick.

The only place I saw the Swedes outside of Night Flight was at the Dicker's bar, Bourbon

Street. It was a one time event when a Night Flight manager called me at work. You should always expect that telephones are bugged, especially in Russia. The manager started by saying "I will completely understand if you have no desire to reply and I will never raise the topic again. Someone with whom you're familiar, the Californian, is hosting a VIP, who does not partake in vodka because of his religion. The Californian asked me to locate chocolate for his guest. I will understand if you want to hang up." I said I would take care of it.

The Californian was in the Metropol Hotel's presidential suite with one of Muamar Qadaffi's sons. I sent O.P. who reported afterwards that Saif Qadaffi excoriated the quality of his marijuana before trying it. He told O.P. that no self-respecting Libyan would smoke anything but top grade hash. He said that what was in the bag looked like something that grew on the side of a Moroccan highway. O.P. apologized but explained that Estonian hothouse weed was the best available in Moscow. Make do with what you get. It's not like you're going to demand Dom Perignon in Tripoli. Qaddafi reluctantly loaded up a pipe and took a couple pulls before sinking into a recliner, where he sat speechless for about twenty minutes. I could relate. The same thing happened to me.

Nelli from the Bolshoi guest bartending at Night Flight.

Banker and Prime Minister

Cerys and her London based banker friend, Howard, hosted a charity fundraiser at the British ambassador's residence. It's located on the opposite side of the Moscow River across from the Kremlin. After visiting in 1994, Elizabeth II supposedly declared it the most beautiful British diplomatic residence in the world. It was a black tie event. The Louse and I stood on the balcony, enjoying the iconic view of the Kremlin and smoking one-hitters out of a dugout.

Mother of my goddaughter, "Oy Astvats," at British Ambassador's residence Moscow

We were pretty convinced that almost no one in Russia knew about the metal cigarette. We'd once been at an outdoor Cyrus Chestnut concert, and didn't know that the American ambassador was in the audience. As the marijuana smell wafted through the crowd, we could see the Russian diplomatic security team scouring the audience, looking for the source. We continued to smoke and they didn't figure it out. We assumed that at a private event, any guards would be forgiving, and if they were strict, they wouldn't know what a dugout was anyway. We didn't know, though, that one of Howard's guests was the prime minister.

I'd met Howard previously. He once shared one of the funniest roof mismatches ever. In 1998 Russia defaulted on her sovereign debt and was a bête noire in the world's financial markets. Mikhail Kasyanov was Minister of Finance at the time. During the turmoil, while everyone was running from Russia, Howard steadfastly supported Russia in any way he could. In 2000 Mr. Kasyanov became prime minister and remembered Howard's loyalty and considered him a friend. As the Russian economy rebounded, Howard's fortunes also improved. Some low-level mafioso wannabe came calling and announced that he was going to be Howard's roof.

Howard told him to piss off, but the man was persistent and increasingly threatening, eventually demanding a razborka. Howard called the prime minister, who good-humoredly accepted his new role as "Roof." They chose to meet at a restaurant. Howard sat with the roof applicant for about 45 minutes. He probably used the term "bitch prostitute." Mr. Bigshot was starting to get annoyed, asking Howard why his valuable time was being wasted. In his mind, there was no way a foreigner who barely spoke Russian was going to attract a heavier hitter than him, right? Howard remained calm and assured the little thug that his patience would be abundantly rewarded. When the advance security detail swept the room, the roof wannabe knew he was outgunned. He couldn't go anywhere. When Prime Minister Kasyanov walked in, smiling and greeting his friend, Howard, I can't imagine what went through the idiot's mind. Howard and the P.M. laughed at the "Roof" and thanked him for buying them dinner.

By the time the charity auction started, the Louse and I walked in plenty stoned. A new generation Fabergé egg went up for sale. When I got the bill to pay for it at the end of the night, I didn't remember bidding on it. Matilda and a friend argued over who should get it, so I decided neither of them and gave it to my niece for her sweet sixteen.

A few weeks later Cerys hosted a party that was not connected to the charity dinner. A man I didn't know kept staring at me as if he knew me. I didn't recall ever seeing him. After a half hour or so he clapped his hands and declared, in English, "I remember now! You was the guy what smoke-ed marijuana in front of prime minister."

Russians will embrace any foreign cultural event that involves getting drunk, like Cinco de Mayo and St. Patrick's Day. A slightly more obscure premise to drink was celebrating the birthday of Scottish poet Rabbie Burns. The Louse had several of Burns' poems memorized and could recite them in a Scottish accent. He named his cat, Duncan. Russians claimed a connection with Burns because one of Russia's greatest poets and authors, Mikhail Lermontov, considered himself to have Scottish heritage as well.

Every year in Moscow there's a party celebrating Burns and Lermontov. Male attendees wear kilts, eat haggis, and wash it down with liters of scotch. People recite the words of Burns and Lermontov. I went to several but remember few. At one of the Burns parties, my wife pointed to a man and said, "Hey. That's the dude whose house you smoked up at Cerys's auction. I want to ask him to dance." It was the indeed British ambassador, Anthony Brenton. They danced.

Celtic Hobbles Along

On the business front, IGA made a deal with Russia's #1 gold producer, and top five in the world, Polyus, to take over mining operations at SVMC. They just acted, without any legal basis. Wilson was replaced with their appointee. I'm sure that to Polyus, Celtic looked like a defenseless target. Their lawyers probably looked at the lily white internationally recognized firm that publicly represented us and assumed they would secure any ruling they wanted in Russian courts. What they didn't know was that we also employed a second lawyer who was all the way local, connected, and not afraid to get dirty.

Polyus filed a suit against SVMC in some remote region. Clean counsel deemed Polyus's maneuver sleazy and underhanded. They were surprised that Polyus had actually served true papers. They claimed the action and choice of court was so corrupt, it would have been consistent to send an empty envelope and claim we'd been legally served. The "local" lawyer was impressed with Polyus's skullduggery. He declared it a brilliant tactic, but knew a way to one-up them. He claimed that if we could provide evidence that a Russian citizen with a Russian address owned shares in Celtic, it would supersede any ruling Polyus could expect from the rural judge they'd bribed.

Merrill Lynch in Minneapolis was host to several investment accounts of numerous Russian citizens. I happened to have a power of attorney for many of them. Martha there handled trades for last names starting with certain letters. I placed an order with her in Pablo's name to purchase fifty dollars of ticker symbol CER on London's AIM exchange. It cost us twenty times more to get the certificate authenticated, notarized, translated and express delivered to Moscow. In keeping with the opening salvo Polyus had fired, the local lawyer chuckled as he reported filing a motion in somewhere equally inconvenient like Bashkiria. The court ruled in our favor, which got Polyus's case tossed out as promised. Local lawyer was proud of his brilliant maneuver and parked a little blurb in the financial papers about how he had made Russia's number one gold mining company smell the glove for $50.

It wasn't like Celtic would be able to use the ruling to change anything in Yakutia, a republic whose president held a financial interest in our opponent. Nonetheless, Polyus's CEO, German Pikhoya, was livid and demanded a face to face. Boris, who was not easily intimidated, accompanied the lawyer and me to the meeting. Pikhoya pointed at the name of the shareholder, Pablo, aka our friend in St. Petersburg, and threatened to "find" him. It was an empty bluff. The deed was done. Going after Pablo would change nothing. Our response was, "Why would you waste your time trying to find him? We can get him on the phone for you right now."

The only recourse Polyus had was to throw Pablo's name onto a site called Kompromat.ru (Compromising materials). It was sort of a Russian version of The Smoking Gun. Pablo found out about it before we told him. He had no qualms about helping us, but was not happy that the site showed his unredacted account number. He asked me to close the Merrill Lynch account.

A headhunter asked if I'd be interested in interviewing with Toronto-based Barrick Gold, which was the largest gold producer in the world at the time. The search firm arranged a video conference with Barrick director, Tye Burt. Shortly after the interview it was revealed that he had no interest in me as a candidate but instead used the interview to determine whether or not to invest in Celtic, which Barrick did. London took all the credit for attracting Barrick. I couldn't admit why or how I'd previously met Mr. Burt, but instead told London I looked forward to meeting our new partners.

Barrick introduced itself to Russian society by organizing an exhibit at The Hermitage of one of Canada's most famous painters from the early 1900s, Tom Thomson. From a business perspective, it didn't make any sense to me. However, getting the opportunity to walk the museum after hours in a small group and meet the director, Mikhail Piotrovsky, was a once in a lifetime evening. Pablo had just received a box of freshly published books of poetry with illustrations. Pablo helped a talented friend from Kazakhstan get the book published. He made me promise that I would boldly present a copy to Mr. Piotrovsky, which I did. The Hermitage exhibit reminded me of something White Knights might have done in lieu of bribing. It sent a message, "We can't give you cash, but we can spend loads of money on intangibles."

Eureka Mining

Foo and others in London quietly launched a subsidiary company called Eureka Mining (EKA:AIM). Eureka's only assets were two licenses to mine copper near Chelyabinsk, Russia. The plot twist was that the mines belonged to Joe Pitch, my friend who was helping Celtic launder money to fight KDM. Joe Pitch's partner in Chelyabinsk had found a dishonorable way to convey the licenses to Eureka. It was a legal transaction under the rules of the stock exchange, but there was zero chance of it holding up in Russian court, which had ultimate jurisdiction.

When Joe Pitch found out Foo was behind the scheme, he called me to express his disappointment. Joe and I were scheduled to be in London at the same time. I suggested a meeting with Eureka. Foo wasn't around, but a board member named Euan claimed to be fully versed and agreed to discuss. We went for lunch near Celtic's office, which was not far from the London Eye (Ferris wheel) on the Thames. We were all speaking English, but not the same language. There was no way I would fight Joe, especially in a battle I knew Eureka had already lost. Euan nonetheless continued to ramble on about that which he didn't know, oblivious to the comedy he was providing. Joe Pitch shot me looks that conveyed simultaneously pity and disbelief, as if tacitly asking, "Do you really have to work with this person, and is he for real?"

When Foo was next in Moscow, we went for lunch to discuss the copper mines and Eureka's soon to be terminated ownership of them. Joe started the conversation with, "You can have any assets in the country except these." To Foo that sounded arrogant. It shocked him. But it was true. Eureka had its own CEO, Bartley. I tried to talk sense to him.

A man we nicknamed Shaggy represented the Russian federal regulatory body that controlled mining licenses. We were not only office mates, but neighbors. We explained to Bartley that Eureka's assets could be wiped out with the stroke of Shaggy's pen. Bartley wisely arranged some cash for Shaggy and signed a contract to issue shares in Eureka to him, pending a (temporary) renewal of the licenses. Bartley made a gentleman's deal with me for 25,000 shares to park wherever I chose.

Shaggy and I knew Eureka could not prevail. But we also didn't want to lose free money. We went to dinner with Joe at a restaurant called "Cheese," (Сыр). We honestly reported to him Eureka's offer and gave him the chance to match it. He declined, believing that Shaggy wasn't high enough in the administration. We understood each other perfectly and parted ways with no animosity.

After the copper licenses were (temporarily) transferred to Eureka, Bartley kept his word and issued us shares. I parked mine at Merrill Lynch in one of the many brokerage accounts I controlled under power of attorney with a Russian proxy. It felt surreal selling something I knew would have no value, but there's an ass for every seat. Joe took the mines back and eventually sold them to Gerald Metals, or Gerry, who was always looking for more coppa.

Shaggy called from Washington and asked if I knew any Russian speakers. I connected him with Dan Rapoport. After they went around town, Shaggy called me back and said, "I never expected to have an oligarch as a tour guide."

Simon Wiesenthal—Jerusalem

Out of the blue in April, 2004, Mountain Hebe called and insisted that I meet him in Jerusalem to participate in the groundbreaking ceremony of the Simon Wiesenthal's Center for Human Dignity and Tolerance Museum. It was an enormous honor. Simon Wiesenthal is a personal hero, whose legacy I consider deserves to be placed alongside all others at the pinnacle of humanity. I was a little surprised to see Arnold Schwarzenegger in the group. It was his first trip abroad as governor of California. His movies had never interested me. I had low expectations when he stood to make a speech.

California Governor Arnold Schwarzenegger, speaking on behalf of his constituents and The Simon Wiesenthal Center 2004

The governor's words were correct and moral. Paraphrasing from memory, he said, "I come from Austria, a country that unleashed some of the worst horrors in human history. I now have the privilege of representing the most diverse population on Earth. It is my obligation to be here today to promote tolerance." Every major media outlet was present and filmed his speech. What the media chose to report was that governor Schwarzenegger infuriated Palestinians by visiting Israel.

We were on a tour with Rabbi Marvin Hier, chairman of Wiesenthal Center. As we were about to enter the tunnels beneath the Temple Mount, a reporter from the New York Times approached Rabbi Hier and asked, "Why did you bring that anti-Semite Arnold with you to Israel?" I may be wrong, but I remember that "person" being James Bennet. Rabbi Hier was visibly livid, but considering we were in front of the Western Wall, he maintained more control than I could have, replying only, "How dare you ask that question about my friend? Especially here, at the holiest site in Judaism?" We walked on, ignoring what the filthy propagandist had asked.

The next morning, Rabbi Hier sat alone at breakfast in The King David Hotel. I asked if I could join him, which he allowed. The incident with the reporter intrigued me. I asked if he could provide context for the hostile reaction. Rabbi's Hier's explanation was diplomatic and free of curse words. I prefer to remember it in vernacular terms. What I heard and definitely not what he said was, "That abject cunt from the New York Times does nothing but print lies every day to the detriment of decency. Fuck him forever."

Bennet was consistent with the vile history of the New York Times, whose morals are equivalent to those of holocaust deniers. Stalin murdered more people by starving them to death in the early 1930s (Holodomor) faster than Hitler did Jews in the 1940s. A New York Times "Reporter," Walter Duranty won a Pulitzer Prize for his commentary, writing "Any report of famine in Russia today is an exaggeration or malignant propaganda." Malignant propaganda should be their motto. To contrast what the prize-winning reporter from the New York Times wrote, I'll cite Boris Pasternak's observations on the Ukrainian Holodomor, "What I saw there could not be expressed in words. There was such inhuman, unimaginable misery, such a terrible disaster, that it began to seem almost abstract. It could not fit within the bounds of consciousness." The way Bennet and the New York Times covered Israel showed they were simply carrying Duranty's torch.

The real story that I remember hearing from Rabbi Hier, was that he and Arnold became friends because of the governor's conscience. Arnold contacted the Wiesenthal Center to find out if his father was complicit in any Nazi crimes. The Wiesenthal Center is likely the best resource for WWII history in the world. Paraphrasing what I heard, Arnold told the Center "I know what my father told me he did, but I have to know for certain what he did." The Wiesenthal Center researched his past and determined that the senior Schwarzenegger held an innocuous position and did not kill anyone. Arnold was at the peak of career and made a very generous contribution to the Center to support their efforts to bring Nazis to justice. His donation was not for public attention. As usual, the New York Times perverted a beautiful narrative and purposefully printed lies for their easily manipulated readers.

It was a great pleasure to shake hands with Natan Sharansky, who had been an affiliated Soviet dissident with my matchmaker, Arkady Polishchuk. Sharansky's book "The Case For Democracy," and in particular the chapter "Freedom vs. Fear" is top-notch political commentary, in my opinion. I only learned about the Polishchuk - Sharansky connection when Arkady's book was released.

With then Israeli Finance Minister Netanyahu

Mountain Hebe and I with Israel's Minister of Defense, Shaul Mofaz

Soviet dissident and Israeli politician, Natan Sharansky

Blackjack Blacked Out

After Jerusalem, I caught up with Toolshed, the little Dicker (the younger brother), and a guy we called Yuzhafrichard (South African in Russian) at a casino across from Red Square and the Kremlin. Until 2009 there was "VIP Casino" in the basement of the National Hotel. They served free drinks and had a decent wine list. As players won, the pour sizes increased. If a stack of chips got tall, they'd serve you an entire bottle of wine in one glass.

There's a Russian saying, "God protects drunks and idiots." Four of us were all winning at blackjack, for hours. The casino escalated to full bottles of wine as single servings. They switched dealers often, and changed decks. Nothing worked. We continued to win, and drink. When a stranger sat down at our table, we assumed that the casino sent in a spoiler in an attempt to disrupt our winning streak. He appeared Caucasian[1]. Toolshed politely asked the stranger, "Excuse me. You wouldn't happen to know how to say 'Fuck your mother' in Italian, would you?" The guy wasn't sure he'd been insulted. Shed repeated it, "I'm sorry. I didn't pose that question properly. What I meant to ask was how to say, "Fuck **YOUR** mother" in Italian?"

To the left of the man's hand was a heavy lead crystal ashtray. He was no interrupter, just a rude blackjack player. With his eyes fixed on Toolshed, who wasn't looking, he was about to lift the ashtray and hit him with it when a bouncer positioned himself between the two. He pushed the insulted man away and out. We played another half hour until closing time, 5 a.m. I remember putting around $4,000 of winnings in my coat pocket and that all four of us cashed in and all walked out with more money than when we started.

We got to the street. The sun was shining. Yuzhaf and Shed bowed out and went home. Little Dicker suggested we walk up the block to The Metropol Hotel where there was a 24-hour casino. The last thing I remember was suggesting we order drinks for each other and it was not allowed to have the same drink twice. After one or two, someone turned out the lights.

Struggling to open my eyes, a screeching car alarm combined with the urgent ring of an international phone call woke me around 4 p.m. It was June 12, which was a holiday initially declared "Independence Day," but later changed to "Russia Day," because the country had never been conquered by any-

---

[1] Caucasian is some from the region of the Caucasus Mountains. Ironically, Americans use the term to describe white Europeans, whereas Russians consider them black.

one other than domestic socialists. My family was in the U.S. From the couch in a sitting room, I scanned the room, trying to deduce how I ended up where I was. My clothes were strewn on the floor in sequence. The windows to the street were wide open. A beautiful silk carpet was stained with burgundy-red vomit. My slightly swollen upper lip jarred my memory a little. I recalled falling face first onto a marble staircase and not being able to extend my hands to soften the impact, thinking "This is going to hurt." On a bookshelf there was a stack of hundred dollar bills, which appeared to be around forty thousand. Intrigued, I walked to the bookshelf and saw that, in addition to the cash, there were several thousand dollars of chips from The Metropol, mostly hundreds but a few five-hundreds. I had no recollection of gambling there.

Russian ATMs dispensed up to $10,000 cash USD at a time. I guessed that the stack was bank withdrawals. Drunk, I could have easily tried to swing heavy at the house. Little Dicker had likely dragged me out of the casino to stop what would have been a bloodbath. Checking online, it was a relief to see that no withdrawals had been made. I loaded my pockets with the chips and went back to cash them in. At the casino entrance they requested my passport. After entering my name, security said, "Sorry. You're blacklisted." I asked if he could tell me why. I explained that earlier that morning I had been there blackout drunk. "Oh no, it's not because of that. You are on the blacklist for card counting." Card counting?!? I couldn't see the cards, let alone count them.

After appealing the blacklisting to security for several minutes, an Englishman emerged and introduced himself as the manager. If they wouldn't let me in to play, would they at least honor their chips? He said, "You can go back in one time." The casino was deserted. Instead of cashing out, I decided to play again. Midway through the first shoe I was up almost another $3,000. The English manager swooped in, lifted all my chips, walked them to the cashier's cage and instructed her to cash me out. "That's it. Never come back." I saved some of the winnings until October and sent my boys home to the U.S. for Halloween to go surprise trick-or-treating at their grandparent's house.

When Little Dicker finally regained consciousness, I asked if he remembered us being at The Metropol. He responded, "Were we?! You were on fire." He relayed the play that caused them to throw me out. He said I adamantly insisted on hitting a hard eighteen against the dealer's six. He knew I was hammered and begged the dealer to not give me a card. Insisting on taking a card, I loudly declared, "My money. My cards. My choice." This attracted the attention of a pitboss, who watched me take a three. The dealer then hit an ace to 17. If I hadn't taken the three the house would have won three spots from me at $2,000 each. The manager cashed me out against my will, escorted me to the sidewalk, and put me on a citywide blacklist, or at least on the blacklist that twenty or so casinos shared. There were uncashed chips because my friend stuffed them into my jacket that was hanging on the back of my chair.

A Wild Man In Provence

As Cerys and I became better friends, she offered me the use of her home in a village near St. Tropez called La Garde Freinet. It's at the top of a mountain with views of the Mediterranean below in the distance. Just opening the windows to smell the air is a pleasure. My family and I went there often. The house was rustic, secluded and a welcome respite from the chaos of Moscow. After our second extended stay, I felt compelled to pay for the privilege. Cerys refused. I insisted. She refused again. We struck a compromise. In lieu of rent, I could stock the wine cellar. She added, "I only want Provence wines for my Provence house." It was a wonderful mission.

We scoured the region, visiting vineyards and boutique shops from Nice to Aix. After collectively spending weeks and months researching wine, the little shop in La Garde Freinet ended up being our favorite. The owner is known as Wild Man. We invited him to Moscow, where I got him stoned and drunk, and then took him to a casino. He played the worst blackjack I've ever seen. It was as if he intentionally wanted to lose. He broke even anyway and tipped the dealer.

Wild Man reciprocated the next time I was in France. He took me to a poker game in Sainte Maxime in a nightclub that was closed for the off-season. It had the feel of a speakeasy. A Spanish gypsy with a cigar stub in his mouth unlocked the door when he saw Wild Man. He looked at me and asked "Qui est le mec?" (Who's the dude?) Wild said simply "He's with me." He let us in and we played poker until sunrise. One of the players had a pet rat that stayed on his shoulder the entire game. He'd occasionally kiss it.

When it was time to leave, Wild Man stood up and fell forward onto a low cocktail table. Stumbling to his feet, he motioned for me to go, saying "I will drive you back." The road winds about ten miles up a mountain. It's just barely wide enough for two small cars. When I drove that road sober in the daytime, the fastest I dared drive on the straight parts was thirty mph. There are numerous cliffs as well. I begged the other card players to call a taxi. They refused. They said Wild Man might be a little tired, but he'd get me home safe. Besides, it was off season. There weren't any taxis. .

Reluctantly I got in the passenger seat. Before leaving the parking lot Wild Man checked that I had my seatbelt on. As he accelerated out of the parking lot, he said, "Don't worry. I drive this route so often that every stone on the road has a name." We were going up the hill at speeds fluctuating between 50 and 75 mph. On many of the turns, I could feel the car slipping on gravel, sliding towards a cliff, and when it gripped the pavement Wild Man accelerated as fast as the car would go. Even if I'd known that Wild Man wasn't drunk, it would still be the most terrifying ride I'd even been on. He delivered me to Cerys's house and sped off. I stood in the yard, nauseous. When I replayed the vision of the car sliding towards a cliff, I reflexively started vomiting.

Later that morning, we visited the butcher shop in the village owned by Jean Jacques Martini. He's a local legend. His lasagna remains my favorite. Actors Daniel Day Lewis and Liam Neeson spent a lot of time in La Garde Freinet. They hired Jean Jacques to cater the opening of the movie, "Gangs of New York" when it was released in Manhattan. During a previous visit we discussed Russian mustard, which is powerful like wasabi. I promised to bring him a jar and did. I mentioned that Wild Man scared the shit out of me with his driving. Jean Jacques said nothing, took me by the arm and flipped over the "Back in 10 minutes" sign. We walked a block or so to a members-only bar, where just inside the entrance was a framed poster showing #1 in the world. The poster had the faces of Wild Man and his driving partner from a 1989 world championship rally race.

Road that Wild Man drove up around 70mph

Kraftwerk In Moscow

The German pioneers of electronic music, Kraftwerk, performed their first concert in Russia at Moscow's Luzhniki stadium, one of the biggest in Europe. In 1980 Luzhniki held the opening and closing ceremonies of the Olympics. Liosha of Disco Banya often DJ'd. He had to experience Kraftwerk. I hounded him all day until he agreed.

We never talked about business, but I surmised one of his sources of income was selling cars to government officials at inflated prices. There was a time when the Duma's parking lot looked like an Audi dealership. Members paid $80,000 for a $40,000 car. The buyer and seller would split the difference. Liosha also sold luxury boats in which we'd cruise Moscow's extensive reservoir system.

On the day of the Kraftwerk concert, Liosha picked me up at Night Flight's sister restaurant, Skandinavia, which didn't employ COB (a synonym for prostitute, i.e. Coin Operated Beaver). Skandinavia got their food from Sweden as well and was known to serve the best hamburger in all of Russia. Instead of his usual Audi or custom van, Liosha was riding in a stretch BMW that day. Between the back seats there was a well stocked refrigerator that was designed to hold glass bottles in place. He had to show me how to extract a beer from it.

On the way to pick up Nach Nach from a restaurant called Silk, near the stadium, Liosha lit a papirosa with the same lethal Estonian hothouse weed and kief that had set the younger Qadaffi deep into the couch. When we arrived at Silk I was unable to open the window. Nach Nach couldn't see into the car, but suspected it was us. Liosha asked if my friend was standing next to the car. I couldn't respond. Liosha reached over to put my window down. Nach Nach saw my stoned face and said only, "Oh Jesus!" He would be in the same condition a few minutes later.

Consciousness somewhat returned as we arrived at Luzhniki stadium. The sidewalks were teeming with people. At Liosha's instruction, his driver pulled up to a set of gates, manned by armed guards. The guards were confused and waved us to turn around. Liosha rolled down the window and said, "We're looking for the VIP entrance." The guard said, "You need police permission to pass through this gate." Laughing Liosh said, "I've got one of those, or maybe two," and handed him a couple hundred dollar bills. As the gate opened, the guard leaned in and told us not to tell anyone he'd let us through.

We reached a barricade with more guards. They stared at our car approaching them. They were clearly baffled how we got there. They too requested our police pass and Liosh again tossed hundreds until they let us pass. They told us to park near the bus, which was in front of the band's entrance. The guards at the stage entrance didn't ask to see credentials. They assumed that three guys who'd made it all the way there in a stretch BMW should be left alone. Liosha and I went in when we heard the concert start. Nach Nach had to stay in the car for two or three songs before he was able to move.

A stadium concert by four guys on computers with a huge video screen was surprisingly excellent. Near the stage it was so loud I could feel internal organs pulsating. Liosha loved it. I didn't. I sat alone about fifty rows back, where it was still loud. For the first encore human band members were replaced with mechanical mannequins that played the song, "The Robots." Liosha noticed the band departing and decided to follow their bus out of the stadium.

Coon Rapids Native at
Kraftwerk Studio, Dusseldorf

The Trinity Sues

On the Celtic front, London may have signed a deal with the Trinity, or perhaps one was forged. I knew I had agreed to nothing. Either way, they sued Celtic in London for breach of contract, using a company out of The Netherlands, called Arduina. I knew nothing about any deal or the basis for their suit. It should have never happened.

While home on summer break in Minneapolis, the court summoned me to testify in London. I considered myself immaterial to whatever case Arduina didn't have, but I had to be there to confirm under oath that I had signed no deals with them. The judge's knowledge of all the statements impressed me. Arduina's London lawyer had tried to suggest that my Russian was insufficient to understand that I'd made an agreement, yet their Russian lawyer submitted an affidavit wherein he deemed my knowledge of Russian sufficient to understand all topics discussed with Dmitry Yakubovsky and Mr. Shodiev. The court ruled in Celtics's favor. It had been a needless waste of time. How Celtic managed to avoid revealing lawsuits and ownership disputes was interesting.

Since the time I was first issued shares and incentivized with the promise of more, Celtic's share price had increased about fivefold. After closing the court case, I said goodbye to J. Dog and intended to finish Summer break with my family, the return ticket was for July 7, 2005, the day of multiple terror attacks on busses across London. By the time I arrived late at Gatwick airport there was one ticket left to anywhere in America, a United flight to Washington Dulles.

Uncle Marijuana Pioneer

Eventually arriving in Minnesota, I picked up some footlong buds from my uncle Doug, my mom's younger brother. Over the course of at least a decade, he tweaked clones of marijuana that he grew outdoors in a State forest whose border was near his 160 acre property. He named it after the park it was grown in. He called it Nemadji Thunderfuck.

Vancouver was the first jurisdiction in North America to generally decriminalize cannabis. Uncle Doug ordered seeds for various strains from there and developed a clone that was perfectly suited for the local climate. It was illegal to mail activated seeds, but how could anyone check? He had a contact in Vancouver who stamped the seed containers "Degerminated." Working the area since the 1970s, Uncle Doug became a skilled grower.

Auntie Gayle, my dad's younger sister, was the general manager of concessions at Minneapolis - St. Paul International Airport. With her title came a pass that allowed her to enter most areas of the airport without security screening, along with up to five others. She never asked why, but I would occasionally ask her to escort me through the basement to avoid security. She would also be rewarded for the gesture with some of Uncle Doug's products. I flew numerous times without any fear of detection. If the connection was in Amsterdam, the Dutch didn't care at all. Moscow never patted down arriving passengers, and even if they found it, you could just pay them off.

There was one close call, though. Flying from Minneapolis through London to Moscow, there was about a half ounce of Uncle Doug in my jacket pocket. When we exited the plane in London there were border agents lined up every ten or so passengers. An announcement was repeated, "Our security systems are down. All passengers will be searched. We apologise for the inconvenience." English law wasn't so lax. Agents were standing watch. I couldn't throw it away undetected. They were certain to find it. As I neared the pat down station, I made do with what I had, which was a pack of Kleenex from the flight kit. I stuffed the weed into my armpit and surrounded it with tissue paper. As the guard frisked me, I started to sweat. When the agent felt the lump in my armpit, he stopped and asked what it was. I told him that I had a gland problem that caused excessive sweating. He told me to show him. I undid a button on my shirt, put my hand inside and pulled out a wet clump of tissue and showed him. He looked disgusted and waved me through.

When the Dicker wasn't in Moscow, the staff at Bourbon Street let me do pretty much whatever I wanted. There were about a dozen of us there whom I knew appreciated good smoke. There were no outsiders. I decided to lock the doors of the twenty-four hour bar for a while. A Bourbon Street regular named Yuri lived in an apartment next door. Among many other talents, he played the French horn in the orchestra of the Bolshoi Theater. He went home to retrieve a bong. Yuri's girlfriend, Liza, was the piano player at the performance of Nord Ost when the entire theater was taken hostage. She survived, but not without mental scars. I considered Liza and Yuri the best kind of people.

With the doors locked and Yuri's bong got lit up, Liosha finally attained that stupefied look he was so good at dishing out. I'd avenged the Estonian hothouse. Yuri was so stoned he thought he'd smoked chemicals. Uncle Doug became the codeword for potent pot. The music was on random and I distinctly remember being floored by the reaction of a guy nicknamed Chili Rodriguez to Louis Armstrong's version of the song, "Sunny Side of the Street." As soon as he heard the opening lyrics "Grab your coat and grab your hat," Chili jumped out of his chair and pumped his fist. It was great to see how genuinely loved Louis Armstrong was all over the world. Chili moved to Norway and I haven't seen him since.

While possession of marijuana is still a serious criminal offense under Russian law (glory to lax enforcement), it is worth noting that the Russian equivalent of America's DEA is much more honestly named. It's called The Federal Service of the Russian Federation to Control the Turnover from Drugs. Its headquarters in Moscow are on Pokrovka or Maroseika, which is the same street with different names.

To mask the smell of the marijuana fields on my uncle's property, he kept a couple dozen pigs. He fed them with the food thrown away by the enormous buffet from casino complex some forty-five minutes away. It was a win-win for the farmer and the casino. The farmer got free food and the casino didn't have the expense of paying to remove it. I once visited him with my wife and two young sons after he had picked up about a half a pallet of eggs, which I'd estimate was around four thousand. We spent at least an hour throwing eggs at the pigs, which, if they broke on a pig's back, another would lick it off. The boys thought this was hilarious. About the marijuana on the property, Matilda and I assumed the boys knew nothing. Perhaps a year later, we were all walking around Amsterdam when my son Michael stopped cold on the sidewalk and got a befuddled look on his face. When we asked why he has stopped, he announced, "Hey! Amsterdam smells just like uncle Doug's farm!."

Bolshoi Chapter Ends

Later in 2005, the Bolshoi Theater closed for six years of renovations, on which almost $1 billion was spent. The final performance was "Swan Lake." Nadezhda Grachiova miraculously performed both the black and white swan. After the performance, we sipped champagne with Nelli in the projection booth, lamenting the end of an era. From the stage, dancers and directors summoned Nelli to come down. Nelli replied that she had guests and didn't want to be rude. The reply came, "A friend of Nelli is a friend of the Bolshoi. Bring everyone" A Ukrainian pastor and his wife, Lilly, were visiting from Minneapolis. Lilly was giddy about the chance to walk on stage at the Bolshoi (as was I) and asked me to call a mutual friend. The call went through. I handed the phone to Lilly, who was on her third or fourth champagne. Her voice was a little loud when she said, "You will NOT believe where Kesha took us." She got a stunned look on her face when she heard the other person's reply, loudly exclaiming, "No! I'm not in a Swedish whorehouse. I'm on stage at the Bolshoi."

A jazz trio from Minneapolis called The Bad Plus performed four concerts in Moscow. The Bad Plus meant nothing to me, but they were playing the best jazz venue in Moscow, Le Club. Numerous people, whose musical opinions I respected, called to insist I check out their show. The venue was relatively close to my apartment. I went to their opening night alone. The skill level of the musicians was tip-top and the arrangements mesmerizing. The next night I invited O.P. and another jazz aficionado from Gorbushka. They too loved the show.

After Swan Lake, before multiple-year renovation June 29, 2005

For their final concert I booked a table in front of the stage, inviting Cerys, Voronchuk, Yuri the French horn player, others, and most memorably, Nelli Ivanovna from the Bolshoi. She told me several times that she had never been to live jazz. O.P. and others smoked weed from a dugout and blew the fumes onstage, eliciting inquisitive looks from the drummer and the bass player, both of whom reacted positively when they recognized the aroma.

About midway through the concert, Dave King went into a trance for an intense and visibly exhausting drum solo that lasted 2–3 minutes. Noticing beads of sweat on his head, Nelli, La Grande Dame du Bolshoi, stood up, walked on stage and extracted an oversized ornate Spanish hand fan that looked like it came out of the wardrobe of Bizet's Carmen. She used it to cool off the oblivious Dave King, who didn't notice her even after she walked away. The crowd loved it. We took some photos together after the show. Outside Le Club a random horse passed by. We insisted that Dave the drummer mount the horse for another photo. Nelli had to help him up. He'd obviously never been on a horse.

Friends Lilli and Victor, onstage with who likely was the Bolshoi Ballet's only Japanese-born soloist, Morihiro Ivata.

Nelli Ivanovna on stage with The Bad Plus of the now defunct jazz venue, Le Club. Moscow

Bolshoi Ballet staff and Grape (center)

An Unlikely Diplomat

In Denver Mountain Hebe attained a certain level of diplomatic immunity. Zoranbaev from the Almaty days became some kind of government minister in Belgrade. He had the power to bestow diplomatic status in certain jurisdictions in random countries. Mountain Hebe was appointed the Honorary Consul of Yugoslavia to the Western United States, a job at which he's certain to excel. However, with diplomatic license plates, his ambulatory abuses behind the wheel are constant. By riding in the passenger seat of a Yugoslavian diplomat, I learned that there is no such thing as a one-way street.

Diplomatic plates encourage pavement perversion

Arrest Tourists

A Minnesotan named Brad John Buscher who was born at ISJ Hospital in Mankato on October 16, 1955 to Bob and Marilyn called me from Bangkok to ask if KLM flew to Moscow. After I said yes, he asked if I could arrange visas for four people. He and three others had purchased 90-day unlimited flights on KLM to go anywhere the airline went. They were flying around the world with no itinerary. Two of them, Buscher and Harry Johnson from Madison Lake, were notorious pranksters. In college, Harry organized a group of friends to stop traffic on the Golden Gate Bridge. Each participant blocked a lane of traffic at an agreed upon location. When they got out of their cars to pose for photographs, they also captured the faces of enraged drivers who were in a hurry to get somewhere.

The day after Buscher's divorce, Harry placed a bogus full-page nuptial announcement in a local newspaper, stating that Bushbag was already instantly engaged to remarry. He wasn't. The call from Bangkok stemmed from the fact that Bushbag had been set up with, and he fell for, a Thai shemale. They took video of Buscher's reaction as he ran his hand up "her" leg. They turned his shocked face into a loop, which became a source of unlimited laughter. He made it clear that he wanted revenge and asked me, "What can you do to them in Russia?" I replied that anything can be arranged, but I would not entertain anything final.

Buscher stayed true to character and lied to the others that he had to attend an emergency company meeting in London, but in actuality showed up in Moscow to plot. Unbeknownst to me, he had already devised most of his plan. He took a suite in The National Hotel with a view overlooking the Kremlin. For the arrival of the other three, I sent a limo with escort girls to the airport and put their names on the VIP list, so they wouldn't have to stand in passport control and customs lines. They probably expected trouble right away. The fact that no bad thing happened to them likely comforted them and they expected further genuine hospitality.

We gathered in Buscher's suite. He ordered a three thousand dollar bottle of scotch from room service. When it was delivered we toasted Moscow. I didn't know that two of the glasses were dosed with Viagra and Cialis. We finished the bottle and went out for dinner. Buscher made it clear to me who the two targets were. They appeared to suspect nothing. We split into two cars after dinner en route to a nightclub. I instructed the driver of the targets to take them to a place called Three Monkeys, an over-the-top gay men's club. Guests had to be buzzed in, and out. When they noticed there was a buzzer to get out, they stayed for a couple drinks.

The driver waited outside for them and took them to Night Flight, where we were at a table upstairs near a window overlooking the entrance. I warned Gluggen the bouncer to be on the lookout for two guys asking for me and asked him to please lead them to our table. Before they showed up, Buscher informed us that he'd laced their drinks with Viagra and Cialis. They were about to enter a room full of gorgeous women for hire. We told Don Stefano, the general manager, to let the girls downstairs know that their services for two guys who would arrive shortly will be paid for by us. My task was to arrange for them to be arrested as they were about to enter their hotel. That was a piece of cake, or as the saying goes in Russian, "as easy as pissing on two fingers."

The targets arrived and were shown to our table. They commented that the Three Monkeys diversion was sort of cute, but not on par with the level of pranks they usually pull. They thought that they were safe after that. I suggested they go downstairs to check out the scenery, and made sure to point out that their hotel was only about ¼ mile from the club. All they had to do was go out the front door, turn right and keep walking until they ran into it. They went downstairs and were immediately swarmed. While they talked to prostitutes, I went out on the street to make sure that the officers on standby were ready for the cue and knew the script.

When they noticed my eagerness to execute, they decided to use it to drive the price up. They negotiated by saying things like, "I'm not sure about this. It's an urgent job and there are foreigners involved. What if they have a heart attack? Embassies and diplomatic services might be contacted. Maybe we should call it off?" Yadda Yadda. The clock was ticking so I didn't negotiate and paid extra. With the extra ka-ching, the police promised to put on a good show, adding masks and AKs. I went back upstairs to watch the front door.

It seems like I barely sat down when the two walked out the door with lovely escorts. The saying in Russian is that they departed "English style," which is without saying goodbye. They thought they had outsmarted Bushbag. To be certain they'd be hard as steel when they got arrested, I reminded the police to let them get as close to the hotel as possible.

It was a perfect August evening for strolling down Moscow's main street towards the Kremlin and Red Square. When they were just around the corner from the hotel entrance, men in masks jumped out of a car and put machine guns to their heads. Then they were cuffed and hauled off to a local police jail, where they sat until the ED drugs wore off. They were booked on faux charges around midnight. Their holding cell was just off Pushkin Square, the very heart of Moscow. The setting for the aspirant amorous duo was likely not very romantic. I wanted to let them out asap, but Bushbag wouldn't budge and he who pays the band requests the song.

A little after four in the morning, we went to the station to let them out. The police pretended to be a little miffed that we left them there so long and tried to squeeze a little more money. I'd already overpaid, so no. When the ED brothers emerged, Bushbag excoriated them for getting into trouble. "How did you manage to get arrested?! My God you're useless. Do you realize that we had to pay thousands of dollars to get you idiots released? I expect to be reimbursed." They believed it. They paid for their own arrest. At the time, I considered Brad Buscher some kind of legitimate businessman. He has since demonstrated with aplomb that he is a fraudster. Mercifully, I never made any commercial associations with him in Russia. If I had, they likely would have at best resulted in mortal defenestrations.

Zero Gravity Flight

Harry was the kind of person who seems to have infiltrated the best of every city's culture. He studied in Los Angeles and New York City. He seems to know the best of everywhere he goes. In Russia he managed to hook up with me and waltz past the line right into the Hermitage. He has an art collection that contains pieces that have been on loan to major museums in Europe. After surfing in Hawaii with musician Dave Grohl, Harry went helicopter skiing in British Columbia with an Italian couple from Milan. The husband, Aldo, financed his wife Lucrezia's production of images of interesting random sights around the world. Lucrezia mentioned to Harry that she had taken a commission to produce an exhibit of images based on Mikhail Bulgakov's novel, Master and Margarita, which is set mostly in Moscow. Many people believe that "Master and Margarita" was Mick Jagger's inspiration to write the song, "Sympathy for the Devil." The book contains numerous occurrences and references to unnatural powers, sorcery and witchcraft. For an opening Bulgakov lifted an idea from Goethe's Faust, "I am part of that power which eternally wills evil and eternally works good." Harry suggested they contact me to help with the project in Moscow.

Lucrezia had created exhibits of things like Namibia's petrified forests, female victims of Sharia in Afghanistan, and a book of orchid close-ups from an English garden that all resembled faces. Lucrezia and I could only communicate in unpolished French. Conversations with her zigzagged in a way I imagined it would be like trying to keep Salvador Dali focused on a topic, which was not likely. Aldo speaks perfect English. He called to plan Lucrezia's Moscow photoshoot. While making the itinerary, I felt they needed to be warned that schedules and Russian reality are not compatible. After touring places like Namibia and Afghanistan, he assured me they were prepared for irregularities. There's a Russian expression, "In Russia there are no roads. Only destinations." (В России нет дорог. Только направления). Its underlying sentiment, which I didn't translate literally, is that roads limit choices of route. The other meaning is literal. There are no roads, which is true in most of Russia. I recall a statistic that California has more paved roads than in all of Russia's eleven time zones.

The plan for the "Master and Margarita" project went fluid on day two. A friend from Star City called and offered me the chance to go on a zero-gravity training flight with members of the Russian space crew. It sounded like a once in a lifetime opportunity. I didn't hesitate to accept. When they said the flight was two days from then, I had to decline. I'd committed to the Italians. Star City said that it couldn't hurt to ask permission for the Italians also. A few hours later they called back to report that, for a cash fee, the Italians could fly too. Aldo and Lucrezia agreed instantly, except Kucrezia was thinking about how to use a zero gravity setting to improve the Master and Margarita exhibit.

The night before the zero-gravity session we went to Night Flight, but this time not for Swedish steak. Lucrezia wanted to find a nude model willing to pose as a witchlike Margarita. The interviews with prostitutes were comical. While I translated broken French into Russian, the conversation started with a hint that we were about to ask for something out of the ordinary. The girls reacted with a yawn and interrupted, "I get it. You want a French-speaking threesome. No problem."

Lucrezia caught me off guard when she replied, "Not even close. I want you to fly naked on a broom in zero gravity." I had to remind Lucrezia that the space center hadn't approved a naked flying witch, yet. She hit me back with a quote I had used earlier, which is "Nothing is impossible in Russia, if you really want it." My preferred quote about the topic is by Oscar Wilde, "Nothing is impossible in Russia, but reform." But the other quote is a Russian truism. I sheepishly called Star City to ask if we could bring a flying naked hooker. Without asking why, they promised to relay the request.

It was after midnight and we needed to leave Moscow at 6 a.m. to arrive at the military airport in time for a pre-flight medical inspection. We had already departed when the call came in confirming that we could bring the naked witch on her broom, but it was too late. Lucrezia decided to photoshop her into an image afterwards. In the final version, a naked Margarita flies a broom in front of the Russian Ministry of Foreign Affairs building, one of the famous Seven Sisters, the architecture style commonly called Stalin's wedding cake.

To locate a male model with a sinister visage, we went to Liosha's Disco Banya. It was hopping. We met an encouraging-looking character outside. We engaged in an introductory conversation and he quickly revealed that he was hallucinating by pointing out sights that weren't there. O.P. noticed us and invited us in. He recommended to not bother speaking with the other guy because, "He was on wheels." I'd never heard that before. It was slang for tripping on pills. O.P. had said it with a criminally mischievous and experienced expression on his face. Lucrezia picked up on the look and asked O.P. if he'd be willing to make his face devilish. He not only agreed but knew every location of each scene in the book. And more importantly, he knew which buildings to avoid, the ones with renovated exteriors that would betray authentic 1930s Moscow.

The zero-gravity flight was on an Ilyushin-76, a Russian military freight plane and paratrooper drop. Its cavernous cargo bay is large enough to carry tanks. Before takeoff, the flight leader explained that there was no shame in vomiting. They had studied many aspects of every person who had gone through the same training flight. They were unable to draw any conclusions as to why some people blanch and throw up, while others laugh and feel elated. Not gender, not height, not weight, not blood pressure, etc. Nothing could predict a person's reaction to G forces.

Thick canvas straps about 5 inches across spanned the floors, ceilings and walls. Flight operators placed their feet underneath them, so as to remain grounded when the plane switched into zero gravity mode. When the plane started its first rapid ascent, I could feel my entire body being sapped of its strength. The camera I was planning to shoot the first session with became difficult to lift. As the gravitational pull continued to increase for an uncomfortable amount of time, the light suddenly went sunlight bright. After a voice announced, "Regime," I was floating in the middle of the room and a crew member motioned me to raise my arms and make a T shape. He then threw me across the room to another crew member waiting to catch me 25 feet away. The reflex reaction was unbridled laughter. The combination of simultaneous fun and surrealness caused me to cackle like never before and never since.

A world record holder for the most days spent in outer space was on board. His antics in zero gravity caught the attention of Aldo and me. He was like a cosmic gymnast, doing multiple backflips wall to wall and sticking the landings. Aldo and I gestured to one of the crew members that we'd like to attempt copying his back flip. He smiled and shook his head no, but right afterwards indicated he'd laugh at watching us try. We both got suspended mid-air about three feet off the floor. In zero gravity not being able to reach a millimeter away is the same as a mile. Self-propulsion is impossible. The crew members stood idly by smiling and let us fall on our own.

Committing levitation in zero gravity

Still Swinging at Celtic

After seeing the Italians off, it was time for another chapter in the Celtic story. Vladimir Lisin was next to toss his hat in the ring. Lisin many times had been a contender for, and occasionally declared winner of, Russia's richest man. He participated in the Aluminum wars of the 1990's and obviously survived. Ten or so years later, the methods of conveying corporate hostilities had become less physical. Instead of Chechen assassins, one could expect a bag of cocaine to mysteriously appear in your bag going through customs, but the likelihood of taking twenty-five bullets from an AK-47 in a crowded area in daylight with no witnesses had greatly diminished.

Lisin's team started their squeeze on Celtic via loan agreements with Zenit Bank, whose board he sat on. Their lawyers created a flimsy basis for litigation. It was obvious they intended their case to be heard by a pre-paid judge whose ruling was likely already written. Bad press like the linked article started to appear in the financial pages in London and Moscow[1]. It seemed that Lisin's team wanted to take the fight to London. Aggravating information was leaked to the media and Celtic's share price started to drop. Then the message was delivered that Lisin's company, Severstal, intended to buy Celtic outright. We had a small budget for paid press as well. It was amazingly easy (as in under $25,000) to place positive articles in the same media outlets that had just printed negative articles. Celtic's share price started to rise again.

We put word out that we wanted to counter Lisin. A guy who knew a guy said he had determined exactly who controlled the Nezhdaninskoye gold mine, a top official from what's popularly called the Russian Senate (Federation Council). I'd been in Russia for 20 years and didn't even know that there was such a thing as a Russian Senate. We'd always just paid off whatever minister or deputy was relevant. It turns out that not only is there a Senate, but its director is the third most powerful Russian politician, behind the president and prime minister.

My perception is that Russian business is like a mafia nightclub. The first thing is to get past the velvet rope and the bouncers protecting it. I think of the bouncers as low-level officials. Sitting down at a table in the club can be dangerous if you don't know who's who. Or you might ask the wrong girl to dance. Walking

---

1 https://www.independent.co.uk/news/business/news/severstal-savages-celtic-chiefs-in-bid-battle-395418.html

past the velvet rope is chump level. There are VIP entrances, back doors, and underground parking. Real bosses enter through the kitchen and have the maitre d' bring a table from the back room and set it up front. There is always someone higher up and more connected. Then there's the capo di tutti capi, the president, the Tsar. When criminality is involved, every action is delegated. No boss partakes in a hit. They appear innocent and lily white.

Celtic had reached the top of their potential for useful Russian connections. The Nezhdaninskoye gold mine represented a seat at a Senator's table in the mafia nightclub. It was the last chance to keep that 25-year mining license active. A go-between set up a meeting with the Senator, warning me that dinner would not be cheap. They made a reservation in my name at one of Moscow's most expensive restaurants at the time, Grin. The most expensive restaurant in Moscow to build was Turandot. It cost over fifty million dollars. One of the owners bragged that nowhere in America was there a dining space as opulent, to which a Las Vegas based high-end restaurateur replied, "He's right about Turandot. In America people know how to manage a budget and forecast sales."

The chef at Grin had allegedly run the highest rated restaurant in the world in Spain. They advised me to arrive on time, but to expect the group to be at least an hour late. I sat alone and wondered if the meeting would happen at all. It was not unusual for the powerful to abandon meetings without warning.

It happened to me several times, and not just in Moscow. I flew six hours to Irkutsk, for example, only to be told that the person I was to meet had just left and wouldn't return for weeks. They didn't think anything of it. I was considered leaving when five men in Savile Row suits were shown to the table. We shook hands but they didn't share names. They sat down and ordered several bottles of $1,000 Bordeaux and all kinds of frou frou dishes. The chef seemed to be a big fan of foam. He put it on almost everything. They'd racked up about a $15,000 tab without saying one word about the gold mine.

It seemed like a set up or maybe a misunderstanding. I didn't even know who was who. "The" senator suddenly stood up from the other side of the table and sat down next to me. Like a mob boss, he leaned in to ask in a low voice, "What's the thing you need to discuss?" I told him the name Nezhdaninskoye and who our opponents were. He said, "Understood. You will get a number later this week," and returned to the other side of the table. I calculated that it had cost about five hundred dollars a second to speak with him one on one.

When I called Foo to report the promising news, I mentioned in passing that dinner had cost over twenty thousand dollars. Foo's response to the meal tab elicited a giant facepalm. He said, "I thought I hired a problem fixer, not a lunch buyer." He wasn't joking. A day or so later, the office of Herman Gref, minister of economics and trade, contacted me to request a written statement. The unsolicited call indicated that the Celtic story was about to be over in Russia. Gref's office requested our perception and not any factual information. This suggested that the senator made his decision and the administration wanted to get ahead of any negative narratives that might flow from throwing out a foreign mining company. I didn't take the bait and sent no statement. Celtic London was oblivious to the quirks and realities of Russia. I thought they should issue the statement about perceptions.

Lisin's company Severstal bought all of Celtic. His offer was simple and much fairer than it would have been in the 1990s. Essentially it was, "Show us what you spent and we'll double it. Now leave." About the same time as the sale of Celtic was being finalized, someone broke into the apartment I rented from Voloshin, while we were home and we had a friend staying in the guest room.

I recall watching at the time a concert by The Bad Plus on a French TV channel called Mezzo, while someone climbed through the locked kitchen window. They removed knives from their wooden holder and scattered them on the floor. They left a few coins on the countertop and left without a trace.

The timing could have been a coincidence, but I took it as a message to not negotiate. Also, there was an untouched stack of about forty-five hundred dollar bills that was clearly visible through a glass door of a kitchen cabinet still there. Robbery didn't seem to be a motive. Every entrance to the building had a camera. The police arrived with a dog, fingerprint kits, and reviewed the video recordings. Like when Jeffrey Epstein was suicided, all the cameras failed and guards were uncharacteristically off duty.

Water Thief In Provence

While waiting for the Celtic - Severstal deal to close, Cerys lent us her home in Provence again. Aldo insisted I borrow his Hummer instead of renting a car. I accepted, but the thing was a curse. Provencal roads are made for skinny cars like Citroens. A Hummer takes up almost the whole road. It was challenging to drive it.

Before I left Moscow, Cerys asked me to look into why her water bill had spiked, from $200 to as high as $5,000 per month. Her pool wasn't even filled. The investigation was concluded instantly. Off the back of her pool house a thick hose about 4" in diameter was pulling water down a hill into a cistern that stood in a neighbor's garden about 350 yards away. The hose was elevated about 3 feet off the ground and supported by Y shaped stakes in the ground. I took photos of the set up and showed them to Wild Man.

He couldn't believe what he saw and asked if he could show them to a couple other locals. The local adhoc justice committee discussed the water theft over a few glasses of wine. The group nodded in unison, concluding that the thief must be fucked in the ass (il faut l'enculer). One suggested reporting the theft to the water company. Wild and the other rejected it. There was probably some legal loophole. There weren't even any police officers in the village. Criminal charges were not likely to work. I wanted to just rip out the hose and throw it away. They agreed that that would send a strong message, but they warned that if I got caught, I could face criminal charges. It had to be done. I resolved to do it solo, so as to not take anyone else down. They advised me to drive about thirty minutes inland to Le Luc, where there was a big set of community dumpsters near the main road.

Aldo's Hummer was great for cargo space. After hauling uphill the first two lengths of hose from the cistern, I worked to remove the sections that were hidden in brush. It took several hours to get a Hummerfull of hose by myself. Midway through the task, I started cutting holes in random places to make sure that the segments I'd already taken were irreparably unusable. I drove across the yard and parked behind the pool house, out of sight of the only neighbor. Winded and sweaty, I loaded as much as the car could hold, leaving behind about a third as much as what had been there at the start.

One would think that a Hummer with Italian license plates, parked alongside a row of community dumpsters in Le Luc, France, out of which cargo was hurriedly being thrown, might generate looks of curiosity, but no one paid attention. Despite successfully executing stage I of the hose removal project, a sense of dread that the police would be waiting gnawed at me all the way back for round two. Alternately, I anticipated being confronted by the irate water thief.

Cautiously peeking my head around the corner of the pool house, I saw no one and there was no sign that the deed had been detected. I chopped up and loaded what was left, went back down the hill and dumped the rest. The next day on the beach we were talking about the water thief at a Norwegian owned restaurant called L'Esquinade. An English-speaking local overheard and joined the conversation. The French seem to enjoy taking any position in a debate, as long as it offends. The local man declared that it was the thief's duty to steal water from rich Americans. He asked, "Don't you like to help the French?" It was hard to tell if he was serious or just yanking chains.

We liked L'Esquinade because it was probably the least pretentious place on Pampelonne beach. When the owners heard I was from Minneapolis, they mentioned that their good friend had moved there from Norway. They wrote him a brief note and sent along a souvenir t-shirt and hat. For the sole purpose of confusing a Norwegian, I delivered a package from his St. Tropez friends to his doorstep, with no address or postage on it.

Body Parts In Our Luggage

Before returning to Moscow, we visited briefly with Juanjo and Anita in Barcelona, where Matilda and I found a Spanish ham so tasty that we bought an entire leg of it. Running late, I first dropped off the family at the departure hall of Cote d'Azur airport. Matilda had my passport and ticket. She got my boarding pass and checked in all our bags. She was waiting with my documents when I entered the airport. From afar, I could see she had a concerned look beyond her usual fear of flying. Then an airport-wide announcement came over the speakers, "Passenger McKinney to Moscow, report immediately to security." Matilda said that was the third time they announced it.

Near the security checkpoint, they had one of our bags on a table by itself. Four or five officials stood nearby. After I declared myself the owner of the bag, they circled around. They pointed to an X-ray image of the bag's contents. It looked like a human leg with a shoe on, and it was riding a scooter. When we realized they had located contraband jamon, we started to laugh. They stared with intent anticipation as I opened the bag to show them what was inside. When they read the corporate stamp, 'Jamon Iberica Real," they also smirked. It took us months to eat the entire leg and it never tasted as good as when an expert shaved pieces as thin as scotch tape.

Sale and De-Listing of Celtic

We emptied Voloshin's apartment and sent dozens of boxes back to Minneapolis. There was a final meeting of Celtic in London. It came as no surprise when Foo announced that he was torpedoing us on the issuance of the shares that he promised on several occasions. If he didn't honor a written commitment to the president of a Republic, why would he keep his word to anyone else? I was grateful for the opportunity that Celtic had provided to visit new places. The short change at the finish was my fault. I should have heeded William S. Burroughs's "Advice for young people," where he says, "If you're doing business with a . . . son of a bitch, get it in writing. His word isn't worth shit."

Loose Ends

When we returned to Minneapolis, the local Russian community was curious to hear a first-person take on modern Russia. At a party hosted by an American who'd represented Land O Lakes in Moscow, his wife looked shocked when I said that Disco Banya at Liosha's house was a definite highlight of Moscow life. She asked me, "Isn't he in the car business?" I confirmed that he was and even mentioned the address of his main showroom. She said she knew exactly where it was, because her friend had tried to start a similar business nearby. She maintained that Liosha firebombed the competitor's lot. I never asked him about it. I wasn't a competitor and he always treated me fantastically.

Liosha called from Southern California, asking if I had any contacts there. I hooked him up with a friend originally from St. Petersburg, who had launched a substantial marijuana company in Los Angeles. Liosha was hiding in Malibu for a while after he put a Russian federal prosecutor in jail for attempting to shake him down. The prosecutor demanded an expensive car for his wife's birthday and another for himself in exchange for uninterrupted operations. Liosha turned the tables and set up an FSB sting. The prosecutor was arrested for extortion and abuse of power.

After his conviction, law enforcement issued a sort of fatwa against Liosha. Sadly, that meant the end of Disco Banya. The Russian weed dealer in L.A. called me after the two met. He reported that Liosha's ability to consume copious amounts of ganja was on par with only one of his other customers, Snoop Dogg.

Some twenty years after Leningrad State U, Olya called from Omaha. She just wanted to visit Minneapolis and chat with Matilda. We were sitting outside on our deck sipping wine, when an Armenian friend answered her phone and said in Russian, "Hello Yiolka." The Armenian had also lived in Leningrad / St. Petersburg. As she spoke with Yiolka on the phone, Olya mentioned that she hadn't heard the name since Leningrad. Olya's next door neighbor in the #6 dormitory was a Lithuanian girl named Yiolka. After the call ended, we told the Armenian about the possible connection. She confirmed that Yiolka studied at Leningrad U at the same time.

Without explaining why, we called Yiolka and invited her to meet us at a Tapas bar in Uptown. My wife, not knowing the term, asked if a "Topless" bar would let us in with children. Her question became a running joke. We arrived first. When Yiolka walked in and spotted Olya, she stood stunned, changing into so many facial expressions that if she had been acting her performance was worthy of a best actress nomination. Her emotions ranged from utter shock, happiness, disbelief to open arms. Afterwards, Yiolka explained that a blast from the past random meeting never happens to Lithuanians in Minneapolis.

Three Bottles of Wine

My bologna-throwing roommate, Dee, announced his wedding in Manhattan to a woman whose parents were Georgian and Lithuanian. I drove to the wedding from Minneapolis and picked up The Dicker on my way there. Joel T said he would meet us in New York. Midway through the reception after the wedding, Joel took a call from his catering company in D.C. When he returned to the table, he announced to the Dicker and me that we needed to go to Washington immediately.

Joel was a prankster. He was a little drunk, So was I. There was no reason to drive to D.C. I was more than hesitant. My car also had a trunk full of baby clothes I'd agreed to deliver to struggling young Russian parents in Brighton Beach. I'd also promised to meet up with my old Minneapolis neighbor, Molly, after the reception. Joel persisted. He was as adamant as I'd ever heard him. He also pointed out that the reception was dying down. He repeatedly promised that what awaited in Washington would be a supremely pleasant surprise.

Taking care of the clothes and crisscrossing with Molly gave me the chance to sober up a bit before hitting the road. Molly suggested we meet at a place called Cafeteria. We got there about 3 a.m. Cafeteria was packed. We waited about a half hour for a table. We knew we were next on the list, when P. Diddy arrived with a small entourage that strutted past us and took our table. It was like being in Leningrad in reverse. I was insulted to the core, but knew that if P. Diddy was on my home turf, I'd expect the staff to give him the same treatment. I remember eating a macaroni and cheese spring roll there, something I'd never seen before.

After Cafeteria, a Russian agreed to pick up the baby clothes at an address not far from the entrance to The Lincoln Tunnel. The Dicker was nodding off in the passenger seat. Joel was stretched out across the back with eyes shut. The Russian arrived. I popped the trunk and got out to help transfer the contents to the other guy's car. When I got back in the car to leave for Washington, the key had been removed from the ignition. No one had walked by. I asked which one took it. Joel and the Dicker both swore they had been asleep and didn't notice anything. Joel berated me as a naïf midwestern bumpkin dumbass, asking, "How could you be so fucking stupid as to leave your keys in the ignition in the middle of Manhattan with the door unlocked?" He was right, but I also thought how useless those two were to not have noticed someone other than me reaching into the car. I started to panic and thought of all the economic downsides of having to order emergency Jaguar key service at 5 a.m. on a Saturday morning in New York City while parked in a tow-away zone. Joel returned the key and mocked me for driving a Jaguar.

All the way to Washington, I imagined what kind of prank Joel was planning. He had already stung me once with the keys and we hadn't even left New York. The best I could hope for was that he wanted a free ride home. He was capable of anything. He once rented an early 1970's Cadillac convertible, put on a cowboy hat and drove to Tennessee with his girlfriend, where they got married without telling anyone. Nothing would surprise me. I was upset with myself for allowing him to set a hook in me, but there we were, speeding down the New Jersey Turnpike en route to D.C.

When we arrived at his catering headquarters in Alexandria, Virginia, I saw an almost identical Jaguar to mine parked in front. Joel laughed when he admitted it was his. Inside, on a black sparkly countertop of a spacious bar, there stood three large format bottles of open wine, two magnums of 1961 Chateau Petrus and a Jeroboam of 1961 Chateau La Tour. These wines are considered the pinnacle Bordeaux vintages of the century. Each still contained five or six ounces. Joel T explained, his company had catered an anniversary party for Rush Limbaugh. Those bottles were served at the head table. Joel's staff decanted the bottles and meticulously recorded which pour from which bottle went into which decanter. After dinner Rush and his friends lit cigars. They wouldn't disrespect the wine by drinking after smoking, so they left the bottles behind. That's when Joel took the call and instructed them to leave them for him.

We searched online and found that the bottles had been sold to an "anonymous" buyer at auction. The magnums of Petrus went for $35,000 each. The Jeroboam of Chateau La Tour was just under $150,000. I had done a long distance introduction to Joel when Wild Man the wine merchant visited Washington a year earlier. After they went out for dinner, Joel called me in a panic to report that "my" Frenchman jumped in his rental car, very drunk, and announced he wanted to reach Chicago in six hours. Joel wasn't concerned about the speed, but that he had put on the razzle dazzle and Wild Man shouldn't drive at all. When I asked Wild about it, he said that he got stopped near the Pentagon, but they didn't want to deal with a foreigner and let him go. He made it to Chicago untouched.

We sent a photo of the three bottles to him in France. Wild texted back several questions: Where are you? Did you win the lottery? Do you understand what those bottles represent? Fabrik lived near Joel's office. I called him to sample some vintage Bordeaux. He promptly showed up with a couple of joints. After reading Mr. Wild's questions, Joel came up with a plan to rile him all the way up. He refilled the bottles with cheap Chilean red wine, recorked them and replaced the foil. Joel staged a video of him opening the Jeroboam of La Tour, which he poured without decanting directly into a pint glass that I was holding. He filled it almost to the top. I immediately chugged as much as I could. Before setting the glass down, they stopped the video and sent it to France. Wild Man believed it and lost his mind, writing back. "You fucking savages are dead to me! You do not treat wine like that. I am done with you forever. Fuck you all. If you ever dare to come to France again, I will greet you at the airport with my knife and cut you."

Joel read the message and beamed with pride. Also, he was stoned from Fabrik's joints. We should have let Wild Man simmer, but Fabrik wanted to torture a French wine patriot too. We took a photo of him swigging straight from a magnum of Petrus. Wild didn't react. We figured he'd either blocked us or had a heart attack. Joel let the cat out of the bag that it was a hoax when he wrote in French that he found the three bottles behind a stove and after we got too drunk to finish them, we gave the rest to some Mexicans so they could marinade goat meat with it.

Jeroboam Chateau la Tour 1961 w/Fabrik

Joel T fake overpouring Petrus 1961 to make Wild Man insane

First Jew In Outer Space

Mrs. Dicker, daughter of cosmonaut Boris Volynov, used to get calls from various Jewish organizations and Synagogues, asking her to speak about how their family suffered as Soviet Jews. The Volynovs never considered themselves Jewish and were not religious. Also, they were treated like celebrities and did not suffer. Compared to most of the country, they lived well. It has been comical to watch the myth of suffering persecuted Soviet Jews expand and take hold. People want to believe so badly in a narrative, they no longer want to hear a person's experience when it differs from their preformed opinion. Writing about "The first Jew in space" is a more intriguing headline than "Guy from Irkutsk orbits the planet."

Random Meeting New Orleans

Masiagin and the Dickers stayed with us before Christmas 2006. From Minneapolis, they went to New Orleans, where they randomly ran into Joel in a bar. It was not planned or discussed. They all called me simultaneously to see whose call I'd answer first. I thought they were joking, until they sent a photo of them together. An hour or so after the first phone call, Joel called me. In a believable drunken voice, he said he lost his passport at the airport and missed his flight to Mexico, asking "Why did I try to drink with that Russian?" He pleaded for me to send the others' numbers so that he could see if they had his passport. They were all sitting together, having a laugh as I tried to solve the predicament that Joel wasn't in.

A chance meeting in New Orleans of my friends from D.C., Moscow, and Indianapolis. Not planned. They didn't have one another's numbers.

Texan Teaches Russians

Just after New Year 2007 I took a short-term contract to secure steel pipe for a company that was building an oil pipeline in the Western U.S. They were having difficulty finding construction materials and needed guidance to access them in Russia. All I had to do was arrange a meeting. The U.S company had tried but the Russians were not responsive. The CEO would be in Moscow mid-February, so we wouldn't have to fly extra hours to the factory. He warned that he was extremely busy and the most he could spare was a window from 11 a.m. to 1 p.m. on a Tuesday.

The pipeline CEO flew into Minneapolis and we met for dinner. I learned that he was a gun fan so I took him over to see the arsenal of our local gunsmith, Bernie White, who among other things had designed The Desert Eagle. It was always a pleasure to visit with Bernie. The Texan was with the variety of arms he had. Bernie made entry-breach shotguns for SWAT teams, which he called "Doorknockers."

When we arrived in Moscow for the pipeline project, Masiagin invited me to the 50th birthday party of his good friend, Peter Podgorodetsky, the keyboard player in the band "Time Machine," which had multiple hits for years. I wanted to go, but because on was on the clock, I shouldn't. Masiagin told me to bring the Texan too. It was the evening before our only important meeting, the whole reason for the trip. I warned him not to go shot for shot with people at the party, he declared, "I'm going to show these Russian fucks how to drink."

We had been at the party for several hours. The Texan sat with some English speakers. They seemed to be enjoying a cordial conversation. The band was about to play Louis Armstrong's "What A Wonderful World" and I was going to sing it. As they played the intro, I dedicated the song to the Texan for his gumption to try and drink with "Russian fucks." I stared at him, trying to make eye contact. He looked through to somewhere else, oblivious to where he was. I felt OK and knew I'd be ready for the next day's meeting, but Texas was toast. I asked Masiagin to send him back to the hotel and make sure he got to his room. When he stood up to leave, he fell over. There was a short staircase up to street level and I saw him fall face first into the stairs on the way out. Two guys lifted him up and carried him out. Forty-five minutes later they returned and reported that he had been put in his bed and was out like a light.

The meeting was twenty minutes away from our hotel, but Moscow traffic can be the worst in the world, sometimes it takes hours to go only a couple miles. To be safe I got up at 8:30 and was ready to go. I was debating how long to give Mr. certain to be hungover to get ready. I thought 9:30 would be about as late as he should start. I called his room and there was no answer. I went to knock on his door. No reply. Eventually I was knocking so loud that security came and told me to stop. I explained to security what had happened and asked if they could review the video to ensure that he had returned. They said they would not give any information about their guests. The only way was to present a search warrant.

I went back to my room and called over and over. I scoured the restaurants and coffee shops. He was nowhere. We were now officially late. I called the Pipe Company and reported that my counterpart was missing. By noon, I was in full panic. The trip was about to be a waste. I found it a bit ironic. It was usually Russians who disappear for important meetings. The pipe company wasn't shocked.

After the scheduled meeting had gone and went, I started calling some resourceful types to see what could be done to break down the Hotel's security stonewall. Masiagin was totally trustworthy. There was zero doubt that the man had reached his hotel room. An FSB officer called around 5 p.m. and said he would stop by the hotel by 6 p.m. to see if he could get info from the hotel's security. As I waited for him in the lobby, the Texan staggered by and when he saw me simply said "Sorry."

I was furious and relieved. What happened was he woke up early, went to the hotel's restaurant. He saw someone sipping on one of Russia's most popular breakfast beverages, cognac. He'd never had cognac for breakfast and tried it. He overcured his hangover. With the shampoo effect, he was drunk again. Forgetting everything, he just took off and wandered around Moscow all day. He eventually got tired and took a taxi back to the hotel. The meeting wasn't even on his mind. For a souvenir of his outing, he cracked a bone in his hand, got a fat lip from the fall on the stairs, and chipped a tooth.

Stock Forger Resurfaces

About ten years had passed since the Ballistica stock certificate forgery. Ugen mailed to my home address a cd recording of his musings about Jesus Christ, with a cover letter apologizing, sort of. I was intrigued and listened briefly, but couldn't take more than thirty seconds of it. My lawyer friend, the Yooper, was familiar with the Ugen story. I made the Yooper smell the glove by telling him that Ugen's Jesus wheezer musings recording might seem tedious, but if he just continued listening, I promised that it would turn a corner and get really interesting, which of course it never did. The Yooper appreciated the prank. After writing about it just now, I asked him if he remembered me doing that to him. His reply was terse, "The guy thinks AIDS can be cured with prayer." That was proof he had actually listened.

Chance Meeting In Cannes

Some time around 2010 I got a phone call from Cannes. Yarmo, the "beretta" oil trader and Celtic's creative lawyer had just met for the first time by making small talk drinking in a bar. Somehow, they got on the topic of foreigners who spoke Russian and did outrageous things. Both were convinced that they owned this space until they determined they were talking about me. I took it as a compliment that Andrei and Igor remembered me. It was a fun conversation.

MMA Heavyweight

Working on a project with a Dagestani nicknamed Shark, we agreed to meet for lunch with two of his contacts. When I arrived at the restaurant, the hostess informed me that a member of our party had already been seated. She asked if I'd like to join right away, or wait for the others. I asked to be seated immediately. When I approached the table, instead of Shark's familiar face, I saw what appeared to be an assassin. Thoughts were running through my mind about whom I'd pissed off and I couldn't think of anything I'd done to merit that type of force. I sized him up and concluded there was nothing I could do to hurt him. I was scrambling for a reason why someone was after me. I also refused to believe that Shark would set me up. For whatever I'd done, they'd sent a solid enforcer.

I sat down and he started the conversation by asking, "You are from Minneapolis, right?" I said yes. He continued, "Can you get in touch with Brett Rogers?" I had no idea who that was. The man sitting across from me was one of Russia's top rated heavyweight MMA fighters, Magomed Malikov. The reason he wanted to see me was that he had lost an MMA match in Moscow to Rogers, who trained in Minneapolis. During the fight, Magomed kicked Brett across his shin, but Magomed broke his own leg and had to forfeit. He hadn't been able to connect with Brett's management and asked me to set up a re-match when I got home. Magomed told me he held Brett in high esteem because of his reaction to the broken leg. Instead of jubilation over his victory, he said that Brett had shown genuine concern and it spoke a lot about his character. I found Rogers' gym, but we never got the chance to arrange a rematch.

Like most people, who can knock you to the ground, using about 5% of their power, Mr. Magomed Malikov was pleasant and kind. I took him on my team.

U.S.—Russia Foundation

In 2016 an executive search firm in D.C. called Russell Reynolds Associates offered me a CEO position for something called, "U.S. Russia Foundation for Economic Advancement and The Rule of Law." The title didn't seem particularly diplomatic. It struck me as intentionally insulting. The position spec sheet was full of pointless gibberish. For example, "U.S. Russia Foundation believes that a productive and cooperative relationship is in the long-term best interest of both countries. . ." If the foundation's mission was to improve relations with Russia, they were colossal failures and admitted as much in their spec sheet. Also, the foundation's offices were in Ukraine. I laughed out loud when I read Kiev! What an exceptional display of incompetence and uselessness. The spec sheet read, "In December 2015, USRF was designated an "undesirable foreign organization" by the Russian government and is currently unable to conduct activities within the jurisdiction of the Russian Federation."

These are the same types of people who scampered out to condemn Donald Trump for delicately asking newly elected president Zelensky how obvious American losers in Ukraine could continue to siphon budgets for failing at their jobs. Their mission was to engage Russia. They'd been kicked out of Russia. They continued to operate anyway, because they considered getting kicked out a "cooperative relationship?" Moral people would return the money, ashamed, and admit they had totally failed. Not USRF.

For comedy, here's more from the position specification:

Establish Strategic Vision "Given its current status in Russia as an "*undesirable foreign organization,*" and the resulting challenges of working with Russian institutions and private citizens, USRF must define a revised strategy for advancing the goals for which the Foundation stands." As I re-read the entire position spec for amusement, I envisioned a circle jerk committee of pompous know-nothings gathered somewhere like in a conference room in the Harvard library or the office of Adam Schiff, deluding themselves that what they were doing was important. I pictured a man with an embarrassing resumé like Lieutenant Vindmann contributing text like the real one, "Development of the rule of law and development of democratic institutions and market economy." After each line of drivel was added, some clown of a peer would praise him for his brilliant vision. Meanwhile, their claim to be seeking a candidate capable of "Building Relationships and Using Influence" was demonstrable, as they say in diplomatic circles, bullshit. The only thing missing was a framed portrait of a somber buffoon like John Kerry to lend it an air of gravity.

If this job had been a potential wife, she would have had multiple children from unknown fathers and untreated STDs. I was curious what their reaction would be, so I offered to consider the "U.S. - Russia" position if they let me first try to reinstate their status in Russia. The reply was instant and that engaging Russia was a non-starter. No one on the board would approve, they said. I got it. Everything they wrote and did was a ruse. Also, why is it that people whose principal skill is pilfering from the public's purse like to feign support for market economies?

I considered it my patriotic duty to sabotage them. I referred them to someone, whose intellect was commensurate with the author of the foundation's mission statement. At my recommendation I believe they hired a guy whose resumé included managing a Moscow nightclub where he arranged prostitutes for patrons. He texted me afterwards and asked why I had turned it down.

The money wasted by the foundation would have been better spent leaving decoy poisoned vodka for invading Russian troops to steal. But of course they didn't expect any hostile troops, because they had been so successful at engaging in constructive dialogue with their Russian counterparts.

I Know a Guy

I took my daughter and her friend to D.C. in August, 2018. I wanted to quickly take a tourist photo with her in front of The White House and move on. August is peak tourist season. There was nowhere to park anywhere near. I remembered my days at the St. Regis (Carlton) two blocks away. I knew that the doormen were always amenable to ignoring the "No Parking" sign for a fee. I decided to try that. Not only could I, and did I, park there, but Luther was on duty. He was part of the crew that I'd worked with in the late 1980s. He refused to take a cent and told me that in 45 minutes J.T. would arrive too, another former co-worker. It was a pleasure to reconnect. It's good to make and keep friends.

Former colleagues and forever part of the network, J.T. and Luther. They've got a chip with me.

Backstory

I started life in Coon Rapids, Minnesota. It was then more a rural community than the suburb of 65,000 people that it's morphed into. There was no highway to nearby Minneapolis, only a local road that followed the east bank of the Mississippi River. If someone needed directions around Coon Rapids, it was not uncommon to tell them, "Take the dirt road." If you asked a local what the world's main religions were, they'd tell you Lutheran and Catholic. Jewish for us was an accent from New York. A common pastime for kids was walking through a pathless prairie with sandy soil that was full of burrs to railroad tracks that we placed various items on. After a freight train passed, we inspected the damage that the steel wheels had done. Occasionally someone might show up with a gun and a few dozen rounds. We would shoot up the same things that we placed on the train tracks to see whether a gun or train did more damage. I remember someone bringing a batch of puppies to the field, which was a similarly big event as a gun.

When I turned twelve, my family moved about two miles away. The Mississippi River was about an 80-yard walk from the back door of our new house. When the water was still, we practiced skipping stones, in pursuit of an elusive forty or more, (the number of times the rock skimmed). We'd meticulously select every rock. My friends and I became experts in river bank geology. The neighbor next door put in a retaining wall and covered the bank with boulders. This was a devastating blow to our skipping rock quarry. After the wall was completed, the best stones were either underwater or under boulders. We stole cigarettes from our parents (or from stores, where tobacco was on shelves like gum and candy) and got dizzy smoking them while fishing for carp.

A new neighbor moved in on the other side, away from the boulders. The new owner, Stanley, immediately set to converting his modest home into some kind of bizarre mansion. He built three towers, a tunnel, and added a second floor. It was completely out of place for Coon Rapids. My mother generally could befriend anyone, but her outreaches to Stanley failed. She instructed us to leave him alone and respect his wishes, which in translation meant that she considered Stanley an asshole.

On the other side of Stanley lived our classmate, Narf. We played basketball in his driveway. Not walking across Stanley's yard added approximately two hundred fifty yards to our walk. After several months of construction, Stanley uncharacteristically feigned to be cordial. He came to our front door and attempted to engage in friendly chit chat, like most neighbors in our town did. After Stanley left, my mother declared, "I do not like or trust that man." She had an outstanding crap detector.

Eventually the source of Stanley's veer towards civility was revealed. He wasn't building a home, but a church. The architectural plans of his proposed shrine included towers for each earthly direction. My parent's house was to his north. He had already built the east, west, and south. To build the north tower, he needed a variance (permission) from my parents. Stanley claimed to be a minister of something I recall sounding like, "The Charismatic Pentecostal Assemblies of God."

I listened to the debate about Stanley's variance. My dad's view was commercial. He would grant the variance in exchange for a ridiculously large payment. Mom's position was simple. Stanley was an asshole and because of that she would do everything she could to thwart his plans. Mom won.

My friend Charlie and I overheard through a door Narf's mother confiding to my mom that her nine-year old son, Joey, had been diagnosed with terminal spinal cancer. Then we heard Joey's mother repeat what Stanley had told her. The exchange was initiated because one of Joey's dying wishes was to have a kitten, which they bought for him. The kitten often got loose and walked on Stanley's property. Stanley approached the mother to complain that the kitten was not welcome and went so far as to say that if he finds the kitten near his house again, he'll kill it. She added, Stanley also told me that if my faith in the Lord was stronger, my son wouldn't be ill. The kitten disappeared and Joey passed away not long after.

Charlie and I hadn't walked through Stanley's yard to Narf's all winter. But after overhearing what he'd said to Joey's mother, all respect for Stanley's wishes was gone. As we approached the property line between Stanley and Narf's, we spotted the lifeless kitten on Stanley's territory in the final remnants of that year's snow. Its head was deformed and looked like it had possibly been hit with a hammer. Charlie and I left it there and went to see Narf, the deceased boy's older brother.

We shared our discovery about the kitten and discussed what action to take. Narf was consumed with grief and had no interest in our desire for justice. We returned to my house. To each other, Charlie and I declared war on Stanley. We weighed the merits and disadvantages of numerous plans. Setting fire to Stanley's house in the middle of the night was initially at the top of our list. But because my house and Narf's were so close to his it was likely we'd also catch on fire. Arson was abandoned. Then Charlie suggested a brilliant opening attack, "Let's drill holes in his roof!"

When we plotted the plan's execution, we only knew about electric drills. Extension cords long enough to reach could be arranged. We were sure that we could get volunteers to help, but the noise from the drill was likely to catch someone's attention. If the police arrived, it would be difficult to explain why someone was on the neighbor's roof with a drill. During school lunch, we asked others how to theoretically execute the idea. Someone told us about his dad's hand-held drills and how well they worked. We borrowed two. Stage I of Operation Stanley was successfully concluded.

Stanley built a tunnel from the main house to what I suppose was a church sanctuary. If the structure had been attached to the house, it would have intersected with the south tower. The tunnel allowed people to get to the sanctuary without going outside. Stanley held what some might call sermons. They seemed to us like seances. In the winter, my friend and I would watch through the windows as attendees flopped on the floor like fish out of water. Some flailed their arms like those nylon advertising aids that have high-speed air blowing through them, convulsing like a person tripping on flakka. There was plenty of loud gibberish, or speaking in tongues. The flopping and flailing were allegedly the result of various spirits passing through their bodies.

When it warmed, the sight of wide-open windows and Stanley's sanctuary with his congregation inside was too much temptation. We had not forgotten about Joey's kitten. Fireworks were illegal to sell, possess, or use in Minnesota. My older brother and a friend had recently returned from a drive to South Dakota, where fireworks were, and are, totally legal. The two stuffed the trunk of the car with contraband fireworks. The Fourth of July was not far off and they knew that they would be able to at least quadruple their investment by re-selling them in Minnesota.

When my brother showed me the stash in his trunk, I was flabbergasted. Before then, a strip of 24 firecrackers was a big deal to have. I was in awe, looking at multiple bricks, each containing 1,280. He had rockets, roman candles, and things I didn't even know existed. I immediately called Charlie and told him to quickly bring as much cash as possible. We pooled all our money and spent everything we had on fireworks. We rationed them pretty well, partially because lighting more than one or two during a regular weekday was likely to catch the attention of the police. The sound of explosions was uncommon.

On a Friday before the Fourth of July, Stanley had a crowd of approximately thirty people in his sanctuary. All the windows and sliding doors were open. Charlie saw the scene and said to me, "We've got to hit 'em. Get the rockets." The mission demanded stealth and precision. Stanley's back yard was fairly well illuminated. If we were close enough to aim, we'd be close enough to be seen. Charlie and I went into my dad's workshop and found sections of plastic pipe. We rigged up a variation of a rotary cannon that could launch four rockets at once.

At the edge of the darkness in Stanley's back yard, we tried to calculate the trajectory of the rockets and plotted our escape route along the river. The plan was to light the four rockets, flee to the river and throw the "cannon" into the water. The river's current would take it downstream. Then we'd run as fast as possible three houses to the north and hide behind a neighbor's pigeon coop, which was about fifteen yards from the river's edge. From there, we could watch for someone coming after us. If necessary, we could sneak into the water and swim away.

It was exhilarating to light the rockets and drop them into the tubes. We both lit two. The first went left and high, exploding so far away above my front yard, it was barely audible. The second flew high and exploded above Stanley's front yard, also barely audible. The third was a jackpot. It flew perfectly through the center of the open sliding door and exploded on the sanctuary's wall, dispersing multiple colors across the room and leaving a smoky haze. The fourth's fuse was delayed. We knew it had definitely been lit, but it didn't come out. We were looking at each other with panic. If we left the pipes, my father could certainly identify us as the source. If we took a lit rocket with us, it might explode on us. Before we could decide, it finally took off. Like the second, it went high. One out of four was pretty good for beginners.

We couldn't hear a single comment, but the collective sound was that of thoroughly stunned people. I tossed the pipes in the river and ran as fast as I could in the direction of the pigeon coop. About 30 feet away from it my left shin smacked into a square metal crossbar of an iron chair that was on the neighbor's lawn. How do I know? I returned in the daylight to see what I had run into. I did a front flip after hitting it, but can't remember how I landed. It was so unexpected and hurt so much, I couldn't believe my leg wasn't broken. After the initial shock, I focused on reaching the pigeon coop, where Charlie was waiting.

I started to tell him about my possibly broken leg. He told me to keep quiet and stay alert. We sat there in silence for what seemed like an hour. We didn't see even a flashlight and walked back. That we could have seriously injured innocent people never entered our minds. Another thing that we never thought about was that Stanley and his church could be under investigation and that law enforcement agents were part of his congregation. The lack of reaction to the rocket and fact that they didn't call the police was disconcerting. We still wanted to push Stanley out of the neighborhood, but vowed to use more subtle tactics.

While returning from a boat ride, I noticed that Stanley had put in a dock, but didn't yet have a boat. I mentioned this to the operation Stanley team (aka Justice for Joey). Someone suggested that when he did get a boat, we should let it loose so the river's current could take it a few miles south where it would be smashed going over a dam. Stanley eventually parked about an eighteen-foot Glastron in the dock. I declined to let it loose, but advised others to "Go for it," which they did.

Unfortunately, the boat floated downstream only about half a mile and got caught up in the branches of a willow tree. The boat was returned to Stanley unharmed. A few weeks later, I was floating down the middle of the river in our boat with only my dog, a spaniel. We were near a community college, next to which on shore was a popular swimming place with a rope swing. The boat's stern was facing south. As I looked in that direction, I noticed a boat headed straight towards me. Its bow was up. I estimated its speed at about twenty-five miles per hour. Boats of that size tend to plane out around thirty mph. Its course didn't change and continued straight at us. I stood up and started waving my hands over my head. The driver did not seem to notice. Once it became clear that a collision was unavoidable, I picked up my dog and jumped off the starboard side into the river.

From the water, I watched the other boat's raised bow crash into our stern and launch about ten feet into the air. It splashed down without any other contact. Once idle, I could see Stanley at the helm. He was unfazed. He stared at me and calmly said, "I'm sorry. I could have killed you." The slight stress he placed on the word "killed" caught my attention. The sound of approaching sirens got louder on both shores of the river. I could see a Sheriff's boat speeding towards us from the South. Accidents on that section of the river were so rare that I can't recall ever hearing of another one.

I reported to my friends what Stanley had done, said, and how he acted and suggested maybe we should back off for a while. Instead of retreating or taking a break, the consensus was that an escalation of hostilities was in order. Up until that point, all of our attacks had been in his backyard. It seemed logical that he wouldn't expect one from the front.

The driveway was his congregation's parking lot. It was about two and a half cars wide and about 60 yards long. The borders on either side were lined with fairly mature lilac bushes that were at least fifteen feet tall. The plan was to put sugar in as many gas tanks in the cars of Stanley's guests as quickly as possible and be gone. The evening that cars started rolling in, Charlie and I called every volunteer on our list and reminded them to bring sugar and to wear dark clothes. Every cool kid in the neighborhood came to help.

We took our positions in the lilacs. A lookout in the back sent a flashlight signal once all the people were in the sanctuary. We emerged from the bushes, walking with quick short strides, crouched over trying not to stand taller than the cars. The vehicular ambush had begun. In total, I'd estimate that we hit seventeen or eighteen cars, but nowhere near the thirty or forty that was our goal.

Perhaps a coincidence, but the operation seemed to be a success. Early the next week a "For Sale" sign went up in front of Stanley's house and he was gone shortly thereafter. The couple who bought the place lived there for at least 40 years and encountered no similar problems, except for one time on the Fourth of July when we were jointly celebrating. A mortar accidentally fell over and launched in the direction of the former sanctuary and missed high.

My journey started in Frau Vickerman's seventh grade German class. Learning about the nuances of ways to express oneself fascinated me like no other subject. By ninth grade, I'd finished the entire high school curriculum and wanted more. With a dictionary in hand, I read my first foreign language novel, Friedrich Durenmatt's "Der Richter und sein Henker" (The Judge and his Hangman). Topics related to Germany's terrible recent history drew me towards politics as well. When I was ready for college, my mom told me to study a real language, saying "like Chinese or Russian." I wanted to show her I was up to the challenge and chose to apply at George Washington University, only because in some book it was rated number one for Russian. The combination of a Russian education and real life living conditions in a political capital sent me down the rabbit hole of "Alice in Wonderland" that can also be called "Sovok".

Arthur Schopenhauer wrote "The first forty years of life give us the text; the next thirty supply the commentary on it." I'm not convinced there won't still be more commentary just on the text I've omitted, not to mention what I've been up to since.

The Grape

Dooch, orchestrator and facilitator from Nakhodka to Murmansk. He always made sure things ran harmoniously.

Russian Consul General at home in San Francisco

With Bibi

WTF is in that bowl?

Ready to fly from Vladivostok to North Korean border town, Hasan.

American drummer Dave King exhibiting a unique method to mount a horse near Taganka Square in Moscow.

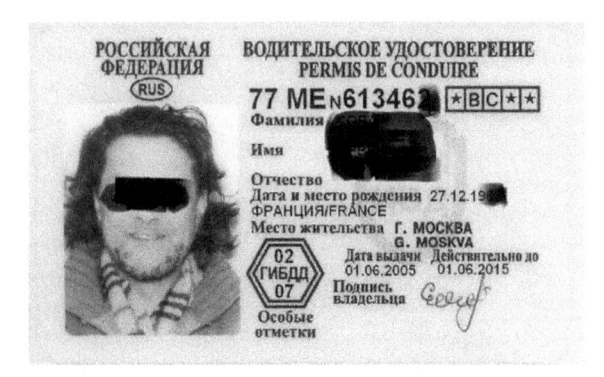

France revoked the Wild Man's driver's license for too many speeding violations, so we found a more amenable jurisdiction to issue him another one, which was valid in France.

A double moon over the Moscow River in front of the Kremlin.

Karl, the Australian freight forwarder rep. who used his pass to let me through the gate unchecked onto the Vladivostok airport tarmac.

Onstage with who likely was the Bolshoi Ballet's only Japanese-born soloist, Morihiro Ivata.

Deceased, but never forgotten, friend I. Masyagin at "The Garage" in Minneapolis. Larry's wearing a KGB hat, given to him by Nach Nach.

In the bologna launchpad with Shed

St. Catherine's Catholic Church in Saint Petersburg. Son Michael, with parents and godparents, was the first foreigner to be baptized there since before the Russian Revolution.

The greeter of the "Green Lamp," Vladivostok's premier cabaret.

Lilli and Victor @ Bolshoi Theater

Outskirts of Raduzhniy

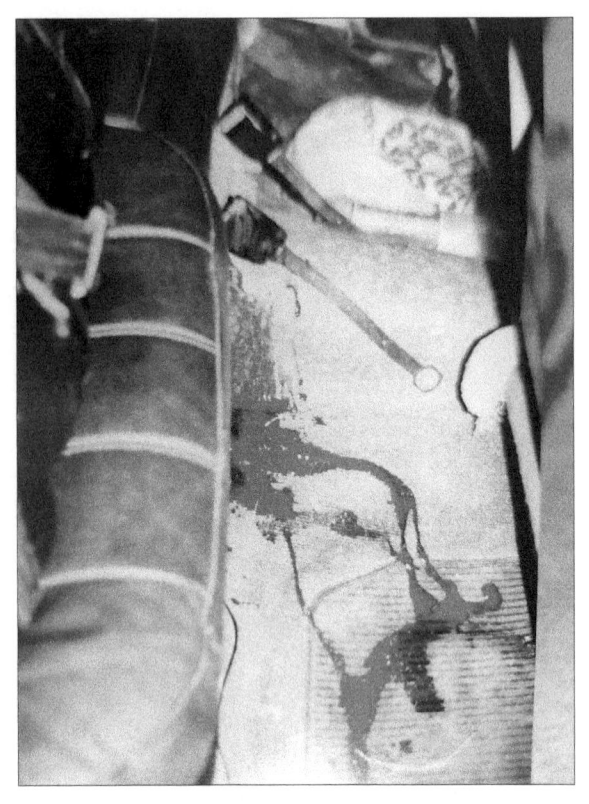

Blood from the accident victim after I dropped her off at the military hospital.

British Ambassador to Russia Tony Brenton & Matilda

Grape and ballerina

With Arnold

"The" German trader

Nakhodka Port commercial director, who made me sit and wait for hours.

Professor Filippov and American program administrators Brad and Edna

The artist who created this book's cover in the home of a great friend in Moscow.

Always with the CD player

With Shimon Peres

Two dear friends from different worlds.
Love this photo!

These two had a thing going on
before they even knew what it was.

One of numerous homes made out of segments from the oil pipeline.

Mechanical street sweepers remain a rarity today.

Alphonso: His kind likes standing in front of Soviet maps

Leader of the eponymous band, Ruth Adams was an accordionist extraordinaire, who made thousand of people happy for decades.

I'm proud to have served the role of "Executive Mixologist" on the Live At Nye's CD

Mountain Hebe in the machine shop of gunmaker, Bernie White, most famous for designing the Desert Eagle for Minneapolis' Magnum Research.

Karen (L) and Jean (R). Karen's 1970's boat of a Cadillac had a custom horn that played the melody of "Quando Quando Quando." One knew who arrived if she chose to press the horn.

First Soviet baseball team to compete in the USA. They did not fare well.

After a couple of decades of not speaking, Pubic surfaced. In Chechnya he clearly perfected the skill of not offending the mother of the host. I can tell, because he's still alive.

At a ceremony for the Simon Wiesenthal Tolerance Museum. (L – R) Frank Gehry, Rabbi Marvin Hier, California Governor Arnold Schwarzenegger, Rabbi Meyer May, and Larry Mizel.

Leonid Vorobyev, leader of "Chicago" cover band, Leonid and Friends, holding a copy of Sovok.

FSB agent who seemed to spend way too much time trying to figure out how Toolshed was spying, or was he?

Some of the ladies from the rail yard dispatch in Nizhnevartovsk

Former Soviet dissident Natan Sharansky, who is mentioned in the writings of Arkady Polishchuk.

The pilot is drunk.

Konda

White Nights' New Year's Eve party

On campus cafeteria

Nitz and I with a Nye's waitress in front of a poster of Al Nye, founder and owner of "America's Best Bar."

Soviet decision maker

Mountain Hebe and I with Israel's minister of Defense, Shaul Mofaz

The building where Lip's Office was in Moscow on Petrovka.

WE WOULD LIKE TO THANK THE FOLLOWING PEOPLE:

. . . Gennady A. Golovachev, Director of the Tchaikovsky Hall, for his support of charity work and help in the organization of this evening.

. . . Igor Moiseyev and his Dance Troop for tonight's performance.

. . . Larry and Tammy Hershfield and Kevin McKinney for making this unprecedented Charity Night at the Tchaikovsky Hall possible.

. . . Laura McNeil, Tammy Hershfield, Eileen O'Connor, Sveta Puzachenko, Katya Borisova, Maria Sullivan, Elena Berezovskaya, and Ludmila Tiurina for all of their efforts in planning and organizing this event.

. . . all of our guests tonight for choosing to pay a little bit more for an evening at the Tchaikovsky and supporting charitable efforts in Russia.

THANK YOU!!!

Ingram Content Group UK Ltd.
Milton Keynes UK
UKHW051157180423
420361UK00008B/743